MW00812430

CLYMER
MANUALS

HONDA
CB 550 & 650 NIGHTHAWK • 1983-1985

WHAT'S IN YOUR TOOLBOX?

More information available at haynes.com
Phone: 805-498-6703

Haynes Group Limited
Haynes North America, Inc.

ISBN-10: 0-89287-420-1
ISBN-13: 978-0-89287-420-0

© Haynes North America, Inc. 1986
With permission from Haynes group Limited

Clymer is a registered trademark of Haynes North America, Inc.

Common spark plug conditions

NORMAL

Symptoms: Brown to grayish-tan color and slight electrode wear. Correct heat range for engine and operating conditions.
Recommendation: When new spark plugs are installed, replace with plugs of the same heat range.

WORN

Symptoms: Rounded electrodes with a small amount of deposits on the firing end. Normal color. Causes hard starting in damp or cold weather and poor fuel economy.
Recommendation: Plugs have been left in the engine too long. Replace with new plugs of the same heat range. Follow the recommended maintenance schedule.

CARBON DEPOSITS

Symptoms: Dry sooty deposits indicate a rich mixture or weak ignition. Causes misfiring, hard starting and hesitation.
Recommendation: Make sure the plug has the correct heat range. Check for a clogged air filter or problem in the fuel system or engine management system. Also check for ignition system problems.

ASH DEPOSITS

Symptoms: Light brown deposits encrusted on the side or center electrodes or both. Derived from oil and/or fuel additives. Excessive amounts may mask the spark, causing misfiring and hesitation during acceleration.
Recommendation: If excessive deposits accumulate over a short time or low mileage, install new valve guide seals to prevent seepage of oil into the combustion chambers. Also try changing gasoline brands.

OIL DEPOSITS

Symptoms: Oily coating caused by poor oil control. Oil is leaking past worn valve guides or piston rings into the combustion chamber. Causes hard starting, misfiring and hesitation.
Recommendation: Correct the mechanical condition with necessary repairs and install new plugs.

GAP BRIDGING

Symptoms: Combustion deposits lodge between the electrodes. Heavy deposits accumulate and bridge the electrode gap. The plug ceases to fire, resulting in a dead cylinder.
Recommendation: Locate the faulty plug and remove the deposits from between the electrodes.

TOO HOT

Symptoms: Blistered, white insulator, eroded electrode and absence of deposits. Results in shortened plug life.
Recommendation: Check for the correct plug heat range, over-advanced ignition timing, lean fuel mixture, intake manifold vacuum leaks, sticking valves and insufficient engine cooling.

PREIGNITION

Symptoms: Melted electrodes. Insulators are white, but may be dirty due to misfiring or flying debris in the combustion chamber. Can lead to engine damage.
Recommendation: Check for the correct plug heat range, over-advanced ignition timing, lean fuel mixture, insufficient engine cooling and lack of lubrication.

HIGH SPEED GLAZING

Symptoms: Insulator has yellowish, glazed appearance. Indicates that combustion chamber temperatures have risen suddenly during hard acceleration. Normal deposits melt to form a conductive coating. Causes misfiring at high speeds.
Recommendation: Install new plugs. Consider using a colder plug if driving habits warrant.

DETONATION

Symptoms: Insulators may be cracked or chipped. Improper gap setting techniques can also result in a fractured insulator tip. Can lead to piston damage.
Recommendation: Make sure the fuel anti-knock values meet engine requirements. Use care when setting the gaps on new plugs. Avoid lugging the engine.

MECHANICAL DAMAGE

Symptoms: May be caused by a foreign object in the combustion chamber or the piston striking an incorrect reach (too long) plug. Causes a dead cylinder and could result in piston damage.
Recommendation: Repair the mechanical damage. Remove the foreign object from the engine and/or install the correct reach plug.

CONTENTS

QUICK REFERENCE DATA

HOME WORKSHOP TOOLS

Tool	Size or Specification
Screwdrivers	
Slot	5/16×8 in. blade
Slot	3/8×12 in. blade
Phillips	Size 2 tip, 6 in. blade
Pliers	
Gas pliers	6 in. overall
Vise Grips©	10 in. overall
Needlenose	6 in. overall
Channel lock	12 in. overall
Snap ring	–
Wrenches	
Box-end set	10-17, 20, 32 mm
Open-end set	10-17, 20, 32 mm
Crescent (adjustable)	6 and 12 in. overall
Socket set	1/2 in. drive ratchet with 10-17, 20, 32 mm sockets
Allen set	2-10 mm
Cone wrenches	–
Spoke wrench	–
Other Special Tools	
Impact driver	1/2 in. drive with ass't tips
Torque wrench	1/2 in. drive—0-100 ft.-lb.
Tire levers	For moped or motorcycle tires

REPLACEMENT BULBS

Item	Wattage	Number
Headlight (quartz bulb)	12V 60/55	H4 (Phillips 12342/99 or equivalent)
Tail/brakelight	12V 8/27W	SAE No. 1157
Turn signals		
Front	12V 23/8W	SAE No. 1034
Rear	12V 23 W	SAE No. 1073
Instrument lights	12V 3W	SAE No. 57
Indicator lights	12V 3W	SAE No. 57
High beam indicator	12V 3W	SAE No. 57
Neutral indicator	12V 3W	SAE No. 57
Oil pressure warning	12V 3W	SAE No. 57
Gear position light	12V 8W	SAE No. 1034

FRAME TORQUE SPECIFICATIONS

Item	N·m	ft.-lb.
Front axle	55-65	40-47
Front axle pinch bolt	15-25	11-18
Caliper mounting bolts (single-disc models)		
Upper mounting bolt	35-45	25-33
Lower mounting bolt	20-25	14-18
Caliper bolts (dual-disc models)		
Right-hand	30-40	22-29
Left-hand side		
Pivot bolt	25-35	18-22
Mounting bolt	20-25	14-18
Piston pin bolt	20-25	14-18
Caliper bracket bolt	35-45	25-33
Brake system union bolts	25-35	18-25
Brake disc bolts	35-40	25-29
Handlebar holder bolts	20-30	14-22
Fork bridge bolts		
Upper	9-13	7-9
Lower	45-55	33-40
Fork cap bolt	15-30	11-22
Fork brace Allen bolts	18-28	13-20
Fork slider Allen bolt	15-25	11-18
Steering stem nut	90-120	65-87
Rear axle nut	60-80	43-58
Rear axle pinch bolt	20-30	14-22
Shock absorber mounting nut and bolt	30-40	22-29
Brake torque link bolt	18-25	13-18
Final drive unit nuts	60-70	43-51
Swing arm		
Left-hand pivot bolt	80-120	58-87
Right-hand pivot bolt	8-12	6-9
Right-hand pivot locknut	80-120	58-87

FRONT FORK OIL CAPACITY*

CB550	375 cc (12.7 oz.)
CB650	
Left-hand fork leg	465 cc (15.7 oz.)
Right-hand fork leg	450 cc (15.2 oz.)

* Capacity for each fork leg.

FRONT FORK AIR PRESSURE

Normal	Maximum*
0-6 psi (0-0.4 kg/cm²)	43 psi (4 kg/cm²)

* Do not exceed the maximum air pressure or internal parts of the fork will be damaged.

STATE OF CHARGE

Specific gravity	State of Charge
1.110-1.130	Discharged
1.140-1.160	Almost discharged
1.170-1.190	One-quarter charged
1.200-1.220	One-half charged
1.230-1.250	Three-quarters charged
1.260-1.280	Fully charged

TUNE-UP SPECIFICATIONS

Compression pressure (at sea level)	12.0 ±1.0 kg/cm² (170 ±14 psi)
Spark plug type	
Standard heat range	ND X24EPR-U9 or NGK DPR8EA-9
Cold weather*	ND X22EPR-U9 or NGK DPR7EA-9
Extended high-speed riding	ND X27EPR-U9 or NGK DPR9EA-9
Spark plug gap	0.8-0.9 mm (0.031-0.035 in.)
Ignition timing	"F" mark @ 1,400 ±200 rpm
Idle speed	1,100 ±100 rpm

* Cold weather climate—below 41° F (5° C).

TIRE PRESSURE (COLD)

Tire size	Normal	Maximum load limit*
Front 100/90-19		
CB550	28 psi (2.00 kg/cm²)	28 psi (2.00 kg/cm²)
CB650	32 psi (2.25 kg/cm²)	32 psi (2.25 kg/cm²)
Rear 130/90-16		
CB550	28 psi (2.00 kg/cm²)	36 psi (2.50 kg/cm²)
CB650	32 psi (2.25 kg/cm²)	40 psi (2.80 kg/cm²)

* Up to maximum load limit of 200 lbs (90 kg) including total weight of motorcycle with accessories, rider(s) and luggage.

FLUID SPECIFICATIONS

Fuel	
CB550	12.0 liters (3.17 U.S. gal., 2.64 Imp. gal.)
CB650	13.0 liters (3.43 U.S. gal., 2.86 Imp. gal.)
Engine oil (with filter change)	2.5 liter (2.6 U.S. qt., 2.2 Imp. qt.)
Engine oil (at overhaul)	3.2 liter (3.4 U.S. qt., 2.8 Imp. qt.)
Final drive oil capacity	
1983	170 cc (5.78 oz.)
1984	150 cc (4.9 oz.)
Final drive oil viscosity	
1983	
Above 5° C (41° F)	SAE 90
Below 5° C (41° F)	SAE 80
1984	SAE 80

SERVICE INTERVALS*

Every 1,000 km (600 miles) or 6 months
- Check engine oil level
- Check battery specific gravity and electrolyte level
- Check hydraulic fluid level in brake master cylinder
- Check hydraulic fluid level in clutch master cylinder
- Lubricate rear brake pedal and shift lever
- Lubricate side and centerstand pivot points
- Inspect front steering for looseness
- Check wheel bearings for smooth operation
- Check wheel runout

Every 6,400 km (4,000 miles)
- Clean air cleaner element
- Replace spark plugs
- Change engine oil and replace oil filter
- Check and adjust the carburetors
- Check and synchronize the carburetors
- Check and adjust the choke
- Check and adjust throttle operation and free play
- Adjust rear brake pedal height and free play
- Clean fuel shutoff strainer
- Check hydraulic fluid level in brake master cylinder
- Check hydraulic fluid level in clutch master cylinder
- Inspect brake pads and linings for wear
- Inspect crankcase breather hose for cracks or loose hose clamps; drain out all residue
- Inspect fuel line for chafed, cracked or swollen ends
- Check engine mounting bolts for tightness
- Check all suspension components

Every 12,800 km (8,000 miles)
- Check ignition timing
- Run a compression test
- Inspect fuel lines for wetness or damage
- Inspect entire brake system for leaks or damage
- Change front fork oil
- Inspect oil level in final drive unit
- Inspect wheel bearings
- Inspect and repack the steering head bearings
- Lubricate the speedometer drive cable
- Lubricate final drive splines
- Check and adjust headlight aim

Every 24,000 km (38,400 miles) or every 2 years
- Change hydraulic fluid in clutch master cylinder
- Change hydraulic fluid in brake master cyinder
- Change oil in final drive unit

Every 4 years
- Replace all hydraulic brake hoses
- Replace the hydraulic clutch hose assembly

* This Honda factory maintenance schedule should be considered as a guide to general maintenance and lubrication intervals. Harder than normal use or exposure to mud, water, sand, high humidity, etc. will naturally dictate more frequent attention to most maintenance items.

ENGINE OIL CAPACITY

Oil and filter change	2.5 liter (2.6 U.S. qt., 2.2 Imp. qt.)
At overhaul	3.2 liter (3.4 U.S. qt., 2.8 Imp. qt.)

CLYMER®

HONDA

CB550 & 650 NIGHTHAWK • 1983-1985

INTRODUCTION

This detailed, comprehensive manual covers the Honda CB550SC and CB650SC from 1983-on. The expert text gives complete information on maintenance, tune-up, repair and overhaul. Hundreds of photos and drawings guide you through every step. The book includes all you need to know to keep your Honda running right.

A shop manual is a reference. You want to be able to find information fast. As in all Clymer books, this one is designed with you in mind. All chapters are thumb tabbed. Important items are extensively indexed at the rear of the book. All procedures, tables, photos, etc., in this manual are for the reader who may be working on the bike or using this manual for the first time. All the most frequently used specifications and capacities are summarized in the *Quick Reference Data* pages at the front of the book.

Keep the book handy in your tool box. It will help you to better understand how your bike runs, lower repair and maintenance costs and generally improve your satisfaction with the bike.

CHAPTER ONE

GENERAL INFORMATION

The troubleshooting, maintenance, tune-up, and step-by-step repair procedures in this book are written specifically for the owner and home mechanic. The text is accompanied by helpful photos and diagrams to make the job as clear and correct as possible.

Troubleshooting, maintenance, tune-up, and repair are not difficult if you know what to do and what tools and equipment to use. Anyone of average intelligence, with some mechanical ability, and not afraid to get their hands dirty can perform most of the procedures in this book.

In some cases, a repair job may require tools or skills not reasonably expected of the home mechanic. These procedures are noted in each chapter and it is recommended that you take the job to your dealer, a competent mechanic, or a machine shop.

MANUAL ORGANIZATION

This chapter provides general information, safety and service hints. Also included are lists of recommended shop and emergency tools as well as a brief description of troubleshooting and tune-up equipment.

Chapter Two provides methods and suggestions for quick and accurate diagnosis and repair of problems. Troubleshooting procedures discuss typical symptoms and logical methods to pinpoint the trouble.

Chapter Three explains all periodic lubrication and routine maintenance necessary to keep your motorcycle running well. Chapter Three also includes recommended tune-up procedures, eliminating the need to constantly consult chapters on the various subassemblies.

Subsequent chapters cover specific systems such as the engine, transmission, and electrical system. Each of these chapters provides disassembly, inspection, repair, and assembly procedures in a simple step-by-step format. If a repair is impractical for the home mechanic it is indicated. In these cases it is usually faster and less expensive to have the repairs made by a dealer or competent repair shop. Essential specifications are included in the appropriate chapters.

When special tools are required to perform a task included in this manual, the tools are illustrated. It may be possible to borrow or rent these tools. The inventive mechanic may also be able to find a suitable substitute in his tool box, or to fabricate one.

The terms NOTE, CAUTION, and WARNING have specific meanings in this manual. A NOTE provides additional or explanatory information. A

CAUTION is used to emphasize areas where equipment damage could result if proper precautions are not taken. A WARNING is used to stress those areas where personal injury or death could result from negligence, in addition to possible mechanical damage.

SERVICE HINTS

Time, effort, and frustration will be saved and possible injury will be prevented if you observe the following practices.

Most of the service procedures covered are straightforward and can be performed by anyone reasonably handy with tools. It is suggested, however, that you consider your own capabilities carefully before attempting any operation involving major disassembly of the engine.

Some operations, for example, require the use of a press. It would be wiser to have these performed by a shop equipped for such work, rather than to try to do the job yourself with makeshift equipment. Other procedures require precision measurements. Unless you have the skills and equipment required, it would be better to have a qualified repair shop make the measurements for you.

Repairs go much faster and easier if the parts that will be worked on are clean before you begin. There are special cleaners for washing the engine and related parts. Brush or spray on the cleaning solution, let stand, then rinse it away with a garden hose. Clean all oily or greasy parts with cleaning solvent as you remove them.

WARNING
Never use gasoline as a cleaning agent. It presents an extreme fire hazard. Be sure to work in a well-ventilated area when using cleaning solvent. Keep a fire extinguisher, rated for gasoline fires, handy in any case.

Much of the labor charge for repairs made by dealers is for the removal and disassembly of other parts to reach the defective unit. It is frequently possible to perform the preliminary operations yourself and then take the defective unit in to the dealer for repair, at considerable savings.

Once you have decided to tackle the job yourself, make sure you locate the appropriate section in this manual, and read it entirely. Study the illustrations and text until you have a good idea of what is involved in completing the job satisfactorily. If special tools are required, make arrangements to get them before you start. Also, purchase any known defective parts prior to starting on the procedure. It is frustrating and time-consuming to get partially into a job and then be unable to complete it.

Simple wiring checks can be easily made at home, but knowledge of electronics is almost a necessity for performing tests with complicated electronic testing gear.

During disassembly of parts keep a few general cautions in mind. Force is rarely needed to get things apart. If parts are a tight fit, like a bearing in a case, there is usually a tool designed to separate them. Never use a screwdriver to pry apart parts with machined surfaces such as cylinder head or crankcase halves. You will mar the surfaces and end up with leaks.

Make diagrams wherever similar-appearing parts are found. You may think you can remember where everything came from — but mistakes are costly. There is also the possibility you may get sidetracked and not return to work for days or even weeks — in which interval, carefully laid out parts may have become disturbed.

Tag all similar internal parts for location, and mark all mating parts for position. Record number and thickness of any shims as they are removed. Small parts such as bolts can be identified by placing them in plastic sandwich bags that are sealed and labeled with masking tape.

Wiring should be tagged with masking tape and marked as each wire is removed. Again, do not rely on memory alone.

Disconnect battery ground cable before working near electrical connections and before disconnecting wires. Never run the engine with the battery disconnected; the alternator could be seriously damaged.

Protect finished surfaces from physical damage or corrosion. Keep gasoline and brake fluid off painted surfaces.

Frozen or very tight bolts and screws can often be loosened by soaking with penetrating oil like Liquid Wrench or WD-40, then sharply striking the bolt head a few times with a hammer and punch (or screwdriver for screws). Avoid heat unless absolutely necessary, since it may melt, warp, or remove the temper from many parts.

Avoid flames or sparks when working near a charging battery or flammable liquids, such as gasoline.

No parts, except those assembled with a press fit, require unusual force during assembly. If a part is hard to remove or install, find out why before proceeding.

Cover all openings after removing parts to keep dirt, small tools, etc., from falling in.

When assembling two parts, start all fasteners, then tighten evenly.

Wiring connections and brake shoes, drums, pads, and discs and contact surfaces in dry clutches should be kept clean and free of grease and oil.

When assembling parts, be sure all shims and washers are replaced exactly as they came out.

Whenever a rotating part butts against a stationary part, look for a shim or washer. Use new gaskets if there is any doubt about the condition of old ones. Generally, you should apply gasket cement to one mating surface only, so the parts may be easily disassembled in the future. A thin coat of oil on gaskets helps them seal effectively.

Heavy grease can be used to hold small parts in place if they tend to fall out during assembly. However, keep grease and oil away from electrical, clutch, and brake components.

High spots may be sanded off a piston with sandpaper, but emery cloth and oil do a much more professional job.

Carburetors are best cleaned by disassembling them and soaking the parts in a commercial carburetor cleaner. Never soak gaskets and rubber parts in these cleaners. Never use wire to clean out jets and air passages; they are easily damaged. Use compressed air to blow out the carburetor, but only if the float has been removed first.

Take your time and do the job right. Do not forget that a newly rebuilt engine must be broken in the same as a new one. Refer to your owner's manual for the proper break-in procedures.

SAFETY FIRST

Professional mechanics can work for years and never sustain a serious injury. If you observe a few rules of common sense and safety, you can enjoy many safe hours servicing your motorcycle. You could hurt yourself or damage the motorcycle if you ignore these rules.

1. Never use gasoline as a cleaning solvent.

2. Never smoke or use a torch in the vicinity of flammable liquids such as cleaning solvent in open containers.

3. Never smoke or use a torch in an area where batteries are being charged. Highly explosive hydrogen gas is formed during the charging process.

4. Use the proper sized wrenches to avoid damage to nuts and injury to yourself.

5. When loosening a tight or stuck nut, be guided by what would happen if the wrench should slip. Protect yourself accordingly.

6. Keep your work area clean and uncluttered.

7. Wear safety goggles during all operations involving drilling, grinding, or use of a cold chisel.

8. Never use worn tools.

9. Keep a fire extinguisher handy and be sure it is rated for gasoline (Class B) and electrical (Class C) fires.

EXPENDABLE SUPPLIES

Certain expendable supplies are necessary. These include grease, oil, gasket cement, wiping rags, cleaning solvent, and distilled water. Also, special locking compounds, silicone lubricants, and engine and carburetor cleaners may be useful. Cleaning solvent is available at most service stations and distilled water for the battery is available at supermarkets.

SHOP TOOLS

For complete servicing and repair you will need an assortment of ordinary hand tools (**Figure 1**).

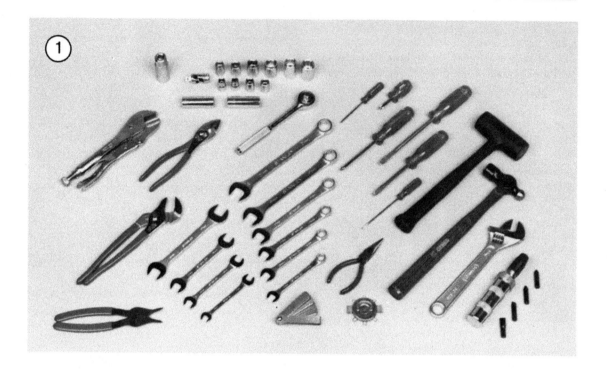

As a minimum, these include:
a. Combination wrenches
b. Sockets
c. Plastic mallet
d. Small hammer
e. Impact driver
f. Snap ring pliers
g. Gas pliers
h. Phillips screwdrivers
i. Slot (common) screwdrivers
j. Feeler gauges
k. Spark plug gauge
l. Spark plug wrench

Special tools required are shown in the chapters covering the particular repair in which they are used.

Engine tune-up and troubleshooting procedures require other special tools and equipment. These are described in detail in the following sections.

EMERGENCY TOOL KITS

Highway

A small emergency tool kit kept on the bike is handy for road emergencies which otherwise could leave you stranded. The tools and spares listed below and shown in **Figure 2** will let you handle most roadside repairs.

a. Motorcycle tool kit (original equipment)
b. Impact driver
c. Silver waterproof sealing tape (duct tape)
d. Hose clamps (3 sizes)
e. Silicone sealer
f. Loctite
g. Flashlight
h. Tire patch kit
i. Tire irons
j. Plastic pint bottle (for oil)
k. Waterless hand cleaner
l. Rags for clean up

Off-Road

A few simple tools and aids carried on the motorcycle can mean the difference between walking or riding back to camp or to where repairs can be made. See **Figure 3**.

A few essential spare parts carried in your truck or van can prevent a day or weekend of trail riding from being spoiled. See **Figure 4**.

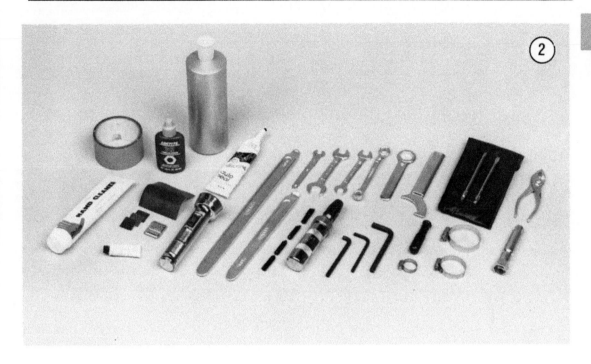

On the Motorcycle

a. Motorcycle tool kit (original equipment)
b. Drive chain master link
c. Tow line
d. Spark plug
e. Spark plug wrench
f. Shifter lever
g. Clutch/brake lever
h. Silver waterproof sealing tape (duct tape)
i. Loctite

In the Truck

a. Control cables (throttle, clutch, brake)
b. Silicone sealer
c. Tire patch kit
d. Tire irons
e. Tire pump
f. Impact driver
g. Oil

> **WARNING**
> *Tools and spares should be carried on the motorcycle — not in clothing where a simple fall could result in serious injury from a sharp tool.*

TROUBLESHOOTING AND TUNE-UP EQUIPMENT

Voltmeter, Ohmmeter, and Ammeter

For testing the ignition or electrical system, a good voltmeter is required. For motorcycle use, an instrument covering 0-20 volts is satisfactory. One which also has a 0-2 volt scale is necessary for testing relays, points, or individual contacts where voltage drops are much smaller. Accuracy should be ± 1/2 volt.

An ohmmeter measures electrical resistance. This instrument is useful for checking continuity (open and short circuits), and testing fuses and lights.

The ammeter measures electrical current. Ammeters for motorcycle use should cover 0-50 amperes and 0-250 amperes. These are useful for checking battery charging and starting current.

Several inexpensive VOM's (volt-ohm-milliammeter) combine all three instruments into one which fits easily in any tool box. See **Figure 5**. However, the ammeter ranges are usually too small fro motorcycle work.

Hydrometer

The hydrometer gives a useful indication of battery condition and charge by measuring the

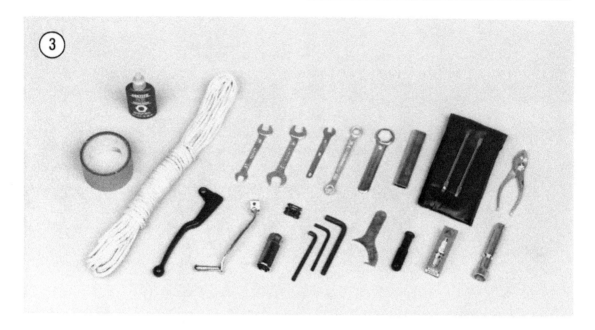

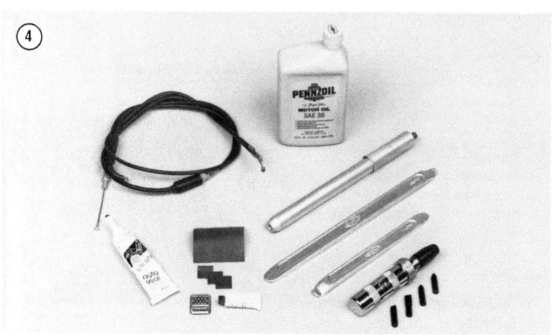

specific gravity of the electrolyte in each cell. See **Figure 6**. Complete details on use and interpretation of readings are provided in the electrical chapter.

Compression Tester

The compression tester measures the compression pressure built up in each cylinder. The results, when properly interpreted, can indicate general cylinder, ring, and valve condition. See **Figure 7**. Extension lines are available for hard-to-reach cylinders.

Dwell Meter (Contact Breaker Point Ignition Only)

A dwell meter measures the distance in degrees of cam rotation that the breaker points remain closed while the engine is running. Since

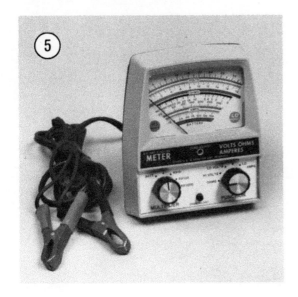

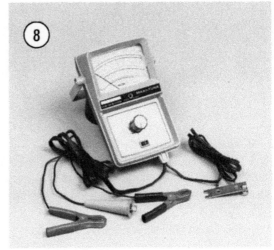

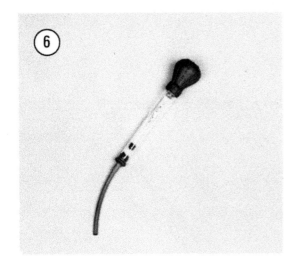

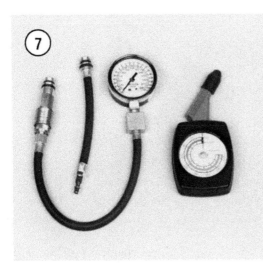

this angle is determined by breaker point gap, dwell angle is an accurate indication of breaker point gap.

Many tachometers intended for tuning and testing incorporate a dwell meter as well. See **Figure 8**. Follow the manufacturer's instructions to measure dwell.

Tachometer

A tachometer is necessary for tuning. See **Figure 8**. Ignition timing and carburetor adjustments must be performed at the specified idle speed. The best instrument for this purpose is one with a low range of 0-1,000 or 0-2,000 rpm for setting idle, and a high range of 0-4,000 or more for setting ignition timing at 3,000 rpm. Extended range (0-6,000 or 0-8,000 rpm) instruments lack accuracy at lower speeds. The instrument should be capable of detecting changes of 25 rpm on the low range.

> NOTE: *The motorcycle's tachometer is not accurate enough for correct idle adjustment.*

Strobe Timing Light

This instrument is necessary for tuning, as it permits very accurate ignition timing. The light flashes at precisely the same instant that No. 1 cylinder fires, at which time the timing marks on the engine should align. Refer to Chapter Three for exact location of the timing marks for your engine.

Suitable lights range from inexpensive neon bulb types to powerful xenon strobe lights. See **Figure 9**. Neon timing lights are difficult to see and must be used in dimly lit areas. Xenon strobe timing lights can be used outside in bright sunlight.

Tune-up Kits

Many manufacturers offer kits that combine several useful instruments. Some come in a convenient carry case and are usually less expensive than purchasing one instrument at a time. **Figure 10** shows one of the kits that is available. The prices vary with the number of instruments included in the kit.

Manometer (Carburetor Synchronizer)

A manometer is essential for accurately synchronizing carburetors on multi-cylinder engines. This tool measures the namifold vacuum for each cylinder simultaneously. A typical mercury manometer (**Figure 11**) can be purchased from a Honda dealership or aftermarket tool supplier.

Fire Extinguisher

A fire extinguisher is a necessity when working on a vehicle. It should be rated for both *Class B* (flammable liquids — gasoline, oil, paint. etc.) and *Class C* (electrical — wiring, etc.) type fires. It should always be kept within reach. See **Figure 12**.

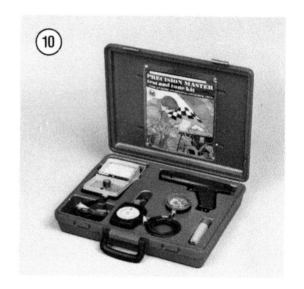

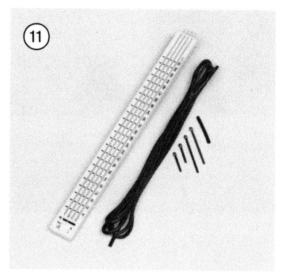

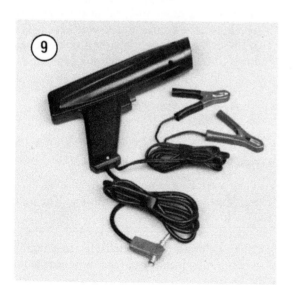

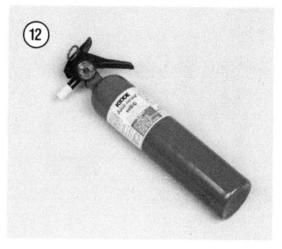

CHAPTER TWO

TROUBLESHOOTING

Troubleshooting motorcycle problems is relatively simple. To be effective and efficient, however, it must be done in a logical step-by-step manner. If it is not, a great deal of time may be wasted, good parts may be replaced unnecessarily, and the true problem may never be uncovered.

Always begin by defining the symptoms as closely as possible. Then, analyze the symptoms carefully so that you can make an intelligent guess at the probable cause. Next, test the probable cause and attempt to verify it; if it's not at fault, analyze the symptoms once again, this time eliminating the first probable cause. Continue on in this manner, a step at a time, until the problem is solved.

At first, this approach may seem to be time consuming, but you will soon discover that it's not nearly so wasteful as a hit-or-miss method that may never solve the problem. And just as important, the methodical approach to troubleshooting ensures that only those parts that are defective will be replaced.

The troubleshooting procedures in this chapter analyze typical symptoms and show logical methods for isolating and correcting trouble. They are not, however, the only methods; there may be several approaches to a given problem, but all good troubleshooting methods have one thing in common — a logical, systematic approach.

ENGINE

The entire engine must be considered when trouble arises that is experienced as poor performance or failure to start. The engine is more than a combustion chamber, piston, and crankshaft; it also includes a fuel delivery system, an ignition system, and an exhaust system.

Before beginning to troubleshoot any engine problems, it's important to understand an engine's operating requirements. First, it must have a correctly metered mixture of gasoline and air (**Figure 1**). Second, it must have an airtight combustion chamber in which the mixture can be compressed. And finally, it requires a precisely timed spark to ignite the compressed mixture. If one or more is missing, the engine won't run, and if just one is deficient, the engine will run poorly at best.

Of the three requirements, the precisely timed spark — provided by the ignition system — is most likely to be the culprit, with gas/air mixture (carburetion) second, and poor compression the least likely.

STARTING DIFFICULTIES

Hard starting is probably the most common motorcycle ailment, with a wide range of problems likely. Before delving into a reluctant or non-starter, first determine what has changed

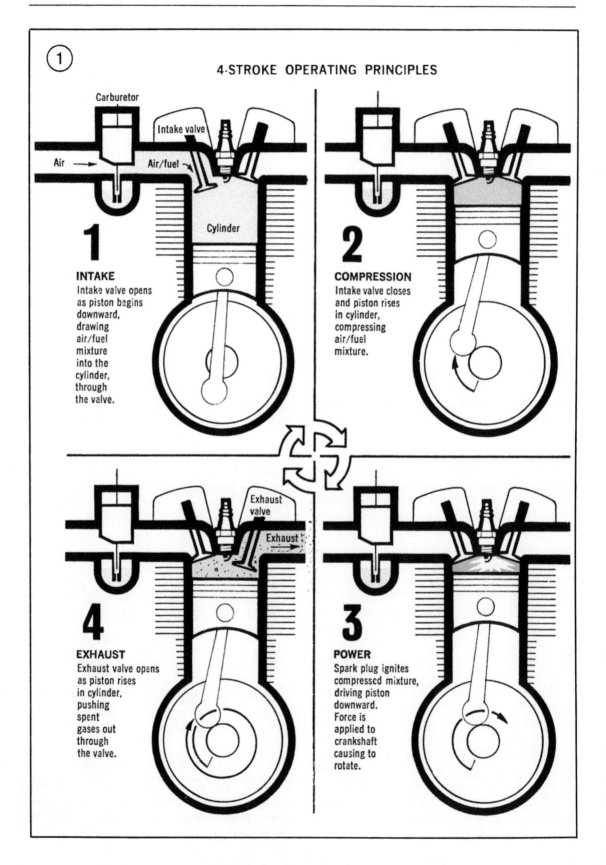

since the motorcycle last started easily. For instance, was the weather dry then and is it wet now? Has the motorcycle been sitting in the garage for a long time? Has it been ridden many miles since it was last fueled?

Has starting become increasingly more difficult? This alone could indicate a number of things that may be wrong but is usually associated with normal wear of ignition and engine components.

While it's not always possible to diagnose trouble simply from a change of conditions, this information can be helpful and at some future time may uncover a recurring problem.

Fuel Delivery

Although it is the second most likely cause of trouble, fuel delivery should be checked first simply because it is the easiest.

First, check the tank to make sure there is fuel in it. Then, disconnect the fuel hose at the carburetor, open the valve and check for flow (**Figure 2**). If fuel does not flow freely make sure the tank vent is clear. Next, check for blockage in the line or valve. Remove the valve and clean it as described in the fuel system chapter.

If fuel flows from the hose, reconnect it and remove the float bowl from the carburetor, open the valve and check for flow through the float needle valve. If it does not flow freely when the float is extended and then shut off when the flow is gently raised, clean the carburetor as described in the fuel system chapter.

When fuel delivery is satisfactory, go on to the ignition system.

Ignition

Remove the spark plug from the cylinder and check its condition. The appearance of the plug is a good indication of what's happening in the combustion chamber; for instance, if the plug is wet with gas, it's likely that engine is flooded. Compare the spark plug to **Figure 3**. Make certain the spark plug heat range is correct. A "cold" plug makes starting difficult.

After checking the spark plug, reconnect it to the high-tension lead and lay it on the cylinder head so it makes good contact (**Figure 4**). Then,

with the ignition switched on, crank the engine several times and watch for a spark across the plug electrodes. A fat, blue spark should be visible. If there is no spark, or if the spark is weak, substitute a good plug for the old one and check again. If the spark has improved, the old plug is faulty. If there was no change, keep looking.

Make sure the ignition switch is not shorted to ground. Remove the spark plug cap from the end of the high-tension lead and hold the exposed end of the lead about ⅛ inch from the cylinder head. Crank the engine and watch for a spark arcing from the lead to the head. If it's satisfactory, the connection between the lead and the cap was faulty. If the spark hasn't improved, check the coil wire connections.

If the spark is still weak, remove the ignition cover and remove any dirt or moisture from the points or sensor. Check the point or air gap against the specifications in the *Quick Reference Data* at the beginning of the book.

If spark is still not satisfactory, a more serious problem exists than can be corrected with simple adjustments. Refer to the electrical system chapter for detailed information for correcting major ignition problems.

Compression

Compression — or the lack of it — is the least likely cause of starting trouble. However, if compression is unsatisfactory, more than a simple adjustment is required to correct it (see the engine chapter).

An accurate compression check reveals a lot about the condition of the engine. To perform this test you need a compression gauge (see Chapter One). The engine should be at operating temperature for a fully accurate test, but even a cold test will reveal if the starting problem is compression.

Remove the spark plug and screw in a compression gauge (**Figure 5**). With assistance, hold the throttle wide open and crank the engine several times, until the gauge ceases to rise. Normal compression should be 130-160 psi, but a reading as low as 100 psi is usually sufficient for the engine to start. If the reading is much lower than normal, remove the gauge and pour about a tablespoon of oil into the cylinder.

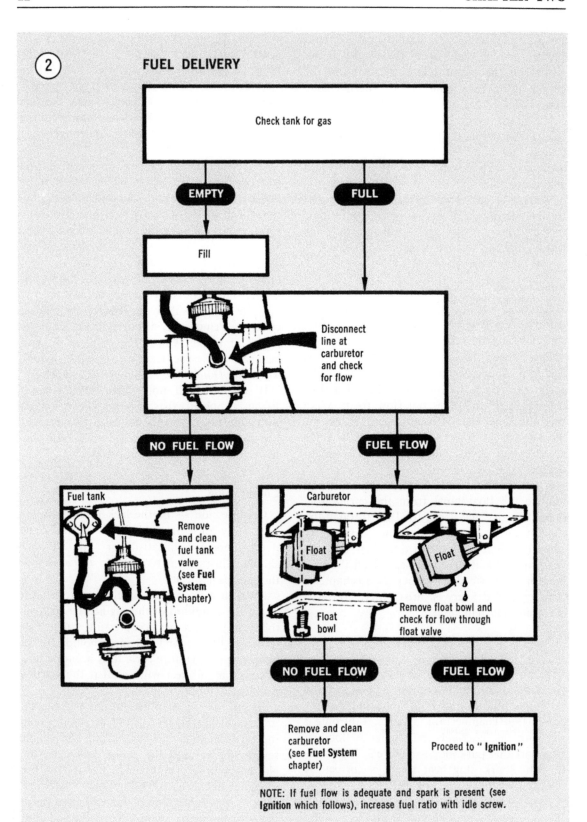

② FUEL DELIVERY

Check tank for gas

EMPTY → Fill

FULL

Disconnect line at carburetor and check for flow

NO FUEL FLOW

FUEL FLOW

Fuel tank

Remove and clean fuel tank valve (see **Fuel System** chapter)

Carburetor

Float

Float

Float bowl

Remove float bowl and check for flow through float valve

NO FUEL FLOW

FUEL FLOW

Remove and clean carburetor (see **Fuel System** chapter)

Proceed to "**Ignition**"

NOTE: If fuel flow is adequate and spark is present (see **Ignition** which follows), increase fuel ratio with idle screw.

2

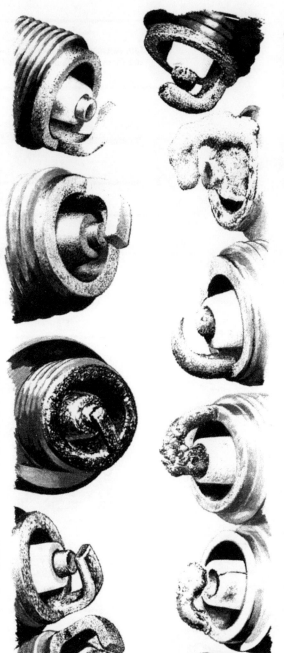

NORMAL
• Appearance—Firing tip has deposits of light gray to light tan.
• Can be cleaned, regapped and reused.

CARBON FOULED
• Appearance—Dull, dry black with fluffy carbon deposits on the insulator tip, electrode and exposed shell.
• Caused by—Fuel/air mixture too rich, plug heat range too cold, weak ignition system, dirty air cleaner, faulty automatic choke or excessive idling.
• Can be cleaned, regapped and reused.

OIL FOULED
• Appearance—Wet black deposits on insulator and exposed shell.
• Caused by—Excessive oil entering the combustion chamber through worn rings, pistons, valve guides or bearings.
• Replace with new plugs (use a hotter plug if engine is not repaired).

LEAD FOULED
• Appearance — Yellow insulator deposits (may sometimes be dark gray, black or tan in color) on the insulator tip.
• Caused by—Highly leaded gasoline.
• Replace with new plugs.

LEAD FOULED
• Appearance—Yellow glazed deposits indicating melted lead deposits due to hard acceleration.
• Caused by—Highly leaded gasoline.
• Replace with new plugs.

OIL AND LEAD FOULED
• Appearance—Glazed yellow deposits with a slight brownish tint on the insulator tip and ground electrode.
• Replace with new plugs.

FUEL ADDITIVE RESIDUE
• Appearance — Brown colored hardened ash deposits on the insulator tip and ground electrode.
• Caused by—Fuel and/or oil additives.
• Replace with new plugs.

WORN
• Appearance — Severely worn or eroded electrodes.
• Caused by—Normal wear or unusual oil and/or fuel additives.
• Replace with new plugs.

PREIGNITION
• Appearance — Melted ground electrode.
• Caused by—Overadvanced ignition timing, inoperative ignition advance mechanism, too low of a fuel octane rating, lean fuel/air mixture or carbon deposits in combustion chamber.

PREIGNITION
• Appearance—Melted center electrode.
• Caused by—Abnormal combustion due to overadvanced ignition timing or incorrect advance, too low of a fuel octane rating, lean fuel/air mixture, or carbon deposits in combustion chamber.
• Correct engine problem and replace with new plugs.

INCORRECT HEAT RANGE
• Appearance—Melted center electrode and white blistered insulator tip.
• Caused by—Incorrect plug heat range selection.
• Replace with new plugs.

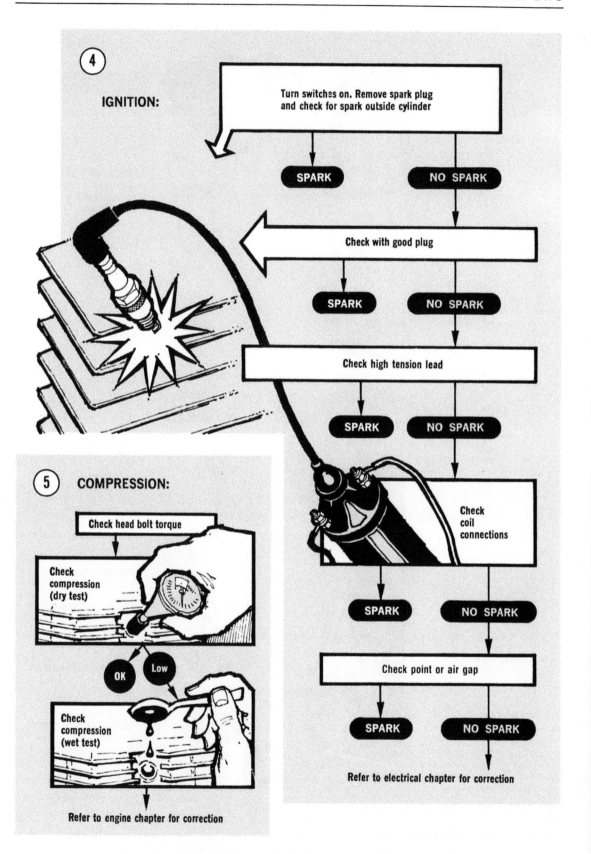

④ IGNITION:

Turn switches on. Remove spark plug and check for spark outside cylinder

SPARK   NO SPARK

Check with good plug

SPARK   NO SPARK

Check high tension lead

SPARK   NO SPARK

Check coil connections

SPARK   NO SPARK

Check point or air gap

SPARK   NO SPARK

Refer to electrical chapter for correction

⑤ COMPRESSION:

Check head bolt torque

Check compression (dry test)

OK   Low

Check compression (wet test)

Refer to engine chapter for correction

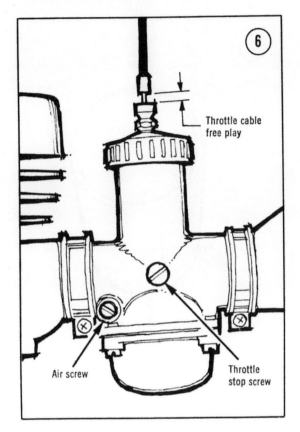

Throttle cable free play

Air screw

Throttle stop screw

Crank the engine several times to distribute the oil and test the compression once again. If it is now significantly higher, the rings and bore are worn. If the compression did not change, the valves are not seating correctly. Adjust the valves and check again. If the compression is still low, refer to the engine chapter.

NOTE: *Low compression indicates a developing problem. The condition causing it should be corrected as soon as possible.*

POOR PERFORMANCE

Poor engine performance can be caused by any of a number of things related to carburetion, ignition, and the condition of the sliding and rotating components in the engine. In addition, components such as brakes, clutch, and transmission can cause problems that seem to be related to engine performance, even when the engine is in top running condition.

Poor Idling

Idling that is erratic, too high, or too low is most often caused by incorrect adjustment of the carburetor idle circuit. Also, a dirty air filter or an obstructed fuel tank vent can affect idle speed. Incorrect ignition timing or worn or faulty ignition components are also good possibilities.

First, make sure the air filter is clean and correctly installed. Then, adjust the throttle cable free play, the throttle stop screw, and the idle mixture air screw (**Figure 6**) as described in the routine maintenance chapter.

If idling is still poor, check the carburetor and manifold mounts for leaks; with the engine warmed up and running, spray WD-40 or a similar light lube around the flanges and joints of the carburetor and manifold (**Figure 7**). Listen for changes in engine speed. If a leak is present, the idle speed will drop as the lube "plugs" the leak and then pick up again as it is drawn into the engine. Tighten the nuts and clamps and test again. If a leak persists, check for a damaged gasket or a pinhole in the manifold. Minor leaks in manifold hoses can be repaired with silicone sealer, but if cracks or holes are extensive, the manifold should be replaced.

A worn throttle slide may cause erratic running and idling, but this is likely only after many thousands of miles of use. To check, remove the carburetor top and feel for back and forth movement of the slide in the bore; it should be barely perceptible. Inspect the slide for large worn areas and replace it if it is less than perfect (**Figure 8**).

If the fuel system is satisfactory, check ignition timing and breaker point gap (air gap in electronic ignition). Check the condition of the system components as well. Ignition-caused idling problems such as erratic running can be the fault of marginal components. See the electrical system chapter for appropriate tests.

Rough Running or Misfiring

Misfiring (see **Figure 9**) is usually caused by an ignition problem. First, check all ignition connections (**Figure 10**). They should be clean, dry, and tight. Don't forget the kill switch; a loose connection can create an intermittent short.

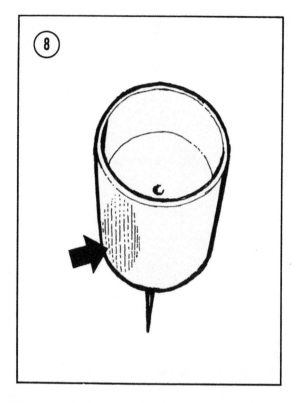

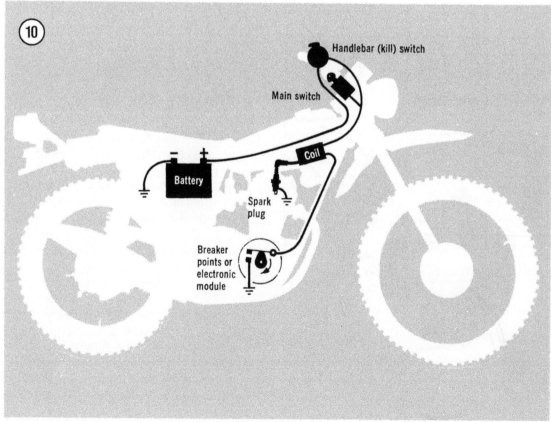

ENGINE RUNS ROUGH AND MISFIRES

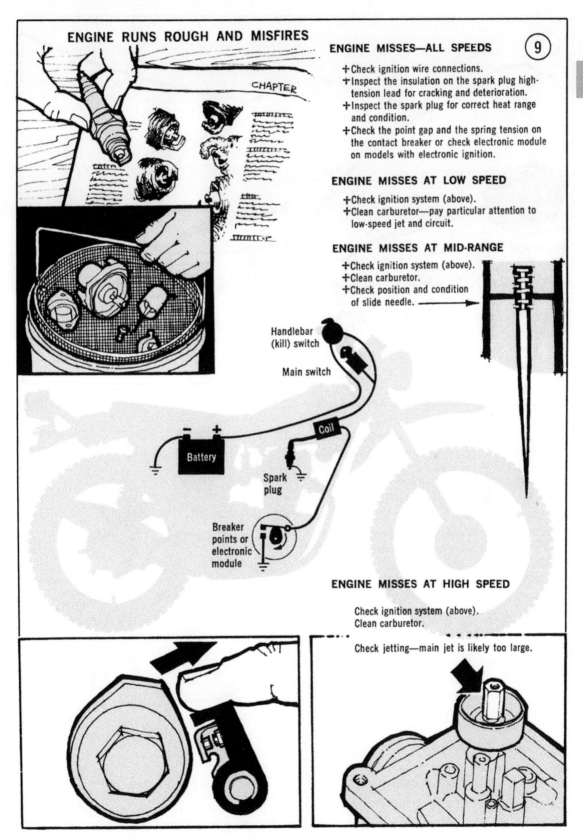

ENGINE MISSES—ALL SPEEDS ⑨

+ Check ignition wire connections.
+ Inspect the insulation on the spark plug high-tension lead for cracking and deterioration.
+ Inspect the spark plug for correct heat range and condition.
+ Check the point gap and the spring tension on the contact breaker or check electronic module on models with electronic ignition.

ENGINE MISSES AT LOW SPEED

+ Check ignition system (above).
+ Clean carburetor—pay particular attention to low-speed jet and circuit.

ENGINE MISSES AT MID-RANGE

+ Check ignition system (above).
+ Clean carburetor.
+ Check position and condition of slide needle. ——————→

Handlebar (kill) switch

Main switch

Coil

Battery

Spark plug

Breaker points or electronic module

ENGINE MISSES AT HIGH SPEED

Check ignition system (above).
Clean carburetor.

Check jetting—main jet is likely too large.

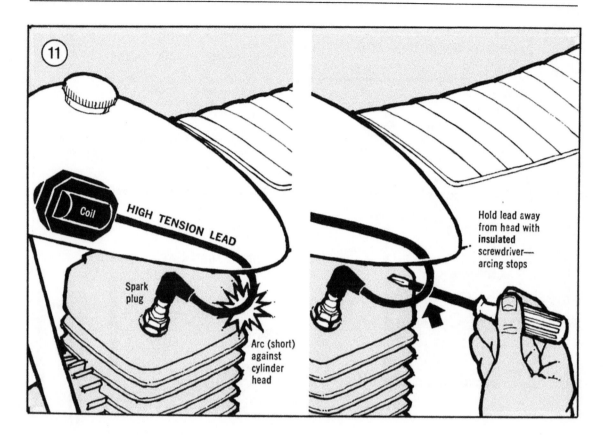

HIGH TENSION LEAD

Coil

Spark plug

Arc (short) against cylinder head

Hold lead away from head with **insulated** screwdriver— arcing stops

Check the insulation on the high-tension spark plug lead. If it is cracked or deteriorated it will allow the spark to short to ground when the engine is revved. This is easily seen at night. If arcing occurs, hold the affected area of the wire away from the metal to which it is arcing, using an insulated screwdriver (**Figure 11**), and see if the misfiring ceases. If it does, replace the high-tension lead. Also check the connection of the spark plug cap to the lead. If it is poor, the spark will break down at this point when the engine speed is increased.

The spark plug could also be poor. Test the system with a new plug.

Incorrect point gap or a weak contact breaker spring can cause misfiring. Check the gap and the alignment of the points. Push the moveable arm back and check for spring tension (**Figure 12**). It should feel stiff.

On models with electronic ignition, have the electronic module tested by a dealer or substitute a known good unit for a suspected one.

If misfiring occurs only at a certain point in engine speed, the problem may very likely be

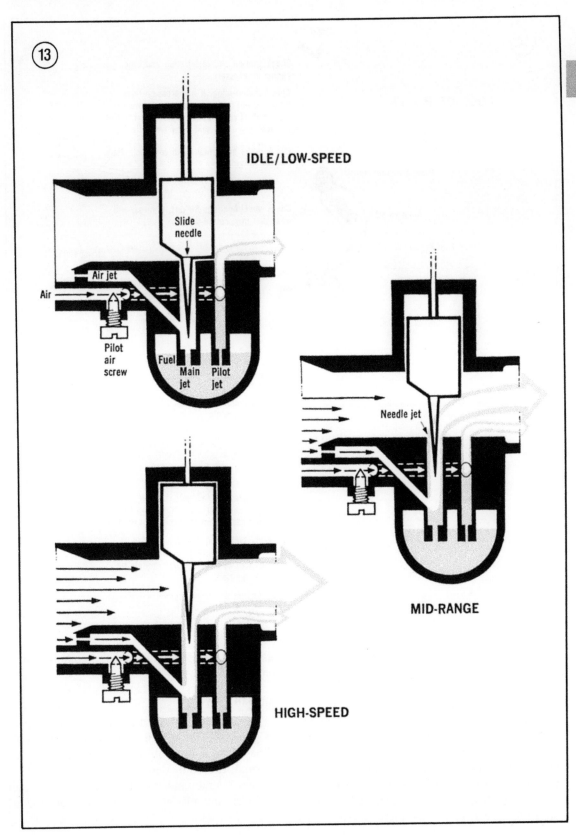

⑬

IDLE/LOW-SPEED

Slide
necdle

Air jet

Air

Pilot
air
screw

Fuel Main Pilot
jet jet

Needle jet

MID-RANGE

HIGH-SPEED

2

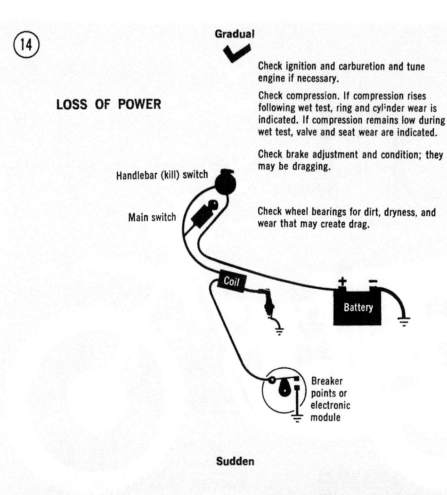

(14)

LOSS OF POWER

Gradual

Check ignition and carburetion and tune engine if necessary.

Check compression. If compression rises following wet test, ring and cylinder wear is indicated. If compression remains low during wet test, valve and seat wear are indicated.

Check brake adjustment and condition; they may be dragging.

Handlebar (kill) switch

Main switch

Check wheel bearings for dirt, dryness, and wear that may create drag.

Coil

Battery

Breaker points or electronic module

Sudden

Check compression (above). If power loss is sudden, damage to rings, piston, and bore or valves and seats are more likely than wear.

Check the ignition system for a failed component, poor contact, or change in timing or point gap. Check electronic module on electronic ignition.

Check the fuel system for an obstruction.

carburetion. Poor performance at idle is described earlier. Misfiring at low speed (just above idle) can be caused by a dirty low-speed circuit or jet (**Figure 13**). Poor midrange performance is attributable to a worn or incorrectly adjusted needle and needle jet. Misfiring at high speed (if not ignition related) is usually caused by a too-large main jet which causes the engine to run rich. Any of these carburetor-related conditions can be corrected by first cleaning the carburetor and then adjusting it as described in the tune-up and maintenance chapter.

Loss of Power

First determine how the power loss developed (**Figure 14**). Did it decline over a long period of time or did it drop abruptly? A gradual loss is normal, caused by deterioration of the engine's state of tune and the normal wear of the cylinder and piston rings and the valves and seats. In such case, check the condition of the

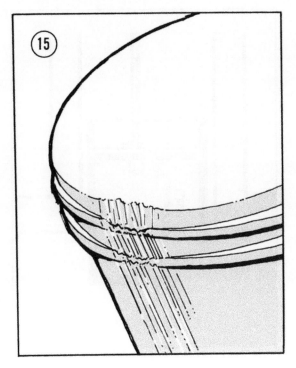

ignition and carburetion and measure the compression as described earlier.

A sudden power loss may be caused by a failed ignition component, obstruction in the fuel system, damaged valve or seat, or a broken piston ring or damaged piston (**Figure 15**).

If the engine is in good shape and tune, check the brake adjustment. If the brakes are dragging, they will consume considerable power. Also check the wheel bearings. If they are dry, extremely dirty, or badly worn they can create considerable drag.

Engine Runs Hot

A modern motorcycle engine, in good mechanical condition, correctly tuned, and operated as it was intended, will rarely experience overheating problems. However, out-of-spec conditions can create severe overheating that may result in serious engine damage. Refer to **Figure 16**.

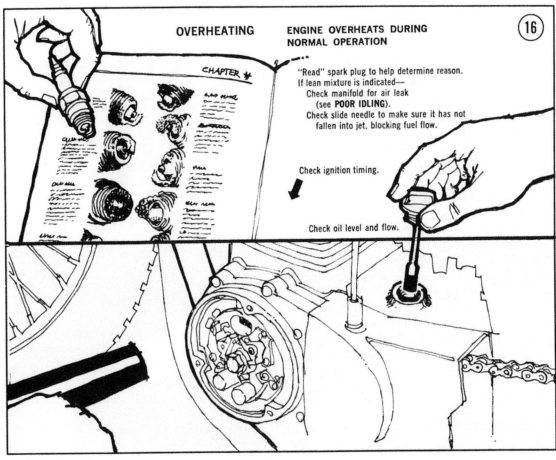

Overheating is difficult to detect unless it is extreme, in which case it will usually be apparent as excessive heat radiating from the engine, accompanied by the smell of hot oil and sharp, snapping noises when the engine is first shut off and begins to cool.

Unless the motorcycle is operated under sustained high load or is allowed to idle for long periods of time, overheating is usually the result of an internal problem. Most often it's caused by a too-lean fuel mixture.

Remove the spark plug and compare it to **Figure 3**. If a too-lean condition is indicated, check for leaks in the intake manifold (see *Poor Idling*). The carburetor jetting may be incorrect but this is unlikely if the overheating problem has just developed (unless, of course, the engine was jetted for high altitude and is now being run near sea level). Check the slide needle in the carburetor to make sure it hasn't come loose and is restricting the flow of gas through the main jet and needle jet (**Figure 17**).

Check the ignition timing; extremes of either advance or retard can cause overheating.

Piston Seizure and Damage

Piston seizure is a common result of overheating (see above) because an aluminum piston expands at a greater rate than a steel cylinder. Seizure can also be caused by piston-to-cylinder clearance that is too small; ring end gap that is too small; insufficient oil; spark plug heat range too hot; and broken piston ring or ring land.

A major piston seizure can cause severe engine damage. A minor seizure — which usually subsides after the engine has cooled a few minutes — rarely does more than scuff the piston skirt the first time it occurs. Fortunately, this condition can be corrected by dressing the piston with crocus cloth, refitting the piston and rings to the bore with recommended clearances, and checking the timing to ensure overheating does not occur. Regard that first seizure as a warning and correct the problem before continuing to run the engine.

CLUTCH AND TRANSMISSION

1. *Clutch slips*—Make sure lever free play is sufficient to allow the clutch to fully engage

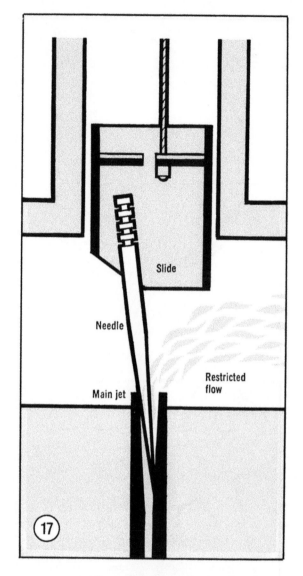

Slide

Needle

Main jet

Restricted flow

(17)

(**Figure 18**). Check the contact surfaces for wear and glazing. Transmission oil additives also can cause slippage in wet clutches. If slip occurs only under extreme load, check the condition of the springs or diaphragm and make sure the clutch bolts are snug and uniformly tightened.

2. *Clutch drags*—Make sure lever free play isn't so great that it fails to disengage the clutch. Check for warped plates or disc. If the transmission oil (in wet clutch systems) is extremely dirty or heavy, it may inhibit the clutch from releasing.

3. *Transmission shifts hard*—Extremely dirty oil can cause the transmission to shift hard.

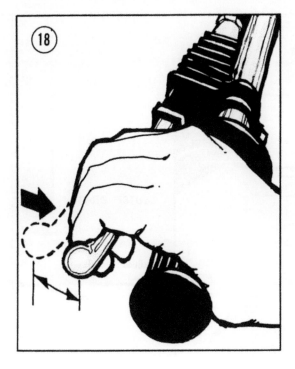

Check the selector shaft for bending (**Figure 19**). Inspect the shifter and gearsets for wear and damage.

4. *Transmission slips out of gear*—This can be caused by worn engagement dogs or a worn or damaged shifter (**Figure 20**). The overshift travel on the selector may be misadjusted.

5. *Transmission is noisy*—Noises usually indicate the absence of lubrication or wear and damage to gears, bearings, or shims. It's a good idea to disassemble the transmission and carefully inspect it when noise first occurs.

DRIVE TRAIN

Drive train problems (outlined in **Figure 21**) arise from normal wear and incorrect maintenance.

CHASSIS

Chassis problems are outlined in **Figure 22**.

1. *Motorcycle pulls to one side*—Check for loose suspension components, axles, steering

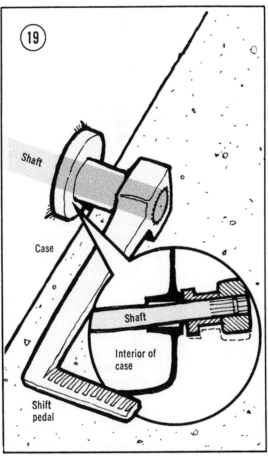

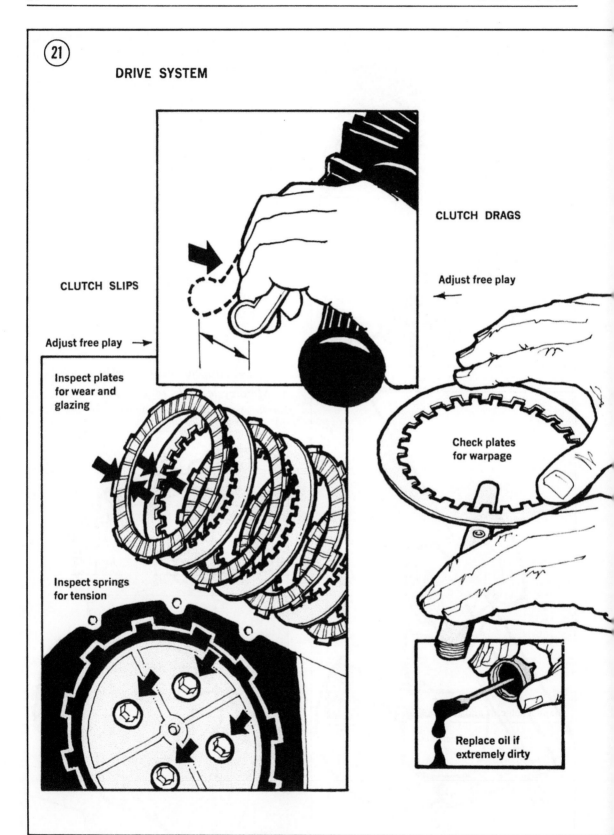

㉑

DRIVE SYSTEM

CLUTCH DRAGS

CLUTCH SLIPS

Adjust free play →

Adjust free play ←

Inspect plates
for wear and
glazing

Check plates
for warpage

Inspect springs
for tension

Replace oil if
extremely dirty

2

TRANSMISSION SLIPS OUT OF GEAR

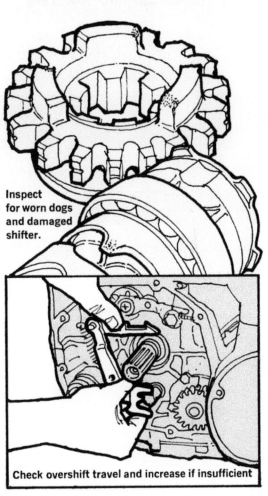

Inspect for worn dogs and damaged shifter.

TRANSMISSION SHIFTS HARD

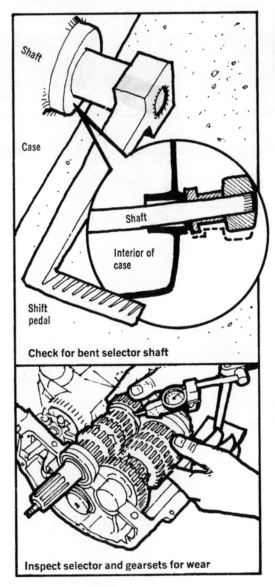

Check for bent selector shaft

Inspect selector and gearsets for wear

Check overshift travel and increase if insufficient

TRANSMISSION IS NOISY

Check oil level

Disassemble and inspect (see Transmission chapter)

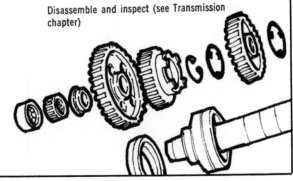

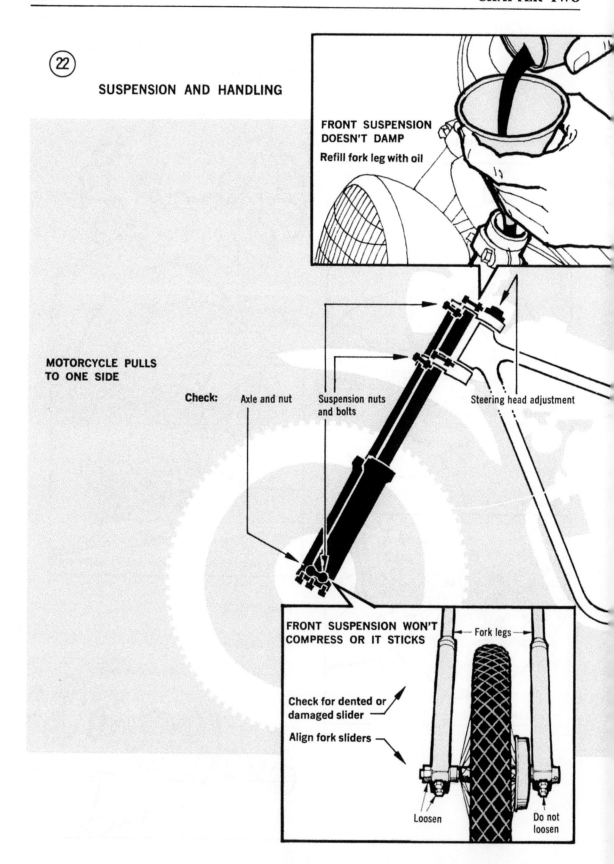

㉒

SUSPENSION AND HANDLING

FRONT SUSPENSION
DOESN'T DAMP
Refill fork leg with oil

MOTORCYCLE PULLS
TO ONE SIDE

Check: Axle and nut   Suspension nuts
and bolts   Steering head adjustment

FRONT SUSPENSION WON'T
COMPRESS OR IT STICKS

Fork legs

Check for dented or
damaged slider

Align fork sliders

Loosen   Do not
loosen

Slider

Replace seals
if fork legs
are oily

SUSPENSION AND HANDLING CONTINUED

2

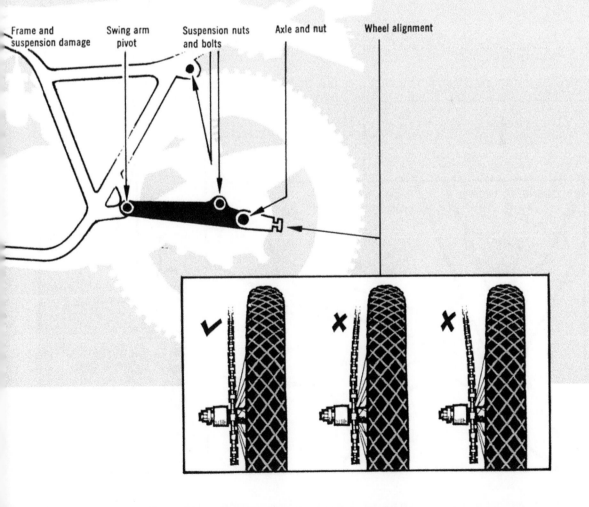

Frame and
suspension damage

Swing arm
pivot

Suspension nuts
and bolts

Axle and nut

Wheel alignment

SUSPENSION AND HANDLING CONTINUED

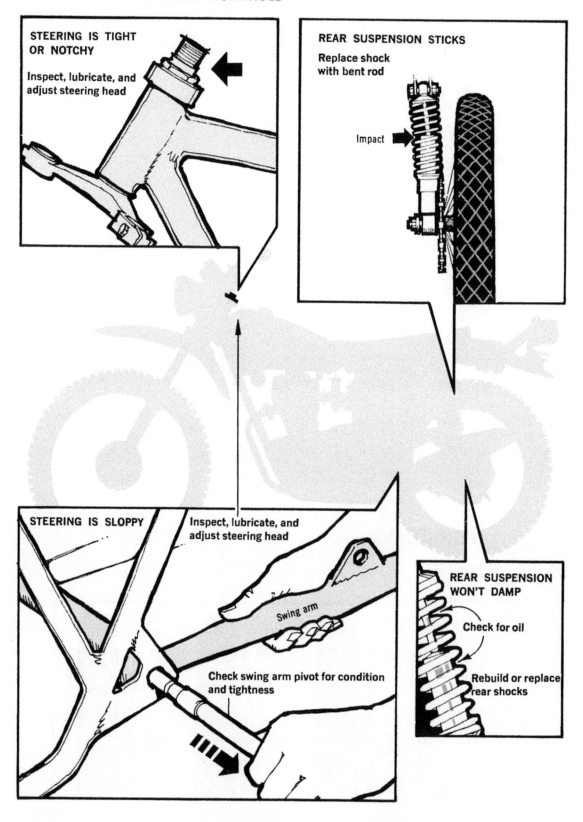

STEERING IS TIGHT OR NOTCHY

Inspect, lubricate, and adjust steering head

REAR SUSPENSION STICKS

Replace shock with bent rod

Impact

STEERING IS SLOPPY

Inspect, lubricate, and adjust steering head

Swing arm

Check swing arm pivot for condition and tightness

REAR SUSPENSION WON'T DAMP

Check for oil

Rebuild or replace rear shocks

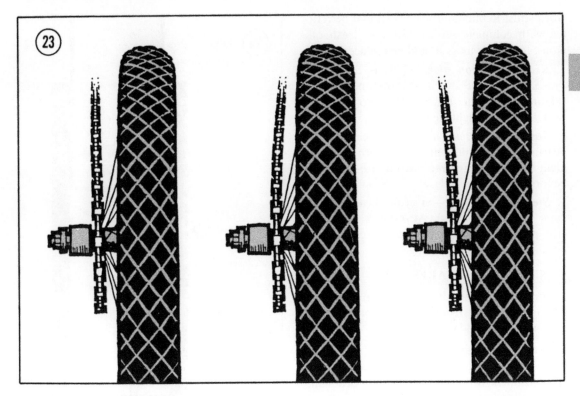

head, swing arm pivot. Check wheel alignment (**Figure 23**). Check for damage to the frame and suspension components.

2. *Front suspension doesn't damp*—This is most often caused by a lack of damping oil in the fork legs. If the upper fork tubes are exceptionally oily, it's likely that the seals are worn out and should be replaced.

3. *Front suspension sticks or won't fully compress*—Misalignment of the forks when the wheel is installed can cause this. Loosen the axle nut and the pinch bolt on the nut end of the axle (**Figure 24**). Lock the front wheel with the brake and compress the front suspension several times to align the fork legs. Then, tighten the pinch bolt and then the axle nut.

The trouble may also be caused by a bent or dented fork slider (**Figure 25**). The distortion required to lock up a fork tube is so slight that it is often impossible to visually detect. If this type of damage is suspected, remove the fork leg and remove the spring from it. Attempt to operate the fork leg. If it still binds, replace the slider; it's not practical to repair it.

4. *Rear suspension does not damp*—This is usually caused by damping oil leaking past

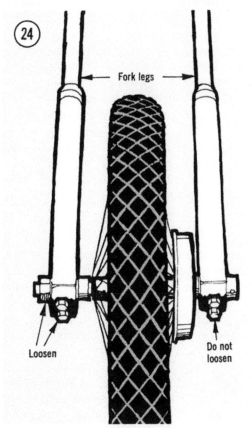

worn seals. Rebuildable shocks should be refitted with complete service kits and fresh oil. Non-rebuildable units should be replaced.

5. *Rear suspension sticks*—This is commonly caused by a bent shock absorber piston rod (**Figure 26**). Replace the shock; the rod can't be satisfactorily straightened.

6. *Steering is tight or "notchy"*—Steering head bearings may be dry, dirty, or worn. Adjustment of the steering head bearing pre-load may be too tight.

7. *Steering is sloppy*—Steering head adjustment may be too loose. Also check the swing arm pivot; looseness or extreme wear at this point translate to the steering.

BRAKES

Brake problems arise from wear, lack of maintenance, and from sustained or repeated exposure to dirt and water.

1. *Brakes are ineffective*—Ineffective brakes are most likely caused by incorrect adjustment. If adjustment will not correct the problem, remove the wheels and check for worn or glazed linings. If the linings are worn beyond the service limit, replace them. If they are simply glazed, rough them up with light sandpaper.

In hydraulic brake systems, low fluid levels can cause a loss of braking effectiveness, as can worn brake cylinder pistons and bores. Also check the pads to see if they are worn beyond the service limit.

2. *Brakes lock or drag*—This may be caused by incorrect adjustment. Check also for foreign matter embedded in the lining and for dirty and dry wheel bearings.

ELECTRICAL SYSTEM

Many electrical system problems can be easily solved by ensuring that the affected connections are clean, dry, and tight. In battery equipped motorcycles, a neglected battery is the source of a great number of difficulties that could be prevented by simple, regular service to the battery.

A multimeter, like the volt/ohm/milliammeter described in Chapter One, is invaluable for efficient electrical system troubleshooting.

See **Figures 27 and 28** for schematics showing

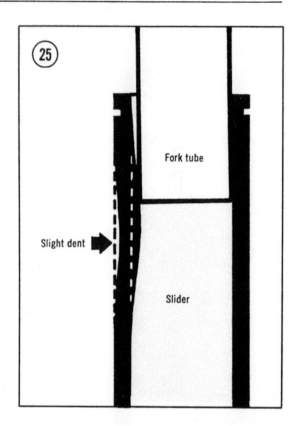

Fork tube

Slight dent

Slider

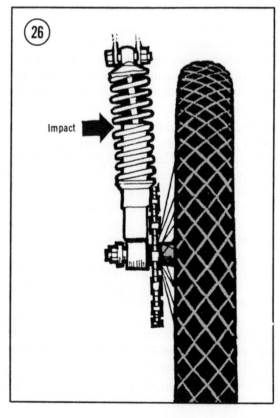

Impact

BASIC IGNITION CIRCUITS

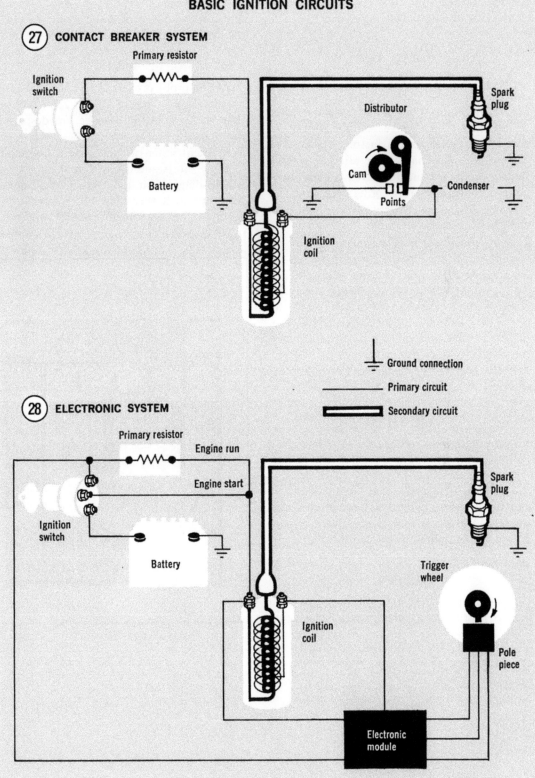

27 CONTACT BREAKER SYSTEM

Primary resistor

Ignition switch

Battery

Distributor

Cam

Points

Condenser

Spark plug

Ignition coil

Ground connection

Primary circuit

Secondary circuit

28 ELECTRONIC SYSTEM

Primary resistor

Engine run

Engine start

Ignition switch

Battery

Ignition coil

Trigger wheel

Spark plug

Pole piece

Electronic module

simplified conventional and electronic ignition systems. Typical and most common electrical troubles are also described.

CHARGING SYSTEM

1. *Battery will not accept a charge*—Make sure the electrolyte level in the battery is correct and that the terminal connections are tight and free of corrosion. Check for fuses in the battery circuit. If the battery is satisfactory, refer to the electrical system chapter for alternator tests. Finally, keep in mind that even a good alternator is not capable of restoring the charge to a severely discharged battery; it must first be charged by an external source.

2. *Battery will not hold a charge*—Check the battery for sulfate deposits in the bottom of the case (**Figure 29**). Sulfation occurs naturally and the deposits will accumulate and eventually come in contact with the plates and short them out. Sulfation can be greatly retarded by keeping the battery well charged at all times. Test the battery to assess its condition.

If the battery is satisfactory, look for excessive draw, such as a short.

LIGHTING

Bulbs burn out frequently—All bulbs will eventually burn out, but if the bulb in one particular light burns out frequently check the light assembly for looseness that may permit excessive vibration; check for loose connections that could cause current surges; check also to make sure the bulb is of the correct rating.

FUSES

Fuse blows—When a fuse blows, don't just replace it; try to find the cause. Consider a fuse

a warning device as well as a safety device. And never replace a fuse with one of greater amperage rating. It probably won't melt before the insulation on the wiring does.

WIRING

Wiring problems should be corrected as soon as they arise — before a short can cause a fire that may seriously damage or destroy the motorcycle.

A circuit tester of some type is essential for locating shorts and opens. Use the appropriate wiring diagram at the end of the book for reference. If a wire must be replaced make a notation on the wiring diagram of any changes in color coding.

Plate is shorted by sulfation

LUBRICATION, MAINTENANCE, AND TUNE-UP

A motorcycle, even in normal use, is subjected to tremendous heat, stress and vibration. When neglected, any bike becomes unreliable and actually dangerous to ride.

To gain the utmost in safety, performance and useful life from your Honda it is necessary to make periodic inspections and adjustments. Frequently, minor problems are found during these inspections that are simple and inexpensive to correct at the time. If they are not found and corrected at this time they could lead to major and more expensive problems later on.

Start out by doing simple tune-up, lubrication and maintenance. Tackle more involved jobs as you become more acquainted with the bike.

This chapter explains lubrication, maintenance and tune-up procedures required for the Honda CB550SC and CB650SC.

Table 1 is a suggested factory maintenance schedule. **Tables 1-8** are located at the end of this chapter.

ROUTINE CHECKS

The following simple checks should be performed at each stop at a service station for gas.

Engine Oil Level

Refer to *Engine Oil Level Check* under *Periodic Lubrication* in this chapter.

General Inspection

1. Quickly inspect the engine for signs of oil or fuel leakage.

2. Check the tires for embedded stones. Pry them out with your ignition key.
3. Make sure all lights work.

NOTE
At least check the brake light. It can burn out at any time. Motorists cannot stop as quickly as you and need all the warning you can give.

Tire Pressure

Tire pressure must be checked with the tires cold. Correct tire pressure varies with the load you are carrying. See **Table 2**.

Battery

Remove the right-hand side cover and check the battery electrolyte level. The level must be between the upper and lower level marks on the case (**Figure 1**).

For complete details see *Battery Removal, Installation and Electrolyte Level Check* in this chapter.

Check the level more frequently in hot weather; electrolyte will evaporate rapidly as heat increases.

Lights and Horn

With the engine running, check the following.
1. Pull the front brake lever on and check that the brake light comes on.
2. Push the rear brake pedal down and check that the brake light comes on soon after you have begun depressing the pedal.

3. Press the headlight dimmer switch to both the HI and LO positions and check to see that both headlight elements are working.

4. Turn the turn signal switch to the left and right positions and check that all 4 turn signals are working.

5. Push the horn button and make sure the horn blows loudly.

6. If the horn or any of the lights failed to operate properly, refer to Chapter Seven.

PRE-CHECKS

The following checks should be performed prior to the first ride of the day.

1. Inspect all fuel lines and fittings for wetness.

2. Make sure the fuel tank is full of fresh gasoline.

3. Make sure the engine oil level is correct.

4. Inspect the oil level in the final drive unit.

5. Check the operation of the clutch. Add hydraulic fluid to the clutch master cylinder or bleed the system if necessary.

6. Check the operation of the front brake. Add hydraulic fluid to the brake master cylinder if necessary.

7. Check the throttle and the rear brake pedal. Make sure they operate properly with no binding.

8. Inspect the front and rear suspension; make sure it has a good solid feel with no looseness.

9. Check tire pressure. Refer to **Table 2**.

10. Check the air pressure in the front forks. Refer to **Table 3**.

11. Check the exhaust system for damage.

12. Check the tightness of all fasteners, especially engine mounting hardware.

SERVICE INTERVALS

The services and intervals shown in **Table 1** are recommended by the factory. Strict adherence to these recommendations will ensure long service from the Honda. If the bike is run in an area of high humidity, the lubrication services must be done more frequently to prevent possible rust damage.

For convenience when maintaining your motorcycle, most of the services shown in the table are described in this chapter. However, some procedures which require more than minor disassembly or adjustment are covered elsewhere in the appropriate chapter.

TIRES AND WHEELS

Tire Pressure

Tire pressure should be checked and adjusted to maintain the smoothness of the tire, good traction

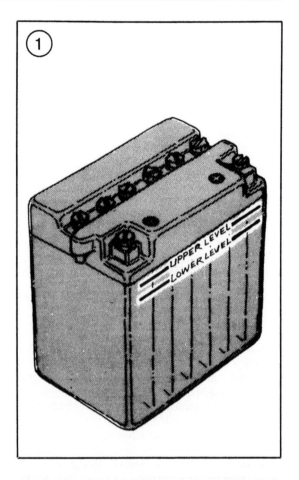

and handling and to get the maximum life out of the tire. A simple, accurate gauge (**Figure 2**) can be purchased for a few dollars and should be carried in your motorcycle tool kit. The appropriate tire pressures are shown in **Table 2**.

Tire Inspection

The tires take a lot of punishment so inspect them periodically for excessive wear, cuts, abrasions, etc. If you find a nail or other object in the tire, mark its location with a light crayon prior to removing it. This will help locate the hole for repair. Refer to Chapter Eight for tire changing and repair information.

Check local traffic regulations concerning minimum tread depth. Measure the tread depth at the center of the tire tread using a tread depth gauge (**Figure 3**) or small ruler. Honda recommends that original equipment tires be replaced when the front tire tread depth is 1.5 mm (1/16 in.) or less, when the rear tread depth is 2.0 mm (3/32 in.) or less or when tread wear indicators appear across the tire indicating the minimum tread depth.

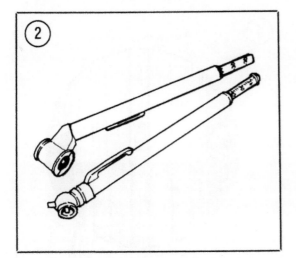

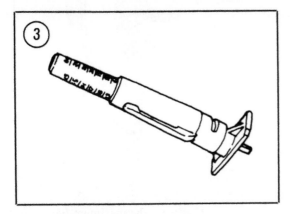

3

Rim Inspection

Frequently inspect the wheel rims. If a rim has been damaged it might be out of alignment. Improper wheel alignment can cause severe vibration and result in an unsafe riding condition. If the rim portion of the alloy wheel is damaged the wheel *must be replaced* as it cannot be repaired.

CRANKCASE BREATHER HOSE (U.S. MODELS ONLY)

Remove both side covers, seat and fuel tank. Inspect the breather hoses for cracks and deterioration and make sure all hose clamps are tight.

EVAPORATION EMISSION CONTROL (1984-ON CALIFORNIA MODELS ONLY)

Inspect the hoses for cracks, kinks and deterioration. Make sure all hoses are tight where they attach to the various components. For correct hose routing, refer to Chapter Six.

BATTERY

Removal, Installation and Electrolyte Level Check

The battery is the heart of the electrical system. It should be checked and serviced as indicated in **Table 1**. The majority of electrical system troubles can be attributed to neglect of this vital component.

The electrolyte level should be maintained between the 2 marks on the battery case (**Figure 1**). If the electrolyte level is low, remove the battery from the bike so it can be thoroughly serviced and checked.

1. Remove the right-hand side cover and the seat.
2. Remove the bolt securing the secondary ground wire to the frame.
3. Remove the bolt securing the battery holder plate.
4. Disconnect the vent tube from the battery. Leave it routed through the bike's frame.
5. Swing the holder plate out of the way.
6. Disconnect the negative (−) lead from the battery.
7. Slide the battery and its lower cover out of the frame. Disconnect the positive (+) lead from the battery.
8. Wipe off any of the highly corrosive residue that may have dripped from the battery during removal.

WARNING
Protect your eyes, skin and clothing. If electrolyte gets into your eyes, flush your eyes thoroughly with clean water and get prompt medical attention.

CAUTION
Be careful not to spill battery electrolyte on painted or polished surfaces. The liquid contains sulfuric acid that is highly corrosive and will damage the finish. If it is spilled, wash it off immediately with soapy water and thoroughly rinse with clean water.

9. Remove the caps from the battery cells and add distilled water to correct the fluid level. Never add electrolyte (acid) to correct the level.

NOTE
If distilled water has been added, reinstall the battery caps and gently shake the battery for several minutes to mix the existing electrolyte with the new water.

10. After the fluid level has been corrected and the battery allowed to stand a few minutes, remove the battery caps and check the specific gravity of the

electrolyte in each cell with a hydrometer (**Figure 4**). See *Battery Testing* in this chapter.

11. After the battery has been refilled, recharged or replaced, install it by reversing these removal steps, noting the following.

12. On 1984-on models, if disconnected, be sure to attach the secondary ground cable (smaller wire) to the frame bolt.

> *CAUTION*
> *If you removed the breather tube from the frame, be sure to route it so residue will not drain onto any part of the bike's frame. The tube must be free of bends or twists as any restriction may pressurize the battery and damage it.*

Testing

Hydrometer testing is the best way to check battery condition. Use a hydrometer with numbered graduations from 1.100 to 1.300 rather than one with color-coded bands. To use the hydrometer, squeeze the rubber ball, insert the tip into the cell and release the pressure on the ball. Draw enough electrolyte to float the weighted float inside the hydrometer. Note the number in line with the surface of the electrolyte; this is the specific gravity for this cell. Squeeze the rubber ball again and return the electrolyte to the cell from which it came.

The specific gravity of the electrolyte in each battery cell is an excellent indication of that cell's condition. A fully charged cell will read from 1.260-1.280, while a cell in good condition reads from 1.230-1.250 and anything below 1.140 is discharged.

Specific gravity varies with temperature. For each 10° the electrolyte temperature exceeds 27° C (80° F), add 0.004 to readings indicated on the hydrometer. Subtract 0.004 for each 10° below 27° C (80° F).

If the cells test in the poor range, the battery requires recharging. The hydrometer is useful for checking the progress of the charging operation. **Table 4** shows approximate state of charge.

Charging

> *WARNING*
> *During the charging process, highly explosive hydrogen gas is released from the battery. The battery should be charged only in a well-ventilated area away from any open flames (including pilot lights on home gas appliances). Do not allow any smoking in the area. Never check the charge of the battery by arcing across the terminals; the resulting spark can ignite the hydrogen gas.*

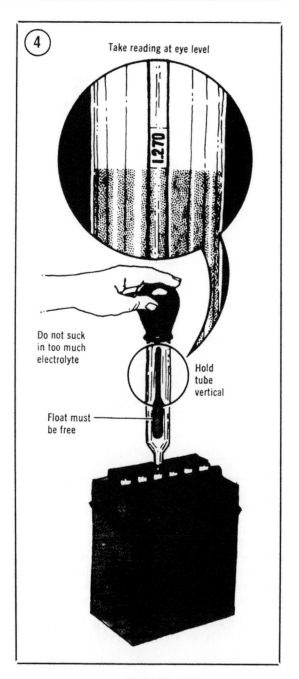

④ Take reading at eye level

L.270

Do not suck in too much electrolyte

Hold tube vertical

Float must be free

> *CAUTION*
> *Always remove the battery from the bike before connecting the battery charger. Never recharge a battery in the bike's frame; the corrosive mist emitted during the charging process will damage the bike.*

1. Connect the positive charger lead to the positive battery terminal (or lead) and the negative charger lead to the negative battery terminal (or lead).

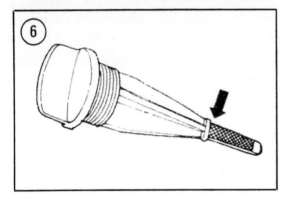

2. Remove all vent caps from the battery, set the charger at 12 volts and switch the charger on. If the output of the charger is variable, it is best to select a low setting—1 1/2 to 2 amps.

CAUTION
The electrolyte level must be maintained at the upper level during the charging cycle; check and refill as necessary.

3. After the battery has been charged for about 8 hours, turn the charger off, disconnect the leads and check the specific gravity. It should be within the limits specified in **Table 5**. If it is, and remains stable for 1 hour, the battery is considered charged.
4. Clean the battery terminals, electrical cable connectors and surrounding case and tray and reinstall them in the bike, reversing the removal steps. Coat the battery terminals with Vaseline or silicone spray to retard corrosion and decomposition of the terminals.

CAUTION
Route the breather tube so it does not drain the bike's frame. The tube must be free of bends or twists as any restriction may pressurize the battery and damage it.

New Battery Installation

When replacing the old battery with a new one, be sure to charge it completely (specific gravity 1.260-1.280) before installing it in the bike. Failure to do so or using the battery with a low electrolyte level will permanently damage the new battery.

PERIODIC LUBRICATION

Oil

Oil is graded according to its viscosity, which is an indication of how thick it is. The Society of Automotive Engineers (SAE) system distinguishes oil viscosity by numbers. Thick oils have higher viscosity numbers than thin oils. For example, an SAE 5 oil is a thin oil while an SAE 90 oil is relatively thick.

Grease

A good quality grease (preferably waterproof) should be used. Water does not wash grease off parts as easily as it washes oil off. In addition, grease maintains its lubricating qualities better than oil on long and strenuous rides. In a pinch, though, the wrong lubricant is better than none at all. Correct the situation as soon as possible.

Engine Oil Level Check

Engine oil level is checked with the dipstick located at the left-hand side of the engine just above the shift lever (**Figure 5**).
1. Place the bike on level ground and on the centerstand.
2. Start the engine and let it idle for 2-3 minutes.
3. Shut off the engine and let the oil settle.
4. Unscrew the dipstick and wipe it clean. Reinsert the dipstick onto the threads in the hole; do not screw it in.
5. Remove the dipstick and check the oil level. The level should be between the 2 lines (**Figure 6**) and not above the upper one. If the level is below the lower line, add the recommended type engine oil to correct the level.

Engine Oil and Filter Change

The factory-recommended oil and filter change interval is listed in **Table 1**. This assumes the motorcycle is operated in moderate climates. In extreme climates, oil should be changed every 30 days. The time interval is more important than the mileage interval because acids formed by combustion blowby will contaminate the oil even if the motorcycle is not run for several months. If the motorcycle is operated under dusty conditions,

3

the oil will get dirty more quickly and should be changed more frequently than recommended.

Always use oil with the API service classification (**Figure 7**) recommended by the manufacturer. The service classification indicates the oil meets specific lubrication standards. The first letter (S, for example) indicates the oil is for gasoline engines. The second letter indicates the standard the oil satisfies. Current SJ oils, which are designed for automotive applications, may not be suitable for motorcycle applications. Try to use the same brand of oil at each oil change. Refer to **Figure 8** for the correct viscosity to use under the anticipated ambient temperatures (not engine oil temperature).

> *CAUTION*
> *Do not add any friction-reducing additives to the oil as they will cause clutch slippage. Also do not use an engine oil with graphite added.*

To change the engine oil and filter you will need the following:
   a. Drain pan.
   b. Funnel.
   c. Can opener or pour spout.
   d. 3 quarts of oil.
   e. New oil filter

> *NOTE*
> *Never dispose of motor oil in the trash or pour it on the ground, or down a storm drain. Many service stations accept used motor oil. Many waste haulers provide curbside used motor oil collection. Do not combine other fluids with motor oil to be recycled. To find a recycling location contact the American Petroleum Institute (API) at www.recycle.org.*

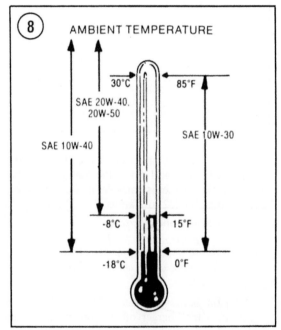

1. Start the engine and let it reach operating temperature; 15-20 minutes of stop-and-go riding is usually sufficient.
2. Turn engine off and place bike on the centerstand.
3. Place a drain pan under the engine.
4. Remove the 17 mm drain plug on the oil pan. Remove the oil filler cap (**Figure 5**); this will speed up the flow of oil.
5. Let the oil drain for at least 15-20 minutes. During this time, push the starter button a couple of times to help drain any remaining oil.

> *CAUTION*
> *Do not let the engine start and run without oil in the crankcase.*

6. Inspect the sealing washer on the crankcase drain plug. Replace if its condition is in doubt.
7. Install the oil pan drain plug and tighten to 30-40 N•m (22-29 ft.-lb.).

> *CAUTION*
> *Before removing the oil filter, thoroughly clean off all road dirt and oil around it.*

8. Move the drain pan under the filter and unscrew the bolt securing the filter cover (**Figure 9**) to the crankcase.
9. Remove the cover and the filter. Discard the old filter and clean out the cover and the bolt with solvent. Make sure all holes in the bolt are open to allow maximum oil flow. Dry all parts thoroughly.
10. Inspect the O-ring seal on the cover. Replace if necessary.

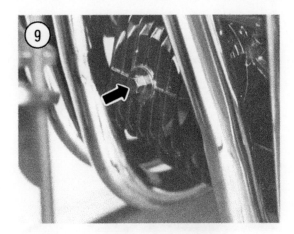

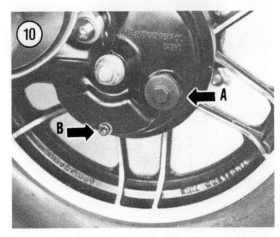

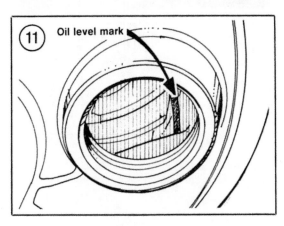

Oil level mark

CAUTION
Prior to installing the oil filter, clean off the mating surface of the crankcase—do not allow any road dirt to enter into the oil system.

11. Insert the bolt into the cover and install the spring and washer. Insert the new filter onto the bolt.

12. Apply a light coat of oil seal on the filter cover and install the filter assembly onto the crankcase.

13. Tighten the cover bolt to 28-32 N•m (20-23 ft.-lb.).

14. Insert a funnel into the oil fill hole and fill the engine with the correct viscosity and quantity of oil. Refer to **Table 5**.

15. Install the oil filler cap.

16. Start the engine, let it run at moderate speed and check for leaks.

17. Turn the engine off and check for correct oil level; adjust as necessary.

Final Drive Oil Level Check

The final drive case should be cool. If the bike has been run, allow it to cool down (minimum of 10 minutes), then check the oil level. When checking or changing the final drive oil, do not allow any dirt or foreign matter to enter the case opening.

1. Place the bike on the centerstand on a level surface.

2. Wipe the area around the oil filler cap clean and unscrew the oil filler cap (A, **Figure 10**).

3. The oil level is correct if the oil is up to the lower edge of the filler cap hole (**Figure 11**). If the oil level is low, add hypoid gear oil API GL-5 until the oil level is correct. Refer to **Table 6** for recommended oil weight for various ambient temperatures.

4. Inspect the O-ring seal on the oil filler cap. If it is deteriorating or starting to harden it must be replaced.

5. Install the oil filler cap.

Final Drive Oil Change

The factory-recommended oil change interval is listed in **Table 1**.

To change the oil you will need the following:
  a. Drain pan.
  b. Funnel.
  c. Approximately 150-170 cc (5-6 oz.) of hypoid gear oil.

Discard old oil as outlined under *Engine Oil and Filter Change* in this chapter.

1. Ride the bike until normal operating temperature is obtained. Usually 15-20 minutes of stop-and-go riding is sufficient.

2. Place the bike on the centerstand.

3. Place a drain pan under the drain plug.

4. Remove the oil filler cap (A, **Figure 10**) and drain plug (B, **Figure 10**).

5. Let the oil drain for at least 15-20 minutes to ensure that most of the oil has drained out.

6. Inspect the sealing washer on the drain plug; replace the washer if necessary.

7. Install the drain plug and tighten it securely.

8. Insert a funnel into the oil filler cap hole.

9. Add the recommended viscosity and quantity of hypoid gear oil; refer to **Table 6**. Remove the funnel and make sure the oil level is correct.

> *NOTE*
> *To measure the correct amount of fluid, use a plastic baby bottle. These have measurements in cubic centimeters (cc) and fluid ounces (oz.) on the side.*

10. Install the oil filler cap.

11. Test ride the bike and check for oil leaks. After the test ride recheck the oil level as described in this chapter and readjust if necessary.

Front Fork Oil Change

There is no factory-recommended fork oil change interval but it's a good practice to change the oil every 12,800 km (8,000 miles) or when it becomes contaminated.

1. Remove each fork top cover (**Figure 12**) and bleed off *all* air pressure from each fork by depressing the valve stem (**Figure 13**).

> *WARNING*
> *Always bleed off all air pressure; failure to do so may cause personal injury when disassembling the fork.*

> *WARNING*
> *Release the air pressure gradually. If released too fast, fork oil will spurt out with the air. Protect your eyes and clothing accordingly.*

2. Place wood block(s) under the engine to support the bike securely with the front wheel off the ground.

3. Unscrew the fork top cap slowly as it is under pressure from the fork spring.

4. Remove the fork spacer from the fork tube.

5A. On models equipped with the TRAC system, place a drain pan under the drain screw and remove the drain screw. Refer to **Figure 14** for the left-hand fork leg and **Figure 15** for the right-hand fork leg. Allow the oil to drain for at least 5 minutes. *Never* reuse the oil.

5B. On all other models, place a drain pan under the drain screw (**Figure 15**) and remove the drain screw. Allow the oil to drain for at least 5 minutes. *Never* reuse the oil.

> *CAUTION*
> *Do not allow the fork oil to come into contact with any of the brake components.*

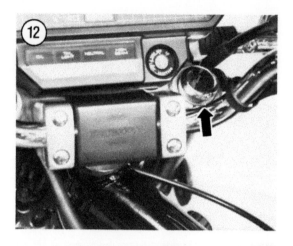

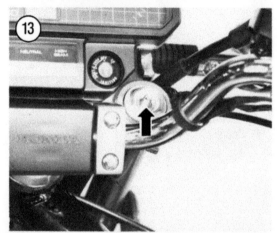

6. Inspect the gasket on the drain screw; replace it if necessary. Install the drain screw.

7. Repeat Steps 3-6 for the other fork.

8. Refill each fork leg with the specified quantity of DEXRON automatic transmission fluid or 10W fork oil. Refer to **Table 7** for specified quantity.

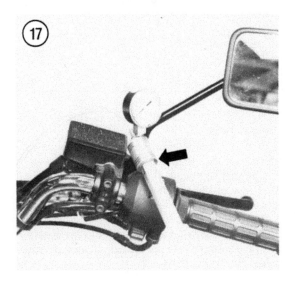

CAUTION
On models equipped with the TRAC system, remember the fork oil capacity is different on each fork leg due to the anti-dive feature on the left-hand fork. Be sure to put the correct amount of fluid into the correct fork leg.

NOTE
In order to measure the correct amount of fluid, use a plastic baby bottle. These have measurements in cubic centimeters (cc) and fluid ounces (oz.) on the side.

9. Inspect the O-ring seal (**Figure 16**) on the fork top cap; replace if necessary.
10. Install the fork spacer and the fork top cap while pushing down on the spring. Start the fork top cap slowly; don't cross-thread it. Tighten the fork top cap to 15-30 N•m (11-22 ft.-lb.).
11. Inflate the front forks to 0-40 kPa (0-6 psi). Do not use compressed air; only use a small hand-operated air pump (**Figure 17**).

WARNING
Never use any type of compressed gas as a lethal explosion may be result. Never heat the fork assembly with a torch or place it near an open flame or extreme heat as this will also result in an explosion.

12. Install the fork top cover on each fork leg.
13. Road test the bike and check for leaks.

Throttle and Choke
Control Cable Lubrication

The throttle and choke control cables should be lubricated at the interval indicated in **Table 1**. They should also be inspected at this time for fraying and the cable sheath should be checked for chafing. The cables are relatively inexpensive and should be replaced when found to be faulty.

The throttle and choke control cables can be lubricated either with oil or with any of the popular cable lubricants and a cable lubricator. The first method requires more time and complete lubrication of the entire cable is less certain.

Examine the exposed end of the inner cable. If it is dirty or the cable feels gritty when moved up and down in its housing, first spray it with a lubricant/solvent such as LPS-25 or WD-40. Let this solvent drain out, then proceed with the following steps.

Oil method

1. On the throttle control cables, remove the screws that clamp the throttle control/switch housing together to gain access to the cable ends. Disconnect the cables from the throttle grip assembly (**Figure 18**).

2. On the choke control cable, remove the screws that clamp the choke control/switch housing together to gain access to the cable end. Disconnect the cable from the choke lever assembly (**Figure 19**).

3. Make a cone of stiff paper and tape it to the end of the cable sheath (**Figure 20**).

4. Hold the cable upright and pour a small amount of thin oil (SAE 10W-30) into the cone. Work the cable in and out of the sheath for several minutes to help the oil work its way down to the end of the cable.

> *NOTE*
> *To avoid a mess, place a shop cloth at the end of the cable to catch the oil as it runs out.*

5. Remove the cone, reconnect the cable and adjust the throttle and choke cables as described in this chapter.

Lubricator method

1. On the throttle control cables, remove the screws that clamp the throttle control/switch housing together to gain access to the cable ends. Disconnect the cables from the throttle grip assembly (**Figure 18**).

2. On the choke control cable, remove the screws that clamp the choke control/switch housing together to gain access to the cable end. Disconnect the cable from the choke lever assembly (**Figure 19**).

3. Attach a lubricator following the manufacturer's instructions.

4. Insert the nozzle of the lubricant can in the lubricator, press the button on the can and hold it down until the lubricant begins to flow out of the other end of the cable.

> *NOTE*
> *Place a shop cloth at the end of the cables to catch all excess lubricant that will flow out.*

5. Remove the lubricator, reconnect the cables and adjust the cables as described in this chapter.

Speedometer Cable Lubrication

Lubricate the cable every year or whenever needle operation is erratic.

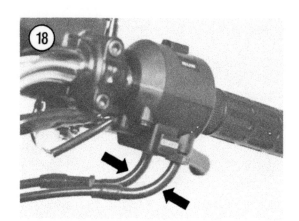

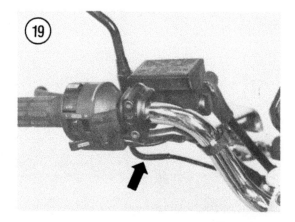

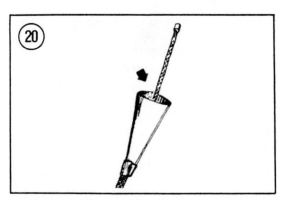

1. Remove the headlight case as described in Chapter Seven.

2. Unscrew the retaining collar and remove the cable from the instrument.

3. Pull the cable from the cable sheath.

4. If the grease on the cable is contaminated, thoroughly clean off all old grease.

5. Thoroughly coat the cable with a good grade multipurpose grease and reinstall into the sheath.

6. Make sure the cable is correctly seated into the drive unit at the wheel.

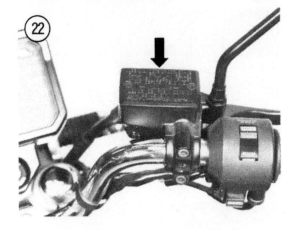

7. Insert the cable into the instrument and screw the retaining collar on securely.

8. Install the headlight case as described in Chapter Seven.

PERIODIC MAINTENANCE

Disc Brake Fluid Level

The fluid level in the front brake reservoir should be up to the upper mark within the reservoir. This upper level mark is only visible when the master cylinder top cover is removed. If the brake fluid level reaches the lower level mark (**Figure 21**), visible through the viewing port on the side of the master cylinder reservoir, the fluid level must be corrected by adding fresh brake fluid.

1. Place the bike on level ground and position the handlebars so the master cylinder reservoir is level.

2. Clean any dirt from the area around the top cover prior to removing the cover.

3. Remove the top cover (**Figure 22**) and the diaphragm. Add brake fluid until the level is to the upper level line within the master cylinder body. Use fresh brake fluid from a sealed brake fluid container.

WARNING
Use brake fluid from a sealed container clearly marked DOT 3 (specified for disc brakes). Others may vaporize and cause brake failure. Do not intermix different brands or types of brake fluid as they may not be compatible. Do not intermix a silicone based (DOT 5) brake fluid as it can cause brake component damage leading to brake system failure.

CAUTION
Be careful when handling brake fluid. Do not spill it on painted or plated surfaces or plastic parts as it will destroy the surface. Wash the area immediately with soapy water and thoroughly rinse it off.

4. Reinstall the diaphragm and the top cover. Tighten the screws securely.

Disc Brake Lines

Check brake lines between the master cylinder and the brake caliper(s). If there is any leakage, tighten the connections and bleed the brakes as described in Chapter Ten. If this does not stop the leak or if a brake line is obviously damaged, cracked or chafed, replace the brake line and bleed the system.

Disc Brake Pad Wear

Inspect the brake pads for excessive or uneven wear, scoring and oil or grease on the friction surface. Look at the pads through the slot in the top of the caliper assembly. Replace the pads if the wear line on the pads reaches the brake disc.

NOTE
On dual disc models, always replace all pads in both caliper assemblies at the same time.

If any of these conditions exist, replace the pads as described in Chapter Ten.

Disc Brake Fluid Change

Every time the reservoir cap is removed, a small amount of dirt and moisture enters the brake fluid. The same thing happens if a leak occurs or any part of the hydraulic system is loosened or disconnected. Dirt can clog the system and cause unnecessary wear. Water in the brake fluid vaporizes at high temperature, impairing the hydraulic action and reducing the brake's stopping ability.

To maintain peak performance, change the brake fluid as indicated in **Table 1**. To change brake fluid, follow the *Bleeding the Brake System* procedure in Chapter Ten. Continue adding new fluid to the master cylinder and bleeding out at the calipers until the fluid leaving the calipers is clean and free of contaminants.

> *WARNING*
> *Use brake fluid from a sealed container clearly marked DOT 3 (specified for disc brakes). Others may vaporize and cause brake failure. Do not intermix different brands or types of brake fluid as they may not be compatible. Do not intermix a silicone based (DOT 5) brake fluid as it can cause brake component damage leading to brake system failure.*

Rear Drum Brake Lining

Check the rear brake linings for wear. If the arrow on the brake arm aligns with the raised index mark on the brake backing plate (**Figure 23**) when the brake pedal is applied, the brake linings require replacement.

If replacement is necessary, refer to Chapter Ten.

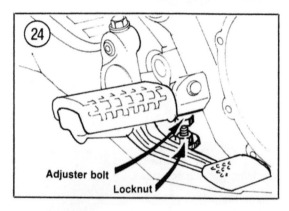

Adjuster bolt

Locknut

Rear Brake Pedal Height Adjustment

The rear brake pedal should be adjusted as indicated in **Table 1**.
1. Place the bike on the centerstand.
2. Check that the brake pedal is in the at-rest position.
3. Adjust the pedal height so the brake pedal is 7 mm (1/4 in.) below the top surface of the front footpeg.
4. To change height position, loosen the locknut and turn the adjuster bolt (**Figure 24**). Tighten the locknut.

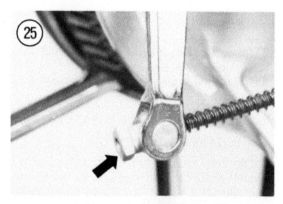

Rear Brake Pedal Free Play

Free play is the distance the rear brake pedal travels from the at-rest position to the applied position when the pedal is depressed by hand.
1. Place the bike on the centerstand with the rear wheel off the ground.
2. Adjust the brake pedal to the correct height as described in this chapter.
3. Turn the adjust nut on the end of the brake rod (**Figure 25**) until the pedal has 20-30 mm (3/4-1 1/4 in.) free play.
4. Rotate the rear wheel and check for brake drag.

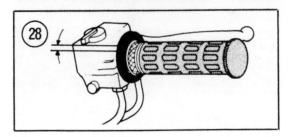

5. Operate the brake pedal several times to make sure the pedal returns to the at-rest position immediately after release.

Clutch Fluid Level Check

The clutch is hydraulically operated and requires no routine adjustment.

The hydraulic fluid in the clutch master cylinder should be checked as listed in **Table 1** or whenever the level drops, whichever comes first. Bleeding the clutch system and servicing clutch components are covered in Chapter Five.

> *CAUTION*
> *If the clutch operates correctly when the engine is cold or in cool weather, but operates erratically (or not at all) after the engine warms up or in hot weather, there is air in the hydraulic line and the clutch must be bled. Refer to Chapter Five.*

The fluid level in the reservoir should be up to the upper mark within the reservoir. This upper level mark is only visible when the master cylinder top cover is removed. If the fluid level reaches the lower level mark (**Figure 26**), visible through the viewing port in the master cylinder reservoir, the fluid level must be corrected by adding fresh hydraulic (brake) fluid.

1. Place the bike on level ground and position the handlebars so the master cylinder reservoir is level.
2. Clean any dirt from the area around the top cover prior to removing the cover.

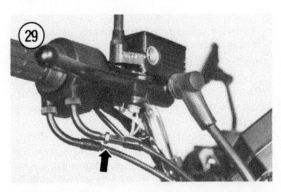

3. Remove the top cover (**Figure 27**) and the diaphragm. Add clutch fluid until the level is to the upper level line within the master cylinder body. Use fresh hydraulic fluid from a sealed hydraulic fluid container.

> *WARNING*
> *Use hydraulic fluid from a sealed container clearly marked DOT 3. Do not intermix different brands or types of hydraulic fluid as they may not be compatible. Do not intermix a silicone based (DOT 5) hydraulic fluid as it can cause clutch component damage leading to clutch release system failure.*

> *CAUTION*
> *Be careful when handling hydraulic fluid. Do not spill it on painted or plated surfaces or plastic parts as it will destroy the surface. Wash the area immediately with soapy water and thoroughly rinse it off.*

4. Reinstall the diaphragm and the top cover. Tighten the screws securely.

Clutch Hydraulic Lines

Check clutch lines between the master cylinder and the clutch slave cylinder. If there is any leakage, tighten the connections and bleed the clutch as described in Chapter Five. If this does not stop the leak or if a clutch line is obviously damaged, cracked or chafed, replace the clutch line and bleed the system.

Throttle Adjustment and Operation

The throttle grip should have 2-6 mm (1/8-1/4 in.) rotational free play (**Figure 28**). If adjustment is necessary, loosen the locknut and turn the adjuster (**Figure 29**) at the throttle grip in or out to achieve proper free play rotation. Tighten the locknut.

NOTE
*Minor adjustments can be made at the throttle grip. Major adjustments can be made where the throttle cables attach to the carburetor assembly (**Figure 30**).*

Check the throttle cables from grip to carburetor. Make sure they are not kinked or chafed. Replace as necessary.

Make sure the throttle grip rotates freely from a fully closed to fully open position. Check with the handlebar at center, at full right and at full left. If necessary, remove the throttle grip and apply a lithium base grease to it.

Air Filter Element Cleaning

The air filter element should be removed and cleaned as indicated in **Table 1**.

The air filter removes dust and abrasive particles from the air before the air enters the carburetors and engine. Without the air filter, very fine particles could enter into the engine and cause rapid wear of the piston rings, cylinders and bearings. They might also clog small passages in the carburetors. Never run the bike without the air filter element installed.

Proper air filter servicing can do more to ensure long service from your engine than almost any other single item.

1. Remove the right-hand side cover (**Figure 31**).
2. Pull the starter solenoid (**Figure 32**) from its rubber mount on the air filter cover.
3. Remove the screws (**Figure 33**) securing the air filter cover and remove the cover.
4. Pull the filter set spring out (**Figure 34**).
5. Remove the air filter element from the air box (A, **Figure 35**).
6. Wipe out the interior of the air box with a shop rag dampened with cleaning solvent. Remove any foreign matter that may have passed through a broken element.

7. Gently tap the air filter element. Apply compressed air to the *outside* of the element to remove all loosened dirt and dust from the element.
8. Inspect the element; if it is torn or broken in any area it should be replaced. Do not run with a damaged element as it may allow dirt to enter the engine.
9. Apply a light coat of wheel bearing grease to the rubber sealing edges (B, **Figure 35**) of the filter to provide an air tight seal between the filter and the air box.
10. Install the air filter element assembly into the air box and slide in the set spring.

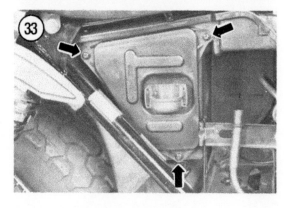

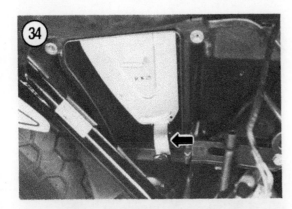

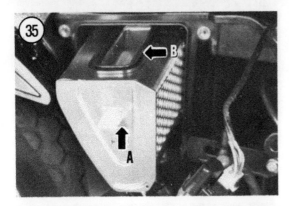

11. Inspect the gasket (**Figure 36**) on the air filter cover. If it is damaged in any way, replace the gasket.

12. Install the air filter cover and secure it with the screws.

13. Install the right-hand side cover.

Fuel Line Inspection

Inspect the fuel line from the fuel tank to the shutoff valve and to the carburetor assembly. If any are cracked or deteriorating they must be replaced. Make sure the small hose clamps are in place and holding securely.

WARNING
A damaged or deteriorated fuel line presents a very dangerous fire hazard to both the rider and the bike if fuel should spill onto a hot engine or exhaust pipe.

Wheel Bearings

There is no factory-recommended mileage interval for cleaning and repacking the wheel bearings. They should be serviced when they are removed from the wheel hub or when water contamination is likely. The correct service procedures are covered in Chapter Eight and Chapter Nine.

Steering Head Adjustment Check

The steering head is fitted with assembled bearings. It should be checked as indicated in **Table 1**.

Place the bike up on wood block(s) so the front wheel is off the ground. Hold onto the front fork tubes and gently rock the fork assembly back and forth. If you can feel looseness, the steering stem must be disassembled and adjusted; refer to Chapter Eight.

Front Suspension Check

1. Apply the front brake and pump the forks up and down as vigorously as possible. Check for smooth operation and check for any oil leaks.

2. Make sure the upper and lower fork bridge bolts are tight (**Figure 37**).

3. Make sure the bolts securing the handlebar holders (**Figure 38**) are tight and the handlebar is secure.

4. Make sure the front axle and axle pinch bolt are tight (**Figure 39**).

> *CAUTION*
> *If any of the previously mentioned bolts and nuts are loose, refer to Chapter Eight for correct procedures and torque specifications.*

Rear Suspension Check

1. Place the bike on the centerstand.

2. Push hard on the rear wheel (sideways) to check for side play in the swing arm bushings.

3. Check the tightness of the upper and lower mounting bolts or nuts (**Figure 40**) on each shock absorber.

4. Make sure the rear axle nut is tight (**Figure 41**).

5. Check the tightness of the rear brake torque arm bolt (**Figure 42**). Make sure the cotter pin is in place.

> *CAUTION*
> *If any of the previously mentioned bolts and nuts are loose, refer to Chapter Ten for correct procedures and torque specifications.*

Nuts, Bolts and Other Fasteners

Constant vibration can loosen many of the fasteners on the motorcycle. Check the tightness of all fasteners, especially those on:

    a. Engine mounting hardware.
    b. Engine crankcase covers.
    c. Handlebar and front forks.
    d. Gearshift lever.
    e. Brake pedal and lever.
    f. Exhaust system.

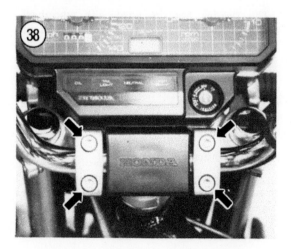

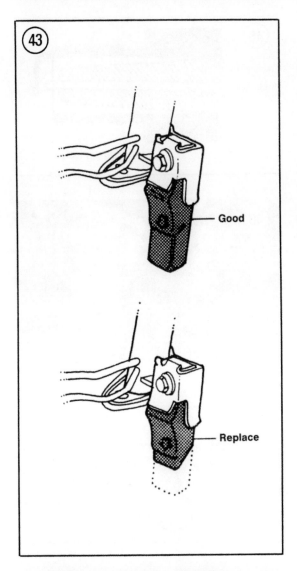

Good

Replace

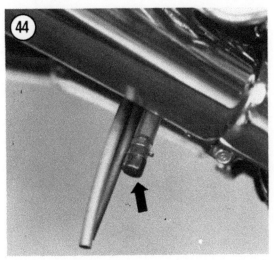

Sidestand Rubber

The rubber pad on the sidestand kicks the sidestand up if you should forget. If it wears down to the molded line (**Figure 43**), it will no longer be effective and must be replaced.

Remove the bolt and replace the rubber pad with a new one. Be sure the new rubber pad is marked "Over 260 lbs. Only."

Crankcase Breather
(U.S. Models Only)

At the interval indicated in **Table 1** or sooner if a considerable amount of riding is done at full throttle or in the rain, the residue in the breather drain tube should be drained.

Remove the drain plug (**Figure 44**) and drain out all residue. Install the cap; make sure the clamp is tight.

Refer to Chapter Six for complete details on the breather system.

TUNE-UP

A complete tune-up should be performed at the interval indicated in **Table 1** for normal riding. More frequent tune-ups may be required if the bike is ridden primarily in stop-and-go traffic. The purpose of the tune-up is to restore the performance lost due to normal wear and deterioration of parts.

Table 8 summarizes tune-up specifications.

The spark plugs should be replaced at every tune-up. In addition, this is a good time to clean the air filter element. Have the new parts on hand before you begin.

The cam chain tensioner is completely automatic and does not require any periodic adjustment. There are no provisions for tensioner adjustment on the engine.

The engine is equipped with hydraulic valve tappets and requires no periodic valve adjustment. There are no provisions for valve adjustment on this engine. If valve clearance problems are suspected, remove and inspect the tappets as described in Chapter Four.

The air filter element should be cleaned or replaced prior to doing other tune-up procedures, as described in this chapter.

Because different systems in an engine interact, the procedure should be done in the following order:

   a. Clean or replace the air filter element.

   b. Run a compression test.

   c. Check or replace the spark plugs.

   d. Check the ignition timing.

e. Synchronize the carburetors.

f. Adjust the carburetor idle speed.

To perform a tune-up on your Honda, you will need the following tools:

a. 18 mm spark plug wrench.

b. Socket wrench and assorted sockets.

c. Compression gauge.

d. Spark plug wire feeler gauge and gapper tool.

e. Ignition timing light.

f. Tune-up tachometer.

g. Manometer (carburetor synchronization tool).

Compression Test

At every other tune-up check cylinder compression. Record the results and compare them at the next tune-up. A running record will show trends in deterioration so that corrective action can be taken before complete failure occurs.

The results, when properly interpreted, can indicate general cylinder, piston ring and valve condition.

1. Warm the engine to normal operating temperature. Shut off the engine. Make sure the choke valve and throttle valve are completely open.

2. Place the bike on the centerstand.

3. Disconnect the spark plug wires from all spark plugs.

4. Remove the spark plugs.

5. Connect the compression tester to one cylinder following manufacturer's instructions.

6. Using the starter, crank the engine over until there is no further rise in pressure. Maximum pressure is usually reached within 4-7 seconds of engine cranking.

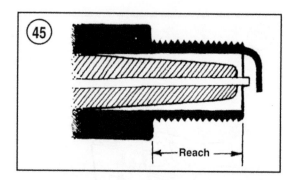

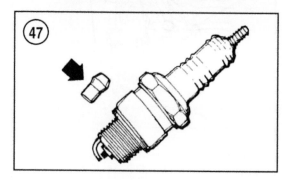

NOTE
Do not turn the engine over more than absolutely necessary. When spark plug leads and disconnected, the electronic ignition will produce the highest voltage possible and the coils may overheat and be damaged.

7. Remove the tester and record the reading.

8. Repeat Steps 5-7 for the other cylinder.

When interpreting the results, actual readings are not as important as the difference between the readings. Readings should be about 11-13 kg/cm2 (156-184 psi). A maximum difference of 4 kg/cm2 (57 psi) between any 2 cylinders is acceptable. Greater differences indicate worn or broken rings, defective hydraulic valve adjuster(s), leaking or sticking valve(s), a blown head gasket or a combination of all.

If compression readings do not differ between any 2 cylinders by more than specified, the rings and valves are in good condition.

If two adjacent cylinders read low, the head gasket may be defective.

If a low reading (10% or more) is obtained on one of the cylinders, it indicates valve, hydraulic valve tappet or ring trouble. To determine which, insert a small funnel into the spark plug hole and pour about a teaspoon of engine oil through it onto the top of the piston. Turn the engine over once to distribute the oil, then take another compression test and record the reading. If the compression increases significantly, the valves are good

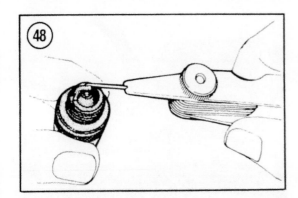

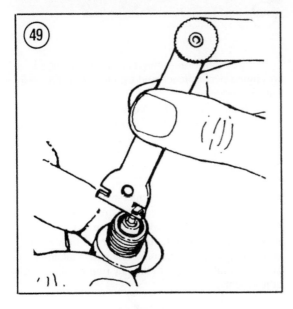

the portion of the insulator within the cylinder after the plug has been in service.

In areas where seasonal temperature variations are great, the factory recommends a "2-plug system"—cold plugs for hard summer riding and hot plugs for slower winter operation.

The reach (length) of a plug is also important. A longer than normal plug could interfere with the valves and pistons, causing permanent and severe damage. Refer to **Figure 45**. The recommended spark plugs are listed in **Table 8**.

Spark Plug Removal/Cleaning

1. Grasp the spark plug lead (**Figure 46**) as near to the plug as possible and pull it off the plug. If the boot is stuck to the plug, twist it slightly to break it loose.

2. Blow away any dirt that has accumulated in the spark plug wells.

CAUTION
The dirt could fall into the cylinders when the plugs are removed, causing serious engine damage.

3. Remove spark plugs with an 18 mm spark plug wrench.

NOTE
If plugs are difficult to remove, apply penetrating oil around base of plugs and let it soak in about 10-20 minutes.

4. Inspect spark plug carefully. Look for a plug with broken center porcelain, excessively eroded electrodes and excessive carbon or oil fouling. Replace such plugs. If deposits are light, the plug may be cleaned in solvent with a wire brush or in a special spark plug sandblast cleaner. Regap the plug as explained in this chapter.

Spark Plug Gapping and Installation

New plugs should be carefully gapped to ensure a reliable, consistent spark. You must use a special spark plug gapping tool with a wire feeler gauge.

Be sure to replace all 4 spark plugs at the same time; all 4 plugs must be of the same heat range.

1. Remove the new plugs from the box. Do *not* screw in the small piece that may be loose in the box (**Figure 47**); it is not used.

2. Insert a wire feeler gauge between the center and the side electrode of each plug (**Figure 48**). The correct gap is 0.8-0.9 mm (0.031-0.035 in.). If the gap is correct, you will feel a slight drag as you pull the wire through. If there is no drag or the gauge won't pass through, bend the side electrode *with the gapping tool* (**Figure 49**) to set the proper gap.

but the rings are defective on that cylinder. If compression does not increase, the valve train requires servicing. A valve could be hanging open or a piece of carbon could be on a valve seat.

Spark Plug Selection

Spark plugs are available in various heat ranges, hotter or colder than plugs originally installed at the factory.

Select plugs of a heat range designed for the loads and temperature conditions under which the bike will be run. The use of incorrect heat ranges can cause seized pistons, scored cylinder walls or damaged piston crowns.

In general, use a hot plug for low speeds, low engine loads and low temperatures. Use a cold plug for high speeds, high engine loads and high temperatures. The plug should operate hot enough to burn off unwanted deposits, but not so hot that it is damaged or causes preignition. A spark plug of the correct heat range will show a light tan color on

3. Put a *small* drop of oil or aluminum anti-seize compound on the threads of each spark plug.
4. Screw each spark plug in by hand until it seats. Very little effort is required. If force is necessary, you have a plug cross-threaded; unscrew it and try again.
5. Tighten the spark plugs an additional 1/2 turn after the gasket has made contact with the head. If you are reinstalling old, regapped plugs and are reusing the old gasket, only tighten an additional 1/4 turn.

> *NOTE*
> *Do not overtighten. This will only squash the gasket and destroy its sealing ability.*

6. Install each spark plug lead; make sure the lead is on tight.

Reading Spark Plugs

Much information about engine and spark plug performance can be determined by careful examination of the spark plugs. This information is more valid after performing the following steps.
1. Ride the bike a short distance at full throttle in any gear.
2. Turn the engine kill switch (**Figure 50**) to the OFF position before closing the throttle and simultaneously pull in the clutch or shift to NEUTRAL; coast and brake to a stop.
3. Remove the spark plugs and examine them. Compare them to **Figure 51**. If the insulator is white or burned, the plug is too hot and should be replaced with a colder one.

A too-cold plug will have sooty or oily deposits ranging in color from dark brown to black. Replace with a hotter plug and check for too-rich carburetion or evidence of oil blowby at the piston rings.

If the plug has a light tan or gray colored deposit and no abnormal gap wear or electrode erosion is evident, the plug and the engine are running properly.

If the plug exhibits a black insulator tip, a damp and oil film over the firing end and a carbon layer over the entire nose, it is oil fouled. An oil fouled plug can be cleaned, but it is better to replace it.

If any one plug is found unsatisfactory, discard and replace all plugs.

Ignition Timing

Your Honda is equipped with a capacitor discharge ignition (CDI) system. This system uses no breaker points and is non-adjustable. The timing should be checked to make sure all ignition components are operating correctly.

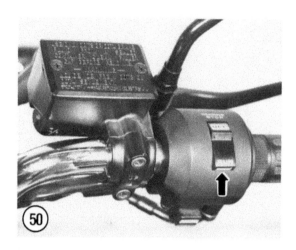

Incorrect ignition timing can cause a drastic loss of engine performance and efficiency. It may also cause overheating.

Before starting on this procedure, check all electrical connections related to the ignition system. Make sure all connections are tight and free of corrosion and that all ground connections are tight.
1. Start the engine and let it reach normal operating temperature. Shut the engine off.
2. Place the bike on the centerstand.
3. Remove the screws securing the pulse generator cover and remove the cover (**Figure 52**).
4. Connect a portable tachometer following the manufacturer's instructions. The bike's tachometer is not accurate enough in the low rpm range for this adjustment.

> *NOTE*
> *The cylinders are numbered 1-4 starting with the No. 1 cylinder on the left-hand side and working across from left to right with the No. 2, No. 3 and No. 4 cylinder. The left-hand side refers to a rider sitting on the seat looking forward.*

5. Connect a timing light to either the No. 1 or No. 4 cylinder following the manufacturer's instructions.
6. Fill in the timing marks on the pulse generator rotor with white grease pencil or typewriter white correction fluid. This will make the marks more visible.
7. Start the engine and let it idle at the idle speed listed in **Table 8**. If necessary, readjust the idle speed as described in this chapter.
8. Aim the timing light at the timing mark on the crankcase and pulse generator rotor and pull the trigger. If the timing mark "F" aligns with the fixed

SPARK PLUG CONDITION

NORMAL
- Identified by light tan or gray deposits on the firing tip.
- Can be cleaned.

GAP BRIDGED
- Identified by deposit buildup closing gap between electrodes.
- Caused by oil or carbon fouling. If deposits are not excessive, the plug can be cleaned.

OIL FOULED
- Identified by wet black deposits on the insulator shell bore and electrodes.
- Caused by excessive oil entering combustion chamber through worn rings and pistons, excessive clearance between valve guides and stems, or worn or loose bearings. Can be cleaned. If engine is not repaired, use a hotter plug.

CARBON FOULED
- Identified by black, dry fluffy carbon deposits on insulator tips, exposed shell surfaces and electrodes.
- Caused by too cold a plug, weak ignition, dirty air cleaner, too rich a fuel mixture, or excessive idling. Can be cleaned.

LEAD FOULED
- Identified by dark gray, black, yellow, or tan deposits or a fused glazed coating on the insulator tip.
- Caused by highly leaded gasoline. Can be cleaned.

WORN
- Identified by severely eroded or worn electrodes.
- Caused by normal wear. Should be replaced.

FUSED SPOT DEPOSIT
- Identified by melted or spotty deposits resembling bubbles or blisters.
- Caused by sudden acceleration. Can be cleaned.

OVERHEATING
- Identified by a white or light gray insulator with small black or gray brown spots and with bluish-burnt appearance of electrodes.
- Caused by engine overheating, wrong type of fuel, loose spark plugs, too hot a plug, or incorrect ignition timing. Replace the plug.

PREIGNITION
- Identified by melted electrodes and possibly blistered insulator. Metallic deposits on insulator indicate engine damage.
- Caused by wrong type of fuel, incorrect ignition timing or advance, too hot a plug, burned valves, or engine overheating. Replace the plug.

pointer on the crankcase (**Figure 53**), the timing is correct.

9. If the timing is incorrect, refer to Chapter Seven and check the spark unit and the pulse generator. There is no method for adjusting ignition timing.

10. Shut off the engine and disconnect the timing light and portable tachometer. Install the timing cover.

Carburetor Idle Mixture

The idle mixture (pilot screw) is preset at the factory and is *not* to be reset. This pertains to all 4 carburetors. Do not adjust the pilot screws unless the carburetors have been overhauled; refer to Chapter Six.

Carburetor Synchronization

When the carburetors are properly synchronized the engine will warm up faster and there will be an improvement in throttle response, performance and mileage.

Prior to synchronizing the carburetors, the air filter element must be clean and the ignition timing must also be checked to make sure all components are operating correctly.

This procedure requires special tools. You will need a mercury manometer (carb-sync tool). This is a tool that measures the manifold vacuum for all cylinders simultaneously. A carb-sync tool can be purchased from a Honda dealer, a motorcycle supply store or mail order firm.

> *NOTE*
> *When purchasing this tool, check that it is equipped with restrictors. These restrictors keep the mercury from being drawn into the engine when engine rpm is increased during the adjustment procedure. If the mercury is drawn into the engine the tool will have to be replaced.*

1. Start the engine and let it warm up to normal operating temperature. Ten minutes of stop-and-go riding is usually sufficient. Shut off the engine.

2. Place the bike on the centerstand.

3. Remove both side covers and the seat.

4. Remove the fuel tank as described in Chapter Six. There should be enough fuel left in the float bowls to run the bike for this procedure.

> *WARNING*
> *Do **not** rig up a temporary fuel supply as this presents a real fire danger. If you start to run out of fuel during the test, shut off the engine and momentarily install the fuel tank to refill the carburetor float bowls, then proceed with the test.*

5. Remove the vacuum plug (consisting of a screw and flat washer) from carburetor insulator at each cylinder (**Figure 54**).

6. Install the vacuum line adaptors into the vacuum hole in each insulator.

7. Connect the vacuum lines from the carb-sync tool, following the manufacturer's instructions. Be sure to route the vacuum lines to the correct cylinder. Most carb-sync tools have the cylinder number indicated on them next to each tube containing mercury.

NOTE
The No. 2 carburetor has no synchronization screw; the rest of the carburetors must be synchronized to it. The carburetors are numbered 1-4 starting with the No. 1 cylinder on the left-hand side and working across from left to right with the No. 2, No. 3 and No. 4 cylinder. The left-hand side refers to a rider sitting on the seat looking forward.

8. Start the engine and let it idle at the idle speed listed in **Table 8**. If necessary, readjust the idle speed as described in this chapter.

9. If the difference in gauge readings is 40 mm Hg (1.6 in. Hg) or less between all 4 cylinders, the carburetors are considered synchronized. If not, proceed as follows.

10. Turn the synchronization adjusting screw on the No. 1 carburetor (**Figure 55**) until the reading is the same as that on the No. 2 carburetor. Open the throttle a little and close it back down after each adjustment.

NOTE
Figure 55 is shown with the carburetor assembly removed for clarity. Do not remove the carburetor assembly for this procedure.

CAUTION
If your carb-sync tool is not equipped with restrictors, open and close the throttle very gently to avoid sucking mercury into the engine. If this happens, it will not harm the engine but will render the tool useless.

11. Repeat Step 10 for the No. 3 and No. 4 carburetors. Repeat Step 10 until all carburetors have the same gauge readings as the No. 2 carburetor.

NOTE
To gain the utmost in performance and efficiency from the engine, adjust the carburetors so that the gauge readings are as close to each other as possible.

12. Shut off the engine and remove the vacuum lines and adaptors. Install the screws and washers into the vacuum ports in the carburetor insulators. Make sure they are in tight to prevent a vacuum leak.

13. Install the fuel tank.

14. Install the seat and the side covers.

15. Restart the engine and readjust the idle speed as described in this chapter.

Idle Speed Adjustment

Before making this adjustment, the air filter element must be clean, the carburetors must be synchronized and the engine must have adequate compression. Otherwise, this procedure cannot be done properly.

1. Attach a portable tachometer following the manufacturer's instructions.

NOTE
The bike's tachometer is not accurate enough in the low rpm range for this adjustment.

2. Start the engine and let it warm up to normal operating temperature.

3. Set the idle speed by turning the large black plastic idle speed stop screw (**Figure 56**) in to increase or out to decrease idle speed. The correct idle speed is listed in **Table 8**.

NOTE
Figure 56 is shown with the carburetor assembly partially removed for clarity. Do not remove the carburetor assembly for this procedure.

4. Open and close the throttle a couple of times; check for variations in idle speed. Readjust if necessary.

WARNING
*With the engine idling, move the handlebar from side to side. If idle speed increases during this movement, the throttle cables may need adjusting or they may be incorrectly routed through the frame. Correct this problem immediately. Do **not** ride the bike in this unsafe condition.*

5. Shut off the engine and disconnect the portable tachometer.

Table 1 SERVICE INTERVALS*

Every 1,000 km (600 miles) or 6 months	• Check engine oil level • Check battery specific gravity and electrolyte level • Check hydraulic fluid level in brake master cylinder • Check hydraulic fluid level in clutch master cylinder • Lubricate rear brake pedal and shift lever • Lubricate side and centerstand pivot points • Inspect front steering for looseness • Check wheel bearings for smooth operation • Check wheel runout
Every 6,400 km (4,000 miles)	• Clean air cleaner element • Replace spark plugs • Change engine oil and replace oil filter • Check and adjust the carburetors • Check and synchronize the carburetors • Check and adjust the choke • Check and adjust throttle operation and free play • Adjust rear brake pedal height and free play • Clean fuel shutoff strainer • Check hydraulic fluid level in brake master cylinder • Check hydraulic fluid level in clutch master cylinder • Inspect brake pads and linings for wear • Inspect crankcase breather hose for cracks or loose hose clamps; drain out all residue • Inspect fuel line for chafed, cracked or swollen ends • Check engine mounting bolts for tightness • Check all suspension components
Every 12,800 km (8,000 miles)	• Check ignition timing • Run a compression test • Inspect fuel lines for wetness or damage • Inspect entire brake system for leaks or damage • Change front fork oil • Inspect oil level in final drive unit • Inspect wheel bearings • Inspect and repack the steering head bearings • Lubricate the speedometer drive cable • Lubricate final drive splines • Check and adjust headlight aim

(continued)

Table 1 SERVICE INTERVALS* (continued)

Every 24,000 km (38,400 miles) or every 2 years	• Change hydraulic fluid in clutch master cylinder • Change hydraulic fluid in brake master cyinder • Change oil in final drive unit
Every 4 years	• Replace all hydraulic brake hoses • Replace the hydraulic clutch hose assembly

* This Honda factory maintenance schedule should be considered as a guide to general maintenance and lubrication intervals. Harder than normal use or exposure to mud, water, sand, high humidity, etc. will naturally dictate more frequent attention to most maintenance items.

Table 2 TIRE PRESSURE (COLD)

Tire size	Normal	Maximum load limit*
Front 100/90-19		
CB550	28 psi (2.00 kg/cm²)	28 psi (2.00 kg/cm²)
CB650	32 psi (2.25 kg/cm²)	32 psi (2.25 kg/cm²)
Rear 130/90-16		
CB550	28 psi (2.00 kg/cm²)	36 psi (2.50 kg/cm²)
CB650	32 psi (2.25 kg/cm²)	40 psi (2.80 kg/cm²)

* Up to maximum load limit of 200 lbs (90 kg) including total weight of motorcycle with accessories, rider(s) and luggage.

Table 3 FRONT FORK AIR PRESSURE

Normal	Maximum*
0-6 psi (0-0.4 kg/cm²)	43 psi (4 kg/cm²)

* Do not exceed the maximum air pressure or internal parts of the fork will be damaged.

Table 4 STATE OF CHARGE

Specific gravity	State of Charge
1.110-1.130	Discharged
1.140-1.160	Almost discharged
1.170-1.190	One-quarter charged
1.200-1.220	One-half charged
1.230-1.250	Three-quarters charged
1.260-1.280	Fully charged

Table 5 ENGINE OIL CAPACITY

Oil and filter change	2.5 liter (2.6 U.S. qt., 2.2 Imp. qt.)
At overhaul	3.2 liter (3.4 U.S. qt., 2.8 Imp. qt.)

Table 6 FINAL DRIVE OIL

Capacity	Viscosity	Temperature
1983 170 cc (5.78 oz.)	SAE 90	Above 5° C (41° F)
	SAE 80	Below 5° C (41° F)
1984-on 150 cc (4.9 oz.)	SAE 80	All temperatures

Table 7 FRONT FORK OIL CAPACITY*

CB550	375 cc (12.7 oz.)
CB650	
Left-hand fork leg	462-467 cc (15.6-15.8 oz.)
Right-hand fork leg	447-452 cc (15.2-15.3 oz.)

* Capacity for each fork leg.

Table 8 TUNE-UP SPECIFICATIONS

Compression pressure (at sea level)	12.0 ± 1.0 kg/cm² (170 ± 14 psi)
Spark plug type	
Standard heat range	ND X24EPR-U9 or NGK DPR8EA-9
Cold weather*	ND X22EPR-U9 or NGK DPR7EA-9
Extended high-speed riding	ND X27EPR-U9 or NGK DPR9EA-9
Spark plug gap	0.8-0.9 mm (0.031-0.035 in.)
Ignition timing	"F" mark @ 1,400 ± 200 rpm
Idle speed	1,100 ± 100 rpm

* Cold weather climate—below 41° F (5° C).

4

ENGINE

The engine in the Honda 550-650 is an air-cooled, 4-stroke, inline 4-cylinder unit with double overhead camshafts. The crankshaft is supported by 5 main bearings and the camshafts are chain-driven from the timing sprockets on the crankshaft. The camshafts operate rocker arms above each of the 4 valves per cylinder. Hydraulic valve tappets maintain the correct valve clearance automatically.

Engine lubrication is by wet sump with a frame mounted oil cooler. The oil supply is housed in the crankcase. The chain-driven oil pump supplies oil under pressure throughout the engine.

The starter motor is behind the cylinder block on the right-hand side and drives the starter clutch that is located in the crankcase.

This chapter provides complete service and overhaul procedures for the Honda engine. Although the clutch and the transmission are located within the engine, they are covered separately in Chapter Five to simplify the presentation of this material.

Before begining engine work, reread the service hints in Chapter One. You will do a better job with this information fresh in your mind.

Table 1 provides complete engine specifications. **Tables 1-8** are located at the end of this chapter.

ENGINE PRINCIPLES

Figure 1 explains how the engine works. This will be helpful when troubleshooting or repairing your engine.

HYDRAULIC VALVE TAPPET SYSTEM

The hydraulic valve tappet system is designed to create an automatic zero valve clearance setting throughout the engine's rpm range and to eliminate any routine valve adjustment. Valve clearance remains the same when the engine is cold or hot. The system is basically a tensioning system and does not contain hydraulic valve lifters like those used in many automobile engines. The hydraulic tappets are supplied with engine oil from the oil control pipes and chambers that are located within the cylinder head.

a. When there is no cam lift on the rocker arm, the hydraulic tappet plunger is in the at-rest position. In this position, the oil inlet hole of the plunger aligns with the oil inlet in the tappet body. Engine oil enters the tappet reservoir through these holes.

b. As the camshaft turns, the cam lobe pushes down on the rocker arm and begins to depress the hydraulic tappet plunger (**Figure 2**).

c. When the tappet plunger is depressed the oil pressure in the tappet high-pressure chamber increases and moves the check ball onto its seat (**Figure 3**).

d. When the cam lobe reaches its maximum lift, pressure within the tappet high-pressure chamber is very high and keeps the check ball closed.

e. As the rocker arm presses on the tappet, some of the oil within the high-pressure chamber is

4-STROKE OPERATING PRINCIPLES

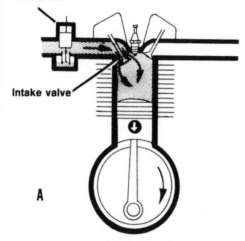

A

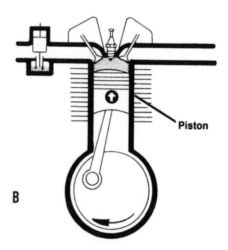

B

As the piston travels downward, the exhaust valve is closed and the intake valve opens, allowing the new air-fuel mixture from the carburetor to be drawn into the cylinder. When the piston reaches the bottom of its travel (BDC), the intake valve closes and remains closed for the next 1 1/2 revolutions of the crankshaft.

While the crankshaft continues to rotate, the piston moves upward, compressing the air-fuel mixture.

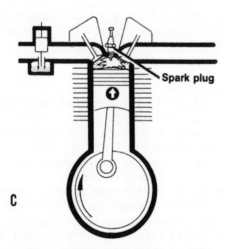

C

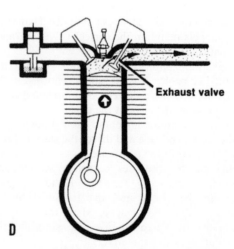

D

As the piston almost reaches the top of its travel, the spark plug fires, igniting the compressed air-fuel mixture. The piston continues to top dead center (TDC) and is pushed downward by the expanding gases.

When the piston almost reaches BDC, the exhaust valve opens and remains open until the piston is near TDC. The upward travel of the piston forces the exhaust gases out of the cylinder. After the piston has reached TDC, the exhaust valve closes and the cycle starts all over again.

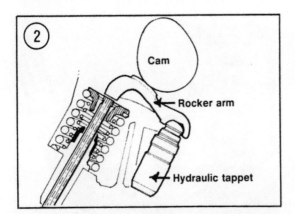

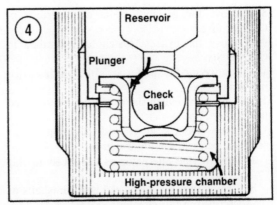

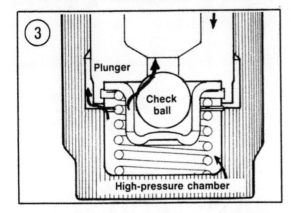

c. Cylinder block.

d. Pistons.

e. Clutch assembly (partial).

f. Alternator.

g. Carburetor assembly.

h. External shift mechanism.

forced out. This allows the plunger in the tappet to absorb some of the load when the cam lobe is at its maximum lift.

f. As the cam lobe moves past its maximum lift, the valve springs apply force on the other end of the rocker arm and the rocker arm moves in the other direction.

g. As the rocker arm shaft moves in the other direction, the spring within the tappet pushes the plunger upward (**Figure 4**).

h. The oil pressure within the high-pressure chamber decreases, allowing the check ball to leave its seat.

i. And the sequence starts all over again. The interaction of all of these parts maintains zero valve clearance up to 8,000 rpm.

SERVICING ENGINE IN FRAME

The following components can be serviced while the engine is mounted in the frame (the bike's frame is a great holding fixture for breaking loose stubborn bolts and nuts):

a. Camshafts.

b. Cylinder head.

ENGINE REMOVAL/INSTALLATION

This procedure includes the removal of many of the engine's external components to reduce the total weight in order to make removal easier. Removal of these components is necessary if the lower end of the engine is going to be serviced. If the engine is not going to be serviced, just removed, then these external components can be left in place. This will take less time but the weight of the engine is much greater.

WARNING
The total engine weight (no external components removed) is 75 kg (165 lb.). Due to this weight it is essential that a minimum of 2, preferably 3, persons be used during the removal and installation procedure.

1. Place the bike on the centerstand.

2. Remove the side covers and seat as described in Chapter Eleven.

3. Disconnect the battery negative and positive leads.

4. Remove the fuel tank as described in Chapter Six.

5. Drain the engine oil as described under *Engine Oil and Filter Change* in Chapter Three.

6. Disconnect the spark plug wires and tie them up out of the way.

7. Remove the ignition coils as described in Chapter Seven.

8. Remove the gearshift pedal as described in Chapter Five.

9. Remove the exhaust system as described in Chapter Six.

10. Remove the carburetor assembly as described in Chapter Six.

11. Remove the clutch slave cylinder as described in Chapter Five.

12. If the engine's lower end is going to be serviced, perform the following:

   a. Remove the alternator as described in this chapter.

   b. Remove the cylinder head and camshafts as described in this chapter.

   c. Remove the cylinder block as described in this chapter.

   d. Remove the clutch as described in Chapter Five.

   e. Remove the external shift mechanism as described in Chapter Five.

   f. Remove the starter as described in Chapter Seven.

13. Disconnect the engine ground strap at the starter motor.

14. Disconnect the alternator stator assembly connector, oil pressure and pulse generator wire connector and the gear location indicator switch wire.

15. Remove the oil cooler and oil filter housing as described in this chapter.

16. Take a final look all over the engine to make sure everything has been disconnected.

17. Loosen, but do not remove, all engine mounting bolts and nuts.

18. Place a jack, with a piece of wood to protect the crankcase, under the engine. Apply a *small amount* of jack pressure up on the engine.

> *WARNING*
> *Due to the weight of the complete engine assembly the following steps must be taken slowly and carefully to avoid dropping the engine out of the frame, causing damage not only to the engine but to yourself and your helpers. Have a good supply of wood blocks on hand to support the engine as it is being removed from the frame.*

19. Pull back the rubber boot on the left-hand side of the swing arm. Have a helper hold the universal joint back and into mesh with the drive shaft during engine removal.

20. On the right-hand side, perform the following:

   a. Remove the bolts (A, **Figure 5**) securing the engine rear hanger bracket.

   b. Remove the nut on the rear mounting bolt (B, **Figure 5**).

   c. Remove the bolts securing the upper front hanger brackets (C, **Figure 5**).

21. On the left-hand side, remove the front upper mounting bolt on each side (A, **Figure 6**).

22. On the right-hand side, remove the bolts (D, **Figure 5**) securing the lower front hanger bracket.

23. On the left-hand side, remove the lower front mounting bolt (B, **Figure 6**) on each side.

24. Remove the rear through bolt (C, **Figure 6**).

> *WARNING*
> *The engine assembly is very heavy. This final step requires a minimum of 2, preferably 3, persons to safely remove the engine from the frame.*

25. Jack the engine up a little more and carefully and slowly pivot the engine (on the wood blocks) toward the left-hand side of the frame. Move it out

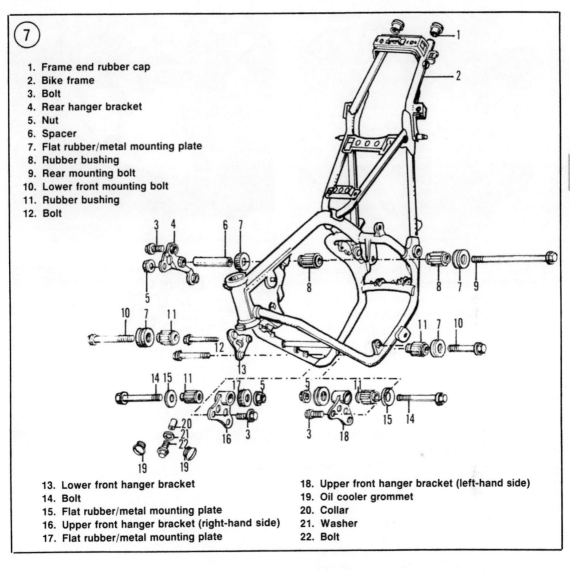

7

1. Frame end rubber cap
2. Bike frame
3. Bolt
4. Rear hanger bracket
5. Nut
6. Spacer
7. Flat rubber/metal mounting plate
8. Rubber bushing
9. Rear mounting bolt
10. Lower front mounting bolt
11. Rubber bushing
12. Bolt

4

13. Lower front hanger bracket
14. Bolt
15. Flat rubber/metal mounting plate
16. Upper front hanger bracket (right-hand side)
17. Flat rubber/metal mounting plate

18. Upper front hanger bracket (left-hand side)
19. Oil cooler grommet
20. Collar
21. Washer
22. Bolt

far enough so everyone can get a good hand hold on the engine.

26. Move the engine out of the frame area on the left-hand side.

27. Place the engine in an engine stand or take it to a work bench for further disassembly.

28. Install by reversing these removal steps, noting the following.

NOTE
Due to the weight of the complete engine assembly, it is suggested that all components removed be left off until the crankcase assembly is in the frame. If you choose to install a completed engine assembly, it requires a minimum of 3 persons.

29. There are many small uniquely shaped metal/rubber laminated washers and rubber spacers that fit between the engine and the mounting areas of the frame. Refer to **Figure 7** for correct placement.

30. Make sure the rear mounting bolt rubber bushings are in place in the crankcase (**Figure 8**) prior to installing the engine in the frame.

31. Be sure to install the upper front hanger brackets with the "IN" mark facing in toward the center of the bike.

32. Tighten the bolts and nuts to the torque specifications listed in **Table 2**.

33. When installing the gear position switch, perform the following:

   a. Make sure the transmission is in the NEUTRAL position.

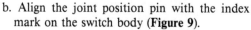

b. Align the joint position pin with the index mark on the switch body (**Figure 9**).

c. Align the joint position pin with the notch in the gearshift drum joint (**Figure 10**).

34. Fill the crankcase with the recommended type and quantity of engine oil. Refer to Chapter Three.

35. Start the engine and check for leaks.

CAMSHAFT

Removal

1. Place the bike on the centerstand.

2. Remove both side covers and the seat as described in Chapter Eleven.

3. Remove the fuel tank as described in Chapter Six.

4. Remove the ignition coils as described in Chapter Seven.

5. Remove all 4 spark plugs. This will make it easier to rotate the engine by hand.

6. Remove the bolts securing the cylinder head cover (**Figure 11**). Remove the cover and gasket. Don't lose the locating dowels.

7. Remove the oil hole covers (**Figure 12**).

8. Remove the oil pipe set bolts (A, **Figure 13**) and the oil control bolt (B, **Figure 13**) securing each oil pipe assembly to the cylinder head.

9. Remove the right- and left-hand oil pipe assemblies. Make sure the O-ring fitted to each oil pipe does not remain in the receptacle in the cylinder head. These O-rings must be replaced each time the oil pipe assembly is removed from the cylinder head.

10. Remove the screws securing the pulse generator cover (**Figure 14**) and remove the cover.

11. Remove the bolts securing the camshaft holders on the right-hand side of the camshaft sprocket bolts. This will make sprocket bolt removal easier.

12. Using the 14 mm bolt (**Figure 15**) on the pulse generator, rotate the engine *counterclockwise* until 2 of the camshaft sprocket bolts are exposed. Remove these 2 bolts (**Figure 16**).

13. To relieve tension on the cam chain, push the cam chain tensioner lock pin down and pull the lock plate up.

14. Using the 14 mm bolt on the pulse generator, rotate the engine *counterclockwise* until the other 2 camshaft sprocket bolts are exposed. Remove these 2 bolts.

15. Using a crisscross pattern, loosen the bolts securing the camshaft holders.

NOTE
The exhaust camshaft holders are marked "EX1" through "EX4" (Figure 17) and the intake camshaft holders are marked "IN1" through "IN4." The "EX1" and the "IN1" holders are for the No. 1 cylinder. The cylinders are numbered 1 through 4 starting on the left-hand side of the bike and working across the engine left to right. The left-hand side refers to a rider sitting on the seat looking forward.

4

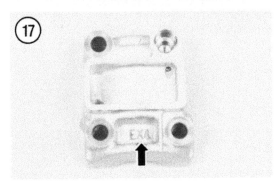

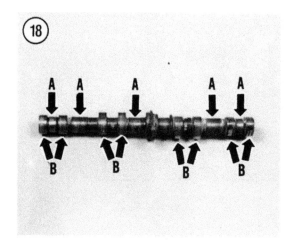

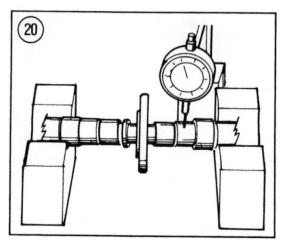

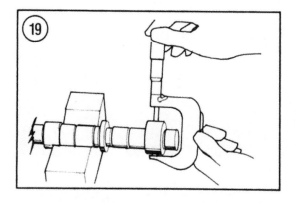

16. Remove the camshaft holders and locating dowels.

17. Slide both camshaft sprockets off the shoulder on the camshafts and remove the cam chain from both sprockets.

18. Withdraw the intake camshaft out through the sprocket and remove the sprocket and camshaft from the left-hand side.

19. To prevent the loose end of the cam chain from falling down into the crankcase, tie a piece of wire to the cam chain and secure the other end of the wire to the exterior of the engine.

20. Withdraw the exhaust camshaft out through the sprocket and remove the sprocket and camshaft from the left-hand side.

CAUTION
If the crankshaft must be rotated when the camshafts are removed, pull up on the cam chain and keep it taut while rotating the crankshaft. Make certain that the chain is positioned onto the crankshaft sprocket. If this is not done, the chain may become kinked and both the cam chain and the sprocket on the crankshaft may be damaged.

Inspection

1. Check the camshaft bearing journals for wear and scoring (A, **Figure 18**).

2. Check the camshaft lobes for wear (B, **Figure 18**). The lobes should not be scored and the edges should be square. Slight damage may be removed with a silicon carbide oilstone. Use No. 100-200 grit initially, then polish with a No. 280-320 grit.

3. Even though the camshaft lobe surface appears to be satisfactory, with no visible signs of wear, the camshaft lobes must be measured with a micrometer as shown in **Figure 19**.

4. Replace the camshaft(s) if worn beyond the service limits listed in **Table 1**.

5. Measure the runout of the camshaft with a dial indicator and V-blocks as shown in **Figure 20**. Divide the total runout in half and compare to the service limits listed in **Table 1**.

6. Check the bearing bores in the cylinder head (**Figure 21**) and camshaft holders (**Figure 22**). They should not be scored or excessively worn. Replace as necessary.

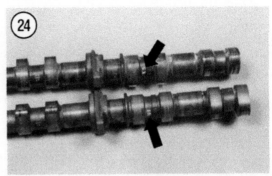

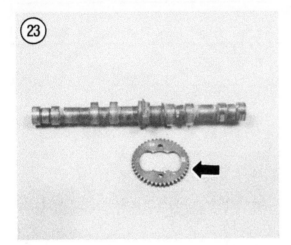

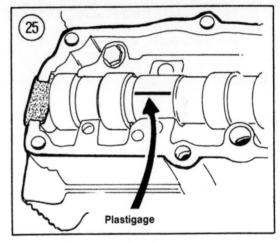

Plastigage

7. Inspect the sprockets (**Figure 23**) for wear; replace if necessary.

8. Inspect the cam chain slipper in the cylinder head cover for wear. If replacement is necessary, remove the bolts securing the slipper and remove the slipper.

Camshaft Bearing
Clearance Measurement

This procedure requires the use of a Plastigage set. The camshafts must be installed into the heads. Prior to installation, wipe all oil residue from each cam bearing journal and bearing surface in the head and all camshaft holders.

1. Each camshaft is marked "IN" (intake) or "EX" (exhaust) as shown in **Figure 24**.

2. Install each camshaft into its correct location in the head.

3. Install all camshaft holder locating dowels into position in the cylinder head.

4. Wipe all oil from cam bearing journals prior to using the Plastigage material.

5. Place a strip of Plastigage material on top of each cam bearing journal, parallel to the cam, as shown in **Figure 25**.

6. Place all camshaft holders into their correct position.

NOTE
The exhaust camshaft holders are marked "EX1" through "EX4" (Figure 17) and the intake camshaft holders are marked "IN1" through "IN4." The "EX1" and the "IN1" holders are for the No. 1 cylinder. The cylinders are numbered 1 through 4 starting on the left-hand side of the bike and working across the engine left to right. The left-hand side refers to a rider sitting on the seat looking forward.

7. Install all camshaft holder bolts only finger-tight at first, then tighten in a crisscross pattern to the final torque specification listed in **Table 2**.

NOTE
Do not rotate either camshaft with the Plastigage material in place.

8. Gradually remove the bolts in a crisscross pattern. Remove the bearing caps carefully.

9. Measure the width of the flattened Plastigage according to manufacturer's instructions (**Figure 26**).

10. If the clearance exceeds the wear limit in **Table 1**, measure the camshaft bearing journals with a micrometer and compare to the wear limits in **Table 1**. If the camshaft bearing journal is less than the dimension specified, replace the cam. If the cam is within specifications, the cylinder head and camshaft holders must be replaced as a set.

> *CAUTION*
> *Remove all particles of Plastigage material from all camshaft bearing journals and bearing caps. This material must not be left in the engine as it can plug up a small oil control orifice and cause severe engine damage.*

Installation

1. Bleed the hydraulic tappets as described in this chapter.

> *NOTE*
> *The hydraulic tappets must be bled even though they were not removed from the cylinder head. Whenever the camshafts are removed, some of the pressure is removed from the tappets. This allows air to enter into the reservoir and high-pressure chamber. These air bubbles must be expelled or the tappet will not operate correctly.*

2. Pull up and make sure the cam chain is properly meshed with the sprocket on the crankshaft. Have an assistant hold the cam chain up while you proceed to Step 3.

3. Using a 14 mm wrench on the pulse generator rotor bolt (**Figure 15**), turn the crankshaft *counterclockwise* until the "T" timing mark aligns with the fixed pointer on the crankcase (**Figure 27**).

4. Lubricate the cam bearing journals, cam lobes and bearing journals in the cylinder head with molybdenum disulfide grease.

5. If removed, install the camshaft holder locating dowels in the cylinder head (**Figure 28**).

6. Position the exhaust camshaft sprocket with the timing marks facing toward the right-hand side of the engine.

7. Install the exhaust camshaft through the camshaft sprocket and position the camshaft in the cylinder head (**Figure 29**) with the lobes for the No. 1 cylinder facing upward, away from the rocker arm.

8. Position the intake camshaft sprocket with the timing marks facing toward the right-hand side of the engine.

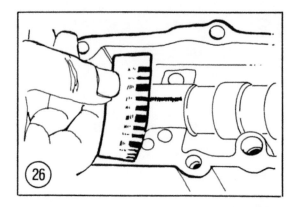

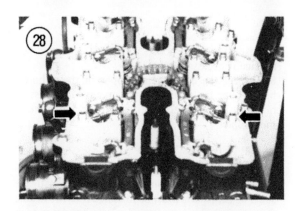

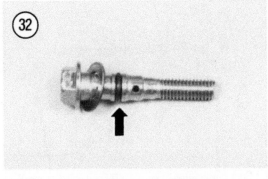

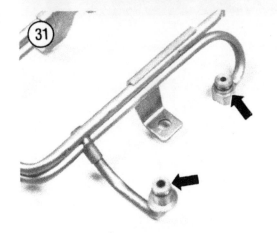

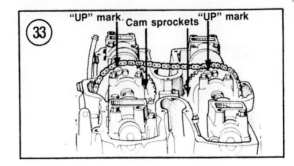

"UP" mark. Cam sprockets "UP" mark

9. Disconnect the piece of wire from the cam chain.

10. Install the intake camshaft through the camshaft sprocket and position the camshaft in the cylinder head (**Figure 30**) with the lobes for the No. 1 cylinder facing upward, away from the rocker arm.

NOTE
*The exhaust camshaft holders are marked "EX1" through "EX4" (**Figure 17**) and the intake camshaft holders are marked "IN1" through "IN4." The "EX1" and the "IN1" holders are for the No. 1 cylinder. The cylinders are numbered 1 through 4 starting on the left-hand side of the bike and working across the engine left to right. The left-hand side refers to a rider sitting on the seat looking forward.*

11. Install the camshaft holders (except for the camshaft holder on the right-hand side of each camshaft sprocket) into their correct position with the arrow facing toward the front of the engine.

12. Using a crisscross pattern, tighten the bolts securing the camshaft holders to the torque specification listed in **Table 2**.

13. Fill the pockets in the camshaft holders with fresh engine oil. Fill each pocket until air bubbles stop coming from the hole in the holder.

14. Install new O-rings (**Figure 31**) onto the oil pipes and apply clean engine oil to the O-rings.

15. Install a new O-ring (**Figure 32**) on the oil control bolt and apply clean engine oil to the O-ring.

16. Install both oil pipes and install the oil control bolt and oil pipe set bolts. Tighten the bolts to the torque specification listed in **Table 2**.

17. Position the exhaust camshaft sprocket so the "EX" mark aligns with the top surface of the cylinder head. With the sprocket in this position, mesh the cam chain onto the sprocket.

18. Pull the sprocket and chain up onto the shoulder of the cam.

19. Position the intake camshaft sprocket so the "IN" mark aligns with the top surface of the cylinder head. With the sprocket in this position, mesh the cam chain onto the sprocket.

20. Pull the sprocket and chain up onto the shoulder of the cam.

CAUTION
Very expensive damage could result from improper camshaft and chain alignment. Recheck your work several times to be sure alignment is correct.

21. Make sure the "UP" marks (**Figure 33**) on both sprockets are facing up.

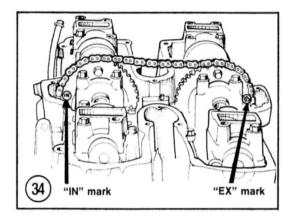

"IN" mark   "EX" mark

22. Again check that the "IN" mark (**Figure 34**) on the intake cam aligns with the top surface of the cylinder head.

23. Using a 14 mm wrench on the pulse generator rotor, turn the crankshaft *clockwise* a small amount until the intake camshaft sprocket bolt holes align. Install the sprocket bolt—only finger-tight at this time.

24. Again check that the "EX" mark (**Figure 34**) on the exhaust cam aligns with the top surface of the cylinder head.

25. Using a 14 mm wrench on the pulse generator rotor, turn the crankshaft a small amount back in the opposite direction (*counterclockwise*) until the exhaust camshaft sprocket bolt holes align. Install the sprocket bolt—only finger-tight at this time (**Figure 35**).

> *NOTE*
> *After the bolts have been installed, rotate the crankshaft back in the opposite direction. The "IN" and "EX" marks should both align with the top surface of the cylinder head (**Figure 36**). If they do not both align at the same point, repeat Steps 17-25 to correct the alignment.*

26. Using a 14 mm wrench on the pulse generator rotor bolt, turn the crankshaft *counterclockwise* until the other sprocket bolt holes are exposed. Apply Loctite Lock N' Seal to the threads and install the 2 remaining sprocket bolts. Tighten to the torque specification listed in **Table 2**.

27. Using a 14 mm wrench on the pulse generator rotor, turn the crankshaft *counterclockwise* until the previously installed sprocket bolts are exposed. Remove the bolts and apply Loctite Lock N' Seal to the threads. Reinstall and tighten the bolts to the torque specification listed in **Table 2**.

28. Install the camshaft holders on the right-hand side of the camshaft sprockets and tighten the bolts to the torque specification listed in **Table 2**.

29. If not already removed, remove both sealing plugs (**Figure 37**) on each side of the cylinder head.

30. Clean off old sealant and apply new liquid sealant (Gasgacinch or equivalent) to the sealing plugs. Reinstall them in the cylinder head.

31. Inspect the lip (**Figure 38**) on each oil hole cover; replace if damaged. Install the oil hole covers on the camshaft holders.

32. If removed, install the cylinder head cover locating dowels.

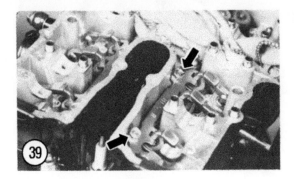

CYLINDER HEAD

Removal

1. Remove the camshafts as described in this chapter.

2. Remove the oil cooler as described in this chapter.

3. Remove the exhaust system as described in Chapter Six.

4. Remove the carburetor assembly as described in Chapter Six.

5. Place a clean shop cloth around the cam chain tensioner assembly to close off the opening that leads down to the crankcase. This will keep any loose parts from falling down into the crankcase.

6. Remove the bolts (**Figure 39**) securing each rocker arm holder and remove each rocker arm holder (**Figure 40**).

7. Remove all rocker arms (**Figure 41**).

8. Remove the hydraulic tappets (**Figure 42**) at this time to avoid an accidental mixup if they should come out while removing the cylinder head.

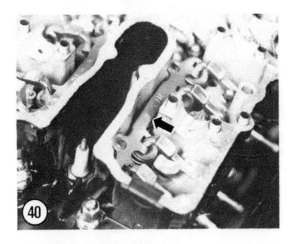

33. Install a new gasket on the cylinder head cover.

34. Install the cover, gasket and bolts. Tighten the bolts securely.

35. Install the pulse generator cover and tighten the screws securely.

36. Install all 4 spark plugs as described in Chapter Three.

37. Install the ignition coils as described in Chapter Seven.

38. Install the fuel tank as described in Chapter Six.

39. Install both side covers and the seat as described in Chapter Eleven.

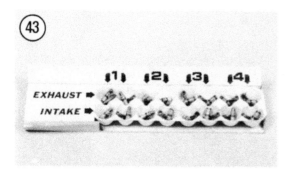

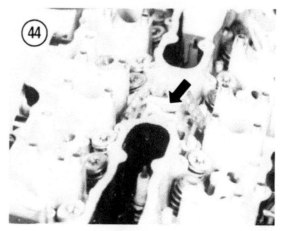

Remove them one at a time and place them into a
container (like an egg carton, see **Figure 43**)
marked with the specific cylinder and "intake" or
"exhaust." The No. 1 cylinder is on the left-hand
side. The left-hand side refers to a rider sitting on
the seat looking forward. The exhaust is at the
front of the engine and the intake is at the rear of
the engine.

> *CAUTION*
> *Because the tappets take a different*
> *wear pattern it is important they be*
> *reinstalled into the same location in the*
> *cylinder head.*

9. Remove the cap nuts and copper washers
securing the cam chain tensioner assembly.

> *NOTE*
> *There are 2 locating dowels on 2 of the*
> *threaded studs holding the cam chain*
> *tensioner in place. Don't let these*
> *dowels fall into the crankcase during*
> *tensioner assembly removal.*

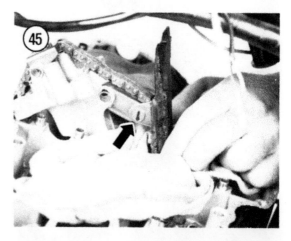

10. Partially pull the cam chain tensioner (**Figure
44**) up and place a clean shop cloth under it to keep
the small parts removed in the next step from
falling into the crankcase.

11. Remove the clip securing the upper pin and
remove the pin (**Figure 45**). Don't drop the clip or
pin into the crankcase.

12. Remove the clip securing the lower pin and
remove the pin (**Figure 46**). Don't drop the clip or
pin into the crankcase.

13. Separate the tensioner slider from the
tensioner body and remove both parts.

14. Remove the cam chain from the tensioner
body and tie a piece of wire to the chain (**Figure
47**). Tie the loose end of the wire to an external
part of the engine.

15. Remove the external oil pipe as follows:

   a. Remove the bolts and sealing washers (A,
     Figure 48) at the rear of the cylinder head.

   b. Remove the bolt and sealing washer (B,
     Figure 48) at the center of the crankcase.

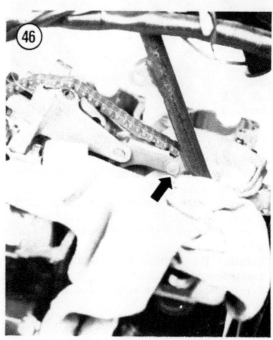

4

c. Remove the bolt and sealing washer (**Figure 49**) at the right-hand side of the crankcase.

d. Remove the oil pipe assembly. Don't lose the 2 sealing washers on each side of all bolts.

16. Remove the bolts (**Figure 50**) securing the cylinder head to the cylinder at the front.

17. Remove the bolt (C, **Figure 48**) securing the cylinder head to the cylinder at the rear.

18. To prevent warpage of the head, loosen the cylinder head inner and outer nuts (**Figure 51**) 1/2 turn at a time in a crisscross pattern in 2-3 stages.

19. After all nuts have been loosened, remove the nuts and their washers.

20. Loosen the head by tapping around the perimeter with a rubber or plastic mallet. If necessary, *gently* pry the head loose with a broad-tipped screwdriver only in the ribbed areas of the fins.

CAUTION
Remember, the fins on the cylinder head are fragile and may be damaged if you tap or pry too hard. Never use a metal hammer.

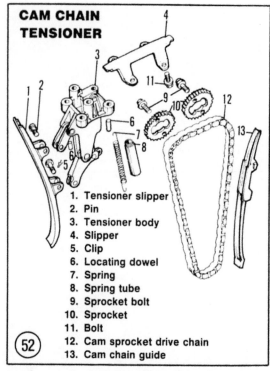

CAM CHAIN TENSIONER

1. Tensioner slipper
2. Pin
3. Tensioner body
4. Slipper
5. Clip
6. Locating dowel
7. Spring
8. Spring tube
9. Sprocket bolt
10. Sprocket
11. Bolt
12. Cam sprocket drive chain
13. Cam chain guide

52

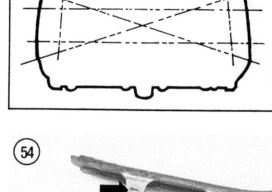

53

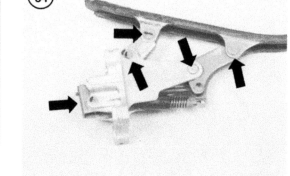

54

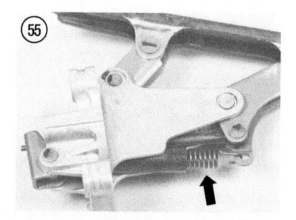

55

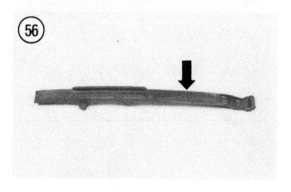

56

21. Untie the wire securing the cam chain and retie it to the cylinder head. Lift the cylinder head straight up and off the cylinder block. Pull the cam chain and wire through the opening in the cylinder head and retie the cam chain to the frame or one of the crankcase studs.

22. Remove the head gasket, dowel pins and the cam chain guide.

23. Place a clean shop rag into the cam chain opening in the block to prevent entry of foreign matter.

Inspection

Refer to **Figure 52** for cam chain tensioner inspection.

1. Remove all traces of gasket material from the cylinder head and the cylinder block mating surface.

2. *Without removing the valves,* remove all carbon deposits from the combustion chambers with a wire brush. A blunt screwdriver or chisel may be used if care is taken not to damage the head, valves and spark plug threads.

3. After all carbon is removed from the combustion chambers and valve intake and exhaust ports, clean the entire head in solvent.

4. Clean away all carbon on the piston crowns. Do not remove the carbon ridge at the top of the cylinder bore.

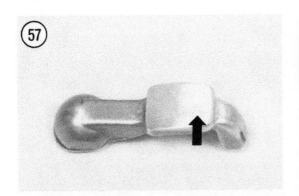

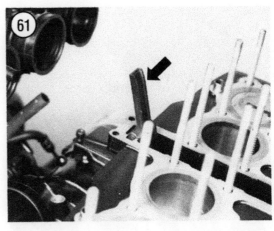

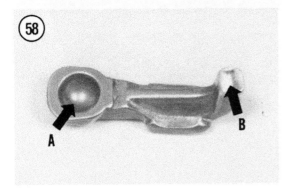

5. Check for cracks in the combustion chamber and exhaust ports. A cracked head must be replaced.

6. After the head has been thoroughly cleaned, place a straightedge across the gasket surface (**Figure 53**) at several points. Measure warp by inserting a flat feeler gauge between the straightedge and the cylinder head at each location. There should be no warpage; if a small amount is present, the head can be resurfaced by a Honda dealer or qualified machine shop.

7. Inspect the valves and valve guides as described in this chapter.

8. Inspect the cam chain tensioner assembly for wear or damage (**Figure 54**). Replace the spring (**Figure 55**) if it is weak or damaged.

9. Inspect the cam chain guide (**Figure 56**) for wear or damage; replace if necessary.

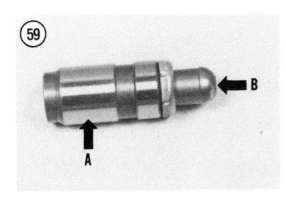

10. Inspect the rocker arm pad (**Figure 57**) for wear or damage where the camshaft rides; replace if necessary.

11. Inspect the rocker arm cup (A, **Figure 58**) where the hydraulic tappet rides and the point where the rocker arm rides on the valve stem (B, **Figure 58**). Check for wear or damage; replace if necessary.

12. Inspect the hydraulic tappet where it rides in the receptacle in the cylinder head (A, **Figure 59**) and where it rides in the rocker arm cup (B, **Figure 59**). Check for wear or damage; replace if necessary.

13. Inspect the receptacle in the cylinder head (**Figure 60**) where the hydraulic tappets ride. Check for wear or damage; replace if necessary.

Installation

1. Clean the cylinder head mating surfaces of any gasket material.

2. Install the cam chain guide (**Figure 61**).

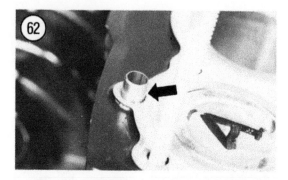

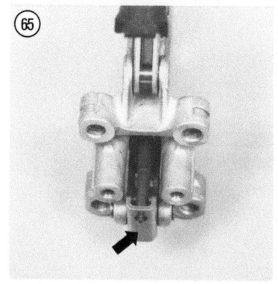

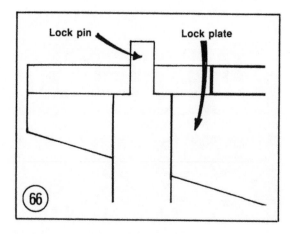

3. Install the locating dowel (**Figure 62**) at each side of the cylinder block and install a new head gasket (**Figure 63**).

4. Untie the wire securing the cam chain to the exterior of the engine. Feed the wire and cam chain up through the opening in the cylinder head and retie the wire to the cylinder head.

5. Install the cylinder head straight down over the crankcase studs and onto the cylinder block (**Figure 64**).

6. To achieve the minimum amount of cam chain tension for assembly, push the tensioner arm toward the tensioner base (**Figure 65**) and lock the arm with the lock pin as shown in **Figure 66**. This will lock the tensioner in place until the cylinder head and camshafts are completely installed.

7. Position the tensioner body into the cam chain cavity and place the cam chain onto the tensioner body (**Figure 67**). Install the tensioner slider to the body.

8. Place a clean shop cloth under the tensioner to keep the small parts to be installed in the next step from falling into the crankcase.

9. Install the lower pin and clip (**Figure 46**) and the upper pin and clip (**Figure 45**) securing the 2 parts together. Make sure the clips are seated correctly so they will not pop out.

Lock pin

Lock plate

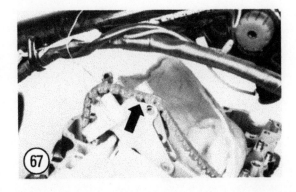

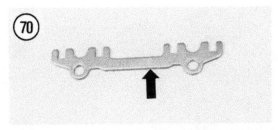

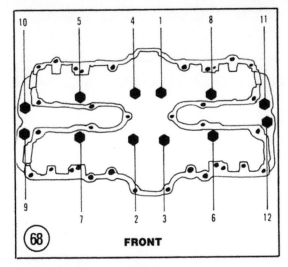

FRONT

10. Apply a light coat of liquid sealant (Gasgacinch or equivalent) to the base of the tensioner prior to installation.

11. Install the locating dowels for the tensioner onto the crankcase studs.

12. Install the tensioner assembly, copper washers and the cap nuts—only finger-tight at this time.

13. Apply a light coat of molybdenum disulfide grease to the crankcase studs prior to installing the cylinder head nuts.

14. Install the copper washers and nuts securing the cylinder head (this includes the cap nuts securing the cam chain tensioner). Tighten the nuts in the pattern shown in **Figure 68** to the torque specification listed in **Table 1**.

15. Install the bolts securing the cylinder head to the cylinder at the front (**Figure 50**) and the rear (C, **Figure 48**). Tighten the bolts to the torque specification listed in **Table 2**.

16. Using compressed air, blow out the external oil line and the oil control bolts. Make sure they are clean and free of any obstructions.

17. Install the external oil pipe to the cylinder and crankcase.

NOTE
The silver bolt is installed on the section of the oil pipe attached at the center of the crankcase (B, Figure 48). Of the 3 black bolts, the longest (30 mm long) is installed on the lower right-hand end of the oil pipe.

18. Be sure to install a sealing washer on each side of the oil control bolts.

19. Install the bolts and sealing washers (**Figure 69**) securing the external oil pipe to the rear of the engine.

20. Bleed the hydraulic tappets as described in this chapter.

21. Install the hydraulic tappets (**Figure 42**) into their original location as noted during removal.

22. Install the rocker arms (**Figure 41**) into the cylinder head.

23. The rocker arm holders are marked with an "R" (right-hand side) or "L" (left-hand side) as shown in **Figure 70**. The holders must be installed on the correct side of the engine.

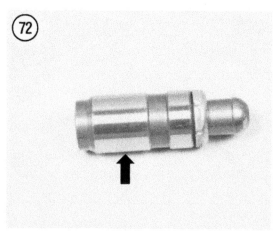

24. Install the locating dowels (**Figure 71**) into the rocker arm holders and install the rocker arm holders into the cylinder head.

25. Install the bolts (**Figure 39**) securing the rocker arm holders and tighten the bolts securely.

26. Install the camshafts as described in this chapter.

27. Install the carburetor assembly as described in Chapter Six.

28. Install the exhaust system as described in Chapter Six.

29. Install the oil cooler as described in this chapter.

HYDRAULIC TAPPETS

NOTE
The tappets are removed and installed during cylinder head removal and installation as described in this chapter.

Inspection

CAUTION
Never attempt to disassemble a tappet; there is internal spring pressure. Never reuse a tappet that has been disassembled or modified in any way.

1. Inspect the exterior of the tappet (**Figure 72**) for wear or damage; replace if necessary.

2. Measure the free length of the tappet as follows:
   a. Bleed the tappet as described in this chapter.
   b. Remove the tappet from the container used for bleeding.
   c. Keep the tappet upright and place it on a flat surface under a dial gauge.
   d. Still keeping the tappet upright, try to quickly compress the tappet with your fingers (**Figure 73**).
   e. You should be able to compress the tappet between 0-0.2 mm (0-0.0078 in.). If it

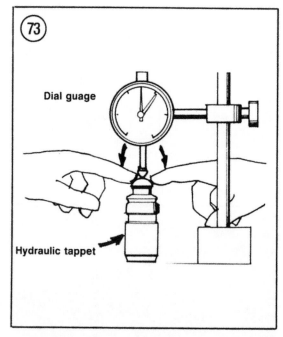

compresses more than the specified dimension, the tappet must be bled again or replaced.

3. If tappet free length is okay, it must be bled again prior to installation.

Bleeding

For proper operation, the hydraulic tappets must be free of air in the high-pressure chamber. A special Honda tool (Hydraulic Tappet Bleeder, Honda part No. 07973-ME90000) or an improvised tool set-up may be used.

CAUTION
Be sure to note the exact location in the cylinder head from which the tappet was removed.

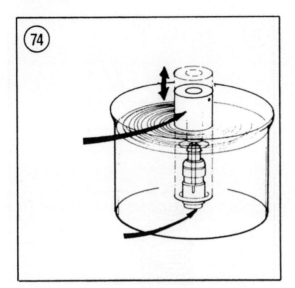

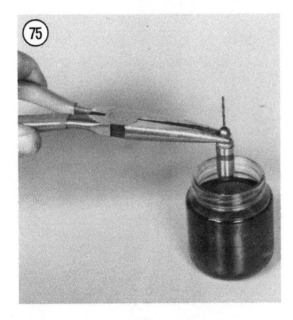

1. Remove the camshafts as described in this chapter.

2. Remove the rocker arms and tappets from the cylinder head one at a time and place them into a container (like an egg container, see **Figure 43**) marked with the specific cylinder number and "intake" or "exhaust." The No. 1 cylinder is on the left-hand side. The left-hand side refers to a rider sitting on the seat looking forward. The exhaust tappets are at the front of the engine and the intake tappets are at the rear.

CAUTION
The tappets must be reinstalled into their original position.

3. Fill a plastic or glass jar (it has to be transparent) with kerosene. Fill the jar with enough kerosene so the tappet is completely covered.

CAUTION
The tappet must be kept submerged and upright during this procedure.

4A. If the special tool is used, perform the following:
  a. Place the tappet right side up within the special tool.
  b. Place the special tool and tappet into the jar filled with kerosene.
  c. Hold the tappet and special tool upright, push down on the special tool and pump the tappet as shown in **Figure 74**. Pump the tappet at a rate of once every second.
  d. Continue to pump until air bubbles stop coming from the high-pressure chamber in the tappet.

4B. If the special tool is not available, perform the following:

CAUTION
Do not use a piece of wire or the sharp end of the drill bit in this procedure as it will damage the check ball in the tappet. This will damage its sealing ability and the tappet will not function properly.

  a. Insert the shank end of a 1/16 in. drill bit into the opening in the top of the tappet.
  b. Place the tappet and drill bit into the jar filled with kerosene (**Figure 75**).
  c. Hold the tappet upright, push down on the drill bit with a piece of metal or wood dowel and pump the tappet. Pump the tappet at a rate of once every second.
  d. Continue to pump until air bubbles stop coming from the high-pressure chamber in the tappet.

NOTE
The small amount of kerosene left in the high-pressure chamber of the tappets will not contaminate the engine's oil.

5. Remove the tappet from the jar filled with kerosene and keep the tappet in the upright position. If the tappet is laid down on an angle or on its side, air will enter the high-pressure chamber and the tappet will have to be bled again.

6. Fill the tappet receptacle in the cylinder head with fresh engine oil.

7. Reinstall the tappet into the correct receptacle in the cylinder head.

8. Repeat this procedure for all tappets.

VALVES AND VALVE COMPONENTS

Removal

Refer to **Figure 76** for this procedure.

1. Remove the cylinder head as described in this chapter.

> *CAUTION*
> *The valve spring outer diameter is relatively small and the area within the cylinder head is very narrow. Make sure the valve spring compressor tool will fit into the cylinder head cavity and onto the valve spring retainer without doing any damage.*

2. Compress springs with a valve spring compressor tool (**Figure 77**). Remove the valve keepers and release compression. Remove the valve compressor tool.

> *CAUTION*
> *To avoid loss of spring tension, do not compress the springs any more than necessary to remove the keepers.*

3. Prior to removing the valves, remove any burrs from the valve stem (**Figure 78**). Otherwise, the valve guides will be damaged.

4. Remove the valve keepers, valve spring retainer and both inner and outer springs (**Figure 79**).

5. Repeat for all valves.

6. Place each valve set into a small box or bag and note its location so it can be reinstalled in the same location in the cylinder head.

Inspection

1. Clean all valves with a wire brush and solvent.

2. Inspect the contact surface of each valve for burning (**Figure 80**). *Minor* roughness and pitting can be removed by lapping the valve as described in this chapter. Excessive unevenness of the contact surface is an indication that the valve is not serviceable.

> *NOTE*
> *The contact surface of the valve **cannot** be ground; the valve must be replaced if this area is damaged.*

3. Measure valve stems for wear (**Figure 81**). Compare with specifications in **Table 1**.

4. Remove all carbon and varnish from the valve guides with a stiff spiral wire brush.

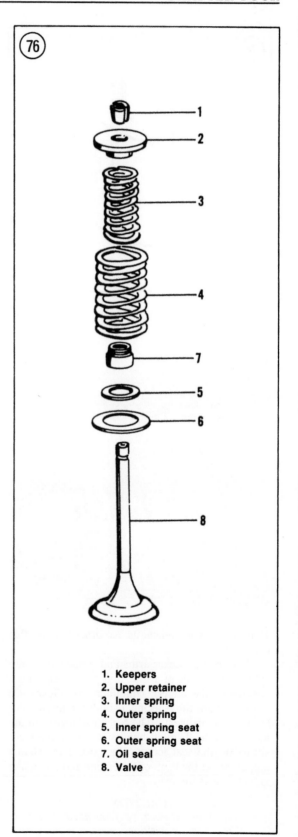

1. Keepers
2. Upper retainer
3. Inner spring
4. Outer spring
5. Inner spring seat
6. Outer spring seat
7. Oil seal
8. Valve

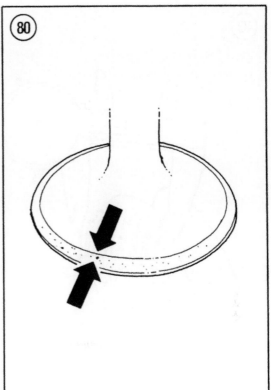

4

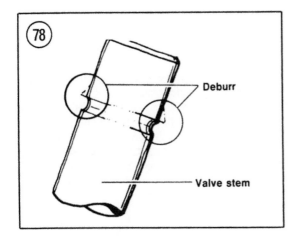

Deburr

Valve stem

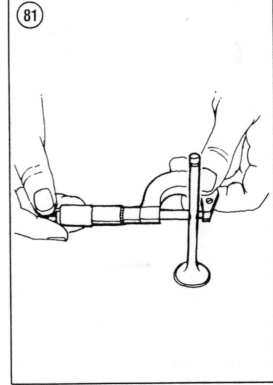

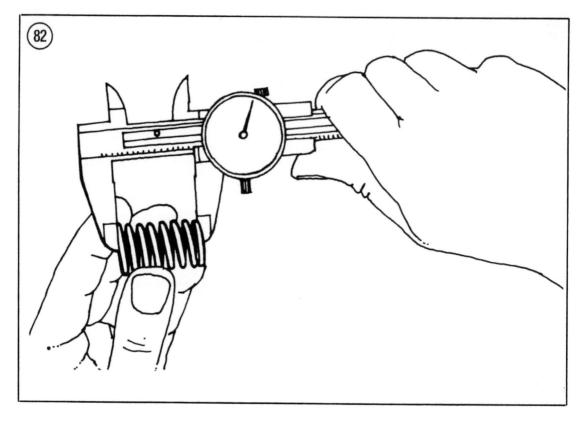

NOTE
The next step assumes all valve stems are within specifications.

5. Insert each valve in its guide. Hold the valve just slightly off its seat and rock it sideways. If it rocks more than slightly, the guide is probably worn and should be replaced. As a final check, take the cylinder head to a dealer and have the valve guides measured.

6. Measure the valve spring heights with a vernier caliper (**Figure 82**). All should be the length specified in **Table 1** with no bends or other distortion. Replace defective springs.

7. Check the valve spring retainer and valve keepers. If they are in good condition, they may be reused.

8. Inspect valve seats. If worn or burned, they must be reconditioned. This should be performed by your dealer or a qualified machine shop. Seats and valves in near-perfect condition can be reconditioned by lapping with a fine carborundum paste. Lapping, however, is always inferior to precision grinding.

Installation

1. Coat the valve stems with molybdenum disulfide grease. To avoid damage to the valve stem seal, turn the valve slowly while inserting the valve into the cylinder head.

2. Install the spring seats and a new seal.

3. Install the valve springs with the narrow pitch end (end with coils closest together) facing the head (**Figure 83**). Install the upper valve spring retainer.

4. Push down on the upper valve spring retainer with the valve spring compressor and install valve keepers.

CAUTION
To avoid loss of spring tension, do not compress the springs any more than necessary to install the keepers.

5. After all keepers have been installed, gently tap the valve stems with a plastic mallet to make sure the keepers are properly seated.

6. Repeat for all valves.

Valve Guide Replacement

When guides are worn so there is excessive stem-to-guide clearance or valve tipping, they must be replaced. Replace all, even if only one is worn. This job should only be done by a dealer, as special tools are required.

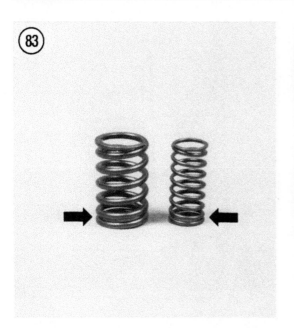

Valve Seat Reconditioning

This job is best left to your dealer or local machine shop. They have the special equipment and knowledge for this exacting job. You can still save considerable money by removing the cylinder head and taking just the head to the shop.

Valve Lapping

Valve lapping is a simple operation which can restore the valve seal without machining if the amount of wear or distortion is not too great.

CAUTION
Do not allow the lapping compound to get into the valve guide area. If it does it will grind away at the guide and valve stem during the lapping operation and cause excessive clearance.

1. Coat the valve seating area in the head with a lapping compound such as Carborundum or Clover Brand.
2. Insert the valve into the cylinder head.
3. Wet the suction cup (**Figure 84**) of the lapping stick and stick it onto the head of the valve. Lap the valve to the seat by rotating the lapping stick in both directions. Every 5 to 10 seconds, rotate the valve 180° in the valve seat; continue lapping until the contact surfaces of the valve and the valve seat are a uniform grey. Stop as soon as they are, to avoid removing too much material.
4. Thoroughly clean the valves and cylinder head in solvent to remove all grinding compound. Any compound left on the valves or the cylinder head will end up in the engine and cause damage.
5. After the lapping has been completed and the valve assemblies have been reinstalled into the head, the valve seal should be tested. Check the seal of each valve by pouring solvent into each of the intake and exhaust ports. The solvent should not flow past the valve seat and the valve head. Perform on all sets of valves. If fluid leaks past any of the seats, disassemble that valve assembly and repeat the lapping procedure until there is no leakage.

CYLINDER BLOCK

Removal

1. Remove the cylinder head as described in this chapter.
2. Remove the nuts at the lower front (**Figure 85**) and lower rear of the cylinder block.

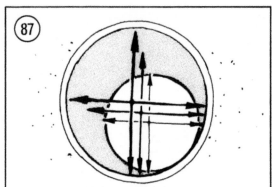

3. If not already removed, remove the front cam chain guide (**Figure 86**).

4. Loosen the cylinder block by tapping around the perimeter with a rubber or plastic mallet. If necessary, *gently* pry the cylinder block loose with a broad-tipped screwdriver only in the ribbed areas of the fins.

> *CAUTION*
> *Remember, the cooling fins are fragile and may be damaged if you tap or pry too hard. Do not use a metal hammer.*

5. Pull the cylinder block straight up and off the pistons and crankcase studs. Work the cam chain wire through the opening in the cylinder block and retie the wire to the crankcase so the cam chain will not fall into the crankcase.

6. Remove the cylinder block base gasket and 2 locating dowels.

Inspection

The following procedures require the use of highly specialized and expensive measuring instruments. If such instruments are not readily available, have the measurements performed by a dealer or qualified machine shop.

1. Soak with solvent any old cylinder head gasket material that may be stuck to the top of the cylinder block. Use a broad-tipped *dull* chisel and gently scrape off all gasket residue. Do not gouge the sealing surfaces as oil and air leaks will result.

2. After the cylinder block has been thoroughly cleaned, place a straightedge across the cylinder block/cylinder head gasket surface at several points. Measure the warpage by inserting a flat feeler gauge between the straightedge and the cylinder block at each location. There should be no warpage; if a small amount is present, it can be resurfaced by a dealer or qualified machine shop. If the cylinder head is warped in any direction by 0.10 mm (0.004 in.) or more it must be replaced.

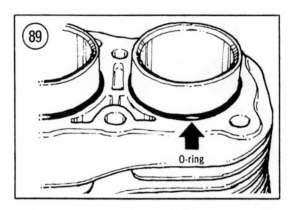

O-ring

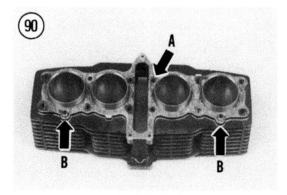

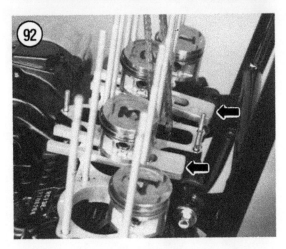

3. Measure the cylinder bores with a cylinder gauge or inside micrometer at the points near the top, in the middle and toward the bottom as shown in **Figure 87**. Measure in 2 axes—in line with the piston pin and at 90° to the pin. If the taper or out-of-round is greater than 0.05 mm (0.002 in.), the cylinders must be rebored to the next oversize and new pistons and rings installed. Rebore all cylinders even though only one may be faulty.

NOTE
The new pistons should be obtained first before the cylinder block is rebored so the pistons can be measured; slight manufacturing tolerances must be taken into account to determine the actual size and the working clearance. Piston-to-cylinder clearance is specified in **Table 1**.

4. Check all cylinder walls (**Figure 88**) for scratches; if evident, the cylinders should be rebored.

NOTE
The maximum wear limit on a cylinder bore is listed in **Table 1**. *If any cylinder is worn to this limit, the cylinder block must be replaced. Never rebore a cylinder if the finished rebore diameter will be this dimension or larger.*

5. Inspect the large O-ring seal at the base of each cylinder (**Figure 89**). Replace all 4 if any are deteriorated.

Installation

1. Check that the top surface of the crankcase and the bottom of the cylinder block are clean prior to installing the base gasket.
2. Install a new cylinder block base gasket (A, **Figure 90**).
3. Install the 2 locating dowels (B, **Figure 90**).
4. Remove the screws securing the pulse generator cover and remove the cover and O-ring seal.
5. Pull up on the camshaft chain and make sure it is properly meshed with the sprocket on the crankshaft.
6. Using the 14 mm bolt on the pulse generator (**Figure 91**), rotate the crankshaft until the No. 2 and No. 3 pistons are at TDC.
7. Install a piston holding fixture (**Figure 92**) under the 2 center pistons.

NOTE
These fixtures may be purchased or may be homemade units of wood. See **Figure 93** *for dimensions.*

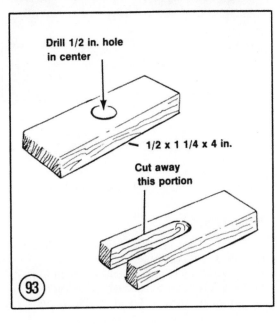

Drill 1/2 in. hole in center

1/2 x 1 1/4 x 4 in.

Cut away this portion

8. Make sure the end gaps of the piston rings are *not* lined up with each other—they must be staggered. Lightly oil the piston rings and cylinder bores with assembly oil or new engine oil.

9. Untie the cam chain wire and retie it to the cylinder block.

> *NOTE*
> *During the following step, you must have an assistant so there is one person on each side of the engine. The engine has such a short stroke that all 4 pistons are entering the cylinder almost at the same time.*

10. Carefully install the cylinder block onto the crankcase studs until it aligns with the 2 uppermost pistons. Untie the wire, feed the cam drive chain up through the opening in the cylinder block and tie it to the cylinder block or frame.

11. Start the cylinder block down over the 2 uppermost pistons. Compress each piston ring as it enters the cylinder either with your fingers, a piston ring compressor or by using aircraft type hose clamps (**Figure 94**) of appropriate size.

> *WARNING*
> *As the cylinder block slides down, watch the top piston ring on the 2 lower pistons. After the cylinder block has moved down over the oil ring of the 2 upper pistons it will start to engage the top ring of the 2 lower pistons. At this point you must watch all 4 pistons at the same time as 1 or 2 pistons rings may be snagged by the cylinder block.*

12. After the cylinder block has moved down over the 2 upper pistons, compress each piston ring on the 2 other pistons as they enter the cylinder either with your fingers, a piston ring compressor or by using aircraft type hose clamps (**Figure 94**) of appropriate size.

13. Slide the cylinder block down until it bottoms on the piston holding fixtures.

14. Remove the piston holding fixtures and push the cylinder block down into place on the crankcase.

15. Install the lower front nuts and lower rear nut. Tighten the nuts securely.

16. Install the pulse generator cover and O-ring gasket. Tighten the screws securely.

17. Install the cylinder head as described in this chapter.

18. Follow the *Break-in Procedure* in this chapter if the cylinder block was rebored or honed or new pistons or piston rings were installed.

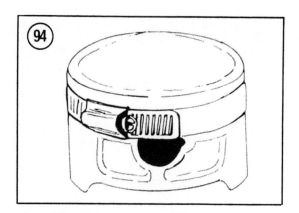

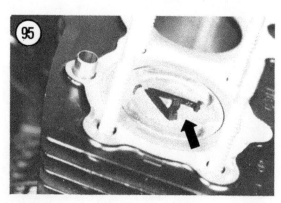

PISTON, PISTON PIN AND PISTON RINGS

The piston is made of an aluminum alloy and is fitted with 2 compression rings and one oil control ring.

Piston Removal

1. Remove the cylinder head and cylinder as described in this chapter.

2. Mark the top of each piston with a number; "1" for the left-hand piston and continuing across from left to right with 2, 3 and 4 (**Figure 95**). The

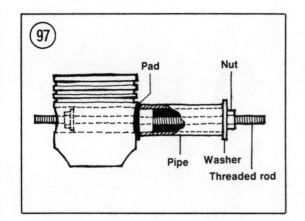

Pad   Nut

Pipe   Washer
Threaded rod

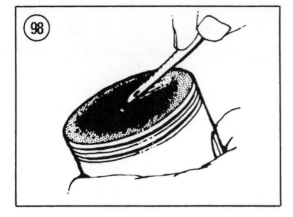

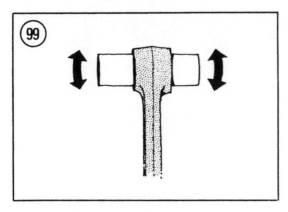

5. Remove the piston pin clips (**Figure 96**) from each side of the piston with a small screwdriver or scribe. Hold your thumb over one edge of the clip when removing it to prevent it from springing out.
6. Use a proper size wooden dowel or socket extension and push out the piston pin.

> *CAUTION*
> *Be careful when removing the pin to avoid damaging the connecting rod. If it is necessary to gently tap the pin to remove it, be sure the piston is properly supported.*

7. If the piston pin is difficult to remove, heat the piston and pin with a small butane torch. The pin will probably push right out. If not, heat the piston to about 60° C (140° F), i.e., until it is too warm to touch, but not excessively hot. If the pin is still difficult to push out, use a special tool as shown in **Figure 97**.

> *NOTE*
> *This special tool, the univeral piston pin extractor, is available from many mail order houses.*

Piston Inspection

1. Carefully clean the carbon from the piston crown with a chemical remover or with a soft scraper (**Figure 98**). Do not remove or damage the carbon ridge around the circumference of the piston above the top ring. If the pistons, rings and cylinders are found to be dimensionally correct and can be reused, removal of the carbon ring from the top of pistons or carbon ridge from the top of cylinder bores will promote excessive oil consumption.

> *CAUTION*
> *Do not wire brush piston skirts.*

2. Examine each ring groove for burrs, dented edges and wide wear. Pay particular attention to the top compression ring groove, as it usually wears more than the others.
3. Measure piston-to-cylinder clearance as described in this chapter. If damage or wear indicates piston replacement, select a new piston as described under *Piston Clearance Measurement* in this chapter.
4. Oil the piston pin and install it in the connecting rod bearing. Slowly rotate the piston pin and check for play (**Figure 99**). If there is play, the piston pin should be replaced, providing the rod bore is in good condition.

left-hand side refers to a rider sitting on the seat looking forward.
3. Remove the cylinder block as described in this chapter.
4. Remove the piston rings as described in this chapter.

> *NOTE*
> *Wrap a clean shop cloth under the piston so the piston pin clip will not fall into the crankcase.*

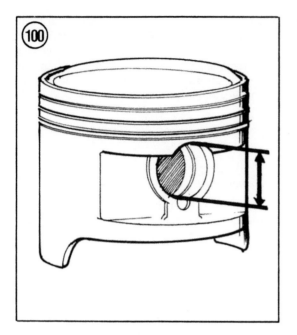

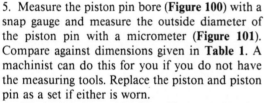

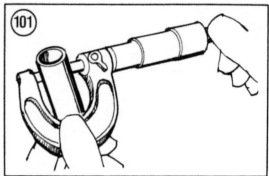

5. Measure the piston pin bore (**Figure 100**) with a snap gauge and measure the outside diameter of the piston pin with a micrometer (**Figure 101**). Compare against dimensions given in **Table 1**. A machinist can do this for you if you do not have the measuring tools. Replace the piston and piston pin as a set if either is worn.

6. Check the piston skirt for galling and abrasion which may have been caused by piston seizure. If light galling is present, smooth the affected area with No. 400 emery cloth and oil or a fine oilstone. However, if galling is severe or if the piston is deeply scored, replace it.

Piston Clearance Measurement

1. Make sure the piston and cylinder walls are clean and dry.

2. Measure the inside diameter of the cylinder bore at a point 13 mm (1/2 in.) from the lower edge with a bore gauge.

3. Measure the outside diameter of the piston across the skirt (**Figure 102**) at right angles to the piston pin. Measure at a distance 14 mm (0.6 in.) up from the bottom of the piston skirt.

4. Piston clearance is the difference between the maximum piston diameter and the minimum cylinder diameter. Subtract the dimension of the piston from the cylinder dimension. If the clearance exceeds the dimension listed in **Table 1**, the cylinder should be rebored to the next oversize and a new piston installed.

NOTE
The new piston should be obtained before the cylinder is rebored so the piston can be measured; slight manufacturing tolerances must be taken into account to determine the actual size and working clearance.

5. To establish a final overbore dimension with a new piston, add the new piston skirt measurement to the specified piston-to-cylinder clearance. This will determine the dimension for the cylinder overbore size. Remember, do not exceed the cylinder maximum inside diameter listed in **Table 1**.

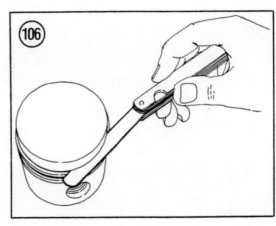

Piston pin clip   Piston cutout

6. There are 4 oversize piston sizes available (0.25 mm, 0.50 mm, 0.75 mm and 1.00 mm oversize).

Piston Installation

1. Apply molybdenum disulfide grease to the inside surface of the connecting rod small end. Apply fresh engine oil to the piston pin and piston pin bore.
2. Insert the piston pin into the piston until its end extends slightly beyond the inside of the boss (**Figure 103**).
3. Align the piston with the "IN" mark (**Figure 104**) toward the rear of the engine (facing toward the carburetors).
4. Be sure to install the piston to the correct connecting rod as marked during removal. Line up the piston pin with the holes in the piston and connecting rod and push the pin into the piston until its ends are even with the clip grooves.

NOTE
If the piston pin does not slide in easily, heat the piston until it is too warm to touch but not excessively hot (60° C/140° F). Continue to drive the piston pin while holding the piston so the rod does not have to take any shock. Drive the piston pin in until it is centered in the rod. If the pin is still difficult to install, use the special tool used during the removal sequence.

NOTE
*In the next step, install the clips with the gap away from the cutout in the piston (**Figure 105**).*

5. Install new piston pin clips in the ends of the pin boss (**Figure 96**). Make sure they are seated in the grooves.
6. Check installation by rocking the piston back and forth around the pin axis and from side to side along the axis. It should rotate freely back and forth but not from side to side.
7. Repeat for all pistons.
8. Install the rings as described in this chapter.
9. Install the cylinder and cylinder head as described in this chapter.

Piston Ring
Removal/Inspection/Installation

WARNING
The edges of all piston rings are very sharp, especially the flat rings of the oil ring assembly. Be careful when handling them to avoid cut fingers.

1. Measure the side clearance of each ring in its groove with a flat feeler gauge (**Figure 106**) and compare with dimensions listed in **Table 1**. If the clearance is greater than specified, the rings must be replaced. If the clearance is still excessive with the new rings, the piston must be replaced.

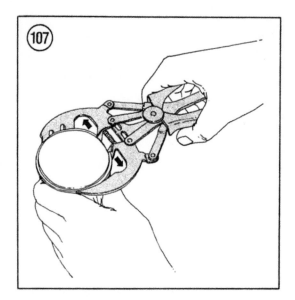

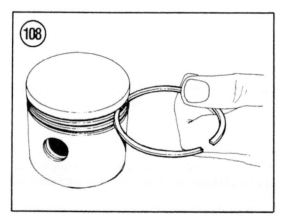

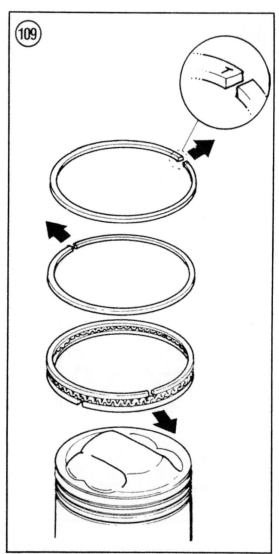

2. Remove the top ring with a ring expander tool or by spreading the ring ends with your thumbs and lifting the ring up and over the piston (**Figure 107**). Repeat for the remaining rings.

3. Carefully remove all carbon from the ring grooves. Inspect grooves carefully for burrs, nicks or broken and cracked lands. Recondition or replace the piston if necessary.

4. Roll each ring around its piston groove as shown in **Figure 108** to check for binding. Minor binding may be cleaned up with a fine-cut file.

5. Measure the rings for wear. Place each ring, one at a time, into the cylinder and push it in about 20 mm (3/4 in.) with the crown of the piston to ensure that the ring is square in the cylinder bore. Measure the gap with a flat feeler gauge and compare with dimensions listed in **Table 1**. If the gap is greater than specified, the ring(s) should be replaced. When installing new rings, measure their end gap in the same manner. If the gap is less than

6. Install the piston rings in the order shown in **Figure 109**.

NOTE
Install all rings with their markings facing up.

7. Install the piston rings—first the bottom, then the middle, then the top ring—by carefully spreading the ends with your thumbs and slipping the ring over the top of the piston. Remember that the piston rings must be installed with the marks on them facing up toward the top of the piston.

8. Make sure the rings are seated completely in their grooves all the way around the piston and that the end gaps are distributed around the piston. specified, carefully file the ends with a fine-cut file until the gap is correct.

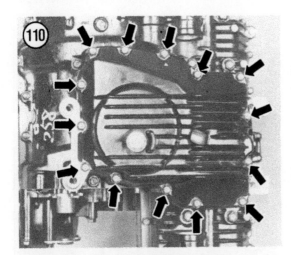

It's important that the ring gaps are not aligned with each other when installed.

9. If new rings are installed, measure the side clearance of each ring in its groove with a flat feeler gauge (**Figure 106**) and compare to dimensions listed in **Table 1**.

OIL PUMP

The oil pump is mounted within the crankcase and can be removed with the engine in the frame. This procedure is shown with the engine removed from the frame for clarity.

Removal/Installation

1. Place the bike on the centerstand.
2. Remove the exhaust system as described in Chapter Six.
3. Drain the engine oil as described in Chapter Three.
4. Remove the bolts (**Figure 110**) securing the oil pan and remove the oil pan and gasket.
5. Remove the oil pressure relief valve (**Figure 111**).
6. Withdraw the oil strainer (**Figure 112**) from the oil pump.
7. Remove the oil pipe (**Figure 113**). Don't lose the O-ring seals (**Figure 114**) on each end where the pipe fits into the oil pump and the crankcase.
8. Tie a piece of wire to the oil pump drive chain and tie the loose end of the wire to the exterior of the engine.
9. Remove the bolts securing the oil pump assembly. Pull the oil pump up slightly, disengage the driven sprocket from the drive chain and

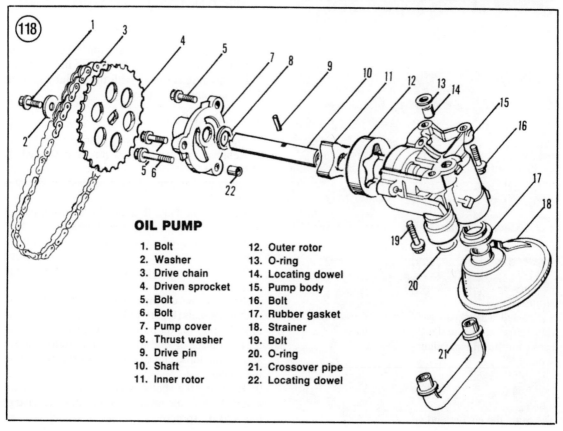

OIL PUMP

1. Bolt
2. Washer
3. Drive chain
4. Driven sprocket
5. Bolt
6. Bolt
7. Pump cover
8. Thrust washer
9. Drive pin
10. Shaft
11. Inner rotor
12. Outer rotor
13. O-ring
14. Locating dowel
15. Pump body
16. Bolt
17. Rubber gasket
18. Strainer
19. Bolt
20. O-ring
21. Crossover pipe
22. Locating dowel

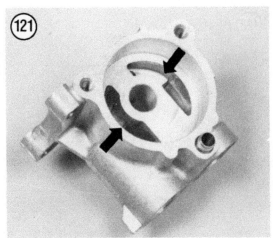

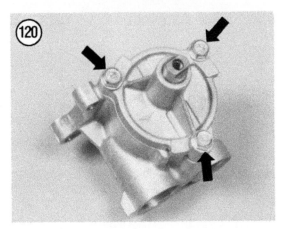

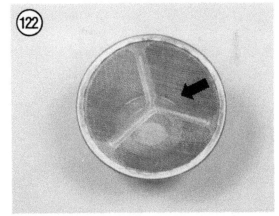

remove the assembly. Don't lose the locating dowel and the O-ring (**Figure 115**) in the crankcase.

10. Install by reversing these removal steps, noting the following.

11. To prime the oil pump, add clean engine oil into one of the openings in the oil pump. Add oil until the oil drains out of the other opening.

12. Make sure the locating dowel and a new O-ring seal (**Figure 115**) are installed in the oil pump.

13. Install new O-ring seals (**Figure 114**) where the crossover pipe is installed into the crankcase.

14. Align the cutout on the strainer with the boss on the oil pump (**Figure 116**) and install the strainer.

15. Install a new pan gasket and the pan. Install the copper washer under the bolt next to the raised arrow on the oil pan (**Figure 117**). Tighten the bolts securely.

16. Refill the engine with the recommended type and quantity of engine oil as described in Chapter Three.

17. Start the engine and check for leaks.

Disassembly/Inspection/Assembly

Refer to **Figure 118** for this procedure.

1. Inspect the outer cover and body for cracks.

2. Remove the bolt (**Figure 119**) securing the driven sprocket and remove the sprocket.

3. Remove the bolts (**Figure 120**) securing the pump cover to the pump body. Remove the pump cover.

4. Withdraw the oil pump drive shaft, thrust washer and pin. Don't lose the drive pin; it will slide out of the shaft.

5. Remove the inner and outer rotors. Check all parts for scratches and abrasion.

6. Clean all parts in solvent and thoroughly dry. Coat all parts with fresh oil prior to installation.

7. Inspect the interior passageways (**Figure 121**) of the oil pump body. Make sure all oil sludge and foreign matter is removed.

8. Inspect the oil strainer (**Figure 122**). Replace if deteriorated or damaged.

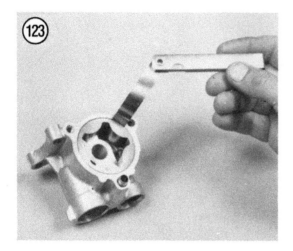

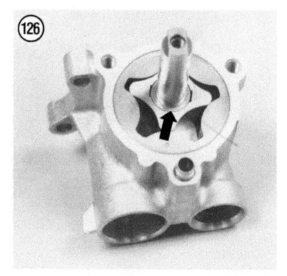

9. Coat all parts with clean engine oil.

10. Install the outer rotor.

11. Check the clearance between the outer rotor and the body (**Figure 123**) with a flat feeler gauge. If the clearance is greater than the service limit in **Table 1**, the oil pump must be replaced.

12. Install the inner rotor with the grooved side up (**Figure 124**).

13. Install the drive pin into the oil pump drive shaft.

14. Align the slots in the inner rotor with the drive pin on the shaft (**Figure 125**) and push the shaft in until it stops.

15. Install the thrust washer (**Figure 126**) into the recess in the inner rotor.

16. Check the clearance between the inner tip and outer rotor (A, **Figure 127**) with a flat feeler gauge. If the clearance is greater than the service limit in **Table 1**, the oil pump must be replaced.

17. Check the rotor side clearance with a straightedge and flat feeler gauge. If the clearance is greater than the service limit in **Table 1**, the oil pump must be replaced.

18. If removed, install the locating dowel (B, **Figure 127**) in the pump body.

19. Install the cover and tighten the screws (**Figure 120**) securely.

20. Align the slot in the driven sprocket with the flat on the shaft and install the driven sprocket. Install the bolt and tighten securely (**Figure 119**).

21. After the oil pump is assembled, turn the shaft and make sure the oil pump turns freely with no binding.

22. Install the oil pump assembly.

NOTE
*If the condition of the oil pump is doubtful, run the **Oil Pump Pressure Test** described in this chapter.*

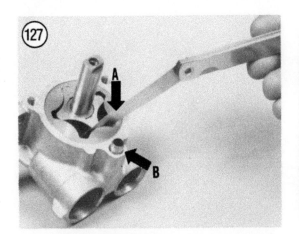

8. Start the engine and run it at 7,000 rpm. The standard pressure is 5.0 kg/cm² (71 psi) at 7,000 rpm and at 80° C (176° F). If the pressure is less than specified the oil pump must be replaced.

9. Turn the engine off.

10. Remove the portable oil pressure gauge.

11. Apply liquid sealant to the switch threads prior to installation. Tighten the switch to the torque specifications listed in **Table 2**. Install the electrical wire to the top of the switch. This connection must be free of oil to make good electrical contact.

12. Install the pulse generator cover and tighten the screws securely.

13. Start the engine. Check that the oil pressure warning light goes out. If the oil pressure warning light stays on, turn the engine off immediately and determine the cause. For oil pressure warning switch test procedure, refer to Chapter Seven.

OIL STRAINER AND PRESSURE RELIEF VALVE

These components can be removed with the engine in the frame. This procedure is shown with the engine removed for clarity.

Refer to **Figure 118** for this procedure.

Removal/Installation

1. Place the bike on the centerstand.

2. Remove the exhaust system as described in Chapter Six.

3. Drain the engine oil as described in Chapter Three.

4. Remove the bolts (**Figure 110**) securing the oil pan and remove the oil pan and gasket.

5. Remove the oil pressure relief valve (**Figure 111**) from the crankcase.

6. Withdraw the oil strainer (**Figure 112**) from the oil pump.

Oil Pump Pressure Test

If the oil pump output is doubtful, the following test can be performed.

1. Warm the engine up to normal operating temperature (80° C/176° F). Shut off the engine.

2. Place the bike on the centerstand.

3. Check the engine oil level. It must be to the upper line; add oil if necessary. Do not run this test with the oil level low or the test readings will be false.

4. Remove the screws securing the pulse generator cover and remove the cover (**Figure 128**).

5. Remove the electrical wire (A, **Figure 129**) from the oil pressure sending switch.

6. Remove the oil pressure sending switch (B, **Figure 129**).

7. Screw a portable oil pressure gauge into the switch hole in the crankcase.

> *NOTE*
> *These can be purchased in an automotive or motorcycle supply store or from a Honda dealer. The Honda parts are No. 07506-3000000 (Oil Pressure Gauge) and No. 07510-MA70000 (Oil Pressure Gauge Attachment).*

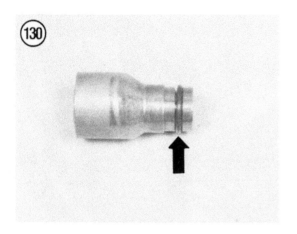

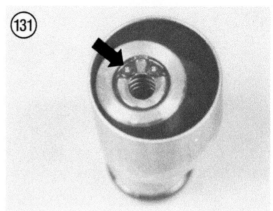

7. Install a new seal ring in the oil pump where the strainer is installed.

8. Align the cutout on the strainer with the boss on the oil pump (**Figure 116**) and install the strainer.

9. Check the O-ring seal (**Figure 130**) on the pressure relief valve. Replace if necessary.

10. Install a new pan gasket and the pan. Install the copper washer under the bolt next to the raised arrow on the oil pan (**Figure 117**). Tighten the bolts securely.

11. Refill the engine with the recommended type and quantity of engine oil as described in Chapter Three.

12. Start the engine and check for leaks.

Inspection

1. Wash all parts in cleaning solvent and thoroughly dry with compressed air. Carefully scrub the strainer screen with a soft toothbrush; do not damage the screen.

2. Inspect the strainer screen for broken areas. This would allow small foreign particles to enter the oil pump and cause damage. If broken in any area, replace the strainer.

3. Remove the circlip (**Figure 131**) securing the pressure relief valve. Remove the dished washer, spring and check valve.

4. Inspect the check valve and the cylinder it rides in for scratches or wear. Replace if defective.

5. Make sure the spring is not broken or distorted; replace if necessary.

6. Assemble by reversing Step 3.

OIL COOLER

Removal/Installation

Refer to **Figure 132** for this procedure.

This procedure is shown with the exhaust system removed for clarity. It is not necessary to remove it for this procedure.

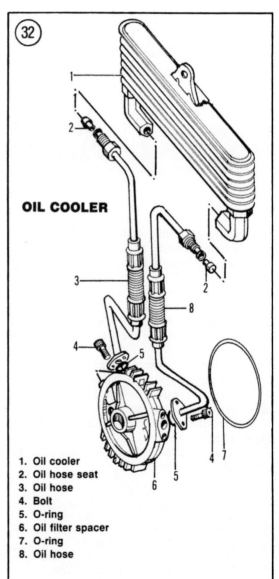

OIL COOLER

1. Oil cooler
2. Oil hose seat
3. Oil hose
4. Bolt
5. O-ring
6. Oil filter spacer
7. O-ring
8. Oil hose

4

1. Place the bike on the centerstand.

2. Drain the engine oil as described in Chapter Three.

3. Place a drain pan under the oil filter housing; residual oil will drain out when the oil filter housing and oil cooler are removed.

4. Remove the oil filter bolt (**Figure 133**).

5A. If the oil cooler is just going to be removed and not disassembled, perform the following:

   a. Remove the oil filter cover, spring, washer and filter.

   b. Remove the bolt (**Figure 134**) securing the oil cooler assembly to the frame.

   c. Pull the oil cooler assembly up and off the locating holes in the frame.

   d. Remove the oil cooler assembly and the oil filter spacer from the frame and engine as an assembly.

5B. If the oil cooler is going to be removed and disassembled, perform the following:

   a. Remove the bolts (**Figure 135**) securing the fittings on the oil cooler hoses to the oil filter spacer. Don't lose the small O-ring seal in each fitting where it attaches to the oil filter spacer.

   b. Hold the elbow (A, **Figure 136**) with an open end wrench and loosen the hose fitting (B, **Figure 136**) on each oil hose where it attaches to the oil cooler.

   c. Remove the bolt (C, **Figure 136**) securing the oil cooler assembly to the frame.

   d. Pull the oil cooler assembly up and off the locating holes in the frame and remove the oil cooler assembly from the frame.

   e. Completely unscrew each hose fitting from the oil cooler and remove the oil hoses and hose fittings from the oil cooler.

6. Install by reversing these removal steps, noting the following.

7A. If the oil cooler was not disassembled, perform the following:

   a. Check the large O-ring seal on the oil filter spacer. Replace if necessary.

   b. If the oil filter was disassembled, install the spring, washer and the oil filter into the oil filter cover.

   c. Check the large O-ring seal on the oil filter cover. Replace if necessary.

   d. Check the O-ring seal on the oil filter bolt. Replace if necessary.

   e. Install the oil filter assembly and tighten the bolt securely.

7B. If the oil cooler was disassembled, perform the following:

   a. Be sure to install the oil hose seat in the end of each oil hose.

   b. Apply liquid sealant to the hose fittings where they attach to the elbow on the oil cooler. Be sure to hold the elbow with an open-end wrench and tighten the hose fitting (B, **Figure 136**) on each oil hose where it attaches to the oil cooler.

8. Refill the engine with the recommended type and quantity of engine oil as described in Chapter Three.

9. Start the engine and check for leaks.

ALTERNATOR

The alternator stator assembly electrical test procedure is covered in Chapter Seven.

Rotor and Stator Removal

1. Place the bike on the centerstand.
2. Remove both side covers.
3. Disconnect the battery negative lead.
4. Disconnect the electrical connector (**Figure 137**) going to the alternator stator assembly.
5. Remove the Allen bolts securing the alternator cover and remove the cover (**Figure 138**).

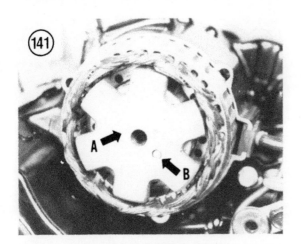

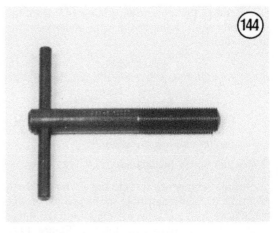

6. Shift the transmission into 6th gear and have an assistant apply the rear brake.

7. Remove the bolt (**Figure 139**) securing the alternator rotor.

8. Remove the cooling fan (**Figure 140**) and the outer rotor (A, **Figure 141**).

9. Pull the stator assembly (A, **Figure 142**), electrical wires and grommet (B, **Figure 142**) out of the crankcase housing.

10. Screw the rotor puller (**Figure 143**) into the inner rotor until it stops. Use a Honda rotor puller (**Figure 144**) (part No. 07933-2160000) or equivalent.

> *CAUTION*
> *Don't try to remove the inner rotor without a puller; any attempt to do so will ultimately lead to some form of damage to the engine or rotor. Many aftermarket pullers are available from motorcycle dealers or mail order houses. The cost of these pullers is low and it makes an excellent addition to any mechanic's tool box. If you can't buy or borrow one, have the inner rotor removed by a dealer.*

11. Shift the transmission into 6th gear and have an assistant apply the rear brake.

12. Turn the rotor puller until the rotor is free.

> *NOTE*
> *If the rotor is difficult to remove, strike the puller with a hammer a few times. This will usually break it loose.*

> *CAUTION*
> *If normal inner rotor removal attempts fail, do not force the puller as the threads may be stripped out of the inner rotor causing expensive damage. Take the bike to a dealer and have the inner rotor removed.*

13. Remove the inner rotor (**Figure 145**) from the alternator shaft. Remove the rotor puller from the inner rotor.

> *CAUTION*
> *Carefully inspect both rotors (**Figure 146**) for small bolts, washers or other metal "trash" that may have been picked up by the magnets. These small metal bits can cause severe damage to the alternator stator assembly.*

Rotor and Stator Installation

1. Install the inner rotor onto the alternator shaft.
2. Align the stator assembly so the painted groove (A, **Figure 147**) on the stator aligns with the upper rear alternator cover bolt hole (B, **Figure 147**).

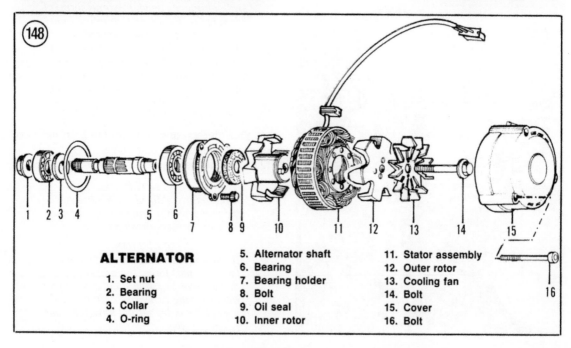

ALTERNATOR

1. Set nut
2. Bearing
3. Collar
4. O-ring
5. Alternator shaft
6. Bearing
7. Bearing holder
8. Bolt
9. Oil seal
10. Inner rotor
11. Stator assembly
12. Outer rotor
13. Cooling fan
14. Bolt
15. Cover
16. Bolt

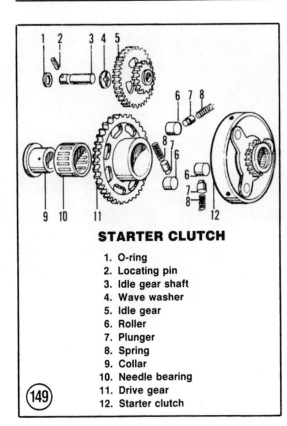

STARTER CLUTCH

1. O-ring
2. Locating pin
3. Idle gear shaft
4. Wave washer
5. Idle gear
6. Roller
7. Plunger
8. Spring
9. Collar
10. Needle bearing
11. Drive gear
12. Starter clutch

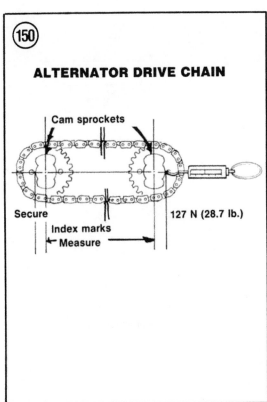

ALTERNATOR DRIVE CHAIN

Cam sprockets

Secure

127 N (28.7 lb.)

Index marks
Measure

Push the stator assembly into place and install the rubber grommet into the groove in the crankcase.

3. Align the hole in the outer rotor with the raised boss on the inner rotor (B, **Figure 141**) and install the outer rotor.

4. Hold the outer rotor in place and install the rotor bolt.

5. Shift the transmission into 6th gear and have an assistant apply the rear brake.

6. Tighten the bolt to the torque specification listed in **Table 2**.

7. Install the alternator cover and bolts. Tighten the bolts securely.

8. Connect the alternator stator electrical connector and route the electrical harness through the frame exactly as before.

9. Connect the battery negative lead.

10. Install both side covers.

Rotor Testing

The rotors are permanently magnetized and cannot be tested except by replacement with rotors known to be good. Rotors can lose magnetism from old age or a sharp blow. If defective, the rotors must be replaced; they cannot be remagnetized. The inner and outer rotors are available only as a set.

STARTER CLUTCH

The starter clutch assembly is located within the upper crankcase half. Refer to **Figure 148**, **Figure 149** and **Figure 150** for this procedure.

Removal

1. Remove the starter as described in Chapter Seven.

2. On the right-hand side of the upper crankcase, perform the following:

    a. Remove the alternator cap (**Figure 151**).

    b. Place the transmission in 6th gear and have an assistant hold the rear brake on.

c. Using a 20 mm deep socket (or spark plug wrench), remove the alternator shaft set nut (**Figure 152**).

3. Remove the alternator as described in this chapter.

4. Remove the engine and separate the crankcase as described in this chapter.

5. Remove both transmission assemblies as described in Chapter Five.

6. Remove the bolt (A, **Figure 153**) securing the alternator drive chain slipper and remove the slipper (B, **Figure 153**).

NOTE
In the following step the alternator shaft and bearing holder may come out of the crankcase as an assembly. This presents no problem.

7. On the left-hand side of the the upper crankcase, perform the following:

a. Remove the bolts securing the alternator shaft bearing holder, bearing and oil seal (**Figure 154**).

b. Remove the bearing holder.

c. Hold onto the starter clutch assembly and withdraw the alternator shaft from the crankcase.

8. Pull the starter clutch assembly up and out of the crankcase, disengage the drive chain and remove the starter clutch assembly.

9. Hold onto the starter idle gear (**Figure 155**) and partially withdraw the starter idle gear shaft (A, **Figure 156**) from the right-hand side of the upper crankcase.

10. Remove the starter idle gear and wave washer from inside the crankcase.

11. Withdraw the starter idle gear shaft. Don't lose the locating pin on the shaft.

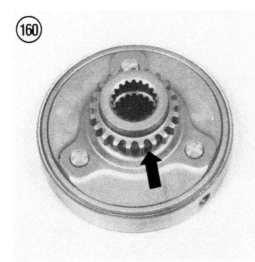

Disassembly/Inspection/Assembly

1. Remove the collar (**Figure 157**) and needle bearing (**Figure 158**) from the starter drive gear.

2. Place the starter clutch assembly with the gear side facing up. Rotate the starter drive gear (**Figure 159**) *clockwise* and pull up at the same time. Remove the starter drive gear from the starter clutch assembly. Keep the starter clutch upright to prevent the roller sets from falling out.

3. Inspect the teeth on the starter drive gear and the starter clutch (**Figure 160**). Check for chipped or missing teeth. Look for uneven or excessive wear on the gear face. Replace if necessary.

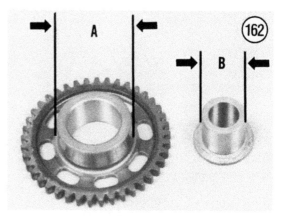

4. Check the needle bearing (**Figure 161**) for wear or damage; it must rotate freely. Replace if necessary.

5. Measure the outside diameter of the drive gear (A, **Figure 162**) and the collar (B, **Figure 162**). Replace if worn to the service limit dimension listed in **Table 1**.

6. Inspect the teeth on the starter idle gear (**Figure 163**). Check for chipped or missing teeth. Look for uneven or excessive wear on the gear face. Replace if necessary.

7. Check the idle gear shaft (A, **Figure 164**) for wear or damage. Make sure the locating pin (B, **Figure 164**) is not bent or damaged.

8. Install a new O-ring seal (C, **Figure 164**) on the idle gear shaft.

9. Check the alternator shaft ball bearing (**Figure 165**) in the upper crankcase half for wear or damage. It must rotate freely or be replaced. Replacement should be entrusted to a dealer as special tools are required.

10. Check the ball bearing (**Figure 166**) in the bearing holder for wear or damage. It must rotate freely or be replaced. Replacement should be entrusted to a dealer as special tools are required.

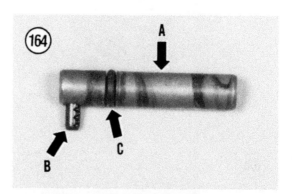

11. Inspect the oil seal and O-ring seal (**Figure 167**) on the bearing holder. Replace if necessary.

12. Inspect the rollers (**Figure 168**) in the starter clutch for uneven or excessive wear; replace as a set if any are bad.

13. To replace the rollers, remove the roller, plunger and spring as a set. Remove all 3 sets.

14. Reinstall the spring, plunger and roller sets into the starter clutch.

Installation

1. Position the starter idle gear with the larger diameter gear toward the crankcase surface (**Figure 155**). Place the wave washer between the idle gear and the crankcase surface. Place these 2 parts in the crankcase and align them with the hole in the crankcase.

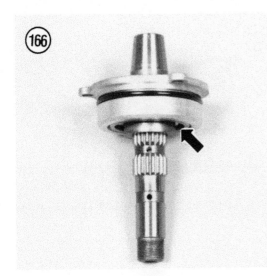

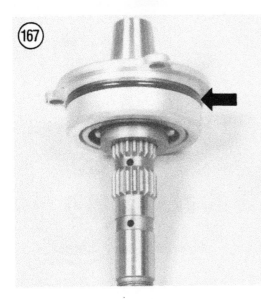

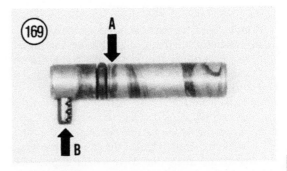

2. Make sure the O-ring seal (A, **Figure 169**) and locating pin (B, **Figure 169**) are installed on the idle gear shaft.

3. Install the idle gear shaft (A, **Figure 156**) into the upper crankcase, through the wave washer and the starter idle gear.

4. Align the locating pin with the groove in the crankcase (B, **Figure 156**). Push the shaft in until it seats completely.

5. To assemble the starter clutch assembly, perform the following:

    a. Place the starter clutch assembly with the exposed roller sets facing upward.

    b. Place the starter drive gear onto the starter clutch.

    c. Rotate the starter drive gear *counterclockwise* and push down at the same time.

    d. Push the drive gear (**Figure 159**) all the way down until it seats completely.

    e. Install the needle bearing (**Figure 158**) and the collar (**Figure 157**).

6. On the left-hand side of the the upper crankcase, perform the following:

    a. Position the starter clutch assembly with the drive gear facing toward the left-hand side of the upper crankcase.

    b. Mesh the drive chain onto the starter clutch assembly (**Figure 170**).

c. Lower this assembly down into the crankcase and align with the hole in the crankcase.

d. Install the alternator shaft through the starter clutch and into the hole in the crankcase on the opposite side. Push the shaft in until it seats completely (**Figure 171**).

e. Make sure the O-ring seal is in place on the bearing holder and install the bearing holder.

f. Align the holes in the bearing holder and install the bolts. Tighten the bolts securely.

7. Install the alternator drive chain slipper (B, **Figure 153**) and bolt (A, **Figure 153**). Tighten the bolt securely.

8. Install both transmission assemblies as described in Chapter Five.

9. Assemble the crankcase halves and install the engine as described in this chapter.

10. On the right-hand side of the upper crankcase, perform the following:

a. Install the alternator shaft set nut (**Figure 152**).

b. Place the transmission in 6th gear and have an assistant apply the rear brake.

c. Tighten the nut to the torque specification listed in **Table 1**.

d. Inspect the O-ring seal on the alternator cap; replace if necessary.

e. Install the alternator cap (**Figure 151**).

11. Install the starter motor.

CRANKCASE AND CRANKSHAFT

Disassembly of the crankcase (splitting the cases) and removal of the crankshaft assembly requires that the engine be removed from the frame.

The crankcase is made in 2 halves of precision diecast aluminum alloy and is of the "thin-walled" type. To avoid damage, do not hammer or pry on any of the interior or exterior projected walls. These areas are easily damaged. The cases are assembled with a coat of gasket sealer between the 2 halves and dowel pins align the halves when they are bolted together.

The procedure which follows is presented as a complete, step-by-step major lower-end rebuild that should be followed if an engine is to be completely reconditioned. However, if you're replacing a known failed part, the disassembly should be carried out only until the failed part is accessible; there's no need to disassemble the engine beyond that point so long as you know the remaining components are in good condition and were not affected by the failed part.

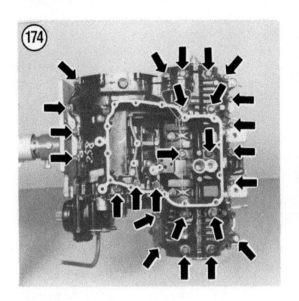

Disassembly

1. Remove all exterior engine assemblies as described in this chapter and other related chapters:
   a. Cylinder head (this chapter).
   b. Cylinder block (this chapter).
   c. Pistons and piston pins (this chapter).
   d. Alternator (this chapter).
   e. External shift mechanism (Chapter Five).
   f. Starter motor (Chapter Seven).
   g. Pulse generator assembly (Chapter Seven).
   h. Clutch assembly (Chapter Five).

2. Remove the engine as described in this chapter and place in an engine stand or work bench.

> *CAUTION*
> *If the engine is going to be set upside down on a workbench, set it on wood blocks to protect the crankcase studs.*

3. Remove the oil pan, oil pump, oil strainer and oil pressure relief valve as described in this chapter.

4. Remove the bolts (**Figure 172**) securing the output gear case to both crankcase halves. Do *not* try to remove the output gear case, just pull the assembly slightly away from both crankcase halves.

> *NOTE*
> *Note the location of the copper washers under some crankcase bolts. There is a raised arrow next to the bolt hole at each location. New copper washers must be reinstalled in these locations.*

5. Leaving the ten 8 mm crankshaft bearing bolts (**Figure 173**) for last, loosen all lower crankcase bolts in 2-3 stages in a crisscross pattern to avoid warpage (**Figure 174**). Remove all bolts and copper washers.

6. Turn the engine right side up on the workbench.

7. Loosen the upper crankcase bolts (**Figure 175**) in 2-3 stages in a crisscross pattern to avoid warpage.

8. Tap around the perimeter of the crankcase halves with a plastic mallet—do not use a metal hammer as it will cause damage.

9. Pull the lower case half off the upper case half. Don't lose the 2 locating dowels.

> *CAUTION*
> *Honda's thin-walled crankcase castings are just that—thin. To avoid damage to the cases do not hammer on the projected walls that surround the clutch. These areas are easily damaged if stressed beyond what they are designed for.*

> *CAUTION*
> *If it is necessary to pry the crankcase apart, do it very carefully so you do not mar the gasket surfaces. If you do, the case will leak and the halves must be replaced as a set. They cannot be repaired.*

10. Remove the transmission assemblies as described in Chapter Five.

11. Remove the starter clutch assembly as described in this chapter.

12. Lift out the crankshaft assembly, alternator drive chain, cam drive chain and oil pump drive chain.

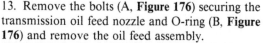

13. Remove the bolts (A, **Figure 176**) securing the transmission oil feed nozzle and O-ring (B, **Figure 176**) and remove the oil feed assembly.

14. Remove the gearshift drum and forks as described in Chapter Five.

15. Remove the bolts (**Figure 177**) securing the crankcase breather plate and remove the plate.

16. Remove the bolts (**Figure 178**) securing the alternator air outlet cover. Remove the cover and gasket.

17. Remove the bolts securing the alternator drive chain tensioner (**Figure 179**) and remove the tensioner.

18. If necessary for replacement, remove the crankcase main bearing inserts from the upper and lower crankcase halves. Mark the backsides of the inserts with a "1," "2," "3" and "4" and "U" (upper) or "L" (lower), so they can be reinstalled into the same position.

NOTE
The No. 1 cylinder is on the left-hand side. The left-hand side refers to the engine as it sits in the bike's frame—not necessarily as it sits on your workbench.

Inspection

1. Thoroughly clean the inside and outside of both crankcase halves with cleaning solvent. Dry with compressed air. Make sure there is no solvent residue left in the cases as it will contaminate the new engine oil.

2. Make sure all oil passages are clean. After cleaning, blow both case halves dry with compressed air.

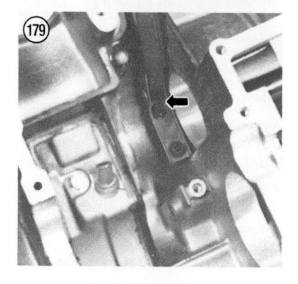

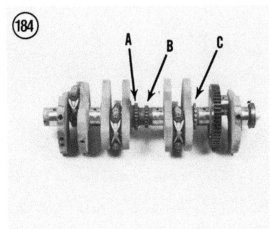

4

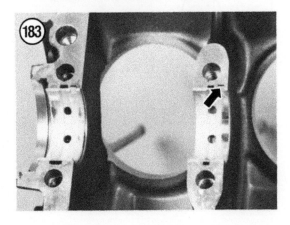

3. Check the crankcases for possible damage such as cracks. Inspect the mating surfaces of both halves. They must be free of gouges, burrs or any damage that could cause an oil leak.

4. Make sure the crankcase studs are not bent and the threads are in good condition. Make sure they are screwed into the crankcase tightly.

5. Remove the rubber isolators (**Figure 180**) from the upper crankcase half. Inspect the rubber isolators (**Figure 181**) for wear or damage; replace as a pair if necessary.

Assembly

Prior to installation of all parts, coat surfaces with assembly oil or engine oil. Assemble with the upper crankcase upside-down and set on wood blocks to protect the crankcase studs.

1. If removed, install the main bearing inserts in both the upper (**Figure 182**) and lower crankcase halves. If reusing old bearings, make sure that they are installed in the same location. Refer to marks made in *Disassembly,* Step 18. Make sure they are locked in place (**Figure 183**).

2. Install the crankcase breather plate and bolts. Tighten the bolts securely.

3. Install the alternator air outlet cover and gasket. Tighten the bolts securely.

4. Install the alternator drive chain tensioner and bolts. Tighten the bolts securely.

5. Install the gearshift drum and forks as described in Chapter Five.

6. Apply assembly oil to the main bearing inserts.

7. Onto the crankshaft sprockets install the alternator drive chain (A, **Figure 184**), the cam drive chain (B, **Figure 184**) and the oil pump drive chain (C, **Figure 184**).

8. Install the crankshaft assembly (**Figure 185**) into the upper crankcase. Make sure the oil seal (**Figure 186**) on the right-hand end is correctly positioned into the groove in the crankcase.

9. Into the lower crankcase half, install the transmission oil feed nozzle assembly and O-ring (B, **Figure 176**). Install the bolts (A, **Figure 176**) and tighten securely.

10. If removed, install the 2 locating dowels (**Figure 187**), one on each side, in the upper crankcase.

11. Install the alternator drive chain tensioner and bolts (**Figure 153**). Tighten the bolts securely.

12. Install the starter clutch assembly as described in this chapter.

13. Install both transmission assemblies as described in Chapter Five.

14. Make sure the case half sealing surfaces are perfectly clean and dry. As a final touch, spray the surfaces with contact cleaner and let air dry.

15. Apply a light coat of gasket sealer to the sealing surfaces of both halves. Cover only flat surfaces, not curved bearing surfaces. Make the coating as thin as possible or the case can shift and hammer out the bearings. Apply sealant only to within 1 mm (0.04 in.) of the edge of the inserts (**Figure 188**). If the sealant is applied any closer it will restrict oil flow.

> *NOTE*
> *Use Gasgacinch Gasket Sealer, 4-Three Bond or equivalent. When selecting an equivalent, avoid thick or hard setting materials.*

> *NOTE*
> *Make sure the crankshaft main bearing inserts are in place and correctly positioned.*

16. In the upper crankcase, position the shift drum into neutral. The shift forks should be positioned so the fingers are straight up as shown in **Figure 189**.

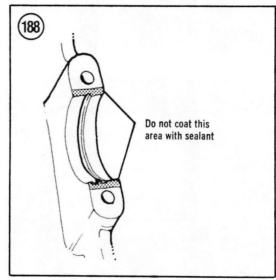

Do not coat this area with sealant

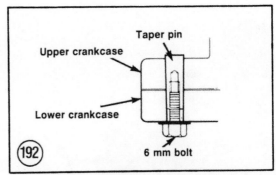

17. Make sure the output gear case is backed away from both crankcase halves.

18. Apply a coat of molybdenum disulfide grease to the shift fork gooves in the main shaft 2nd/3rd gear, the countershaft 5th gear and 6th gears.

19. To ensure proper alignment of the upper and lower crankcase halves 2 special tools (2 assembly pins—Honda part No. 07973-ME5000) are necessary. Install the bolt hole end of the tapered pins into the front outer holes of the upper crankcase. Refer to **Figure 190** and **Figure 191**. *Lightly* tap the tapered pins into place so they will not fall out during assembly.

20. Install the lower crankcase as follows:
   a. Position the lower crankcase onto the upper crankcase.
   b. Set the front portion down first and lower the rear while making sure the shift forks engage properly into the transmission assembly gear groves.
   c. Make sure the cam drive chain slider and the alternator drive chain slider align with the grooves in the lower case.
   d. Lower the crankcase completely, making sure the outer bearing races on the main shaft are still engaged into the dowel pin and set ring. If they are not seated correctly this will keep the crankcase halves from completely seating.

CAUTION
Do not install any crankcase bolts until the sealing surface around the entire crankcase perimeter has seated completely.

21. Prior to installing the bolts, slowly spin the transmission main shaft and shift the transmission through all 6 gears. This is done to check shift fork engagement.

22. Into the tapered pins installed in Step 19, install 2 of the clutch spring bolts (or 6×20 mm bolts) as shown in **Figure 192**. Tighten the bolts (**Figure 193**) to 10-14 N•m (7-10 ft.-lb.).

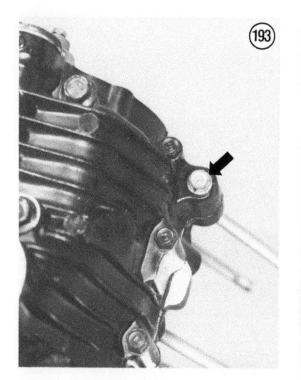

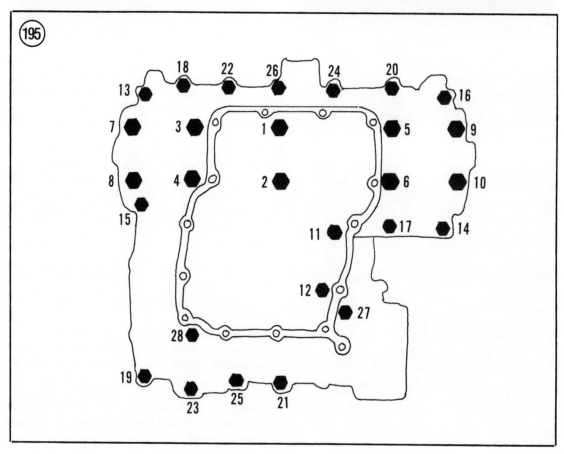

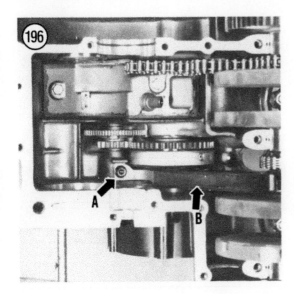

23. Apply molybdenum disulfide grease to the threads and flanges of the 8 mm bolts (crankshaft bearing bolts). Install these bolts only finger-tight at this time.

24. Apply oil to the threads of the remaining lower crankcase bolts.

25. Install a *new* copper sealing washer under the 6 mm bolts marked with a raised arrow on the crankcase (**Figure 194**).

26. Install the lower crankcase 6 mm bolts only finger-tight at this time.

27. Tighten all bolts in 2-3 stages in the torque sequence shown in **Figure 195**. Tighten to the torque specification listed in **Table 2**.

28. Turn the crankcase assembly over and install all upper crankcase bolts only finger-tight (**Figure 175**). Tighten the bolts in 2-3 stages to the torque specification listed in **Table 2**.

> *CAUTION*
> *Do not damage the crankcase halves while tapping the tapered pin out of the upper crankcase.*

29. Remove the clutch spring bolts (or 6×20 mm bolts) from the tapered pins and *carefully* tap the tapered pins out of the holes in the upper crankcase.

30. Tighten the output gear case bolts to 30-34 N•m (22-25 ft.-lb.).

31. Install all exterior engine assemblies as described in this chapter and other related chapters:

   a. Pulse generator assembly (Chapter Seven).
   b. Starter motor (Chapter Seven).
   c. Oil pan, oil pump, oil strainer and oil pressure relief valve (this chapter).

   d. External shift mechanism (Chapter Five).
   e. Alternator (this chapter).
   f. Pistons and piston pins (this chapter).
   g. Cylinder block (this chapter).
   h. Cylinder head (this chapter).

32. Install the engine as described under *Installation* in this chapter.

33. Fill the crankcase with the recommended type and quantity of engine oil. Refer to Chapter Three.

CRANKSHAFT AND CONNECTING RODS

Crankshaft Removal/Installation

1. Split the crankcase as described in this chapter.

2. Remove the transmission assemblies as described in Chapter Five.

3. Remove the bolt (A, **Figure 196**) securing the alternator drive chain slipper and remove the slipper (B, **Figure 196**).

4. If the connecting rods are going to be removed from the crankshaft, do it now as described in this chapter. It is easier to loosen the rod cap nuts while the crankshaft is in the crankcase.

5. Install by reversing these removal steps.

Crankshaft Inspection

1. Remove the connecting rods as described in this chapter.

2. Clean crankshaft thoroughly with solvent. Clean oil holes (**Figure 197**) with rifle cleaning brushes; flush thoroughly with new solvent and dry with compressed air. Lightly oil all bearing journal surfaces immediately to prevent rust.

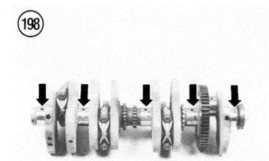

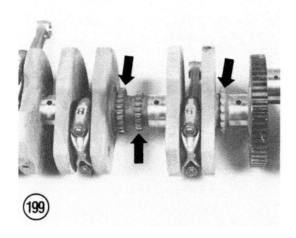

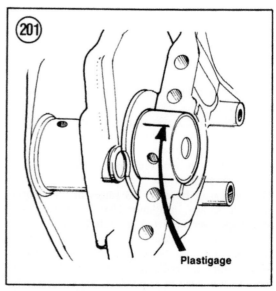

Plastigage

3. Carefully inspect each bearing journal (**Figure 198**) for scratches, ridges, scoring, nicks, etc. Very small nicks and scratches may be removed with fine emery cloth. More serious damage must be removed by grinding—a job for a machine shop or dealer.

4. If the surface on all journals is satisfactory, take the crankshaft to a dealer or machine shop. They can check for out-of-roundness, taper and wear on the bearing journals. They can also check crankshaft runout.

5. Inspect the sprocket teeth for the camshaft, alternator and oil pump chains (**Figure 199**). If damaged, the crankshaft must be replaced.

6. Check the teeth of the final drive gear (**Figure 200**) on the crankshaft. Check for chipped or missing teeth. Look for uneven or excessive wear on the gear face. If damaged, the crankshaft must be replaced.

Crankshaft Main Bearing and Journal Inspection

1. Check the inside and outside surfaces of the bearing inserts for wear, bluish tint (burned), flaking abrasion and scoring. If the bearings are good, they may be reused. If any insert is questionable, replace the entire set.

2. Clean the bearing surfaces of the crankshaft and the main bearing inserts. Measure the main bearing clearance by performing the following steps.

3. Set the upper crankcase upside down on wood blocks on the workbench to protect the crankcase studs.

4. If removed, install the existing main bearing inserts into the upper and lower crankcase halves.

5. Install the crankshaft into the upper crankcase.

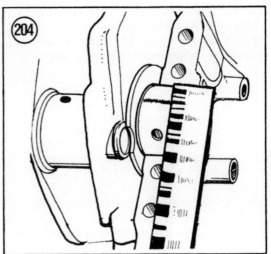

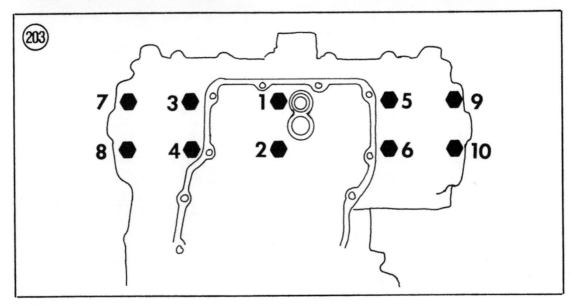

6. Place a strip of Plastigage material over each main bearing journal parallel to the crankshaft (**Figure 201**). Do not place the Plastigage strip over an oil hole in the crankshaft.

NOTE
Do not rotate the crankshaft while the Plastigage strips are in place.

7. Carefully turn the lower crankcase over and install it onto the upper crankcase.

8. Apply molybdenum disulfide grease to the threads and flanges of the 8 mm lower crankcase bolts (**Figure 202**) next to the crankshaft bearings. Tighten them in 2-3 steps in the torque sequence shown in **Figure 203**. Tighten to a final torque of 21-25 N•m (15-18 ft.-lb.).

9. Remove the 8 mm bolts in the reverse order of installation.

10. Carefully remove the lower crankcase and measure the width of the flattened Plastigage material following manufacturer's instructions. Measure both ends of the Plastigage strip (**Figure 204**). A difference of 0.025 mm (0.001 in.) or more indicates a tapered journal. Confirm with a micrometer. New bearing oil clearance and service limit dimensions are listed in **Table 1**. Remove the Plastigage strips from all bearing journals.

11. If the bearing clearance is greater than specified, use the following steps for new bearing selection.

12. The crankshaft main bearing ID is coded as either "A," "B" or "C" (**Figure 205**). The letters are marked on the right-hand side upper crankcase next to the right-hand main bearing insert.

> *NOTE*
> *The letter on the left-hand end relates to the bearing insert in the left-hand side and continues across from left to right. Remember, the left-hand side relates to the engine as it sits in the bike's frame, not as it sits on your workbench.*

13. The crankshaft main journals are marked "1," "2," "3" or "4" (**Figure 206**). The numbers are marked on the end of the counterbalance weight.

> *NOTE*
> *The number on the left-hand end relates to the bearing journal on the left-hand side and continues across from left to right. Remember, the left-hand side relates to the engine as it sits in the bike's frame, not as it sits on your workbench.*

14. Measure the main journal (**Figure 198**) with a micrometer. If the main journal dimension is within the tolerance stated for its number code in **Table 3**, the bearing can be selected by color code. Select new bearings by cross-referencing the main journal number (**Figure 206**) in the horizontal column of **Table 3** to the the crankcase bearing letter (**Figure 205**) in the vertical column. Where the columns intersect, the new bearing insert color is indicated. **Table 4** gives the bearing color and thickness. Always replace bearing inserts as a set.

15. If any main journal measurements taken during inspection do not fall within the tolerance range for the stamped number code, the serviceability of the crankshaft must be carefully examined. If the main bearing journal in question is not tapered, out-of-round or scored the crankshaft may still be used; however, the bearing selection will have to be made based on the measured diameter of the bearing journal and not by the stamped number code. Honda recommends the crankshaft be replaced whenever a main bearing journal dimension is beyond the specified range on the stamped number code.

16. After new bearings have been installed, recheck clearance by repeating this procedure.

Connecting Rod
Removal/Installation

1. Split the crankcase as described in this chapter.

2. Remove the transmission assemblies as described in Chapter Five.

3. Remove the bolt securing the alternator slipper assembly and remove the assembly.

4. Prior to removing the rods, check the rod side clearance (**Figure 207**) with a flat feeler gauge. Compare to dimensions given in **Table 1**.

> *NOTE*
> *Prior to disassembly, mark the rods and caps. Number them "1," "2," "3" or "4" starting from the left-hand side. The left-hand side refers to the engine sitting in the bike frame—not as it sits on your workbench.*

5. Loosen the cap nuts (**Figure 208**) securing the bearing caps to each connecting rod. Remove the cap nuts and bearing caps.

6. Remove the connecting rods from the crankshaft. Mark the back of each bearing insert with the cylinder number and "U" (upper) or "L" (lower).

7. Install by reversing these removal steps, noting the following.

8. Install the bearing inserts into each connecting rod and cap. Align the oil holes in the upper bearing inserts (**Figure 209**). Make sure they are locked into place correctly (**Figure 210**).

> *NOTE*
> *If the old bearing inserts are reused, be sure they are installed into their original positions; refer to Step 6.*

9. Apply molybdenum disulfide grease to the bearing inserts, crankpins and connecting rod bolt threads. Install the connecting rods and rod caps. Tighten the cap nuts evenly in 2-3 steps to the torque specification listed in **Table 2**.

10. After all rod caps have been installed, rotate the crankshaft several times and check that the bearings are not too tight. Make sure there is no binding.

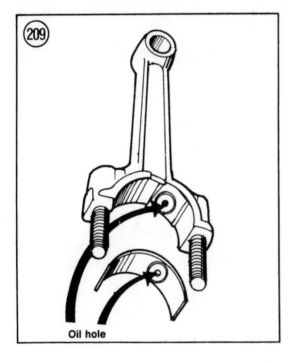

Oil hole

Connecting Rod Inspection

> *NOTE*
> *Prior to disassembly, mark the rods and caps. Number them "1," "2," "3" or "4" starting from the left-hand side. The left-hand side refers to the engine in the bike's frame—not on your workbench.*

1. Clean the connecting rods and inserts in solvent and dry with compressed air.

2. Carefully inspect each rod journal on the crankshaft for scratches, ridges, scoring, nicks, etc. Very small nicks and scratches may be removed

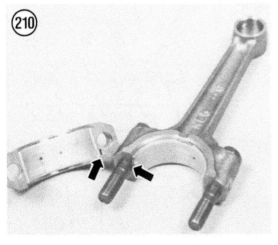

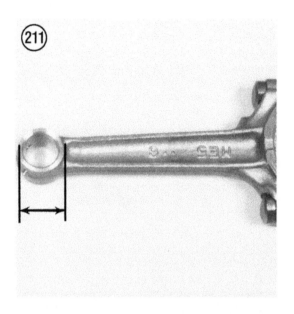

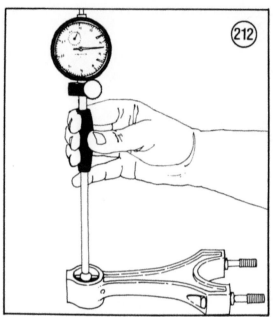

with fine emery cloth. More serious damage must be removed by grinding—a job for a machine shop or dealer.

3. If the surface on all journals is satisfactory, take the crankshaft to a dealer or machine shop. They can check for out-of-roundness, taper and wear on the rod bearing journals.

Connecting Rod Bearing and Journal Inspection

1. Check the inside and outside surfaces of the bearing inserts for wear, bluish tint (burned), flaking abrasion and scoring. If the bearings are good, they may be reused. If any insert is questionable, replace the entire set.

2. Measure the inside diameter of the small end (**Figure 211**) of the connecting rods with an inside dial gauge (**Figure 212**). Check against dimension listed in **Table 1**; replace the rod if necessary.

3. If removed, install the crankshaft into the upper crankcase.

4. Clean the rod bearing surfaces of the crankshaft and the rod bearing inserts. Measure the rod bearing oil clearance by performing the following steps.

5. Place a strip of Plastigage material over each rod bearing journal parallel to the crankshaft (**Figure 213**). Do not place the Plastigage material over an oil hole in the crankshaft.

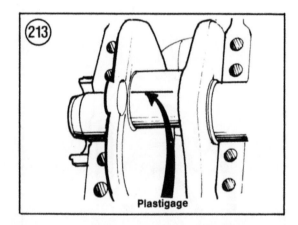

Plastigage

> *NOTE*
> *Do not rotate the crankshaft while the Plastigage strips are in place.*

6. Install the rod cap and tighten the cap nuts to the torque specification listed in **Table 2**.

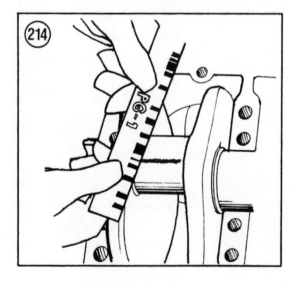

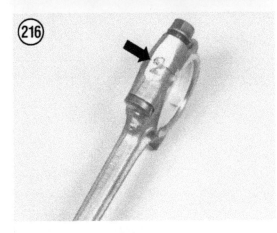

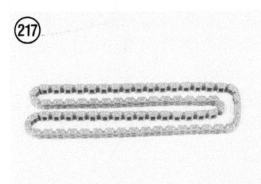

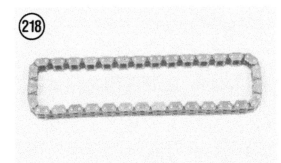

7. Remove the rod cap and measure the width of the flattened Plastigage material following manufacturer's instructions. Measure both ends of the Plastigage strip (**Figure 214**). A difference of 0.025 mm (0.001 in.) or more indicates a tapered journal. Confirm with a micrometer. New bearing oil clearance and service limit are listed in **Table 1**. Remove the Plastigage material from the connecting rods and crankshaft journals.

8. If the rod bearing clearance is greater than specified, use the following steps for new bearing selection.

9. The crankshaft rod journals are marked with letters "A," "B" or "C" (**Figure 215**) on the counterbalance weights. The connecting rod and cap are marked with numbers "1," "2" or "3" (**Figure 216**).

10. Select new bearings by cross-referencing the rod journal letter (**Figure 215**) in the horizontal column of **Table 6** or **Table 7** to the rod bearing number (**Figure 216**) in the vertical column. Where the 2 columns intersect, the new bearing color is indicated. **Table 8** gives the bearing insert color and thickness.

11. If any rod bearing journal measurements taken during inspection do not fall within the tolerance range for the stamped letter code, the serviceability of the crankshaft must be carefully examined. If the main bearing journal in question is not tapered, out-of-round or scored the crankshaft may still be used; however, the bearing selection will have to be made based on the measured diameter of the bearing journal and not by the stamped number code. Honda recommends the crankshaft be replaced whenever a main bearing journal dimension is beyond the specified range on the stamped number code.

12. After new bearings have been installed, recheck clearance by repeating this procedure.

13. Repeat Steps 5-12 for the other 3 cylinders.

CAMSHAFT AND ALTERNATOR CHAIN INSPECTION

1. Split the crankcase and remove the crankshaft as described in this chapter.

2. Inspect the links on both the camshaft chain (**Figure 217**) and alternator chain (**Figure 218**).

3. Place the cam chain onto the intake and exhaust cam sprockets. Secure one sprocket and attach a scale (a portable fish scale will do) to the other sprocket. Apply 29 lb. (13 kg) of tension on the components. Measure the distance between the 2 sprockets as shown in **Figure 150**. Replace the chain if the length exceeds the service wear limit listed in **Table 1**.

4. Place the alternator chain onto the sprocket on the crankshaft and the starter clutch driven gear (**Figure 219**). Attach a scale (a portable fish scale will do) and apply 29 lb. (13 kg) of tension on the components. Measure the distance between the centerline of the 2 sprockets as shown in **Figure 220**. Replace the chain if the length exceeds the service wear limit listed in **Table 1**.

5. Inspect the links on the oil pump chain (**Figure 221**) for wear or damage. Honda does not provide a wear limit measurement for this chain.

BREAK-IN PROCEDURE

If the rings were replaced, new pistons installed, the cylinders rebored or honed or major lower end work performed, the engine should be broken in just as though it were new. The performance and service life of the engine depends greatly on a careful and sensible break-in.

For the first 800 km (500 miles), no more than one-third throttle should be used and speed should be varied as much as possible within the one-third throttle limit. Prolonged steady running at one speed, no matter how moderate, is to be avoided as is hard acceleration.

Following the *800 km (500 miles) Service* described in this chapter, more throttle should not be used until the motorcycle has covered at least 1,600 km (1,000 miles) and then it should be limited to short bursts of speed until 2,400 km (1,500 miles) have been logged.

The mono-grade oils recommended for break-in and normal use provide a better bedding pattern for rings and cylinders than do multi-grade oils. As a result, piston ring and cylinder bore life are greatly increased. During break-in, oil consumption will be higher than normal. It is therefore important to frequently check and correct oil level. At no time during the break-in or later should the oil level be allowed to drop below the bottom line on the dipstick; if the oil level is low, the oil will become overheated resulting in insufficient lubrication and increased wear.

800 km (500 Mile) Service

It is essential the oil and filter be changed after the first 800 km (500 miles). In addition, it is a good idea to change the oil and filter at the completion of the break-in (about 2,400 km/1,500 miles) to ensure all of the particles produced during break-in are removed from the lubrication system. The small added expense may be considered a smart investment that will pay off in increased engine life.

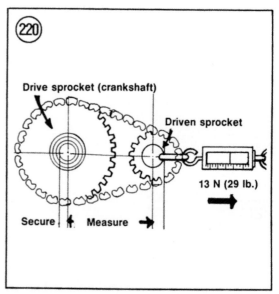

Drive sprocket (crankshaft)

Driven sprocket

13 N (29 lb.)

Secure   Measure

Table 1 ENGINE SPECIFICATIONS

Item	Specification	Wear limit
General		
Engine type	Air-cooled, 4-stroke, DOHC, inline four	
Bore and stroke		
550 cc	60.0×50.6 mm (2.36×1.99 in.)	
650 cc	60.0×58.0 mm (2.36×2.28 in.)	
Displacement		
550 cc	572 cc (23 cid)	
650 cc	655 cc (39.9 cid)	
Compression ratio	9.5 to 1	
Valve train	Hi-Vo multi-link drive chain, DOHC	
	4 valves per cylinder with hydraulic tappets	
Maximum horsepower		
CB550	62 HP @ 9,500 rpm (47.7 kw @ 9,500 rpm)	
CB650	73 HP @ 9,500 rpm (53.7 kw @ 9,500 rpm)	
Lubrication	Wet sump	
Air filtration	Paper element type	
Engine weight (dry)	75 kg (165 lb.)	
Cylinders		
Bore	60.000-60.010 mm (2.3622-2.3626 in.)	60.10 mm (2.367 in.)
Out of round	—	0.05 mm (0.002 in.)
Taper	—	0.05 mm (0.002 in.)
Piston/cylinder clearance	0.01-0.050 mm (0.0003-0.0020 in.)	0.10 mm (0.004 in.)
Pistons		
Diameter	59.97-59.99 mm (2.3610-2.3618 in.)	59.90 mm (2.36 in.)
Clearance in bore	0.01-0.05 mm (0.0003-0.0020 in.)	0.10 mm (0.004 in.)
Piston pin bore	15.002-15.008 mm (0.5906-0.5909 in.)	15.05 mm (0.592 in.)
Piston pin outer diameter	14.994-15.000 mm (0.5903-0.5906 in.)	14.98 mm (0.589 in.)
Piston rings		
Number per piston		
Compression	2	
Oil control	1	
Ring end gap		
Top and second	0.15-0.30 mm (0.0059-0.012 in.)	0.50 mm (0.02 in.)
Oil (side rail)	0.30-0.90 mm (0.012-0.035 in.)	1.10 mm (0.04 in.)
Ring side clearance		
Top and second	0.015-0.045 mm (0.0006-0.0018 in.)	0.06 mm (0.002 in.)
Oil (side rail)	—	—
Connecting rod		
Small end inner diameter	15.016-15.034 mm (0.5912-0.5909 in.)	15.07 mm (0.593 in.)

(continued)

Table 1 ENGINE SPECIFICATIONS

Item	Specification	Wear limit
Crankshaft		
Runout	—	0.05 mm (0.002 in.)
Main bearing oil clearance	0.019-0.043 mm (0.0007-0.0017 in.)	0.06 mm (0.002 in.)
Connecting rod oil clearance	0.024-0.057 mm (0.0009-0.0022 in.)	0.07 mm (0.003 in.)
Connecting rod big end side clearance	0.05-0.20 mm (0.002-0.0079 in.)	0.3 mm (0.010 in.)
Camshaft chain length	323.05-324.05 mm (12.750-12.758 in.)	327.0 mm (12.87 in.)
Alternator chain length	136.50-136.70 mm (5.374-5.382 in.)	137.8 mm (5.43 in.)
Camshaft		
Cam lobe height		
Intake and exhaust	31.901 mm (1.2559 in.)	31.85 mm (1.252 in.)
Runout	—	0.03 mm (0.001 in.)
Bearing journal OD @		
IN1, IN4, EX1, EX4	22.939-22.970 mm (0.9031-0.9043 in.)	22.91 mm (0.902 in.)
IN2, IN3, EX2, EX3	22.909-22.930 mm (0.9019-0.9028 in.)	22.88 mm (0.901 in.)
Oil clearance @		
IN1, IN4, EX1, EX4	0.030-0.072 mm (0.0012-0.0028 in.)	0.13 mm (0.005 in.)
IN2, IN3, EX2, EX3	0.070-0.112 mm (0.0028-0.0044 in.)	0.16 mm (0.006 in.)
Tappet compression stroke in kerosene	—	0.20 mm (0.0079 in.)
Valves		
Valve stem outer diameter		
Intake	4.975-4.990 mm (0.1959-0.1965 in.)	4.97 mm (0.195 in.)
Exhaust	4.955-4.970 mm (0.1951-0.1957 in.)	4.94 mm (0.194 in.)
Valve guide inner diameter		
Intake and exhaust	5.0-5.012 mm (0.1969-0.1973 in.)	5.04 mm (0.198 in.)
Stem to guide clearance		
Intake	0.010-0.037 mm (0.0004-0.015 in.)	0.07 mm (0.003 in.)
Exhaust	0.030-0.057 mm (0.0012-0.0022 in.)	0.09 mm (0.004 in.)
Valve seat width		
Intake and exhaust	1.41-1.98 mm (0.056-0.078 in.)	2.0 mm (0.08 in.)
Valve springs free length		
Intake and exhaust		
Outer	34.61 mm (1.363 in.)	33.4 mm (1.31 in.)
Inner	33.90 mm (1.335 in.)	32.7 mm (1.29 in.)

(continued)

Table 1 ENGINE SPECIFICATIONS (continued)

Item	Specification	Wear limit
Cylinder head warpage	—	0.10 mm (0.004 in.)
Oil pump		
Inner rotor tip to outer clearance	0.10 mm (0.004 in.)	0.15 mm (0.006 in.)
Outer rotor to body clearance	0.15-0.22 mm (0.006-0.009 in.)	0.35 mm (0.014 in.)
End clearance to body	0.02-0.07 mm (0.001-0.003 in.)	0.10 mm (0.004 in.)
Oil pump pressure (at switch)	5.0 kg/cm² (71.0 psi)	
Oil pump delivery	36 liters/min. @ 7,000 rpm (38.05 U.S. qt./min. @ 7,000 rpm)	
Starter clutch		
Drive gear OD	42.175-42.200 mm (1.6604-1.6614 in.)	42.16 mm (1.660 in.)
Collar OD	24.987-25.000 mm (0.9837-0.9843 in.)	24.96 mm (0.983 in.)

Table 2 ENGINE TORQUE SPECIFICATIONS

Item	N•m	ft.-lb.
Engine mounting bolts		
8 mm hanger bolts	20-30	14-22
10 mm	45-60	33-43
Cylinder head nuts and cam chain tensioner	20-24	14-17
Cam sprocket bolts *	18-22	13-16
Camshaft holder bolts	11-13	8-9
Oil control bolt	13-16	9-12
External oil pipe		
8 mm	12-16	9-12
10 mm	16-20	12-14
Crankcase bolts		
6 mm	10-14	7-10
8 mm	21-25	15-18
Connecting rod cap nuts	30-34	22-25
Alternator		
Rotor bolt	31-39	22-28
Shaft nut	38-42	27-30
Oil pressure switch **	16-22	12-14
Oil filter bolt	28-32	20-23
Oil drain plug	30-40	22-29

* Apply Loctite to the threads prior to installation.
**Apply liquid sealing agent to the threads prior to installation.

Table 3 MAIN JOURNAL BEARING SELECTION (CB550)

Main journal OD size code letter and dimension				
	Number 1 31.994-32.000 mm (1.2596-1.2598 in.)	Number 2 31.988-31.994 mm (1.2594-1.2596 in.)	Number 3 31.982-31.988 mm (1.2591-1.2594 in.)	Number 4 31.976-31.982 mm (1.2589-1.2591 in.)
Crankcase inside dimension Letter A 35.000-35.006 mm (1.3780-1.3782 in.)	Pink	Yellow	Green	Brown
Letter B 35.006-35.012 mm (1.3782-1.3784 in.)	Yellow	Green	Brown	Black
Letter C 35.012-35.018 mm (1.3784-1.3787 in.)	Green	Brown	Black	Blue

Table 4 MAIN JOURNAL BEARING SELECTION (CB650)

Main journal OD size code letter and dimension				
	Number 1 32.994-33.000 mm (1.2990-1.2992 in.)	Number 2 32.988-32.994 mm (1.2987-1.2990 in.)	Number 3 32.982-32.988 mm (1.2985-1.2987 in.)	Number 4 32.976-32.982 mm (1.2983-1.2985 in.)
Crankcase inside dimension Letter A 36.000-36.006 mm (1.4173-1.4176 in.)	Pink	Yellow	Green	Brown
Letter B 36.006-36.012 mm (1.4176-1.4178 in.)	Yellow	Green	Brown	Black
Letter C 36.012-36.018 mm (1.4178-1.4180 in.)	Green	Brown	Black	Blue

Table 5 MAIN JOURNAL BEARING INSERT THICKNESS (ALL MODELS)

Color	mm	in.
Blue	1.511-1.514	0.0595-0.0596
Black	1.508-1.511	0.0594-0.0595
Brown	1.505-1.508	0.0593-0.0594
Green	1.502-1.505	0.0591-0.0593
Yellow	1.499-1.502	0.0590-0.0591
Pink	1.496-1.499	0.0589-0.0590

Table 6 CONNECTING ROD BEARING SELECTION (CB550)

Crankpin journal OD size code letter and dimension		
Letter A 31.992- 32.000 mm (1.2595- 1.2598 in.)	Letter B 31.992- 31.984 mm (1.2592- 1.2595 in.)	Letter C 31.976- 31.984 mm (1.2589- 1.2592 in.)
Connecting rod ID code number and dimension		
Number 1 35.000-35.008 mm Brown (1.3780-1.3783 in.)	Yellow	Green
Number 2 35.008-35.016 mm Black (1.3783-1.3786 in.)	Green	Brown
Number 3 35.016-35.024 mm Blue (1.3786-1.3789 in.)	Brown	Black

Table 7 CONNECTING ROD BEARING SELECTION (CB650)

Crankpin journal OD size code letter and dimension		
Letter A 37.000-37.008 mm (1.4567-1.4570 in.)	Letter B 37.008-37.016 mm (1.4570-1.4573 in.)	Letter C 37.016-37.024 mm (1.4573-1.4576 in.)
Connecting rod ID code number and dimension		
Number 1 40.000-40.008 mm (1.5748-1.5751 in.)	Yellow	Green	Brown
Number 2 40.008-40.016 mm (1.5751-1.5754 in.)	Green	Brown	Black
Number 3 40.016-40.024 mm (1.5754-1.5757 in.)	Brown	Black	Blue

Table 8 CONNECTING ROD BEARING INSERT THICKNESS (ALL MODELS)

Color	mm	in.
Blue	1.502-1.506	0.0591-0.0593
Black	1.498-1.502	0.0590-0.0591
Brown	1.494-1.498	0.0588-0.0590
Green	1.490-1.494	0.0587-0.0588
Yellow	1.486-1.490	0.0585-0.0587

CLUTCH AND TRANSMISSION

This chapter contains repair and service information for the clutch and the 6-speed transmission.

Tables 1-5 are located at the end of this chapter.

CLUTCH

The clutch is a wet, multiplate type which operates immersed in the engine oil. It is mounted on the right-hand end of the transmission main shaft. The clutch center is splined to the main shaft and the outer hub can rotate freely on the main shaft. The outer housing is geared to the primary drive gear on the right-hand end of the crankshaft.

In order to remove the outer housing, the engine must be removed from the frame and the crankcase must be disassembled.

The clutch release mechanism is hydraulic and requires no routine adjustment. The mechanism consists of a clutch master cylinder on the left-hand handlebar, a slave cylinder on the left-hand side of the engine just below the alternator and a pushrod that rides within the channel in the transmission main shaft.

The clutch is activated by hydraulic fluid pressure and is controlled by the clutch master cylinder. The hydraulic pressure generated by the master cylinder activates the clutch slave cylinder which in turn pushes the clutch pushrod. The clutch pushrod pushes on the lifter guide thus moving the pressure plate which disengages the clutch mechanism.

Refer to **Table 1** for all clutch torque specifications. Refer to **Figure 1** for the clutch assembly.

Removal/Disassembly

1. Place the bike on the centerstand.
2. Drain the engine oil as described under *Engine Oil and Filter Change* in Chapter Three.

NOTE
Do not operate the clutch lever after the clutch assembly or slave cylinder are removed from the engine. If the lever is applied it will force the slave cylinder piston out of the body and make slave cylinder installation difficult.

3. Place a block of wood between the clutch lever and the hand grip to hold the lever in the released position. Secure the wood with a rubber band or duct tape. This will prevent the clutch lever from being applied accidentally after the clutch slave cylinder is removed from the crankcase.
4. Remove the rear brake lever as described in Chapter Ten.
5. Remove the bolts securing the clutch cover (**Figure 2**) and remove the cover and O-ring seal.
6. Using a crisscross pattern, remove the clutch bolts, washers and the clutch springs (**Figure 3**) securing the pressure plate.
7. Remove the pressure plate, release bearing and lifter guide.

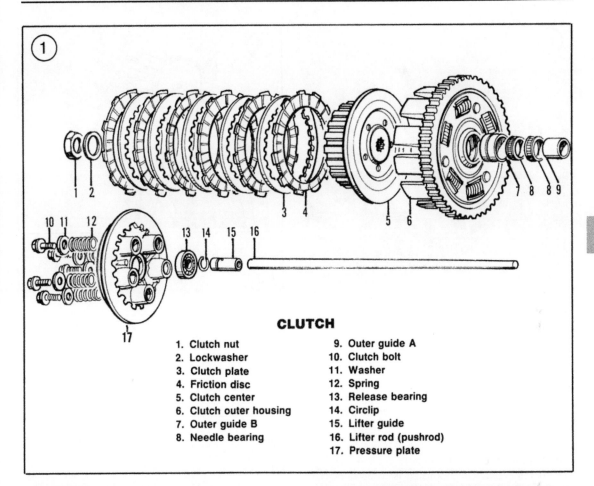

CLUTCH

1. Clutch nut
2. Lockwasher
3. Clutch plate
4. Friction disc
5. Clutch center
6. Clutch outer housing
7. Outer guide B
8. Needle bearing
9. Outer guide A
10. Clutch bolt
11. Washer
12. Spring
13. Release bearing
14. Circlip
15. Lifter guide
16. Lifter rod (pushrod)
17. Pressure plate

5

8. Remove the clutch pushrod, the friction discs and the clutch plates.

9. Remove the clutch nut and the lockwasher.

> *NOTE*
> *To keep the clutch housing from turning, use the "Grabbit" special tool (part No. 969103) available from Joe Bolger Products Inc., Barre, MA. 01005.*

10. Remove the clutch center.

11. If the clutch outer housing is to be removed, perform the following:

  a. Remove the engine as described in Chapter Four.

  b. Disassemble the crankcase as described in Chapter Four.

  c. Remove the transmission main shaft and clutch outer housing as an assembly from the lower crankcase half (**Figure 4**).

  d. Slide the outer housing, outer housing guides and needle bearings from the transmission main shaft. It is not necessary to remove the washer from the end of the main shaft.

Inspection

Refer to **Table 2** for clutch specifications.

1. Clean all clutch parts in petroleum-based solvent such as kerosene and thoroughly dry with compressed air.

2. Measure the thickness of each friction disc at several places around the disc as shown in **Figure 5**. Compare to the specifications listed in **Table 2**. Replace any disc that is worn to the service limit or less.

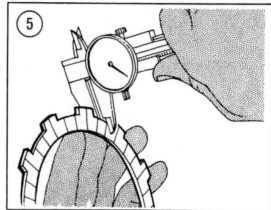

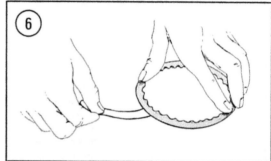

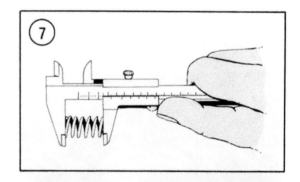

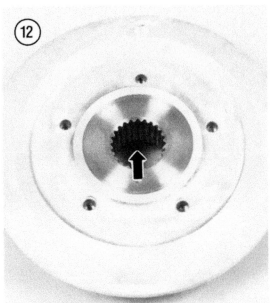

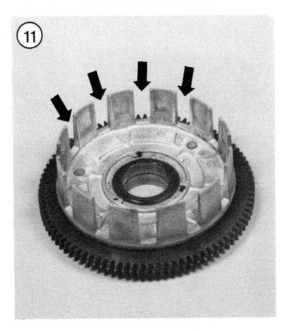

3. Check the clutch plates for warpage on a surface plate such as a piece of plate glass (**Figure 6**). Compare to the specifications listed in **Table 2**. Replace any plates that warped to the service limit or more.

4. Measure the free length of each clutch spring as shown in **Figure 7**. Compare to the specifications listed in **Table 2**. Replace any springs that have sagged to the service limit or less.

> *NOTE*
> *If any of the friction discs, clutch plates or clutch springs require replacement, you should consider replacing all of them as a set to retain maximum clutch performance.*

5. Inspect the teeth of split gear (**Figure 8**) on the outer housing for damage. If damage is severe, the housing must be replaced. Also check the teeth on the crankshaft final drive gear (**Figure 9**); if damaged, the crankshaft may also need replacing.

6. Inspect the needle bearings (**Figure 10**) within the clutch outer housing. Make sure they rotate smoothly with no signs of wear; replace as a pair if necessary.

7. Inspect the slots in the clutch outer housing (**Figure 11**) for cracks, nicks or galling where they come in contact with the friction disc tabs. If any severe damage is evident, the housing must be replaced.

8. Inspect the inner splines (**Figure 12**) of the clutch center. Check the outer grooves (A, **Figure**

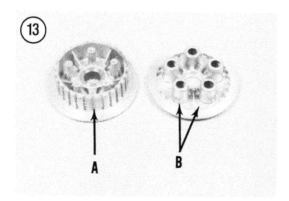

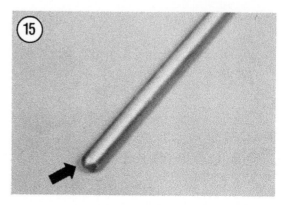

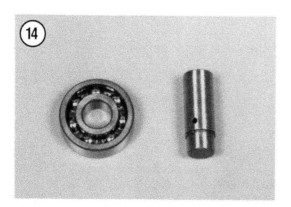

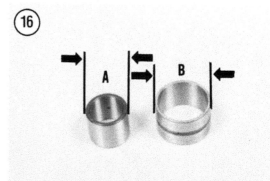

13) of the clutch center. Replace the clutch center if necessary.

9. Check the posts and grooves (B, **Figure 13**) in the pressure plate. Replace if necessary.

10. Check the bearing and lifter guide (**Figure 14**). Make sure the bearing rotates smoothly with no signs of wear or damage. Replace if necessary.

11. Check each end of the clutch pushrod (**Figure 15**) for wear or damage. Replace if necessary.

12. Measure the outside diameter of the clutch outer housing guide A (smaller) and guide B (larger) (**Figure 16**). If either are worn to the service limit listed in **Table 2** they must be replaced.

Assembly/Installation

1. If the clutch outer housing was removed, perform the following:

    a. If removed, install the clutch outer guide A (**Figure 17**).

    b. If removed, install the washer with the "OUT" mark facing out (**Figure 18**).

    c. If removed, slide on clutch outer guide B (**Figure 19**), both needle bearings (**Figure 20**) and the outer guide B.

    d. Lift the transmission shaft out of the crankcase and slide the outer housing onto the outer guide B and the main shaft (**Figure 4**).

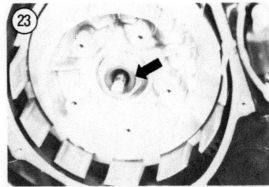

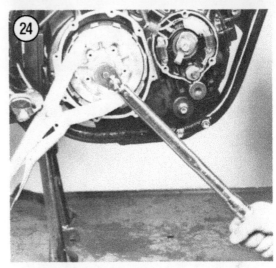

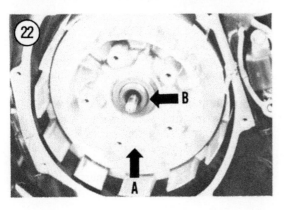

e. Install the main shaft into the crankcase lower half as described in this chapter.

f. Assemble the crankcase as described in Chapter Four.

g. Install the engine as described in Chapter Four.

> *CAUTION*
> *If either or both friction discs and clutch plates have been replaced with new ones, apply new engine oil to all surfaces to avoid having the clutch lock up when used for the first time.*

2. Install the clutch pushrod (**Figure 21**).

3. Install the clutch center (A, **Figure 22**) and the lockwasher (B, **Figure 22**) with the dished side facing out.

4. Install the clutch locknut (**Figure 23**) and tighten to the torque specification listed in **Table 1**. To keep the clutch housing from turning, use the same tool set-up used in Step 9, *Removal/Disassembly*. See **Figure 24**.

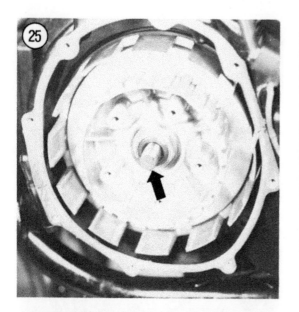

5. Install the lifter guide (**Figure 25**) on the clutch pushrod.

6. Install a friction disc (**Figure 26**), a clutch plate and a friction disc. Continue to install a clutch plate and then a friction disc; alternate them until all are installed. The last item installed is a friction disc (**Figure 27**).

7. Align the index marks on the pressure plate and the clutch outer housing (**Figure 28**). Install the clutch pressure plate.

8. Install the clutch springs (**Figure 29**), washers and bolts (**Figure 30**). Tighten the bolts in a crisscross pattern in 2 or 3 stages.

9. Install a new O-ring seal (**Figure 31**) on the clutch cover. Install the cover and tighten the bolts securely.

10. Install the rear brake lever as described in Chapter Ten.

11. Fill the crankcase with the recommended type and quantity of engine oil. Refer to Chapter Three.

CLUTCH HYDRAULIC SYSTEM

The clutch is actuated by hydraulic fluid pressure and is controlled by the hand lever on the clutch master cylinder. As clutch components wear, the fluid level drops in the reservoir and automatically adjusts for wear. There is no routine adjustment necessary or possible.

When working on the clutch hydraulic system, it is necessary that the work area and all tools be absolutely clean. Any tiny particles of foreign matter and grit in the clutch slave cylinder or the clutch master cylinder can damage the components. Also, sharp tools must not be used inside the slave cylinder or on the piston. If you

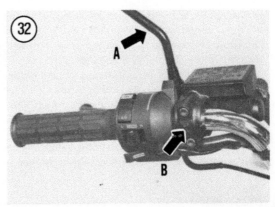

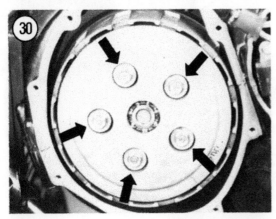

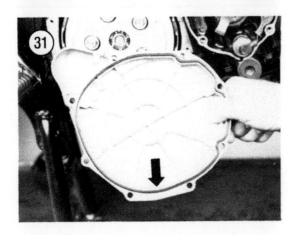

have any doubt about your ability to correctly and safely carry out major service on the clutch hydraulic components, take the job to a dealer.

CAUTION
*Throughout the text, reference is made to hydraulic fluid. Hydraulic fluid is the same as DOT 3 brake fluid. Use only DOT 3 brake fluid; do **not** use other types of fluids as they are not compatible. Do not intermix silicone based (DOT 5) hydraulic fluid as it can cause clutch component damage leading to clutch system failure.*

MASTER CYLINDER

Removal/Installation

1. Remove the rear view mirror (A, **Figure 32**) from the clutch master cylinder.

CAUTION
Cover the fuel tank and instrument cluster with a heavy cloth or plastic tarp to protect them from accidental hydraulic fluid spills. Wash fluid off any painted or plated surfaces or plastic parts immediately, as it will destroy the finish. Use soapy water and rinse completely.

2. Disconnect the electrical wires from the clutch switch (**Figure 33**).
3. Pull back the rubber boot (A, **Figure 34**) and remove the union bolt (B, **Figure 34**) securing the clutch hose to the clutch master cylinder. Remove the clutch hose; tie the hose up and cover the end to prevent entry of foreign matter.
4. Remove the clamping bolts and clamp (B, **Figure 32**) securing the clutch master cylinder to the handlebar and remove the clutch master cylinder.
5. Install by reversing these removal steps, noting the following.

6. Install the clamp (B, **Figure 32**) aligning the end of the clamp with the punch mark on the handlebar (**Figure 35**). Tighten the upper bolt first, then the lower. Tighten the bolts securely.

7. Install the clutch hose onto the clutch master cylinder. Be sure to place a sealing washer on each side of the fitting and install the union bolt. Tighten the union bolt to the torque specification listed in **Table 1**.

8. Connect the electrical wires to the clutch switch.

9. Bleed the clutch as described in this chapter.

Disassembly

Refer to **Figure 36** for this procedure.

1. Remove the clutch master cylinder as described in this chapter.

2. Remove the bolt and nut securing the clutch lever and remove the lever.

3. Remove the screws securing the cover and remove the cover and diaphragm; pour out the hydraulic fluid and discard it. *Never reuse hydraulic fluid.*

4. Remove the pushrod and end piece.

5. Remove the rubber boot from the area where the hand lever pushrod actuates the internal piston.

6. Using circlip pliers, remove the internal circlip from the body.

7. Remove the secondary cup and the piston assembly.

8. Remove the primary cup and spring.

9. Remove the clutch switch if necessary.

Inspection

1. Clean all parts in denatured alcohol or fresh hydraulic fluid. Inspect the cylinder bore and piston contact surfaces for signs of wear and damage. If either part is less than perfect, replace it.

2. Check the end of the piston for wear caused by the hand lever pushrod. Replace the piston if necessary.

3. Check both the primary and secondary cup for damage. Replace as necessary. Replace the piston if the secondary cup requires replacement.

4. Check the hand lever pivot bore in the clutch master cylinder. If worn or elongated, the master cylinder must be replaced.

5. Inspect the pivot bore in the hand lever. If worn or elongated it must be replaced.

6. Make sure the passages in the bottom of the fluid reservoir are clear. Check the reservoir cap and diaphragm for damage and deterioration and replace as necessary.

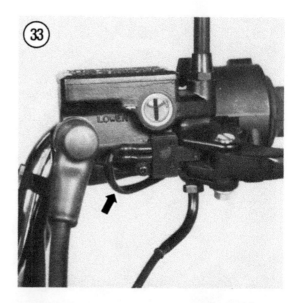

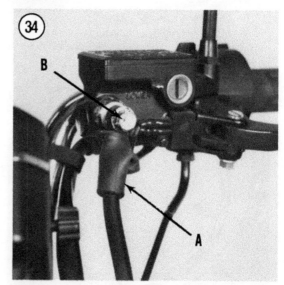

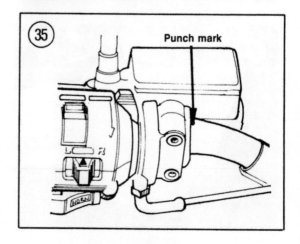

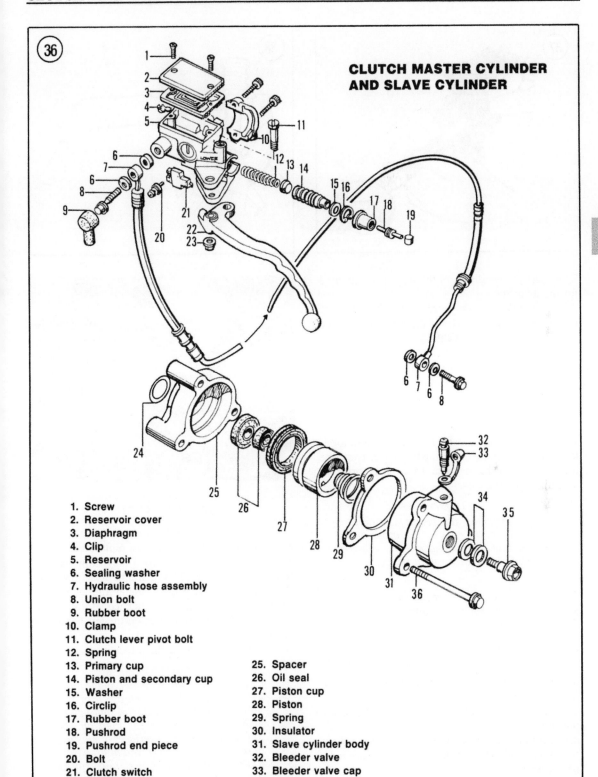

CLUTCH MASTER CYLINDER AND SLAVE CYLINDER

5

1. Screw
2. Reservoir cover
3. Diaphragm
4. Clip
5. Reservoir
6. Sealing washer
7. Hydraulic hose assembly
8. Union bolt
9. Rubber boot
10. Clamp
11. Clutch lever pivot bolt
12. Spring
13. Primary cup
14. Piston and secondary cup
15. Washer
16. Circlip
17. Rubber boot
18. Pushrod
19. Pushrod end piece
20. Bolt
21. Clutch switch
22. Clutch lever
23. Nut
24. O-ring

25. Spacer
26. Oil seal
27. Piston cup
28. Piston
29. Spring
30. Insulator
31. Slave cylinder body
32. Bleeder valve
33. Bleeder valve cap
34. Washer
35. Bolt
36. Bolt

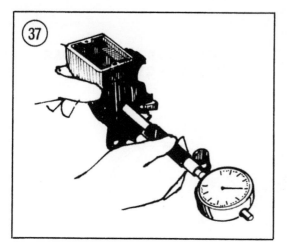

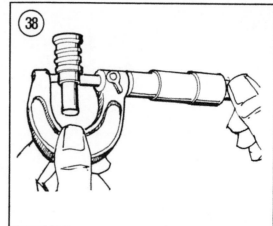

7. Inspect the condition of the threads in the bore for the fluid line.

8. Measure the cylinder bore (**Figure 37**). Replace the clutch master cylinder if the bore exceeds the specifications given in **Table 2**.

9. Measure the outside diameter of the piston as shown in **Figure 38** with a micrometer. Replace the piston assembly if it is less than the specifications given in **Table 2**.

Assembly

1. Soak the new cups in fresh hydraulic fluid for at least 15 minutes to make them pliable. Coat the inside of the cylinder with fresh fluid prior to assembly of parts.

> *CAUTION*
> *When installing the piston assembly, do not allow the cups to turn inside out as they will be damaged and allow clutch fluid leakage within the cylinder bore.*

2. Install the spring, primary cup and piston assembly into the cylinder together.

> *NOTE*
> *Be sure to install the primary cup with the open end in first, toward the spring.*

3. Install the circlip; make sure it seats firmly in the groove.

4. Slide in the rubber boot, the pushrod and the pushrod end piece.

5. Install the diaphragm and cover. Do not tighten the cover screws at this time as fluid will have to be added later.

6. Install the lever onto the master cylinder body.

7. If removed, install the clutch switch.

8. Install the clutch master cylinder and bleed the clutch system as described in this chapter.

HOSE REPLACEMENT

There is no factory-recommended replacement interval but it is a good idea to replace the clutch hoses every four years or when they show signs of cracking or damage. The hydraulic hose assembly consists of one section of metal tubing with a flexible hose permanently attached at each end. The hose assembly is located on the left-hand side of the frame.

Refer to **Figure 36** for this procedure.

> *CAUTION*
> *Cover the front wheel, fender and frame with a heavy cloth or plastic tarp to protect them from accidental spilling of hydraulic fluid. Wash the fluid off of any painted or plated surfaces or plastic parts immediately, as it will destroy the finish. Use soapy water and rinse completely.*

1. Remove the seat as described in Chapter Eleven.

2. Remove both side covers.

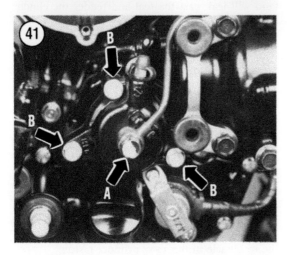

3. Remove the fuel tank as described in Chapter Six.

4. Remove the left-hand rear crankcase cover (**Figure 39**).

5. Attach a hose to the bleed valve on the clutch slave cylinder (**Figure 40**).

6. Place the loose end of the hose into a container and open the bleed valve. Operate the clutch lever until all fluid is pumped out of the system. Close the bleed valve and remove the hose.

WARNING
Dispose of this fluid—never reuse hydraulic fluid. Contaminated fluid can cause clutch failure.

7. Place a container under the clutch hose at the clutch slave cylinder to catch any remaining fluid. Remove the union bolt and sealing washers (A, **Figure 41**) securing the clutch hose to the clutch slave cylinder. Remove the clutch hose and let any remaining fluid drain out into the container.

8. Pull back the rubber boot (A, **Figure 34**) and remove the union bolt (B, **Figure 34**) and sealing washers securing the clutch flexible hose to the clutch master cylinder.

9. Remove the hose assembly from the clips on the engine and frame (**Figure 42**).

10. Remove any bands securing the metal tubing to the frame.

11. Carefully remove the hose assembly from between the carburetors and from the frame.

CAUTION
After removing the hose assembly, wash any hydraulic fluid off of any painted or plated surfaces or plastic parts immediately, as it will destroy the finish.

12. Install the hose assembly, sealing washers and union bolts in the reverse order of removal. Be sure to install new sealing washers in the correct position on each side of each union bolt; refer to **Figure 36**.

13. Tighten all union bolts to torque specifications listed in **Table 1**.

14. Refill the clutch master cylinder with fresh hydraulic fluid clearly marked DOT 3 only. Bleed the clutch system as described in this chapter.

SLAVE CYLINDER

Removal and installation are covered in 2 different ways. The first procedure is for removing the slave cylinder from the crankcase intact when no service procedures are going to be performed. The second procedure is for when the slave cylinder is going to be disassembled, inspected and serviced. Follow the correct procedure for your specific needs.

Refer to **Figure 36** for both procedures.

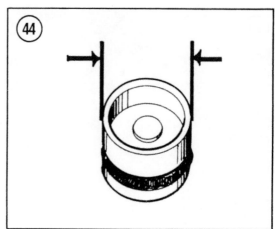

Removal/Installation (Intact)

This procedure is for removal and installation only—not for disassembly, inspection and service.

1. Place a piece of wood between the clutch lever and the hand grip to hold the lever in the released position. Secure the piece of wood with a rubber band or duct tape. This will prevent the clutch lever from being applied accidentally after the clutch slave cylinder is removed from the crankcase.

> *NOTE*
> *Do not operate the clutch lever after the slave cylinder is removed from the crankcase. If the clutch lever is applied it will force the piston out of the slave cylinder body and make installation difficult.*

2. Remove the left-hand rear crankcase cover.
3. Unhook the flexible hose from the clamp on the frame.
4. Remove the bolts (B, **Figure 41**) securing the clutch slave cylinder to the crankcase and withdraw the unit from the crankcase. Don't lose the O-ring seal on the backside of the slave cylinder.
5. Tie the clutch slave cylinder up and out of the way.
6. Apply a light coat of high-temperature silicone grease (or hydraulic fluid) to the piston seal and the oil seal prior to installing the assembly.

> *NOTE*
> *Inspect the piston seal and the oil seal. Replace if their condition is doubtful. If either seal is removed from the piston it must be replaced with a new seal.*

7. Make sure the piston seal is still correctly seated in the groove in the piston. If not seated correctly,

fluid will leak past the seal and render the clutch useless.

> *NOTE*
> *Sometimes the piston will move out slightly from the slave cylinder body when the body is withdrawn from the crankcase during removal.*

8. Withdraw the clutch pushrod from the transmission main shaft and use it to push the piston as far back in the slave cylinder body as possible. Reinstall the clutch pushrod in the transmission main shaft (**Figure 43**).
9. Make sure the O-ring is in place on the backside of the slave cylinder and install the slave cylinder on the crankcase.
10. Make sure the pushrod is inserted correctly in the receptacle in the slave cylinder piston.

> *NOTE*
> *After being positioned correctly in the crankcase the slave cylinder assembly may stick out by about 3/8 in. from the mating surface of the crankcase. This is due to the pressure within the hydraulic system.*

11. Install the bolts securing the slave cylinder and gradually tighten the bolts in a crisscross pattern. Continue to tighten until the slave cylinder has bottomed on the mating surface of the crankcase. Tighten the bolts securely.
12. Install the left-hand rear crankcase cover.

Removal (For Disassembly)

This procedure is for a complete service procedure of removal, disassembly, inspection, assembly and installation of the slave cylinder.

1. Remove the bolt securing the left-hand rear crankcase cover and remove the cover.

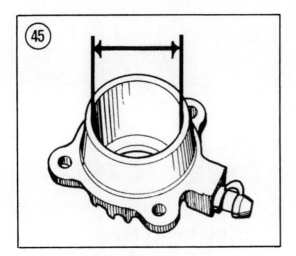

2. Attach a hose to the bleed valve on the clutch slave cylinder (**Figure 40**).

3. Place the loose end of the hose into a container and open the bleed valve. Operate the clutch lever until all fluid is pumped out of the system. Close the bleed valve and remove the hose.

WARNING
Dispose of this fluid—never reuse hydraulic fluid. Contaminated fluid can cause clutch failure.

4. Place a container under the clutch flexible hose at the clutch slave cylinder to catch any remaining fluid. Remove the union bolt and sealing washers (A, **Figure 41**) securing the clutch flexible hose to the clutch slave cylinder. Remove the clutch hose and let any remaining fluid drain out into the container.

5. Remove the bolts (B, **Figure 41**) securing the clutch slave cylinder to the crankcase and withdraw the unit from the crankcase. Don't lose the O-ring seal on the backside of the slave cylinder.

Disassembly/Inspection

1. Remove the spacer and insulator from the backside of the slave cylinder body.

2. To remove the piston, hold the slave cylinder body in your hand with the piston facing away from you. Place a clean shop cloth behind the piston. Carefully apply a *small* amount of compressed air in short spurts into the hole where the union bolt was attached. The air pressure will force the piston out of the body.

CAUTION
Catch the piston when it is pushed out of the body. Failure to do so will result in damage to the piston.

3. Remove the spring from the piston.

4. Check the spring for damage or sagging. Honda does not provide service limit dimensions for this spring. Replace the spring if its condition is doubtful.

5. Remove the oil seal and the piston seal from the piston; discard both seals.

6. Use a vernier caliper and measure the outside diameter of the piston as shown in **Figure 44**. Replace the piston if it is worn to the service limit listed in **Table 2**.

7. Use a vernier caliper and measure the inside diameter of the slave cylinder body as shown in **Figure 45**. Replace the body if it is worn to the service limit listed in **Table 2**.

Assembly/Installation

1. Apply a light coat of high-temperature silicone grease (or hydraulic fluid) to the new piston seal and the oil seal prior to installation.

2. Install both seals on the piston. Make sure the piston seal is correctly seated in the groove in the piston. If not seated correctly, fluid will leak past the seal and render the clutch useless.

NOTE
A new piston seal and oil seal must be installed every time the slave cylinder is removed.

3. Install the piston and spring in the body (spring end first).

4. Withdraw the clutch pushrod from the transmission main shaft and use it to push the piston all the way into the slave cylinder body. Reinstall the clutch pushrod.

5. Install the insulator and spacer on the slave cylinder body.

6. Install the slave cylinder on the crankcase.

7. Install the bolts and tighten in a crisscross pattern in 2-3 stages. Tighten the bolts securely.

8. Install the union bolt and sealing washers to the slave cylinder. Tighten the union bolts to the torque specification listed in **Table 1**.

9. Clean the top of the clutch master cylinder of all dirt. Remove the cap and diaphragm. Fill the reservoir with DOT 3 hydraulic fluid almost to the top lip; insert the diaphragm and install the cap loosely.

10. Bleed the clutch as described in this chapter.

BLEEDING THE CLUTCH

This procedure is not necessary unless the clutch feels spongy, the clutch is not operating correctly when the engine is warmed up, there has been a

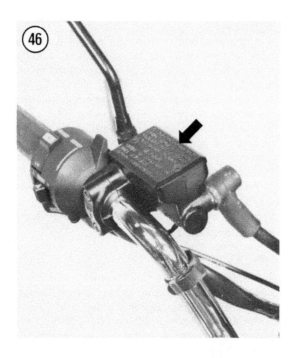

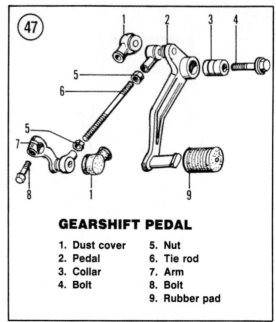

GEARSHIFT PEDAL

1. Dust cover   5. Nut
2. Pedal   6. Tie rod
3. Collar   7. Arm
4. Bolt   8. Bolt
                 9. Rubber pad

leak in the system, a component is being replaced or the hydraulic fluid has been replaced.

> *CAUTION*
> *Throughout the text reference is made to hydraulic fluid. Hydraulic fluid is the same as DOT 3 brake fluid. Use only DOT 3 fluid; do **not** use other fluids as they are not compatible. Do not intermix silicone based (DOT 5) hydraulic fluid as it can cause clutch component damage leading to clutch system failure.*

1. Remove the dust cap from the bleed valve on the clutch slave cylinder.
2. Connect a length of clear tubing to the bleed valve (**Figure 40**).
3. Place the other end of the tube into a clean container. Fill the container with enough fresh hydraulic fluid to keep the end submerged. The tube should be long enough so a loop can be made higher than the bleed valve to prevent air from being drawn into the clutch slave cylinder during bleeding.

> *CAUTION*
> *Cover the clutch slave cylinder and lower frame with a heavy cloth or plastic tarp to protect them from accidental fluid spills. Wash any fluid off painted or plated surfaces or plastic parts immediately, as it will destroy the finish. Use soapy water and rinse completely.*

4. Clean the top of the clutch master cylinder of all dirt and foreign matter. Remove the cap and diaphragm (**Figure 46**). Fill the reservoir almost to the top lip; insert the diaphragm and install the cap loosely.

> *CAUTION*
> *Failure to install the diaphragm on the master cylinder will allow fluid to spurt out when the clutch lever is applied.*

> *CAUTION*
> *Use hydraulic fluid clearly marked DOT 3 only. Others may vaporize and cause clutch failure. Always use the same brand name; do not intermix as many brands are not compatible. Do not intermix silicone based (DOT 5) hydraulic fluid as it can cause clutch component damage leading to clutch system failure.*

5. Insert a 20 mm (3/4 in.) spacer between the handlebar grip and the clutch lever. This will prevent over-travel of the piston within the clutch master cylinder.
6. Slowly apply the clutch lever several times. Hold the lever in the applied position. Open the bleed valve about one-half turn. Allow the lever to travel to its limit against the installed spacer. When this limit is reached, tighten the bleed valve. As the fluid enters the system, the level will drop in the reservoir. Maintain the level at the top of the reservoir to prevent air from being drawn into the system.

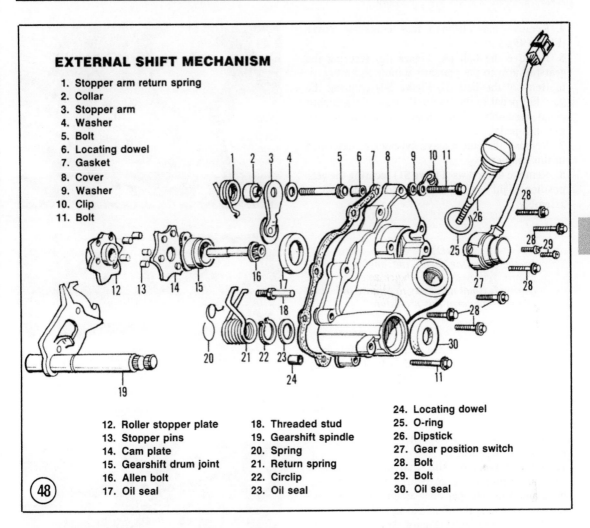

EXTERNAL SHIFT MECHANISM

1. Stopper arm return spring
2. Collar
3. Stopper arm
4. Washer
5. Bolt
6. Locating dowel
7. Gasket
8. Cover
9. Washer
10. Clip
11. Bolt

12. Roller stopper plate	18. Threaded stud
13. Stopper pins	19. Gearshift spindle
14. Cam plate	20. Spring
15. Gearshift drum joint	21. Return spring
16. Allen bolt	22. Circlip
17. Oil seal	23. Oil seal

24. Locating dowel
25. O-ring
26. Dipstick
27. Gear position switch
28. Bolt
29. Bolt
30. Oil seal

48

7. Repeat Step 6 until the fluid emerging from the hose is completely free of bubbles.

NOTE
Do not allow the reservoir to empty during the bleeding operation or air will enter the system. If this occurs, the entire procedure must be repeated.

8. Hold the lever in, tighten the bleed valve, remove the bleed tube and install the bleed valve dust cap.
9. If necessary, add fluid to correct the level in the reservoir. It should be to the upper level line.
10. Install the reservoir cap.
11. Test the feel of the clutch lever. It should be firm and should offer the same resistance each time it's operated. If it feels spongy, there is still air in the system and it must be bled again. When all air has been bled from the system and the fluid level is correct in the reservoir, double-check for leaks and tighten all the fittings and connections.

EXTERNAL SHIFT MECHANISM

The external shift mechanism is located on the same side of the engine as the clutch assembly and can be removed with the engine in the frame. To remove the shift drum and shift forks it is necessary to remove the engine and disassemble the crankcase. That procedure is covered under *Gearshift Drum and Forks* in this chapter.

Refer to **Figure 47** and **Figure 48** for this procedure.

Removal

1. Remove the seat as described in Chapter Eleven.
2. Remove both side covers.
3. Drain the engine oil as described under *Engine Oil and Filter Change* in Chapter Three.

4. Remove the left-hand rear crankcase cover (**Figure 49**).

5. Remove the bolt (A, **Figure 50**) securing the gearshift arm to the gearshift spindle assembly.

6. Remove the bolt (B, **Figure 50**) securing the gearshift pedal to the frame. Remove the gearshift pedal assembly. Don't lose the collar in the gearshift pedal.

7. Remove the clutch slave cylinder as described in this chapter.

8. Remove the screws (**Figure 51**) securing the gear position light switch and remove the switch assembly.

NOTE
In the following steps, the engine is shown removed from the frame for clarity. It is not necessary to remove the engine to perform this procedure.

9. Remove the bolts securing the gearshift linkage cover and remove the cover and gasket (**Figure 52**). Don't lose the dowel pins in the crankcase.

10. Disengage the gearshift fingers from the gearshift drum and withdraw the gearshift spindle assembly (**Figure 53**) from the crankcase.

11. Remove the Allen bolt (**Figure 54**) securing the gearshift drum joint.

12. Using a piece of wire, pull the stopper arm back and remove the gearshift drum joint, cam plate and roller stopper plate assembly. Don't lose the small locating dowel in the shift drum.

13. Remove the bolt (**Figure 55**) securing the stopper arm and remove the stopper arm, washer, spacer and spring.

Inspection

1. Inspect the return spring on the gearshift arm assembly (A, **Figure 56**). If broken or weak it must be replaced.

2. Inspect the shift arm assembly spring (**Figure 57**). If broken or weak, remove and replace the spring.

3. Inspect the gearshift spindle assembly shaft (B, **Figure 56**) for bending, wear or other damage; replace if necessary.

4. Inspect the roller stopper plate ramps (A, **Figure 58**) and cam plate (B, **Figure 58**) for wear; replace if necessary.

5. Check the stopper pins (C, **Figure 58**) for wear or damage. Replace as a set if any are damaged.

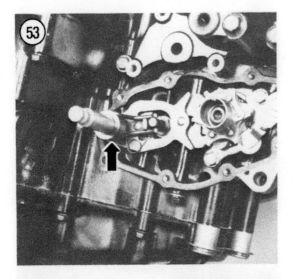

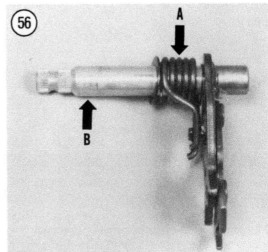

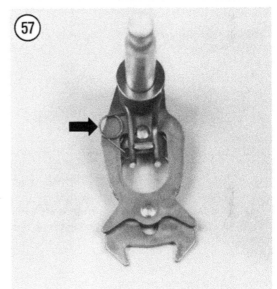

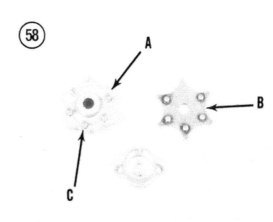

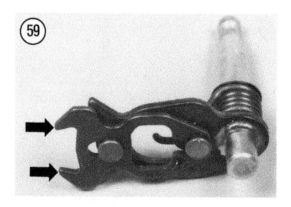

6. Check the stopper pin engagement fingers (**Figure 59**) on the gearshift spindle assembly for wear or damage. Replace the spindle assembly if they are damaged.

Installation

1. Install the spring, spacer, washer, stopper arm and bolt (**Figure 55**). Do not completely tighten the bolt at this time.
2. If removed, install the small locating dowel (A, **Figure 60**) in the shift drum. Align the slot (B, **Figure 60**) in the backside of the roller stopper plate with this dowel.
3. Engage the spring onto the stopper arm and pull the stopper arm back with a piece of wire (**Figure 61**).
4. Install the roller stopper plate, cam plate and gearshift drum joint assembly (**Figure 62**).
5. Align the hole in the gearshift drum joint with the raised boss on the cam plate and install the gearshift drum joint. Install the Allen bolt and tighten securely.
6. Engage the stopper arm with the roller stopper plate. Tighten the stopper arm securely.
7. Make sure the thin thrust washer (**Figure 63**) is in place on the gearshift spindle assembly and install the gearshift spindle assembly. Make sure the return spring is correctly positioned onto the stopper plate bolt (**Figure 64**).
8. Rotate the gearshift spindle and check the linkage for smooth operation.
9. Make sure the locating dowels (A, **Figure 65**) are in place and install a new gasket (B, **Figure 65**).
10. Install the gearshift linkage cover and tighten the bolts securely.
11. Make sure the transmission is in NEUTRAL.
12. Align the switch joint pin with the neutral position index mark on the switch (**Figure 66**).
13. Align the joint pin with the notch in the shift drum joint (**Figure 67**) and install the gear position light switch assembly. Tighten the screws securely.

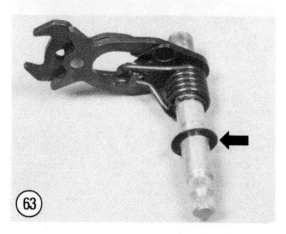

14. Install the clutch slave cylinder as described in this chapter.

15. Align the punch marks (**Figure 68**) on the gearshift arm and the gearshift spindle and install the gearshift arm onto the gearshift spindle assembly. Install and tighten the clamping bolt.

16. Install the gearshift pedal onto the frame and tighten the bolt securely.

17. Install the left-hand rear crankcase cover and both side covers.

18. Install the seat as described in Chapter Eleven.

19. Refill the engine with oil as described in Chapter Three.

TRANSMISSION

The transmission is located within the engine crankcase. To gain access to the transmission and internal shift mechanism it is necessary to remove the engine and disassemble the crankcase. The output gear case also has to be removed. Once the crankcase is split, removal of the transmission main shaft requires pulling the assembly up and out of the crankcase. The countershaft must be partially disassembled prior to removing the shaft and the remainder of its gears from the crankcase.

Pay particular attention to the location of spacers, washers and bearings during disassembly. If disassembling a used, well run-in engine (high mileage) for the first time by yourself, pay particular attention to any shims added by a previous owner. These may have been added to take up the tolerance of worn components. If all of the existing components are going to be reinstalled, these shims must be reinstalled in the same position as the shims have developed a wear pattern. If new parts are going to be installed these shims may be eliminated. This is something you will have to determine upon reassembly.

Specifications for the transmission components are listed in **Table 3**.

Removal/Installation

1. Remove the engine from the frame as described in Chapter Four.
2. Disassemble the crankcase as described in Chapter Four.
3. Remove the clutch outer housing and main shaft assembly (**Figure 69**).
4. To remove the countershaft assembly, perform Steps 1-7 of *Countershaft Disassembly/Inspection/Assembly* in this chapter.

> *NOTE*
> *Prior to installing any components, coat all bearing surfaces with assembly oil.*

5. To install the countershaft, perform Steps 29-37 of *Countershaft Disassembly/Inspection/Assembly* in this chapter.
6. Install the main shaft and clutch outer housing assembly as follows:

   a. Make sure the bearing set ring (**Figure 70**) and locating dowel (**Figure 71**) are positioned correctly in the upper crankcase.
   b. If removed from the main shaft, install the clutch outer guide A (**Figure 72**), then the washer with the "OUT" mark facing out (**Figure 73**). Install the clutch outer guide B (**Figure 74**) and both needle bearings (**Figure 75**) onto the mainshaft.
   c. Lift the transmission assembly out of the crankcase and slide the clutch outer housing onto the transmission shaft.
   d. Install the main shaft and clutch outer housing assembly into the upper crankcase. Make sure the set ring and dowel pin are properly seated into both bearings on the main shaft.

7. Assemble the crankcase as described in Chapter Four.
8. Install the engine as described in Chapter Four.

Main Shaft Disassembly/Inspection/Assembly

Refer to **Figure 76** for this procedure.

> *NOTE*
> *A helpful "tool" that should be used for transmission disassembly is a large egg flat (the type restaurants get their eggs in). As you remove a part from the shaft, set it in one of the depressions in the same position from which it was removed. This is an easy way to remember the correct relationship of all parts.*

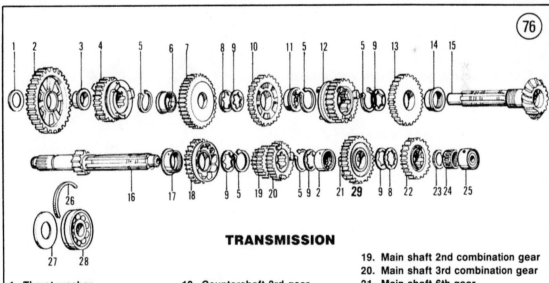

TRANSMISSION

1. Thrust washer
2. Countershaft 1st gear
3. Countershaft 1st gear bushing
4. Countershaft 5th gear
5. Circlip
6. Countershaft 2nd gear
7. Countershaft 2nd gear bushing
8. Splined lockwasher
9. Splined washer
10. Countershaft 3rd gear
11. Countershaft 3rd gear bushing
12. Countershaft 6th gear
13. Countershaft 4th gear
14. Countershaft 4th gear bushing
15. Countershaft
16. Main shaft/1st gear
17. Main shaft 5th gear bushing
18. Main shaft 5th gear
19. Main shaft 2nd combination gear
20. Main shaft 3rd combination gear
21. Main shaft 6th gear
22. Main shaft 4th gear
23. Washer
24. Needle bearing
25. Needle bearing outer race
26. Set ring
27. Thrust washer
28. Bearing
29. 6th gear bushing

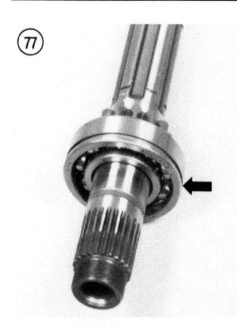

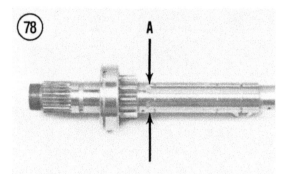

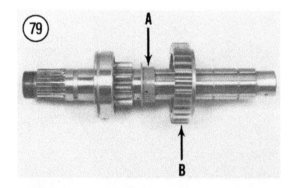

1. Place the assembled shaft into a large can or plastic bucket and thoroughly clean with solvent and a stiff brush. Dry with compressed air or let it sit on shop rags to drip dry.

2. Slide off the bearing outer race, needle bearing, washer and the 4th gear.

3. Slide off the splined lockwasher. Rotate the splined washer in either direction to disengage the tangs from the grooves in the transmission shaft. Slide off the splined washer.

4. Slide off the 6th gear, the 6th gear splined bushing and the splined washer.

5. Remove the circlip and slide off the 2nd/3rd combination gear.

6. Remove the circlip and splined washer; slide off the 5th gear and the 5th gear bushing.

7. Check each gear for excessive wear, burrs, pitting or chipped or missing teeth.

8. Make sure the gear dogs are in good condition.

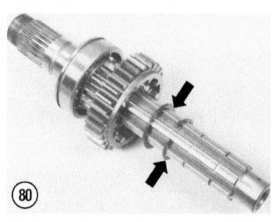

> *NOTE*
> *Defective gears should be replaced. It is a good idea to replace the mating gear on the countershaft even though it may not show as much wear or damage.*

> *NOTE*
> *The 1st gear is part of the main shaft. If the gear is defective, the shaft must be replaced.*

9. Make sure all gears and bushings slide smoothly on the main shaft splines.

10. Check the ball bearing (**Figure 77**). Make sure it rotates smoothly with no signs of wear or damage. Replace if necessary.

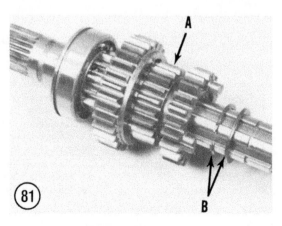

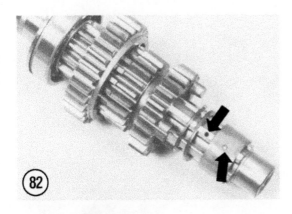

(82)

(83)

(84)

(85)

(86)

5

11. Measure the inside diameter of the 5th and the 6th gears. Compare with the dimensions listed in **Table 3**.

12. Measure the outside diameter of the 5th and the 6th gear bushings and the inside diameter of the 5th gear bushing. Compare with the dimensions listed in **Table 3**.

13. Measure the outside diameter of the shaft at the location of the 5th gear bushing (A, **Figure 78**). Compare with the dimensions listed in **Table 3**.

NOTE
It is a good idea to replace the circlips every other time the transmission is disassembled to ensure proper gear alignment.

14. Slide on the 5th gear bushing (A, **Figure 79**) and slide on the 5th gear (B, **Figure 79**).

15. Slide on the splined washer and circlip (**Figure 80**).

16. Position the 2nd/3rd combination gear with the smaller diameter 2nd gear going on first (A, **Figure 81**). Slide on the 2nd/3rd combination gear and install the circlip and splined washer (B, **Figure 81**).

17. Align the oil hole in the 6th gear bushing with the oil hole in the main shaft (**Figure 82**). This alignment is necessary for proper oil flow.

18. Slide on the 6th gear (**Figure 83**).

19. Slide on the splined washer (**Figure 84**). Rotate the splined washer in either direction so its tangs are engaged in the transmission shaft groove.

20. Slide on the splined lockwasher (**Figure 85**) so the tangs go into the open areas of the splined washer and lock the washer into place.

21. Slide on the 4th gear and the washer (**Figure 86**).

22. Slide on the needle bearing (**Figure 87**).

23. Install the bearing outer race (**Figure 88**).

24. After assembly is complete, refer to **Figure 89** for correct placement of all gears. Make sure all circlips are seated correctly in the main shaft grooves.

25. Make sure each gear engages properly with the adjoining gears where applicable.

**Countershaft Disassembly/
Inspection/Assembly**

The countershaft must be partially disassembled within the upper crankcase before the shaft assembly and the remainder of the gears can be removed.

Refer to **Figure 76** for this procedure.

> *NOTE*
> *Use the same large egg flat (used on the main shaft disassembly) during the countershaft disassembly. This is an easy way to remember the correct relationship of all parts.*

1. Remove the 6 mm and 8 mm bolts (**Figure 90**) securing the output gear case to the upper crankcase assembly.

2. Partially pull the countershaft assembly out of the crankcase enough to remove the transmission gears outlined in Step 3 through Step 6.

3. Slide off the thrust washer, 1st gear and the 1st gear bushing.

4. Slide off the 5th gear.

5. Remove the circlip.

6. Slide off the 2nd gear and the 2nd gear splined bushing.

7. Withdraw the countershaft assembly and output gear case from the upper crankcase half and

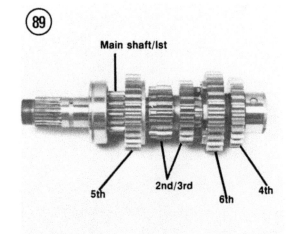

Main shaft/1st

5th   2nd/3rd   6th   4th

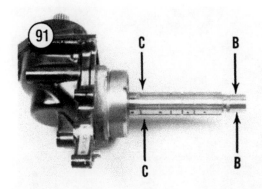

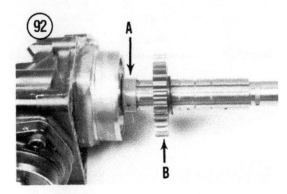

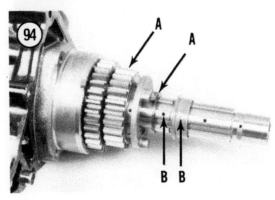

continue to remove the remaining parts from the shaft. Don't lose the locating dowel on the output gear case.

8. Slide off the splined lockwasher. Rotate the splined washer in either direction to disengage the tangs from the grooves on the transmission shaft. Slide off the splined washer.

9. Slide off the 3rd gear and the 3rd gear splined bushing.

10. Remove the circlip and slide off the 6th gear.

11. Remove the circlip and slide off the splined washer.

12. Remove the 4th gear and the 4th gear bushing.

13. Check each gear for excessive wear, burrs, pitting or chipped or missing teeth. Make sure the lugs are in good condition.

NOTE
Defective gears should be replaced. It is a good idea to replace the mating gear on the main shaft even though it may not show signs of wear or damage.

14. Make sure all gears and gear bushings slide smoothly on the countershaft splines.

15. Check the bearings in the output case. Make sure they rotate smoothly with no signs of wear or damage. Replacement should be entrusted to a dealer as special tools are required.

16. Measure the inside diameter of the 1st, 2nd, 3rd and 4th gears. Compare with the dimensions listed in **Table 3**.

17. Measure the outside diameter of the 1st, 2nd, 3rd and 4th gear bushings. Compare with the dimensions listed in **Table 3**.

18. Measure the inside diameter of the 1st and the 4th gear bushings. Compare with the dimensions listed in **Table 3**.

19. Measure the outside diameter of the shaft at the location of the 1st gear bushing (B, **Figure 91**) and 4th gear bushing (C, **Figure 91**). Compare with dimensions listed in **Table 3**.

20. Install a new gasket onto the output gear case. Make sure the locating dowel is in place.

21. Slide on the 4th gear bushing (A, **Figure 92**). No special alignment is necessary.

22. Slide the 4th gear into place (flush side on first) (B, **Figure 92**).

23. Slide on the splined washer and install the circlip (**Figure 93**).

24. Slide on the 6th gear and install the circlip (A, **Figure 94**).

25. Align the oil hole in the 3rd gear bushing with the oil hole in the shaft (B, **Figure 94**). This alignment is necessary for proper oil flow.

26. Slide on the 3rd gear (**Figure 95**).

27. Slide on the splined washer (**Figure 96**) and rotate it in either direction to engage the tangs in the groove in the transmission shaft.

28. Slide on the lockwasher so that the tangs go into the open areas of the splined washer and lock the splined washer in place (**Figure 97**).

29. Install the countershaft assembly into the crankcase (**Figure 98**).

30. Slide on the 2nd gear (A, **Figure 99**).

31. Align the oil hole in the 2nd gear bushing with the oil hole in the shaft (B, **Figure 99**). This alignment is necessary for proper oil flow.

32. Install the circlip (**Figure 100**).

33. Slide on the 5th gear (**Figure 101**).

34. Slide the 1st gear bushing (**Figure 102**) onto the shaft.

35. Position the 1st gear with the flange side on first and slide on the 1st gear (A, **Figure 103**).

36A. If the output gear case has *not* been serviced, reinstall the original thrust washer (B, **Figure 103**).

36B. If the output gear case has been serviced and any of the internal shims replaced, a thrust washer of a different thickness must be installed. Refer to *Output Gear Case Thrust Washer Selection* in this chapter.

37. Push the countershaft assembly into place (**Figure 104**) leaving a small gap between the output case and the crankcase. Install the 6 mm and 8 mm bolts (**Figure 90**) securing the output gear case to the upper crankcase. Do not tighten the bolts at this time. They will be tightened after the crankcase halves are assembled.

OUTPUT GEAR CASE

Removal/Installation

1. Remove the engine from the frame as described in Chapter Four.

2. Remove the bolt (**Figure 105**) securing the oil feed line.

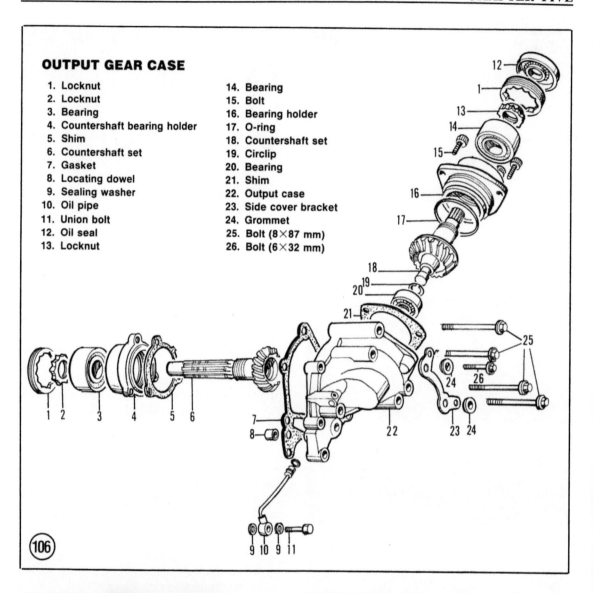

OUTPUT GEAR CASE

1. Locknut
2. Locknut
3. Bearing
4. Countershaft bearing holder
5. Shim
6. Countershaft set
7. Gasket
8. Locating dowel
9. Sealing washer
10. Oil pipe
11. Union bolt
12. Oil seal
13. Locknut
14. Bearing
15. Bolt
16. Bearing holder
17. O-ring
18. Countershaft set
19. Circlip
20. Bearing
21. Shim
22. Output case
23. Side cover bracket
24. Grommet
25. Bolt (8×87 mm)
26. Bolt (6×32 mm)

106

107

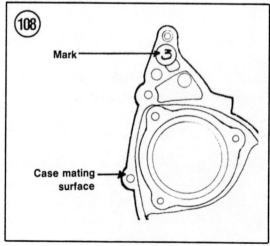

108

Mark

Case mating surface

3. Withdraw the oil feed line from the output gear case. Don't lose the O-ring on the end of the oil line.

4. Separate the crankcase as described in Chapter Four.

5. Remove the output gear case assembly as described under *Countershaft Disassembly/ Inspection/Assembly* in this chapter.

> *CAUTION*
> *Do not try to remove the bolts and the output gear case assembly at the same time. The gear case bolts must be removed first then some of the transmission gears must be removed from the shaft assembly. There is an interference fit between some of the transmission gears and the crankcase. The output gear case will not come out of the crankcase until the crankcase is separated and the countershaft partially disassembled. If force is used at this time the entire countershaft assembly will try to come out along with the gear case; damage will occur to both the crankcase and the transmission components.*

6. Install by reversing these removal steps, noting the following.

7. Install the bolts and tighten finger-tight; there must be a gap between the output gear case and the crankcase for assembly.

8. Assemble the crankcase as described in Chapter Four.

9. After all bolts are finger-tight and the output gear case is snug against the crankcase, torque all bolts in a crisscross pattern to 30-34 N•m (22-25 ft.-lb.).

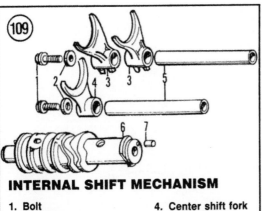

INTERNAL SHIFT MECHANISM

1. Bolt
2. Washer
3. Right- and left-hand shift fork
4. Center shift fork
5. Shift fork shaft
6. Shift drum
7. Pin

10. Install a new ring on the end of the oil feed line where it goes into the output gear case.

11. Install the engine in the frame as described in Chapter Four.

Inspection

Output gear case disassembly and assembly requires a considerable number of special Honda tools. The price of all of these tools could be more than the cost of most repairs by a dealer.

Figure 106 shows the internal components of the output gear case.

> *CAUTION*
> *Do not try to disassemble the gear case with make-shift tools. Approximately 20 special tools and a hydraulic press are required to disassemble and assemble the unit. If assembled incorrectly, the gear tooth contact pattern and set-up tolerance will be incorrect and the unit will be damaged.*

1. Inspect the splines on the cross shaft (A, **Figure 107**) where it mates with the drive shaft. If they are damaged or worn, the cross shaft gears must be replaced.

> *NOTE*
> *If these splines are damaged also inspect the splines on the drive shaft universal joint; it may also have to be replaced. Refer to Chapter Nine.*

2. Check the oil seal (B, **Figure 107**) for damage or traces of oil leakage. Have the oil seal replaced by a dealer if necessary.

3. Check the entire output gear case for cracks or damage, especially around the bolt hole bosses. Replace if necessary.

Thrust Washer Selection

If the output gear case has been serviced and the internal gear backlash shim has been replaced, the thrust washer on the right-hand end of the countershaft must be replaced with one of a different thickness.

If the backlash shim has been replaced, the identifying mark on the case must be revised with a new number. This number is located on the inside surface of the mounting flange as shown in **Figure 108**. This number relates to the correct thrust washer thickness as listed in **Table 4**. These thrust washers are available from Honda dealers.

**GEARSHIFT DRUM
AND FORKS**

Refer to **Figure 109** for this procedure.

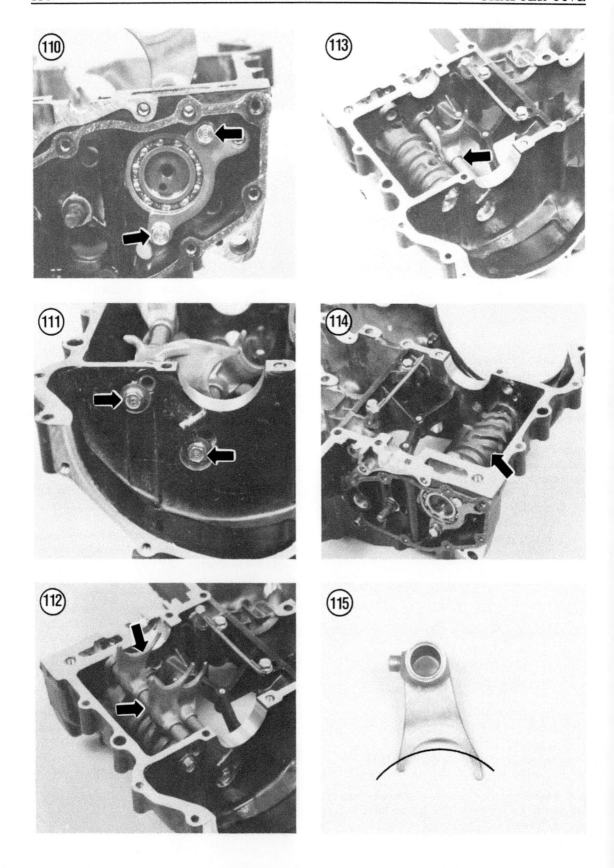

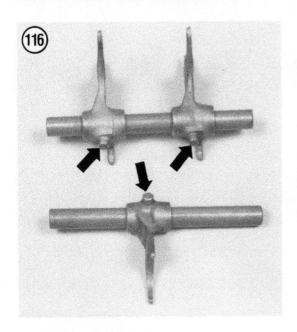

Removal

1. Remove the external shift mechanism as described in this chapter.
2. Separate the crankcase as described in Chapter Four.
3. Remove the bolts (**Figure 110**) securing the shift drum bearing stopper plate and remove the stopper plate.
4. Remove the bolts and washers (**Figure 111**) securing the shift fork shafts.
5. Hold the 2 shift forks while withdrawing the rear shift fork shaft (**Figure 112**) from the left-hand side. Remove the shift forks. Reinstall the shift forks on the shaft in their original position.
6. Hold the shift fork while withdrawing the front shift fork shaft (**Figure 113**) from the left-hand side. Remove the shift fork. Reinstall the shift fork on the shaft in its original position.
7. Withdraw the shift drum (**Figure 114**) from the right-hand side.

Inspection

Refer to **Table 5** for shift fork and shaft specifications.
1. Inspect each shift fork for wear or cracking. Replace any worn forks.

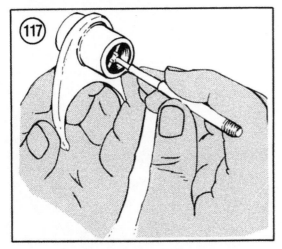

> *NOTE*
> *Check for any arc-shaped wear or burn marks on the shift forks (**Figure 115**). If apparent, the shift fork has come in contact with the gear, indicating that the fingers are worn beyond use and the fork must be replaced.*

2. Roll the shift fork shafts on a flat surface such as a piece of plate glass and check for bends. If the fork shaft is bent, it must be replaced.
3. Check the cam pin followers (**Figure 116**) in each shift fork for wear or burrs. If worn or damaged, the shift fork must be replaced.
4. Measure the inside diameter of the shift forks with an inside micrometer (**Figure 117**). Replace any worn beyond the limit in **Table 5**.
5. Measure the width of the gearshift fingers with a micrometer (**Figure 118**). Replace any worn beyond the limit in **Table 5**.
6. Make sure all shift forks slide easily on their shafts. If there is any binding either the shift fork(s) or the shaft(s) must be replaced.
7. Check the shift drum bearing. Make sure it operates smoothly with no signs of wear or damage.

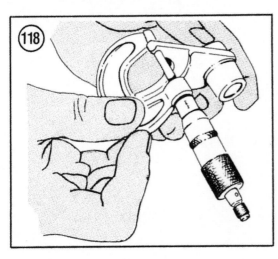

8. Check the grooves in the shift drum (**Figure 119**) for wear or roughness. If any of the groove profiles have excessive wear or damage, replace the shift drum.

9. Inspect all bearing surfaces in the upper crankcase where the shift fork shafts and shift drum ride. Check for scoring or scratches. If severely damaged, the crankcase half must be replaced.

Installation

1. Coat all bearing and sliding surfaces with assembly oil.

2. Install the shift drum from the right-hand side. Push it in until it seats completely.

3. Position the front shift fork and insert the guide pin into the groove in the shift drum. Insert the shift fork shaft through the crankcase and into the shift fork.

4. Position the left-hand rear shift fork and push the rear shift fork shaft through it.

5. Install the right-hand shift fork and insert the guide pin into the groove in the shift drum.

6. Push the rear shift fork shaft through the right-hand shift fork and all the way in until it completely seats in the right-hand side of the crankcase.

7. Make sure the shift forks are properly installed as shown in **Figure 120**.

> *NOTE*
> *Apply Loctite Lock N' Seal to the threads of the screws and bolts prior to installation.*

8. Install the bolts and washers (**Figure 111**) securing the shift fork shafts.

9. Install shift drum stopper plate and bolts (**Figure 110**) securing the shift drum bearing. Tighten the bolts securely.

10. Assemble the crankcase halves as described in Chapter Four.

11. Install the external shift mechanism as described in this chapter.

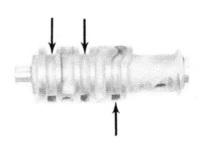

Tables are on the following pages.

Table 1 CLUTCH AND GEARSHIFT MECHANISM TORQUE SPECIFICATIONS

Item	N·m	ft.-lb.
Clutch locknut	47-53	34-38
Clutch hose union bolts	25-35	18-25
Clutch master cylinder cover screws	1-2	0.7-0.9
Clutch lever pivot nut	5-7	4-5
Slave cylinder bleed valve	4-7	3-5

Table 2 CLUTCH SPECIFICATIONS

Item	Standard	Wear limit
Friction disc thickness	3.22-3.38 mm (0.127-0.133 in.)	2.6 mm (0.10 in.)
Clutch plate warpage	—	0.30 mm (0.012 in.)
Clutch spring free length	35.5 mm (1.40 in.)	34.0 mm (1.34 in.)
Outer guide OD		
Outer guide A	31.984-32.000 mm (1.2592-1.2598 in.)	31.95 mm (1.258 in.)
Outer guide B	41.989-41.000 mm (1.6531-1.6535 in.)	41.95 mm (1.652 in.)
Clutch slave cylinder		
Cylinder ID	38.100-38.162 mm (1.5000-1.5024 in.)	38.18 mm (1.503 in.)
Piston OD	38.036-38.075 mm (1.4975-1.4990 in.)	38.02 mm (1.497 in.)
Clutch master cylinder		
Cylinder bore ID	14.000-14.043 mm (0.5512-0.5524 in.)	14.06 mm (0.553 in.)
Piston OD	13.957-13.984 mm (0.5495-0.5506 in.)	13.94 mm (0.549 in.)

5

Table 3 TRANSMISSION SPECIFICATIONS

Item	Specification	Wear limit
Gear backlash		
1st, 2nd and 3rd	0.044-0.133 mm (0.0017-0.0052 in.)	0.20 mm (0.008 in.)
4th	0.034-0.102 mm (0.0013-0.0040 in.)	0.15 mm (0.006 in.)
5th and 6th	0.046-0.140 mm (0.0018-0.0055 in.)	0.18 mm (0.007 in.)
Gear ID main shaft		
5th, 6th gear	28.020-28.041 mm (1.1031-1.1041 in.)	28.06 mm (1.105 in.)

(continued)

Table 3 TRANSMISSION SPECIFICATIONS (continued)

Item	Specification	Wear limit
Gear ID countershaft		
1st	24.020-24.041 mm (0.9457-0.9465 in.)	24.06 mm (0.947 in.)
2nd, 3rd and 4th	28.020-28.041 mm (1.1031-1.1040 in.)	28.06 mm (1.105 in.)
Gear bushing OD		
Main shaft		
5th and 6th	27.979-28.000 mm (1.1015-1.1024 in.)	27.96 mm (1.101 in.)
Countershaft		
1st	23.984-24.005 mm (0.9443-0.9451 in.)	23.97 mm (0.944 in.)
2nd, 3rd and 4th	27.979-28.000 mm (1.1015-1.1024 in.)	27.96 mm (1.101 in.)
Gear bushing ID		
Main shaft 5th	24.985-24.006 mm (0.9837-0.9845 in.)	25.04 mm (0.986 in.)
Countershaft		
1st	20.000-20.021 mm (0.7874-0.7882 in.)	20.04 mm (0.789 in.)
4th	24.985-24.006 mm (0.9837-0.9845 in.)	25.04 mm (0.986 in.)
Main shaft OD		
At 5th gear bushing location (A)	24.959-24.980 mm (0.9826-0.9835 in.)	24.90 mm (0.980 in.)
Countershaft OD		
At 1st gear bushing location (B)	19.980-19.993 mm (0.7866-0.7871 in.)	19.93 mm (0.785 in.)
At 4th gear bushing location (C)	24.959-24.980 mm (0.9826-0.9835 in.)	24.90 mm (0.980 in.)
Bushing clearance wear limits		
Main shaft		
5th and 6th gear to shaft	—	0.08 mm (0.003 in.)
4th gear to 4th gear bushing	—	0.08 mm (0.003 in.)
5th gear bushing to shaft	—	0.07 mm (0.003 in.)
Countershaft		
1st gear to 1st gear bushing	—	0.08 mm (0.003 in.)
1st gear bushing to shaft	—	0.06 mm (0.002 in.)
2nd gear to 2nd gear bushing	—	0.08 mm (0.003 in.)
3rd gear to 3rd gear bushing	—	0.08 mm (0.003 in.)
4th gear bushing to shaft	—	0.07 mm (0.003 in.)

Table 4 OUTPUT GEAR THRUST WASHER SELECTION

Output gear case mark	Thrust washer thickness	Thrust washer OD
1	1.0 mm (0.039 in.)	30 mm (1.18 in.)
2	1.0 mm (0.039 in.)	30 mm (1.18 in.)
3	0.9 mm (0.035 in.)	31 mm (1.22 in.)
4	0.9 mm (0.035 in.)	31 mm (1.22 in.)
5	0.8 mm (0.031 in.)	33 mm (1.29 in.)

Table 5 SHIFT FORK AND SHIFT SHAFT SPECIFICATIONS

Item	Specification	Wear limit
Shift fork ID	—	12.04 mm (0.474 in.)
Shift fork fingers	—	4.6 mm (0.18 in.)
Shift fork shaft OD	—	11.90 mm (0.469 in.)

5

CHAPTER SIX

FUEL AND EXHAUST SYSTEMS

The fuel system consists of the fuel tank, shutoff valve, 4 Keihin constant velocity carburetors and the air filter.

The exhaust system consists of 4 exhaust pipes, a common collector and 2 mufflers.

The air filter must be cleaned frequently; the specific procedures and service intervals are covered in Chapter Three.

This chapter includes service procedures for all parts of the fuel and exhaust systems. Carburetor specifications are listed in **Table 1**. **Table 1** and **Table 2** are at the end of this chapter.

The carburetors on all U.S. models are engineered to meet stringent EPA (Environmental Protection Agency) regulations. The carburetors are flow tested and preset at the factory for maximum performance and efficiency within EPA regulations. Altering preset carburetor jet needle and pilot screw adjustments is forbidden by law. Failure to comply with EPA regulations may result in heavy fines.

CARBURETOR OPERATION

An understanding of the function of each of the carburetor components and their relation to one another is a valuable aid for pinpointing a source of carburetor trouble.

The carburetor's purpose is to supply and atomize fuel and mix it in correct proportions with air drawn through the air intake. At the primary throttle opening (idle), a small amount of fuel is siphoned through the pilot jet by the incoming air. As the throttle is opened further, the air stream begins to siphon fuel through the main jet and needle jet. The tapered needle increases the effective flow capacity of the needle jet; as it is lifted, it occupies less of the area of the jet.

At full throttle the carburetor venturi is fully open and the needle is lifted far enough to permit the main jet to flow at full capacity.

The choke circuit is a "bystarter" system in which the choke lever opens a valve rather than closing a butterfly in the venturi area as on many carburetors. In the open position, the slow jet discharges a stream of fuel into the carburetor venturi, enriching the mixture when the engine is cold.

CARBURETOR SERVICE

Carburetor service (removal and cleaning) should be performed when poor engine performance or hesitation is observed. If, after servicing the carburetors and making the adjustments described in this chapter, the motorcycle does not perform correctly (and assuming other factors affecting performance are correct, such as ignition timing and condition, etc.), the motorcycle should be checked by a dealer or a qualified performance tuning specialist.

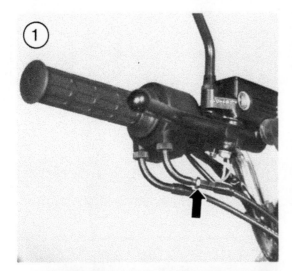

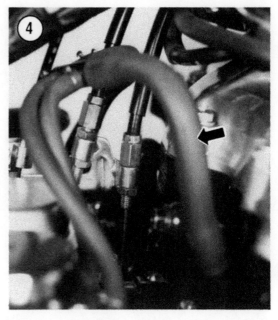

Removal/Installation

1. Place the bike on the centerstand and remove the seat as described in Chapter Eleven.

2. Remove the right- and left-hand side covers.

3. Disconnect the battery negative lead.

4. Remove the fuel tank as described in this chapter.

5. At the hand throttle, loosen the throttle cable locknut and turn the adjusting barrel (**Figure 1**) all the way in. This provides slack for cable removal at the carburetor assembly.

6. Loosen the choke cable clamp screw (**Figure 2**) and disconnect the choke cable from the carburetor assembly.

7. Loosen the clamping screws on the air filter connecting tubes at the carburetors (A, **Figure 3**). Slide the clamping bands off the tubes and away from the carburetor assembly.

8. Loosen the clamping screws on the intake tubes on the cylinder head (B, **Figure 3**). Slide the clamping bands off the tubes and away from the carburetors.

9. Pull the carburetor assembly toward the rear until the assembly is clear of the intake tubes on the cylinder head.

10. On models so equipped, disconnect the main line (**Figure 4**) from the carburetors to the PCV valve.

11. Slowly and carefully pull the carburetor assembly out to the left. Be careful not to damage any of the carburetor components. This is a lot easier if you have one person on each side of the bike.

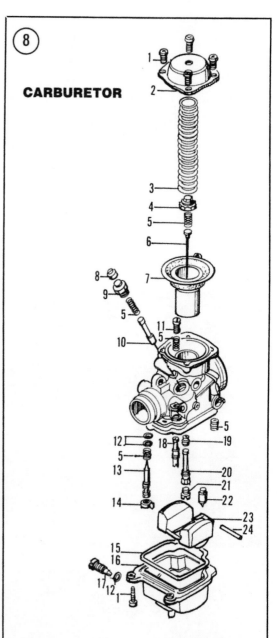

CARBURETOR

1. Screw
2. Top cover
3. Vacuum cylinder spring
4. Needle holder
5. Needle spring
6. Jet needle
7. Vacuum cylinder
8. Clip
9. Cap
10. Choke plunger
11. Screw
12. O-ring
13. Pilot jet
14. Limiter cap
15. Gasket
16. Float bowl
17. Drain screw
18. Slow jet
19. Needle jet
20. Needle jet holder
21. Main jet
22. Float needle
23. Float
24. Float pivot pin

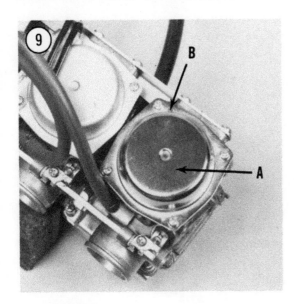

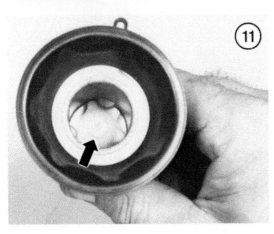

12. Loosen the locknuts (**Figure 5**) securing the throttle cables to the cable bracket.

13. Disconnect the throttle cables (**Figure 6**) from the throttle wheel. Tie the loose ends of the cables out of the way.

14. Remove the carburetor assembly from the frame.

15. Install by reversing these steps, noting the following.

16. Prior to installing the carburetor assembly, coat the inside surface of all intake tubes and air filter connecting tubes with Armor All or rubber lube. This will make it easier to install the carburetor throats into the rubber tubes.

17. Be sure the throttle cables and choke cable are correctly positioned in the frame—not twisted or sharply bent. Tighten the locknuts securely.

18. Attach the "pull" throttle cable to the rear bracket and in the rear slot (A, **Figure 7**) in the throttle wheel.

19. Attach the "push" throttle cable into the front bracket and in the front slot (B, **Figure 7**) in the throttle wheel.

20. Attach the choke cable to its bracket.

21. Adjust the throttle cables as described in Chapter Three.

22. Adjust the choke as described in this chapter.

Disassembly/Cleaning/Inspection

Refer to **Figure 8** for this procedure.

It is recommended that only one carburetor be disassembled and cleaned at a time. This will prevent accidental mixing of parts.

1. Remove the screws securing the carburetor top cover to the main body and remove the cover (A, **Figure 9**).

2. Remove the vacuum cylinder spring and vacuum cylinder assembly (**Figure 10**).

3. Put an 8 mm socket or Phillips screwdriver down in the vacuum cylinder cavity (**Figure 11**). Place the socket or Phillips screwdriver on the needle holder and turn the holder 60° in either direction to unlock it from the tangs in the vacuum cylinder. Remove the needle holder, jet needle spring and jet needle (**Figure 12**).

4. Remove the screws (**Figure 13**) securing the float bowl to the main body and remove the float bowl.

5. Remove the gasket from the float bowl (**Figure 14**).

6. Carefully push out the float pin (**Figure 15**).

7. Lift the float and needle valve (**Figure 16**) out of the main body.

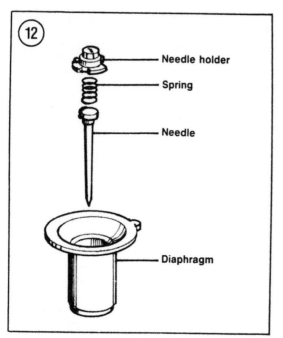

⑫

Needle holder

Spring

Needle

Diaphragm

⑮

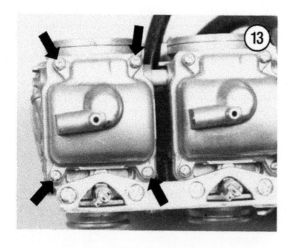

⑬

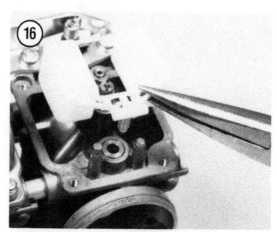

⑯

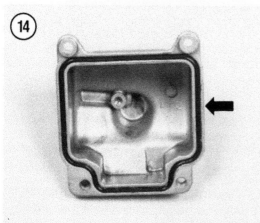

⑭

⑰

8. Remove the slow jet (**Figure 17**).

9. Remove the main jet (**Figure 18**).

10. Remove the main jet holder (**Figure 19**).

11. The starter jet is pressed into place and cannot be removed.

12. The needle jet (A, **Figure 20**) is not removable.

NOTE
Prior to removing the pilot screw, record the number of turns necessary to lightly seat the screw. Record the number of turns for each carburetor. The screws must be reinstalled to the exact same setting.

13. If necessary, remove the pilot screw assembly (**Figure 21**).

14. Remove the drain screw and O-ring in the float bowl. If necessary, clean the drain tube outlet and reinstall the drain screw.

NOTE
Further disassembly is neither necessary or recommended. If throttle shafts or butterflies are damaged, take the carburetor body to a dealer for replacement.

15. Using compressed air, clean the slow air jet (B, **Figure 20**) and the main air jet (C, **Figure 20**) in the vacuum cylinder portion of the carburetor body.

16. Clean all parts, except rubber or plastic parts, in a good grade of carburetor cleaner. This solution is available in a small, resealable tank with a dip basket at most automotive or motorcycle supply stores. If the tank is tightly sealed when not in use, the solution will last for several cleanings. Follow the manufacturer's instructions for correct soak time (usually about 1/2 hour).

NOTE
It is recommended that one carburetor be cleaned at a time to avoid mixing parts.

17. Remove the parts from the cleaner and blow dry with compressed air. Blow out the jets with compressed air. Do *not* use wire to clean them. Minor gouges in a jet can alter flow rate and upset the fuel-air mixture.

18. Inspect the end of the float valve needle (**Figure 22**) and seat for wear or damage; replace either or both parts if necessary.

19. Repeat Steps 1-18 for the remaining carburetors.

20. Replace all O-rings and gaskets upon assembly. O-ring seals become hardened after prolonged use and exposure to heat and lose their ability to seal. Replace as necessary.

Assembly

1. If removed, screw the pilot screw in the same number of turns as recorded during disassembly. If new pilot screws were installed, do not install the limiter caps at this time.

> *NOTE*
> *If new pilot screws were installed, turn them out from the **lightly seated** position the number of turns indicated in **Table 1**.*

2. To assemble the vacuum cylinder (**Figure 23**), insert the jet needle (**Figure 24**) in the vacuum cylinder. Insert the needle holder and spring (**Figure 25**). Using an 8 mm socket or Phillips screwdriver, turn the needle holder 60° in either direction to lock the holder in the vacuum cylinder (**Figure 11**).

3. Install the vacuum cylinder into the carburetor body. Align the tab on the diaphragm with the hole (**Figure 26**) in the carburetor body.

4. Install the vacuum cylinder compression spring in the vacuum cylinder.

5. Align the hole in the vacuum cylinder with the raised boss (B, **Figure 9**) on the top cover. Install the top cover and tighten the screws securely.

6. Install the main jet holder (**Figure 27**) and the main jet (**Figure 28**).

7. Install the slow jet (**Figure 29**).

8. Install the needle valve on the float.

9. Install the float and needle valve and install the float pin (**Figure 15**).

10. Inspect the float height and adjust if necessary as described in this chapter.

11. Install the gasket in the float bowl (**Figure 14**).

12. Install the float bowl and tighten the screws securely (**Figure 13**).

13. After assembly and installation are completed, adjust the carburetors as described in this chapter and Chapter Three.

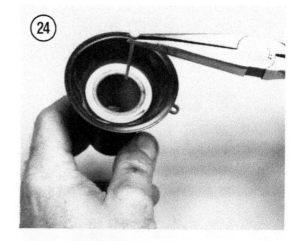

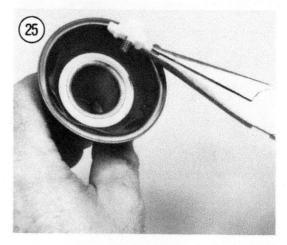

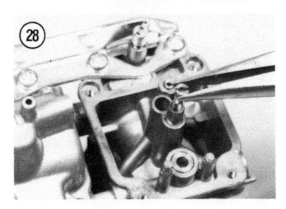

Separation/Assembly

Refer to **Figure 30** for this procedure.

1. Remove the carburetor assembly as described in this chapter.

2. Unhook the choke (bystarter) relief spring (A, **Figure 31**) from the ledge on the carburetor body (B, **Figure 31**).

> *NOTE*
> *Prior to turning any of the synchronizing screws, turn each synchronizing screw in all the way until it seats. Record the number of turns for each individual carburetor as the screw must be turned back to its original setting.*

3. Loosen each synchronizing screw (**Figure 32**) until there is no spring tension.

4. Loosen each choke (bystarter) arm locking screw (A, **Figure 33**).

5. Pull the choke shaft (B, **Figure 33**) out from the right.

6. On models so equipped, disconnect the evaporation hose assembly from each carburetor (C, **Figure 33**).

7. Remove the screws (**Figure 34**) securing the rear bracket and remove the rear bracket.

8. Remove the screws securing the front bracket (A, **Figure 35**) and remove the front bracket.

9. Carefully pull the carburetors apart horizontally and in the same plane. Do not damage the fuel (B, **Figure 35**) and air joint pipes or the choke linkage during separation.

10. Assemble by reversing these steps, noting the following.

11. Install new O-ring seals on the fuel and air joint pipes and coat them with oil.

12. Place the individual carburetors on a flat surface and install the front bracket. Install and tighten the screws only finger-tight at this time.

13. Press the carburetors together tightly and tighten the screws in 2-3 steps in a staggered pattern. Tighten the screws securely.

14. Place the carburetor assembly on a flat surface and install the rear bracket. Install and tighten the screws only finger-tight at this time.

15. Press the carburetors together tightly and tighten the screws in 2-3 steps in a staggered pattern. Tighten the screws securely.

16. Turn the synchronizing screw to its original position. Double check that the throttle valve aligns with the bypass hole in the venturi. This distance must be the same on all carburetors. Adjust, if necessary, by turning the synchronizing screw.

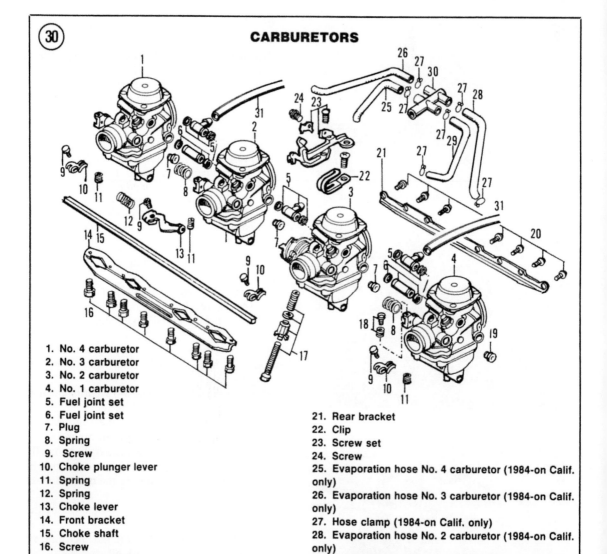

CARBURETORS

1. No. 4 carburetor
2. No. 3 carburetor
3. No. 2 carburetor
4. No. 1 carburetor
5. Fuel joint set
6. Fuel joint set
7. Plug
8. Spring
9. Screw
10. Choke plunger lever
11. Spring
12. Spring
13. Choke lever
14. Front bracket
15. Choke shaft
16. Screw
17. Idle adjust screw
18. Screw and spring
19. Plug
20. Screw

21. Rear bracket
22. Clip
23. Screw set
24. Screw
25. Evaporation hose No. 4 carburetor (1984-on Calif. only)
26. Evaporation hose No. 3 carburetor (1984-on Calif. only)
27. Hose clamp (1984-on Calif. only)
28. Evaporation hose No. 2 carburetor (1984-on Calif. only)
29. Evaporation hose No. 1 carburetor (1984-on Calif. only)
30. Evaporation hose manifold (1984-on Calif. only)
31. Fuel hose

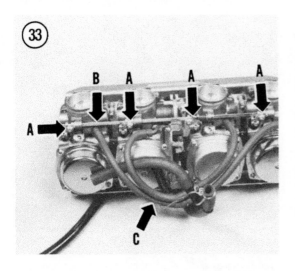

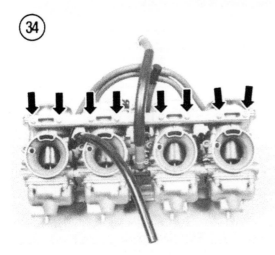

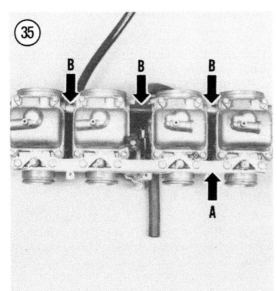

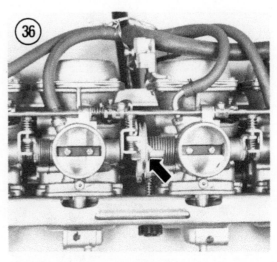

17. Using the throttle linkage (**Figure 36**), open the throttle a little then release it. The throttle should return smoothly with no drag.

18. If there is drag or the throttle does not move smoothly, recheck all previous steps.

> *NOTE*
> *If the carburetors have been reassembled correctly and the throttle still does not operate correctly, there may be internal damage to the throttle shafts or butterfly valves. Take the assembly to a dealer for inspection or replacement.*

19. Install the carburetor assembly as described in this chapter.

CARBURETOR ADJUSTMENTS

Float Adjustment

The carburetor assembly has to be removed and partially disassembled for this adjustment.

1. Remove the carburetors as described in this chapter.

2. Remove the screws (**Figure 37**) securing the float bowls to the main bodies and remove them.

3. Hold the carburetor assembly with the carburetor inclined 15-45° from vertical so the float arm is just touching the float needle. Use a float level gauge (Honda part No. 07401-0010000 or equivalant) and measure the distance from the carburetor body to the bottom surface of the float (**Figure 38**). The correct height is listed in **Table 1**.

4. If the float level is not correct the float assembly will have to be replaced. The float is plastic and cannot be adjusted.

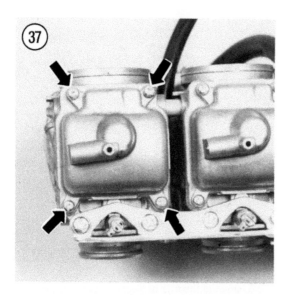

5. If the float level is too high, the result will be a rich fuel-air mixture. If it is too low, the mixture will be too lean.

> *NOTE*
> *The floats on all 4 carburetors must be adjusted to the same height to maintain the same fuel-air mixture to all 4 cylinders.*

6. Reassemble and install the carburetors.

Needle Jet Adjustment

The needle jet is *non-adjustable* on all models.

Choke Adjustment

First make sure the choke cable operates smoothly with no binding. If the cable binds, lubricate it as described in Chapter Three. If the cable still does not operate smoothly, replace it as described in this chapter.
1. Remove both side covers.
2. Remove the seat as described in Chapter Eleven.
3. Remove the fuel tank as described in this chapter.
4. Operate the choke lever and check for smooth operation of the cable and choke mechanism.

> *NOTE*
> *The choke circuit is a "bystarter" system in which the choke lever opens a valve rather than closing a butterfly in the venturi area as on many carburetors. In the open position, the slow jet discharges a stream of fuel into the carburetor venturi to richen the mixture when the engine is cold.*

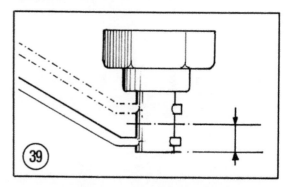

5. At the No. 3 carburetor assembly, move the lever to the fully open position and to the fully closed position Measure the choke valve stroke (**Figure 39**). The correct stroke is 5-7 mm (3/16-1/4 in.).
6. To adjust, loosen the cable clamping screw (**Figure 40**) and move the cable sheath up or down to achieve the correct amount of stroke.
7. Repeat Step 5 and Step 6 until the correct stroke can be achieved.
8. If proper adjustment cannot be achieved using this procedure, the cable has stretched and must be replaced as described in this chapter.
9. Reinstall the fuel tank, seat and side covers.

**Pilot Screw Adjustment and
New Limiter Cap Installation**

Each pilot jet is pre-set at the factory and adjustment is not necessary unless the carburetors have been overhauled or someone has misadjusted them.

In order to comply with U.S. emission control standards, a limiter cap is attached to the end of

each pilot screw. This is to prevent the owner from readjusting the pilot screw from the factory setting. The limiter cap will allow a maximum of 7/8 of a turn of the pilot screw to a leaner mixture only.

CAUTION
Do not try to remove the limiter cap from the pilot screw, as it is bonded in place. It will break off and damage the pilot screw if removal is attempted.

NOTE
The carburetors are numbered in the same sequence as the engine cylinders. The No. 1 carburetor is located on the left-hand side and the numbers continue from left to right. The left-hand side refers to a rider sitting on the seat facing forward.

1. Place the bike on the centerstand.
2. For the preliminary adjustment, carefully turn the pilot screw (**Figure 41**) on each carburetor in until it seats *lightly* and then back it out the number of turns listed in **Table 1**.

CAUTION
The pilot screw seat can be damaged if the pilot screw is tightened too hard against it.

3. Start the engine and let it reach normal operating temperature. Approximately 5-10 minutes of stop and go riding is usually sufficient. Shut the engine off.
4. Connect a portable tachometer following the manufacturer's instructions.
5. Turn the idle speed adjust screw in or out to obtain the idle speed listed in **Table 1**.
6. Turn each pilot screw 1/2 turn *out* from the initial setting in Step 2.
7. If the engine speed increased by 50 rpm or more, turn each pilot screw *out* an additional 1/2

turn at a time until engine speed drops by 50 rpm or less.
8. Turn the idle speed screw to obtain the idle speed listed in **Table 1**.
9. Turn the pilot screw on the No. 1 carburetor *in* 1/2 turn at a time until the idle speed drops by 50 rpm.
10. Turn the pilot screw *out* 1 full turn from the position obtained in Step 9.
11. Turn the idle speed adjust screw in or out again to obtain the idle speed listed in **Table 1**.
12. Repeat Steps 9-11 for the No. 2, 3 and 4 carburetor pilot screws.
13. Open and close the throttle a couple of times and check for variations in idle speed. Readjust if necessary.

WARNING
With the engine idling, move the handlebar from side to side. If idle speed increases during this movement, the throttle cable needs adjustment or may be incorrectly routed through the frame. Correct this problem immediately. Do not ride the bike in this unsafe condition.

14. Disconnect the portable tachometer.
15. Install the limiter caps as follows:
   a. Apply Loctite No. 601 or equivalent to the new limiter cap.
   b. Position the limiter cap against the stop on the float bowl so the pilot screw can only turn *clockwise*.
   c. Install the limiter cap on each pilot screw. Make sure the pilot screw does not move while installing the limiter cap.

High Elevation Adjustment

If the bike is going to be ridden for any sustained period of time at high elevations (2,000 m/6,500

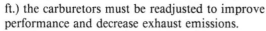

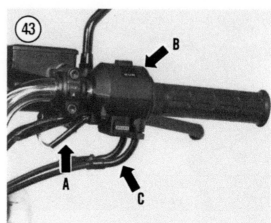

ft.) the carburetors must be readjusted to improve performance and decrease exhaust emissions.

1. Start the engine and let it reach normal operating temperature. Stop-and-go riding for approximately 10 minutes is sufficient. Turn off the engine.

2. Connect a portable tachometer following the manufacturer's instructions. The bike's tach is not accurate enough at low rpm.

NOTE
In the following 2 steps, the carburetor assembly is shown removed for clarity. Do not remove the carburetor assembly for this procedure.

3. Turn each pilot screw 1/2 turn away from the stop on the float bowl (**Figure 41**).

4. Restart the engine and turn the large idle screw (**Figure 42**) to achieve the idle speed listed in **Table 1**.

5. Turn the engine off and disconnect the portable tachometer.

6. When the bike is returned to lower elevations (near sea level), the pilot screws must be returned to their original position and the idle speed readjusted to the specification listed in **Table 1**.

Rejetting The Carburetors

Do not try to solve a poor running engine problem by rejetting the carburetors if all of the following conditions hold true:

  a. The engine has held a good tune in the past with the standard jetting.

  b. The engine has not been modified.

  c. The motorcycle is being operated in the same geographical region under the same general climatic conditions as in the past.

  d. The motorcycle was and is being ridden at average highway speeds.

If those conditions all hold true, chances are the problem is due to a malfunction in the carburetor or another component that needs to be adjusted or repaired. Changing carburetor jet size probably won't solve the problem. Rejetting the carburetors may be necessary if any of the following conditions hold true:

  a. A non-standard type of air filter element is being used.

  b. A non-standard exhaust system is installed on the motorcycle.

  c. Any of the top end components in the engine (pistons, cams, valves, compression ratio, etc.) have been modified.

  d. The motorcycle is in use at considerably higher or lower elevations or in a considerably hotter or colder climate than in the past.

  e. The motorcycle is being operated at considerably higher speeds than before and changing to colder spark plugs does not solve the problem.

  f. Someone has previously changed the carburetor jetting.

  g. The motorcycle has never held a satisfactory engine tune.

If it is necessary to rejet the carburetors, check with a dealer or motorcycle performance tuner for recommendations as to the size of jets to install for your specific situation.

If you do change the jets do so only one size at a time. After rejetting, test ride the bike and perform a spark plug test; refer to *Reading Spark Plugs* in Chapter Three.

THROTTLE CABLE REPLACEMENT

1. Remove both side covers.

2. Remove the seat as described in Chapter Eleven.

3. Remove the fuel tank as described in this chapter.

4. Disconnect the front brake light switch electrical connectors (A, **Figure 43**) from the switch.

5. Remove the screws securing the right-hand switch/throttle housing halves together (B, **Figure 43**).

6. Remove the housing from the handlebar and disengage the throttle cables (C, **Figure 43**) from the throttle grip.

7. Partially remove the carburetor assembly as described in this chapter.

NOTE
It may not look like it, but it is practically impossible to remove the throttle cables from the carburetors with the carburetor assembly in place. There is not enough room for 2 hands within the area.

8. Loosen the throttle cable locknuts (**Figure 44**) and remove both cables from the carburetor assembly (**Figure 45**).

NOTE
The piece of string attached in the next step will pull the new throttle cables back through the frame so they will be routed in exactly the same position as the old ones were.

9. Tie a piece of heavy string or cord (approximately 7 ft./2 m long) to the carburetor end of the throttle cables. Wrap this end with masking or duct tape. Do not use an excessive amount of tape as it must be pulled through the frame loop during removal. Tie the other end of the string to the frame or air box.

10. At the throttle grip end of the cables, carefully pull the cables (and attached string) out through the frame, past the electrical harness and from behind the headlight housing. Make sure the attached string follows the same path as the cables through the frame.

11. Remove the tape and untie the string from old cables.

12. Lubricate the new cables as described in Chapter Three.

13. Tie the string to the new throttle cables and wrap it with tape.

14. Carefully pull the string back through the frame, routing the new cables through the same path as the old cables.

15. Remove the tape and untie the string from cables and the frame.

CAUTION
*The throttle cables are the push/pull type and must be installed as described and shown in Step 14 and Step 15. Do **not** interchange the 2 cables.*

16. Attach the throttle "pull" cable to the rear bracket and into the rear hole in the throttle wheel (A, **Figure 46**). The other end is attached to the front receptacle of the throttle/switch housing.

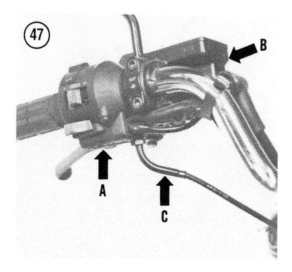

17. Attach the throttle "push" cable to the front bracket and into the front hole in the throttle wheel (B, **Figure 46**). The other end is attached to the rear receptacle of the throttle/switch housing.
18. Install the throttle/switch housing and tighten the screws securely.
19. Attach the front brake light switch connectors.
20. Operate the throttle grip and make sure the carburetor throttle linkage is operating correctly, with no binding. If operation is incorrect or there is binding carefully check that the cables are attached correctly and there are no tight bends in the cables.
21. Install the carburetor assembly, fuel tank and seat.
22. Adjust the throttle cables as described in Chapter Three.
23. Test ride the bike slowly at first and make sure the throttle is operating correctly.

CHOKE CABLE REPLACEMENT

1. Remove both side covers.
2. Remove the seat as described in Chapter Eleven.
3. Remove the fuel tank as described in this chapter.
4. Loosen the choke cable clamp screw (**Figure 40**).
5. Partially remove the carburetor assembly as described in this chapter.

> *NOTE*
> *It may not look like it, but it is practically impossible to remove the choke cable from the carburetors with the carburetor assembly in place. There is just not enough room for 2 hands within the area.*

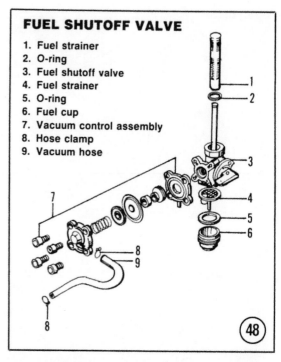

FUEL SHUTOFF VALVE

1. Fuel strainer
2. O-ring
3. Fuel shutoff valve
4. Fuel strainer
5. O-ring
6. Fuel cup
7. Vacuum control assembly
8. Hose clamp
9. Vacuum hose

6. Remove the cable end from the choke linkage.
7. Remove the clutch switch wires at the clutch lever.
8. Remove the screws securing the left-hand switch assembly (A, **Figure 47**) and remove the switch assembly from the handlebar.
9. Remove the clutch master cylinder (B, **Figure 47**) as described in Chapter Five.
10. Remove the choke cable (C, **Figure 47**) from the clutch lever assembly on the handlebar.

> *NOTE*
> *The piece of string attached in the next step will be used to pull the new choke cable back through the frame so it will be routed in the same position as the old cable.*

11. Tie a piece of heavy string or cord (approximately 7 ft./2 m long) to the carburetor end of the choke cable. Wrap this end with masking or duct tape. Do not use an excessive amount of tape as it must be pulled through the frame loop during removal. Tie the other end of the string to the frame or air box.
12. At the choke lever end of the cable, carefully pull the cable (and attached string) out through the frame and from behind the headlight housing. Make sure the attached string follows the same path that the cable does through the frame.
13. Remove the tape and untie the string from the old cable.

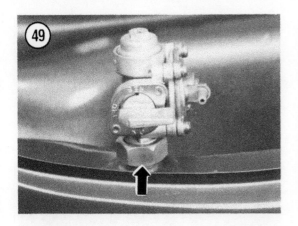

14. Lubricate the new cable as described in Chapter Three.
15. Tie the string to the new choke cable and wrap it with tape.
16. Carefully pull the string back through the frame, routing the new cable through the same path as the old cable.
17. Remove the tape and untie the string from the cable and the frame.
18. Install the choke cable onto the choke lever assembly.
19. Attach the choke cable to the carburetor choke linkage and tighten the clamping screw.
20. Install the clutch master cylinder (B, **Figure 47**) as described in Chapter Five.
21. Install the left-hand switch assembly halves onto the handlebar and install the screws (A, **Figure 47**) securing the halves together.
22. Attach the clutch switch wires to the clutch lever.
23. Operate the choke lever and make sure the carburetor choke linkage is operating correctly, with no binding. If operation is incorrect or there is binding carefully check that the cable is attached correctly and there are no tight bends in the cable.
24. Adjust the choke cable as described in this chapter.
25. Install the carburetor assembly, fuel tank and seat.

AUTOMATIC FUEL SHUTOFF VALVE

The manual override portion of the fuel shutoff valve can be left in the ON or RES position at all times. Engine vacuum opens the valve only when the engine is running and automatically closes the valve when the engine is shut off. The fuel shutoff valve OFF position is used only when the motorcycle is to be stored for any length of time or when servicing the fuel system.

Removal/Cleaning/Installation

Refer to **Figure 48** for this procedure.
1. Remove the fuel tank as described in this chapter.
2. Place a clean, sealable metal container under the fuel shutoff valve. This fuel can be reused if kept clean.
3. Position the fuel tank on block(s) of wood to support the tank in its normal position.
4. Open the fuel filler cap. This will allow air to enter the tank and speed up the flow of fuel. Drain the tank completely. Close the fuel filler cap.
5. Place clean shop cloths or a blanket on the workbench to protect the fuel tank finish.
6. Turn the fuel tank upside down and unscrew the locknut from the tank (**Figure 49**). Remove the valve.
7. After removing the valve, insert a corner of a clean shop rag in the tank opening to stop fuel from dribbling out.
8. Remove the filter cup on the bottom of the valve and remove the filter and O-ring gasket. Clean the filter with a soft toothbrush and blow out with compressed air. Replace if it is defective.
9. Install by reversing these removal steps. Do not forget to install the washer between the valve and the tank.
10. Carefully check for fuel leaks.

Testing

This test is performed with the fuel tank installed on the bike.
1. Turn the manual override portion of the shutoff valve ON.
2. Place a metal container under the fuel line from the fuel shutoff valve to the carburetor assembly.
3. Disconnect the fuel line (A, **Figure 50**) from the T-fitting on the carburetor assembly and drain the remaining fuel from the valve and line into the

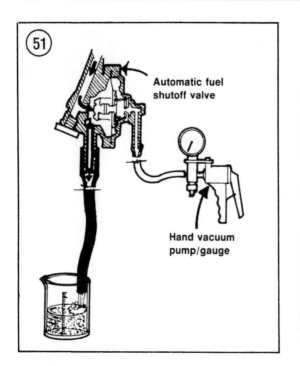

Automatic fuel
shutoff valve

Hand vacuum
pump/gauge

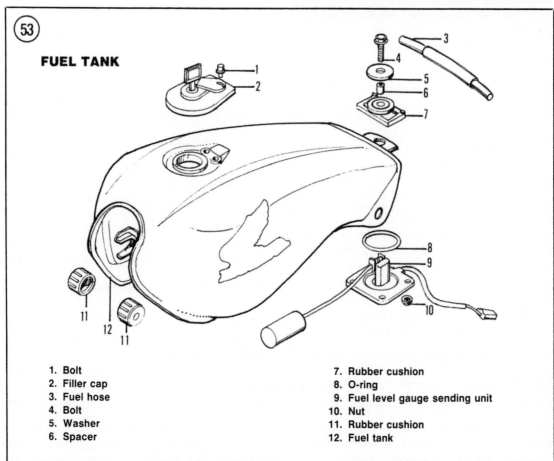

FUEL TANK

1. Bolt
2. Filler cap
3. Fuel hose
4. Bolt
5. Washer
6. Spacer
7. Rubber cushion
8. O-ring
9. Fuel level gauge sending unit
10. Nut
11. Rubber cushion
12. Fuel tank

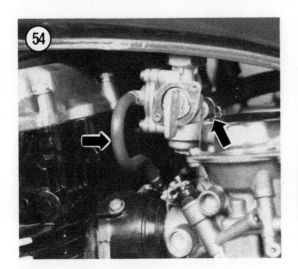

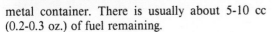

metal container. There is usually about 5-10 cc (0.2-0.3 oz.) of fuel remaining.

4. If the fuel stops draining, the fuel shutoff valve is operating correctly. If the flow does not stop, plug the end of the fuel line with a golf tee to stop the flow of fuel.

5. Remove the vacuum line (B, **Figure 50**) from the shutoff valve to the cylinder head. Clean out the vacuum line and reinstall.

6. Remove the golf tee and check if fuel still drains. If the flow does not stop, again plug the end of the fuel line with a golf tee.

7. Disconnect the vacuum line from the cylinder head (leave it attached to the shutoff valve). Connect a portable hand vacuum pump to the vacuum line as shown in **Figure 51**. Use Honda Vacuum Pump/Gauge (part No. A973X-041-XXXXX) or equivalent.

8. Place a suitable clean metal container under the carburetor fuel line (the one that leads to the carburetor assembly).

NOTE
If this fuel is kept clean it can be reused. If it becomes contaminated during this procedure dispose of it properly. Check with local regulations for proper disposal of gasoline.

9. Turn the manual override portion of the fuel shutoff valve to the ON or RES position. Fuel should *not* flow from the carburetor fuel hose. If fuel does flow, the spring or diaphragm within the shutoff valve may be faulty and the valve must be replaced.

10. Apply vacuum to the diaphragm with the hand pump. Fuel should flow out when 12-20 mm Hg (0.48-0.8 in. Hg) of vacuum is applied and should stop when the vacuum pump is disconnected.

11. If fuel does not flow when vacuum is applied the diaphragm must be disassembled and cleaned.

12. Disconnect the portable hand vacuum pump.

13. To remove the diaphragm assembly, remove the screws (**Figure 52**) securing it to the shutoff valve and remove the assembly. Replacement parts are not available for the diaphragm assembly; it must be replaced as a unit.

14. Turn the fuel shutoff valve OFF and remove the vacuum pump.

15. Install the fuel line to the carburetor assembly and the vacuum line to the cylinder head.

FUEL TANK

Removal/Installation

Refer to **Figure 53** for this procedure.

1. Place the bike on the centerstand.

2. Remove both side covers and the seat as described in Chapter Eleven.

3. Turn the fuel shutoff valve OFF.

4. Remove the fuel line and the vacuum line to the carburetor assembly (**Figure 54**).

5. Disconnect the battery negative lead.

6. Disconnect the electrical wires from the fuel gauge sending unit.

7. Remove the bolt and washer (**Figure 55**) securing the rear of the fuel tank. Don't lose the metal spacer in the rubber cushion.

8A. On models so equipped, lift up and pull the tank to the rear and disconnect the hose going to the fuel evaporation canister. Remove the fuel tank.

8B. On all other models, lift up and pull the tank to the rear and remove the fuel tank.

9. Install by reversing these removal steps.

CRANKCASE BREATHER
SYSTEM (U.S. ONLY)

To comply with air pollution standards, the Honda is equipped with a crankcase breather system. The system draws blowby gases from the crankcase and recirculates them into the fuel-air mixture to be burned.

Inspection/Cleaning

Make sure all hose clamps are tight. Check all hoses for deterioration and replace as necessary.

Slide the drain tube out of the bracket on the battery holder. Remove the clamp and plug (**Figure 56**) from the drain hose and drain out all residue. This cleaning procedure should be done more frequently if a considerable amount of riding is done at full throttle or in the rain.

Install the drain tube in the bracket on the battery holder.

NOTE
Be sure to install the drain plug and clamp.

EVAPORATIVE EMISSION
CONTROL SYSTEM
(1984-ON CALIFORNIA
MODELS ONLY)

Vapor from the fuel tank is routed to a charcoal canister (**Figure 57**). This vapor is stored when the engine is not running. When the engine is running the vapor is drawn through a purge control valve and into the carburetors to be burned. Make sure all hose clamps are tight. Check all hoses for deterioration and replace as necessary (**Figure 58**).

Refer to **Figure 57** for correct hose routing to the PC valve. When removing the hoses from the PC valve, label the hose and the fitting to identify where the hose goes. There are so many vacuum hoses on these models that reconnection can be very confusing.

The charcoal canister and the PC valve are located just forward of the rear wheel.

Removal/Installation

1. Remove both side covers and the seat.
2. Remove the fuel tank as described in this chapter.
3. Remove the rear wheel as described in Chapter Nine.

NOTE
Prior to removing the hoses from the PC valve, label the hose fitting to identify where the hose goes.

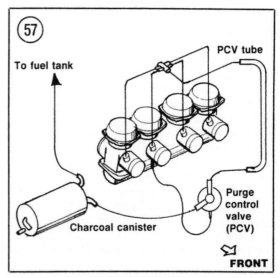

4. Disconnect the hoses going to the charcoal canister from the PC valve.
5. Remove the bolts securing the charcoal canister to the bracket on the frame and remove the assembly.
6. Install by reversing these removal steps. Be sure to install the hoses to their correct place on the PC valve.

EXHAUST SYSTEM

The exhaust system consists of 4 exhaust pipes, an equalizer tube and 2 mufflers. Refer to **Figure 59**.

Removal/Installation

NOTE
This procedure is best done with the aid of a helper. One person can work on each side of the bike.

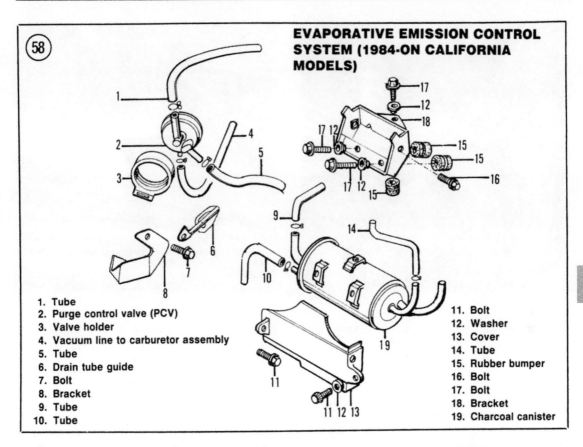

EVAPORATIVE EMISSION CONTROL SYSTEM (1984-ON CALIFORNIA MODELS)

1. Tube
2. Purge control valve (PCV)
3. Valve holder
4. Vacuum line to carburetor assembly
5. Tube
6. Drain tube guide
7. Bolt
8. Bracket
9. Tube
10. Tube
11. Bolt
12. Washer
13. Cover
14. Tube
15. Rubber bumper
16. Bolt
17. Bolt
18. Bracket
19. Charcoal canister

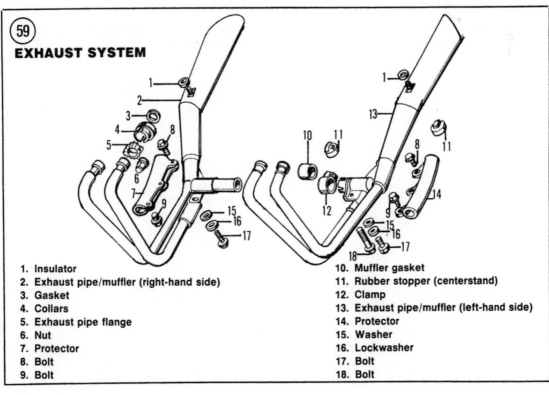

EXHAUST SYSTEM

1. Insulator
2. Exhaust pipe/muffler (right-hand side)
3. Gasket
4. Collars
5. Exhaust pipe flange
6. Nut
7. Protector
8. Bolt
9. Bolt
10. Muffler gasket
11. Rubber stopper (centerstand)
12. Clamp
13. Exhaust pipe/muffler (left-hand side)
14. Protector
15. Washer
16. Lockwasher
17. Bolt
18. Bolt

1. Place the bike on the centerstand.
2. Remove the nuts securing the exhaust pipe flanges (**Figure 60**) to the cylinder head.
3. Slide the flanges down.
4. Remove the rear brake pedal as described in Chapter Ten.
5. Remove the bolt (**Figure 61**) securing the muffler to each rear footpeg bracket.
6. Loosen the bolt clamping the equalizing tube between the mufflers.
7. Remove the bolts and washers securing the muffler to the lower crankcase on each side.
8. Pull the front portion of the exhaust system down and slightly forward and remove from the engine and the frame.

> *NOTE*
> *If difficult to remove, spray some WD-40 or equivalent on the rear clamping bolts to help loosen the rear exhaust pipes from the common collector.*

9. Inspect the gaskets at all joints; replace as necessary.

10. Be sure to install a new gasket in each exhaust port in both cylinder heads.
11. Install the collars on each exhaust pipe and apply 1 layer of transparent tape (do not use duct, masking or other types of tape) to hold the collars together and in place. The tape will burn away after a short ride.
12. If the mufflers were separated, apply a light coat of multipurpose grease to the inside surface of the gaskets in the equalizing tube. This will make insertion of the two tubes easier.
13. Install the exhaust flanges with the arrow pointing down.

14. Install the assembly into position and install all bolts and nuts finger-tight until the exhaust flange nuts and washers are installed and securely tightened. This will minimize an exhaust leak at the cylinder head.

15. Tighten all bolts and nuts to the torque specifications listed in **Table 2**.

16. After installation is complete, make sure there are no exhaust leaks.

Table 1 CARBURETOR SPECIFICATIONS

	CB550	CB650
Carburetor model No.	VE62A	VE54A
		VE75A (Calif.)
Main jet number	No. 110	No. 115
Slow jet	No. 35	No. 35
Jet needle clip setting	Non-adjustable	Non-adjustable
Float level	18.5 mm (0.73 in.)	18.5 mm (0.73 in.)
Idle speed	1,000 ±100 rpm	1,100 ±100 rpm
Pilot screw initial setting	2 5/8 turns out	2 5/8 turns out

Table 2 EXHAUST SYSTEM TORQUE SPECIFICATIONS

Item	N·m	ft.-lb.
Muffler mounting bolt	24-30	17-22
Muffler collector joint bolt	24-30	17-22

6

CHAPTER SEVEN

ELECTRICAL SYSTEM

This chapter constains service and test procedures for the electrical system components. Refer to Chapter Three for battery and spark plug maintenance.

Specifications are in **Table 1-4** at the end of this chapter.

Wiring diagrams are at the end of this book.

ELECTRICAL COMPONENT REPLACMENT

Most motorcycle dealerships and parts suppliers will not accept the return of any electrical part. If you cannot determine the *exact* cause of any electrical system malfunction, have a Honda dealership retest that specific system to verify your test results. If you purchase a new electrical component(s), install it, and then find that the system still does not work properly, you will probably be unable to return the unit for a refund.

Consider any test results carefully before replacing a component that tests on *slightly* out of specification, especially resistance. A number of variables can affect test results dramatically. These include: the testing meter's internal circuitry, ambient temperature and conditions under which the machine has been operated. Successful test results depend to a great extent upon individual accuracy.

CHARGING SYSTEM

The charging system consists of the battery, alternator and a voltage regulator/rectifier (**Figure 1**).

The alternator is a three-phase type that uses two rotors driven by the crankshaft and a fixed stator that consists of a series of wound coils of wire. Cur-

rent is generated by a process of electromagnetic induction, whereby a field coil electromagnetically charges the rotors. The now magnetized rotors, as they revolve inside the fixed stator coils, induce an alternating current from the stator This AC output voltage is regulated and rectified to DC voltage by the regulator/rectifier to operate the electrical component and charge the battery. The rotor also functions as a flywheel to smooth out low speed engine pulsation.

There are no test procedures for the rotors.

Alternator removal and installation procedures are covered in Chapter Four.

Output Test

Whenever charging system trouble is suspected, make sure the battery is in good condition (Chapter Three).

Prior to starting this test, start the bike and let it reach normal operating temperature; shut off the engine.

1. Remove the right-hand side cover and the seat as described in Chapter Eleven.

2. Disconnect the battery negative cable from the battery.

3. Connect a 0-20 V voltmeter as follows:
    a. Connect the voltmeter positive lead to the battery positive terminal on the starter solenoid (A, **Figure 2**).
    b. Connect the voltmeter negative lead to ground.

4. Connect a 0-10 DC ammeter in line with the main fuse connector (fusible link) as follows:
    a. Loosen the screws securing the fusible link (B, **Figure 2**) and remove the fusbile link.

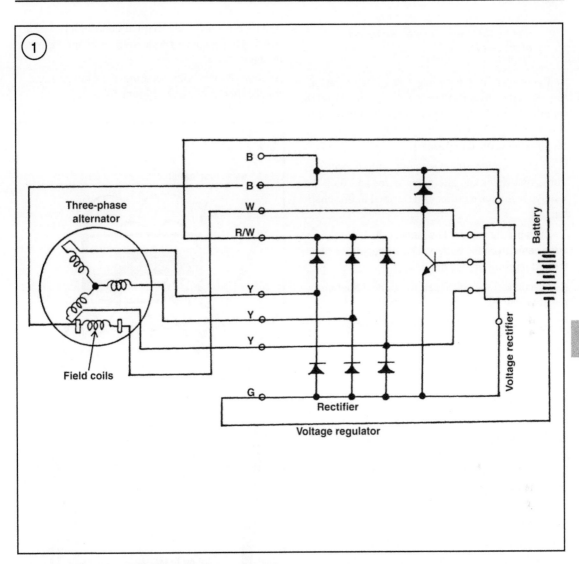

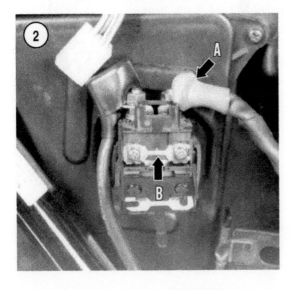

b. Install an inline fuse/fuse holder (available at most most auto supply or electronic supply stores) along with the ammeter as shown in **Figure 3**.

c. Use alligator clips on the test leads for a good electrical connection.

NOTE
Do not try to test the charging system by connecting an ammeter between the positive (+) battery terminal and the starter cable. The ammeter will burn out when the electric starter is operated.

NOTE
During the test, if the needle of the ammeter reads in the opposite direc-

tion on the scale, reverse the polarity of the test leads.

5. Reconnect the battery negative cable to the battery. Start the engine and let it warm up again for 10 minutes at 2,000-2,100 rpm. Allow the voltage to stabilize at 14-15 volts, then check the amperage output as described in **Table 1**.

6. If the charging amerage is not within specifications, first check the alternator stator and then the voltage regulator/rectifier as described in this chapter.

7. Turn off the engine. Disconnect the battery negative cable from the battery. Disconnect the ammeter and reinstall the fusible link.

8. Disconnect the voltmeter. Reconnect the battery negative cable to the battery.

9. Install the seat and the right-hand side cover.

ALTERNATOR

Stator Testing

1. Remove the left-hand side cover and the seat as described in Chapter Eleven.

2. Disconnect the 6-pin alternator electrical connector (**Figure 4**).

3. Calibrate the ohmmeter on the R × 1000 scale and check for continuity between each of the yellow wires and a clean engine ground. There should be no continuity between any of the yellow wires and ground. If continuity is noted, replace the stator.

4. Next, calibrate the ohmmeter on the R × 1 scale and meausre the resistance between eachof the yellow stator wires. The resistance should be 0.4-0.6 ohm. If not, replace the stator.

5. Measure the resistance between the black and white stator wires. The resistance should be 4-6 ohms. If not, replace the stator.

Voltage Regulator/Rectifier Removal/Installation

1. Remove both side covers and the seat as described in Chapter Eleven.

2. Disconnect the battery negative lead.

3. Disconnect the 2 electrical connectors (A, **Figure 5**). One connector contains 5 wires and the other contains 3 wires.

4. Remove the bolts securing the voltage regulator/rectifier in place (B, **Figure 5**).

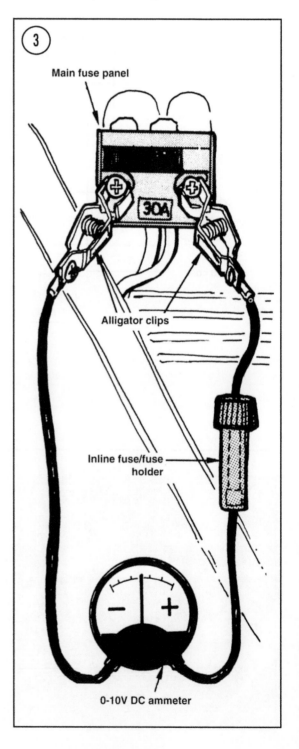

3

Main fuse panel

30A

Alligator clips

Inline fuse/fuse holder

0-10V DC ammeter

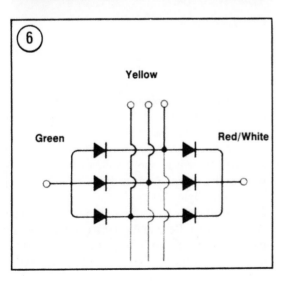

Yellow

Green   Red/White

5. Carefully pull the voltage regulator/rectifier and the 2 electrical connectors and wires out from the frame.

6. Install by reversing these steps. Make sure all connections are tight.

Static Test

To test the voltage regulator/rectifier, disconnect the 2 electrical connectors from the harness. One connector contains 5 wires and the other contains 3 wires.

Make the following measurements using an ohmmeter and referring to **Figure 6**.

The following test should be performed with one of the following ohmmeters with a positive ground:

    a. Sanwa SP-10D.

    b. Kowa TH-5H.

    c. Kowa digital KS-AHM-32-CO3.

If a different ohmmeter is used the test results may be out of specification.

1. Connect the positive (+) ohmmeter lead to the yellow lead and the negative (–) ohmmeter lead to the green lead. There should be continuity (5-40 ohms).

2. Reverse the ohmmeter leads and repeat Step 1. This time there should be high resistance (2,000 ohms minimum).

3. Connect the positive (+) ohmmeter lead to the red/white lead and the negative (–) ohmmeter lead to the yellow lead. There should be continuity (5-40 ohms).

4. Reverse the ohmmeter leads and repeat Step 3. This time there should be high resistance (2,000 ohms minimum).

5. If the voltage regulator/rectifier fails to pass any of these tests the unit is defective and must be replaced.

Performance Test

Perform the following test at the connector containing 5 wires. Do not disconnect the 5 wire connector.

1. Connect a voltmeter positive test lead to the black wire on the harness side of the connector.

2. Connect the voltmeter negative test lead to ground.

3. Start the engine and increase engine speed to 2,500 rpm.

4. The voltage should stabilize between 14.0 and 15.0 volts.

5. At this point, the voltage regulator/rectifier should prevent any further increase in voltage.

6. If this does not happen and voltage increases above specifications, the voltage regulator/rectifier is faulty and must be replaced.

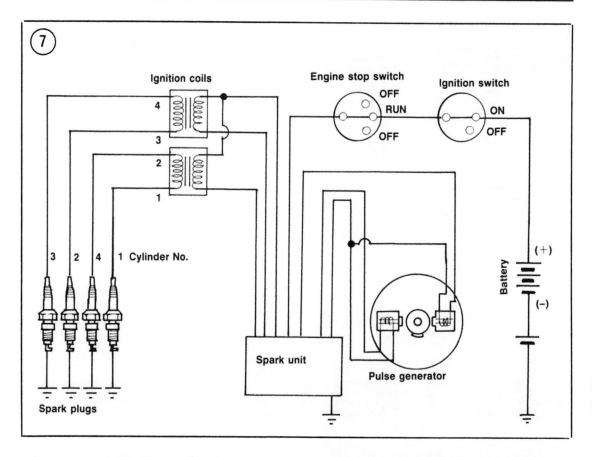

Ignition coils
Engine stop switch
Ignition switch
Cylinder No.
Spark plugs
Spark unit
Pulse generator
Battery

IGNITION SYSTEM

The ignition system consists of 2 ignition coils, one spark unit, an ignition pulse generator and 4 spark plugs. Refer to **Figure 7** for a diagram of the ignition circuit.

The Honda is equipped with a solid state capacitor discharge ignition (CDI) system that uses no breaker points. This system provides a longer life for components and delivers a more efficient spark throughout the entire speed range of the engine. Ignition timing is not adjustable. If ignition timing is incorrect, it is due to a faulty unit within the ignition system.

Direct current charges the capacitor. As the piston approaches the firing position, a pulse from the pulse generator coil triggers the silicone controlled rectifier. The rectifier in turn allows the capacitor to discharge quickly into the primary circuit of the ignition coil, where the voltage is stepped up in the secondary circuit to a value sufficient to fire the spark plugs of the No. 1 and No. 4 cylinders or No. 2 and No. 3 cylinders. The distribution of the pulses from the pulse generator is controlled by the rotation of the crankshaft; it is driven off of the right-hand end of the crankshaft.

NOTE
The spark plugs will fire in pairs (No. 1 and 4 and No. 2 and 3) but only one of the cylinders will be at TDC on the compression stroke. The other cylinder is on the exhaust stroke and the spark in that cylinder has no effect on it.

CDI Precautions

Certain measures must be taken to protect the capacitor discharge system.

1. Never connect the battery backwards. If the connected battery polarity is wrong, damage will occur to the voltage regulator/rectifier, the alternator and the spark units.

2. Do not disconnect the battery when the engine is running. A voltage surge will occur which will damage the voltage regulator/rectifier and possibly burn out the lights.

3. Keep all connections between the various units clean and tight. Be sure the wiring connections are pushed together firmly to help keep out moisture.

4. Do not substitute another type of ignition coil.

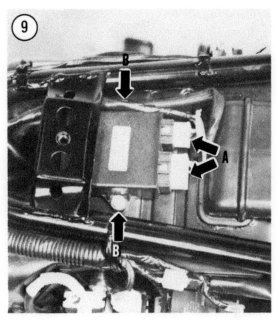

5. Each component is mounted within a rubber vibration isolator. Always be sure the isolator is in place when installing any part of the system.

CDI Troubleshooting

Problems with the capacitor discharge system are usually the production of a weak spark or no spark at all.

1. Check all connections to make sure they are tight and free of corrosion.

2. Check the ignition coils as described in this chapter.

3. Check the pickup coils in the ignition pulse generator with an ohmmeter:

   a. Remove the seat as described in Chapter Eleven.

   b. Disconnect the 6-pin (containing only 4 wires) ignition pulse generator electrical connector from the left-hand side of the spark unit (**Figure 8**).

   c. Connect the ohmmeter leads between the white and the yellow leads (No. 2 and 3 cylinders) and then between the white and the blue leads (No. 1 and 4 cylinders).

   d. The resistance for each coil should be approximately 330 ohms ±10% at 68° F (20° C). If the pickup coils do not meet these specifications, the ignition pulse generator assembly must be replaced as described in this chapter. It cannot be serviced.

4. If the ignition coils and ignition pulse generator assembly check out okay, the spark unit is at fault and must be replaced.

SPARK UNIT

Replacement

1. Remove both side covers and the seat as described in Chapter Eleven.
2. Disconnect the battery negative lead.
3. Disconnect the electrical connectors going to the spark unit (A, **Figure 9**).
4. Remove the bolts (B, **Figure 9**) securing the spark unit to the air filter air box.
5. Install by reversing these removal steps. Make sure all electrical connections are tight and free of corrosion.

Testing

Honda does not provide test procedures nor specifications for the spark unit. If the ignition coils, pulse generator assembly and wiring harness are good and the ignition timing is off, replace the spark unit with a known good unit.

IGNITION COIL

There are 2 ignition coils; one fires the No. 1 and 4 cylinders and the other fires the No. 2 and 3 cylinders.

The ignition coil is a transformer which develops the high voltage required to jump the spark plug gap. The only maintenance required is keeping the electrical connections clean and tight and occasionally checking to see that the coils are mounted securely.

7

Removal/Installation

1. Remove both side covers and the seat as described in Chapter Eleven.
2. Remove the fuel tank as described in Chapter Six.
3. Disconnect the battery negative lead.
4. Disconnect the spark plug leads from the spark plugs.
5. Disconnect the primary wire connectors (A, **Figure 10**) for both coils:
    a. Cylinders No. 2 and 3—yellow and black/white.
    b. Cylinders No. 1 and 4—blue and black/white.
6. Remove the bolts (B, **Figure 10**) securing the ignition coils to the frame and remove both coils.
7. Install by reversing these removal steps; note the following.
8. Make sure all electrical connections are tight and free of corrosion.
9. Route the spark plug wires to the correct cylinder. Original equipment spark plug wires are numbered next to the spark plug rubber boot.

Dynamic Test

Disconnect the high voltage lead from the spark plug. Remove the spark plug from the cylinder head. Connect a new or known good spark plug to the high voltage lead and place the spark plug base on a good ground such as the engine cylinder head (**Figure 11**). Position the spark plug so you can see the electrodes.

> *WARNING*
> *If it is necessary to hold the high voltage lead, do so with an insulated pair of pliers. The high voltage generated could produce serious or fatal shocks.*

Push the starter button to turn the engine over a couple of times. If a fat blue spark occurs, the coil is in good condition; if not, it must be replaced. Make sure you are using a known good spark plug for this test. If the spark plug used is defective the test results will be incorrect.

Reinstall the spark plug in the cylinder head.

Continuity Test

1. Use an ohmmeter set at R×10 and measure between the 2 primary connector lugs on the coil. The specified resistance is 2.8 ohms.
2. Use an ohmmeter set at R×1,000 and measure between the 2 secondary leads (spark plug leads) with the spark plug caps in place. The specified resistance is 21,000-28,000 ohms.

PULSE GENERATOR

NOTE
*Pulse generator testing is described under **CDI Troubleshooting** in this chapter.*

Removal/Installation

1. Remove both side covers and the seat as described in Chapter Eleven.
2. Remove the fuel tank as described in Chapter Six.
3. Remove the bolts securing the pulse generator cover (**Figure 12**) and remove the cover.
4. At the spark unit, disconnect the 6-pin (containing only 4 wires) ignition pulse generator electrical connector (**Figure 8**).
5. Remove the screws securing each pulse generator (A, **Figure 13**) to the crankcase. Note the location of the metal plates (**Figure 14**) on the front pulse generator. These plates must be reinstalled in the same location as they keep the electrical wires in place and out of the path of the pulse generator rotor.
6. Remove the screw (B, **Figure 13**) securing the electrical wire to the oil pressure warning switch. Disconnect the wire from the switch.
7. Carefully remove the rubber grommet (C, **Figure 13**) and electrical wires from the crankcase and remove the assembly from the frame.
8. Install by reversing these removal steps, noting the following.
9. Make sure the screws securing the pulse generators are tight and the wires are routed correctly in the frame.
10. Be sure to install the metals plates in their same location as noted in Step 5.

STARTING SYSTEM

The starting system consists of the starter motor, starter gears, solenoid and starter button.
The layout of the starting system is shown in **Figure 15**. When the starter button is pressed, it allows current to flow through the starter solenoid coil. The solenoid contacts then close, allowing electricity to flow from the battery to the starter motor.

CAUTION
Do not operate the starter for more than 5 seconds at a time. Let it rest approximately 10 seconds, then use it again.

The starter gears and starter clutch assembly are covered in Chapter Four.

3. Use an ohmmeter set at R × 10 and measure between the 2 secondary leads (spark plug leads) with the spark plug caps removed. The specified resistance is 13,600-15,500 ohms.
4. If the coil(s) pass the test in Step 3, but fail Step 2, the spark plug caps may be faulty. Disconnect the spark plug leads from the ignition coil. Use an ohmmeter and check for continuity from the coil end of the spark plug wire to the plug end (plug caps removed). There should be continuity (low resistance). If there is no continuity the spark plug wire is faulty and must be replaced.
5. If the coil(s) fail to pass any of these tests the coil(s) should be replaced.

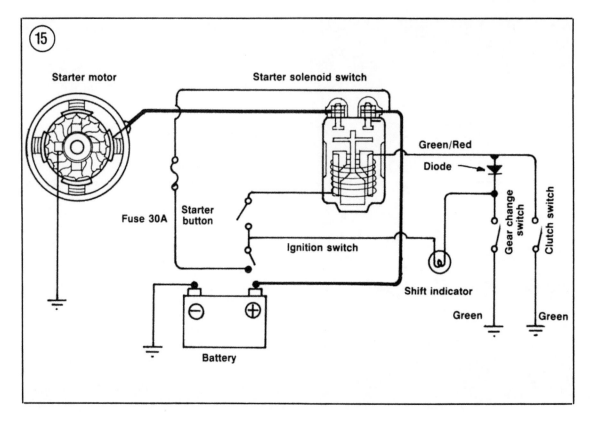

Table 2, at the end of the chapter, lists possible starter problems, probable causes and most common remedies.

STARTER

Removal/Installation

This procedure is shown with some of the engine components removed for clarity.
1. Place the bike on the centerstand.
2. Remove both side covers and the seat as described in Chapter Eleven.
3. Disconnect the battery negative lead.
4. Disconnect the starter cable from the starter (A, **Figure 16**).
5. Remove the bolts (B, **Figure 16**) securing the starter to the crankcase.
6. Pull the starter to the right and remove the starter from the crankcase.
7. Install by reversing these steps. Make sure the connection is free of corrosion and is tight.

Disassembly/Inspection/Assembly

The overhaul of a starter motor is best left to an expert. This procedure shows how to detect a defective starter.
1. Remove the case screws and separate the case and covers.

NOTE
Write down the number of shims used on the shaft next to the commutator. Be sure to install the same number when reassembling the starter.

2. Clean all grease, dirt and carbon from the armature, case and end covers.

CAUTION
Do not immerse brushes or the wire windings in solvent as the insulation may be damaged. Wipe the windings with a cloth lightly moistened with solvent and dry thoroughly.

3. Measure the length of each brush (**Figure 17**) with a vernier caliper. If the length is 6.5 mm (0.26 in.) or less for any one of the brushes, the brush terminal assembly must be replaced.
4. To replace the brush terminal assembly, perform the following:

NOTE
Prior to removing the nuts and washers, write down their positions. This is important. They must be reinstalled in the same order because this set of brushes is insulated from the case.

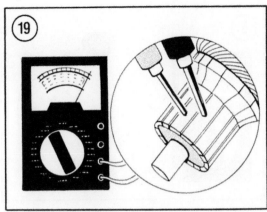

a. Remove the nuts, washers and O-ring (A, **Figure 18**) securing the cable terminal and brush assembly.

b. Slide the armature and brush holder assemblies partially out of the case.

c. Remove the old brush holder and remove the old brush terminal assembly.

d. Install a new brush terminal assembly into the brush holder.

e. Slide the armature and brush holder assembly back into the case.

f. Install the O-ring, nuts and washers in the same order of removal securing the cable terminal and brush assembly.

5. Inspect the commutator. The mica in a good commutator is below the surface of the copper bars. On a worn commutator the mica and copper bars may be worn to the same level. If necessary, have the commutator serviced by a dealer or motorcycle or automotive electrical repair shop.

6. Inspect the commutator copper bars for discoloration. If a pair of bars are discolored, grounded armature coils are indicated.

7. Use an ohmmeter and check for continuity between the commutator bars (**Figure 19**); there should be continuity (low resistance) between pairs of bars. Also check continuity between the commutator bars and the shaft (**Figure 20**); there should be no continuity (infinite resistance). If the unit fails either of these tests the armature is faulty and must be replaced.

8. Use an ohmmeter and inspect the field coil by checking continuity between the starter cable terminal and the starter case; there should be no continuity (infinite resistance). Also check continuity between the starter cable terminal and each brush wire terminal; there should be continuity (low resistance). If the unit fails either of these tests the case/field coil assembly must be replaced.

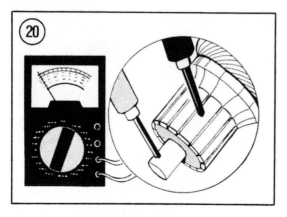

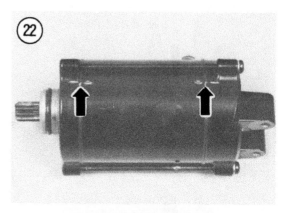

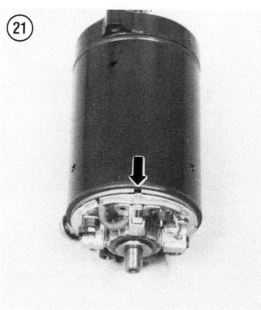

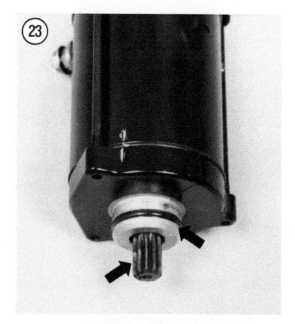

9. Assemble the case as follows:
   a. Align the pin in the brush holder with the notch in the case (**Figure 21**).
   b. Align the slot in the rear cover (B, **Figure 18**) with the pin on the brush holder (C, **Figure 18**).
   c. Align the marks on both the case and end covers (**Figure 22**).
   d. Install and tighten the case screws.

10. Inspect the gear and O-ring seal (**Figure 23**). If the gear is chipped or worn the armature must be replaced. Replace the O-ring if it is hardened or starting to deteriorate.

STARTER SOLENOID

Testing

1. Remove the solenoid as described in this chapter.

2. Connect an ohmmeter to the two large terminals on top of the solenoid. There should be no continuity.

3. Connect a 12 volt battery to the 2 small (starter switch) terminals. As the last connection is made, the solenoid should click and the ohmmeter should show continuity.

4. If the solenoid does not perform as described, replace it.

5. Install the solenoid as described in this chapter.

Removal/Installation

1. Remove both side covers and the seat as described in Chapter Eleven.

2. Disconnect the battery negative lead.

3. Disconnect the electrical connector (**Figure 24**) from the top of the main fuse holder.

should be continuity (low resistance) in one direction and no continuity (infinite resistance) in the other direction. Replace the diode if it fails this test.

5. Install by reversing these removal steps.

LIGHTING SYSTEM

The lighting system consists of a headlight, taillight/brake light combination, turn signals, indicator lights and meter illumination lights. **Table 3** lists replacement bulbs for these components.

Always use the correct wattage bulb. The use of a larger wattage bulb will give a dim light and a smaller wattage bulb will burn out prematurely.

Headlight Replacement

All models are equipped with a quartz halogen headlight. Special handling of the quartz halogen bulb is required as specified in this procedure.

Refer to **Figure 27** for this procedure.

1. Remove the screw (**Figure 28**) on the bottom of the trim bezel securing the headlight assembly.
2. Pull out on the bottom of the headlight assembly and disengage it from the locating tab on top of the headlight housing.
3. Disconnect the electrical connector (**Figure 29**) from the headlight lens unit.
4. Remove the bulb cover.

> *CAUTION*
> *Carefully read all instructions shipped with the replacement quartz halogen bulb. Do not touch the bulb glass with your fingers. Any traces of oil on the quartz halogen bulb will drastically reduce the life of the bulb. Clean any traces of oil from the bulb with a cloth moistened in alcohol or lacquer thinner.*

4. Slide off the rubber protective boots and disconnect the electrical wires (**Figure 25**) from the top terminals of the solenoid.
5. Remove the solenoid from the frame (along with the main fuse holder attached to it).
6. Install by reversing these removal steps.

CLUTCH DIODE

Removal/Testing/Installation

1. Remove both side covers and the seat as described in Chapter Eleven.
2. Remove the fuel tank as described in Chapter Six.
3. Disconnect the clutch diode from the wire harness (**Figure 26**).
4. Use an ohmmeter and check for continuity between the 2 terminals on the clutch diode. There

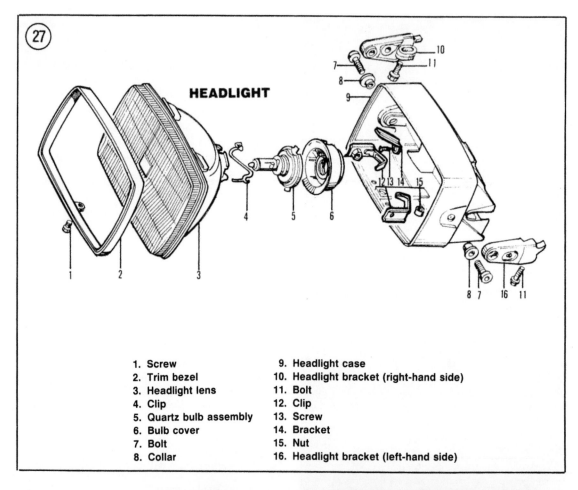

HEADLIGHT

1. Screw
2. Trim bezel
3. Headlight lens
4. Clip
5. Quartz bulb assembly
6. Bulb cover
7. Bolt
8. Collar
9. Headlight case
10. Headlight bracket (right-hand side)
11. Bolt
12. Clip
13. Screw
14. Bracket
15. Nut
16. Headlight bracket (left-hand side)

5. Remove the clip and bulb assembly. Replace with a new bulb assembly—do not touch the bulb with your fingers. Assemble by reversing this sequence.

6. Install by reversing these removal steps.

7. Adjust the headlight as described in this chapter.

Headlight Housing Removal/Installation

Refer to **Figure 27** for this procedure.

1. Remove the headlight lens assembly (A, **Figure 30**) as described in this chapter.

2. Prior to disconnecting the electrical connectors, label with masking tape. Disconnect all electrical connectors within the headlight housing (B, **Figure 30**).

3. Carefully withdraw the electrical connectors through the headlight housing and remove the housing.

4. Remove the Allen bolt on each side securing the headlight case assembly to the case mounting bracket on the forks.

5. To remove the assembly mounting bracket, disconnect all electrical connectors to the instrument cluster and the front turn signals. Remove the bolt securing each headlight bracket/turn signal assembly and remove it from the front forks.

6. Install by reversing these removal steps, noting the following.

7. Prior to installing the headlight lens assembly, check out the operation of the following items controlled by the electrical connections in the headlight housing:

   a. Right and left turn signals.

   b. Headlight dimmer switch.

   c. Horn.

   d. Engine stop switch.

   e. Ignition switch.

8. For a preliminary adjustment, locate the headlight case so the index marks on the case and the bracket align.

9. Adjust the headlight as described in this chapter.

Headlight Adjustment (CB550)

Adjust the headlight horizontally and vertically according to Department of Motor Vehicle regulations in your area.

To adjust the headlight horizontally, loosen the bolts on top of and behind the headlight assembly. Position the headlight correctly. Retighten the bolts.

To adjust the headlight vertically, loosen the bolts on each side of the headlight assembly. Position the headlight correctly. Retighten the bolts.

Headlight Adjustment (CB650)

Adjust the headlight vertically according to Department of Motor Vehicle regulations in your area.

There is no provision for adjusting the headlight horizontally.

To adjust the headlight vertically, loosen the bolts (**Figure 31**) on each side of the headlight assembly. Position the headlight correctly. Retighten the bolts.

Taillight/Brake Light Replacement (CB550)

1. Remove the screws securing the lens and remove the lens.

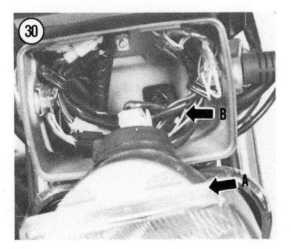

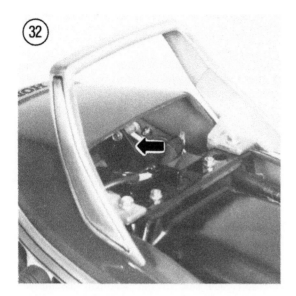

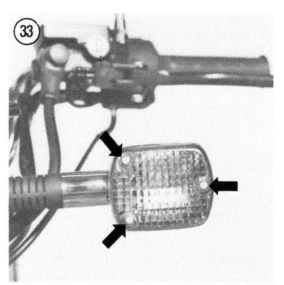

2. Wash the inside and outside of the lens with a mild detergent and wipe dry. Wipe off the reflective base surrounding the bulbs with a soft cloth.
3. Inspect the lens gasket and replace if it is damaged or deteriorated.
4. Replace the bulb and install the lens; do not overtighten the screws as the lens may crack.

Taillight/Brake Light/License Plate Light Replacement (CB650)

1. Remove both side covers and the seat as described in Chapter Eleven.
2. Reach into the rear cavity of the rear fender (**Figure 32**). Push in on the bulb socket assembly and turn clockwise until the socket assembly disengages from the assembly.
3. Remove the bulb from the socket assembly.
4. Replace the bulb and install the socket assembly. Install the seat and side covers.

License Plate Light Replacement (CB550)

1. Remove the nuts behind the license plate light bracket.
2. Remove the license plate light cover and lens.
3. Push in on the bulb and turn clockwise until the bulb disengages from the socket assembly.
4. Wash the inside and outside of the lens with a mild detergent and wipe dry.
5. Inspect the lens gasket and replace if it is damaged or deteriorated.
6. Replace the bulb and install the lens and lens cover; do not overtighten the nuts as the lens may crack.

Turn Signal Light Replacement

1. Remove the screws securing the lens and remove the lens (**Figure 33**).
2. Wash the inside and outside of the lens with a mild detergent and wipe dry.
3. Inspect the lens gasket and replace if it is damaged or deteriorated.
4. Replace the bulb and install the lens; do not overtighten the screws as the lens may crack.

Meter Illumination Light Replacement (CB550)

Refer to **Figure 34** for this procedure.
1. Remove the instrument cluster as described in this chapter.

> *WARNING*
> *In the next step do not allow the instruments to remain upside down any longer than necessary. The needle damping fluid will leak out on the instrument face and lens.*

2. Turn the instrument cluster upside down on the workbench. Remove the screws securing the lower cover and remove the lower cover.
3. Remove the screws securing the meter to the housing and withdraw the meter from the housing.
4. Carefully pull the socket/bulb assembly out of the backside of the housing.
5. Replace the defective bulb(s).
6. Install by reversing these removal steps.

Indicator Light Replacement (CB550)

Refer to **Figure 34** for this procedure.

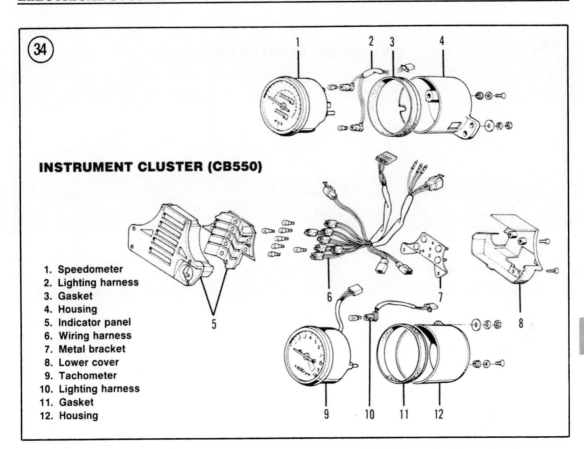

INSTRUMENT CLUSTER (CB550)

1. Speedometer
2. Lighting harness
3. Gasket
4. Housing
5. Indicator panel
6. Wiring harness
7. Metal bracket
8. Lower cover
9. Tachometer
10. Lighting harness
11. Gasket
12. Housing

1. Remove the instrument cluster as described in this chapter.

WARNING
In the next step do not allow the instruments to remain upside down any longer than necessary. The needle damping fluid will leak out on the instrument face and lens.

2. Turn the instrument cluster upside down on the workbench. Remove the screws securing the lower cover and remove the lower cover.
3. Remove the screw securing the indicator panel to the metal bracket. Remove the indicator panel.
4. Carefully pull the socket/bulb assembly out of the backside of the housing.
5. Replace the defective bulb(s).
6. Install by reversing these removal steps.

Meter Illumination Light and Indicator Light Replacement (CB650)

Refer to **Figure 35** for this procedure.
1. Remove the instrument cluster as described for your model in this chapter.

WARNING
In the next step do not allow the instruments to remain upside down any longer than necessary. The needle damping fluid will leak out on the instrument face and lens.

2. Turn the instrument cluster upside down on the workbench. Remove the screws securing the lower cover and remove the lower cover.
3. Remove the nuts and washers securing the bracket to the inner cover and remove the bracket.
4. Carefully pull the socket/bulb assembly out of the backside of the inner cover.
5. Replace the defective bulb(s).
6. Install by reversing these removal steps.

SWITCHES

Ignition Switch Testing

In the following test, connect the ohmmeter leads to the electrical connectors going to the ignition switch—*not* to the wiring harness side of the connectors. Refer to **Figure 36** for this procedure.

1. Remove the right-hand side cover and the seat as described in Chapter Eleven.

7

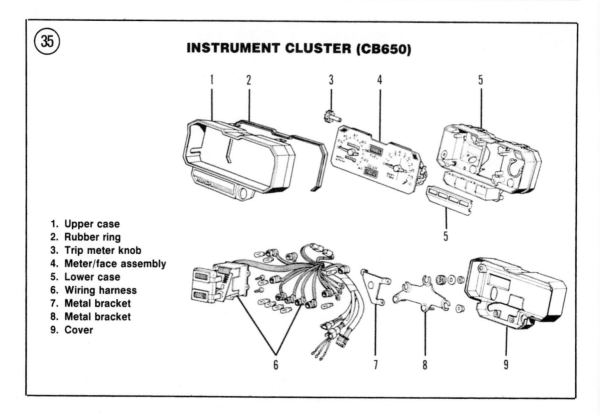

INSTRUMENT CLUSTER (CB650)

1. Upper case
2. Rubber ring
3. Trip meter knob
4. Meter/face assembly
5. Lower case
6. Wiring harness
7. Metal bracket
8. Metal bracket
9. Cover

2. Disconnect the battery negative lead.

3. Remove the headlight and headlight case as described in this chapter.

4. Remove the fuse cover and fuse holder as described in this chapter.

5. Disconnect the 2 electrical connectors from the ignition switch.

6. Turn the ignition switch ON. Use an ohmmeter set at $R \times 10$ and check for continuity between the following terminals:

   a. Red and black: there should be continuity (low resistance).

   b. Brown/white and brown: there should be continuity (low resistance).

7. Turn the ignition switch to the P (park) position. Use an ohmmeter set at $R \times 10$ and check for continuity between the red and brown terminals. There should be continuity (low resistance).

8. With the switch in the OFF and LOCK position there should be no continuity (infinite resistance) between any of the terminals.

Ignition Switch
Removal/Installation

1. Remove the right-hand side cover and the seat as described in Chapter Eleven.

2. Disconnect the battery negative lead.

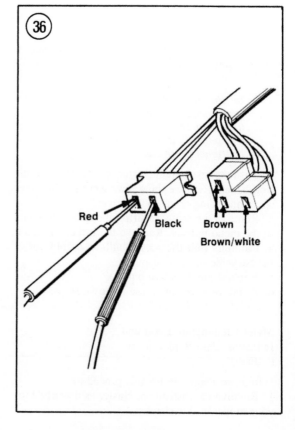

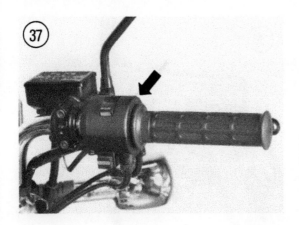

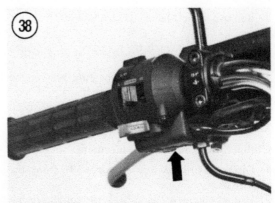

3. Remove the headlight and headlight case as described in this chapter.

4. Remove the fuse cover and fuse holder as described in this chapter.

5. Disconnect the 2 electrical connectors from the ignition switch.

6. Remove the bolt securing the ignition switch to the upper fork bridge.

7. Install by reversing these removal steps.

Ignition Switch
Disassembly/Assembly

1. Open the wire clamp on the wire harness at the base of the switch.

2. Insert the ignition key and turn the tumbler in between the ON and OFF positions. The key must be between the detents.

3. Push in on the lugs of the electrical switch portion, depressing them enough to clear the slots in the mechanical portion of the switch assembly.

4. Withdraw the electrical switch from the mechanical portion of the ignition switch.

5. Replace the defective component.

6. Assemble by reversing these steps.

Right-hand Switch Assembly
Removal/Installation

The right-hand switch assembly contains the engine stop switch and the starter switch. This assembly also contains the wires for the front brake light switch. If any of these parts are faulty the entire assembly must be replaced.

1. Remove the headlight and headlight case as described in this chapter.

2. Remove the fuse cover and fuse holder as described in this chapter.

3. Within the headlight case disconnect the 3-pin white connector.

4. Disconnect the 8-pin and 3-pin electrical connector from the backside of the fuse holder.

5. Remove the screws clamping the right-hand switch assembly together (**Figure 37**).

6. Unhook any straps securing the wires to the handlebar.

7. Remove the right-hand switch and wires from the frame.

8. Install a new switch by reversing these removal steps, noting the following.

9. Make sure to index the locating pin on the switch with the hole in the handlebar.

10. Make sure all connections are free of corrosion and are tight.

Left-hand Switch Assembly
Removal/Installation

The left-hand switch assembly contains the headlight dimmer switch, the horn button and the turn signal switch. This assembly also contains the wires for the clutch switch. If any of these parts are faulty the entire assembly must be replaced.

1. Remove the headlight and headlight case as described in this chapter.

2. Remove the fuse cover and fuse holder as described in this chapter.

3. Within the headlight case disconnect the two 2-pin white connectors and the 3-pin connector going to the headlight.

4. Also within the headlight case disconnect the following individual wires:

   a. Orange/white (left-hand turn signal bulb).

   b. Light blue/white (right-hand turn signal bulb).

   c. Orange (left-hand turn signal indicator).

   d. Light blue (right-hand turn signal indicator).

5. Disconnect the 5-pin connector (containing 4 wires) from the backside of the fuse holder.

6. Remove the screws clamping the left-hand switch assembly together (**Figure 38**).

7. Unhook any straps securing the wires to the handlebar.

7

8. Remove the left-hand switch and wires from the frame.

9. Install a new switch by reversing these steps, noting the following.

10. Make sure to index the locating pin on the switch with the hole in the handlebar.

11. Make sure all connections are free of corrosion and are tight.

Clutch Switch Testing/Replacement

1. Disconnect the wires (**Figure 39**) from the clutch switch.

2. Use an ohmmeter and check for continuity between the 2 terminals on the clutch switch. There should be no continuity (infinite resistance) with the clutch lever released. With the clutch lever applied there should be continuity (low resistance). If the switch fails either of these tests the switch must be replaced.

3. Remove the screw securing the clutch switch and remove the clutch switch from the clutch master cylinder.

4. Install a new switch by reversing these removal steps. Make sure all connections are free of corrosion and are tight.

Oil Pressure Switch Testing/Replacement

1. Remove the screws securing the ignition pulse generator cover (**Figure 40**) and remove the cover.

2. Pull back the rubber boot and remove the screw securing the connector (A, **Figure 41**) to the switch.

3. Unscrew the switch (B, **Figure 41**) from the upper crankcase.

4. Use an ohmmeter and check for continuity between the connector and the base of the switch. There should be continuity (low resistance) with no pressure applied. With 0.2 ± 0.4 kg/cm2 (2.8-5.6 psi) air pressure applied to the bottom of the switch there should be no continuity (high resistance). If it fails either of these tests the switch must be replaced.

5. Apply Loctite to the switch threads. Install the switch and tighten to 16-20 N•m (12-14 ft.-lb.).

6. Attach the wire. Make sure the connection is tight and free from oil.

7. Slide the rubber boot back into position.

8. Install the pulse generator cover and gasket and tighten the screws securely.

Gear Change Switch Testing/Replacement (CB550)

1. Remove the left-hand side cover.

2. Disconnect the 2-pin connector.

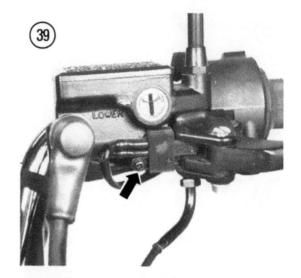

3. Use an ohmmeter and check for continuity between each wire in the connector (going to the gear change switch) as follows:

    a. With the transmission in NEUTRAL, check between the green wire and ground—there should be continuity (low resistance).

    b. With the transmission in OVERDRIVE (6th gear), check between the blue wire and ground—there should be continuity (low resistance).

If either of the wires shows no continuity the switch is faulty and must be replaced.

4. If the switch requires replacement, perform the following:

    a. Remove the left-hand rear crankcase cover (**Figure 42**).

    b. Remove the bolts (**Figure 43**) securing the switch to the external shift mechanism cover and remove the switch.

    c. Disconnect the 2-pin connector (**Figure 44**).

    d. Remove any bands securing the electrical wires to the frame and remove the switch and the wires from the frame.

5. Install by reversing these removal steps, noting the following.

6. Align the switch joint pin with the index mark (neutral position) on the switch (**Figure 45**).

7. Align the switch joint pin with the groove in the gear shift drum joint (**Figure 46**).

Gear Change Switch Testing/Replacement (CB650)

1. Remove the left-hand side cover.

2. Disconnect the 9-pin connector containing 7 wires (**Figure 44**).

3. Use an ohmmeter and check for continuity between each wire in the connector (going to the gear change switch) and ground. In each of the gear positions indicated in **Table 4** there should be continuity (low resistance). If any of the wires shows no continuity the switch is faulty and must be replaced.

4. If the switch requires replacement, perform the following:

    a. Remove the left-hand rear crankcase cover (**Figure 42**).

    b. Remove the bolts (**Figure 43**) securing the switch to the external shift mechanism cover and remove the switch.

    c. If still connected, disconnect the 9-pin connector (**Figure 44**).

    d. Remove any bands securing the wires to the frame and remove the switch and wires from the frame.

7

5. Install by reversing these removal steps, noting the following.

6. Align the switch joint pin with the index mark (neutral position) on the switch (**Figure 45**).

7. Align the switch joint pin with the groove in the gear shift drum joint (**Figure 46**).

Front Brake Light Switch
Testing/Replacement

1. Disconnect the wires to the brake light switch (**Figure 47**).

2. Use an ohmmeter and check for continuity between the 2 terminals on the brake light switch. There should be no continuity (infinite resistance) with the brake lever released. With the brake lever applied there should be continuity (low resistance). If the switch fails either of these tests the switch must be replaced.

3. Remove the screw securing the brake switch and remove the brake switch from the brake master cylinder.

4. Install a new switch by reversing these steps. Make sure all connections are free of corrosion and are tight.

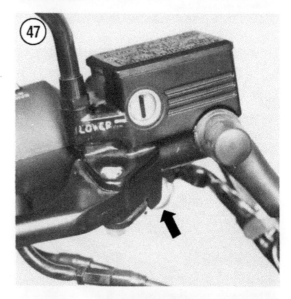

Rear Brake Light Switch
Testing/Replacement

1. Remove the right-hand side cover.

2. Disconnect the 2-pin connector to the rear brake light switch (**Figure 48**).

3. Use an ohmmeter and check for continuity between the 2 terminals on the brake light switch. There should be no continuity (infinite resistance) with the brake pedal released. With the brake pedal down or applied there should be continuity (low resistance). If the switch fails either of these tests the switch must be replaced.

4. Unhook the return spring (**Figure 49**) and unscrew the locknut securing the rear brake light

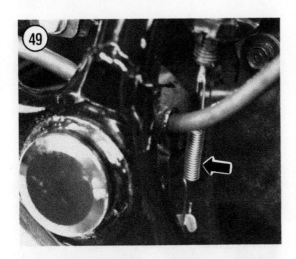

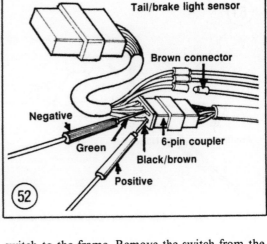

Tail/brake light sensor

Brown connector

Negative

Green

6-pin coupler

Black/brown

Positive

switch to the frame. Remove the switch from the frame.

5. Install a new switch by reversing these steps, noting the following.

6. Make sure all connections are free of corrosion and are tight.

7. Adjust the switch as described in this chapter.

Rear Brake Light Switch Adjustment

NOTE
The brake pedal height and free play must be adjusted prior to adjusting the switch. Refer to Chapter Three.

1. Turn the ignition switch ON.

2. Depress the brake pedal. The light should come on after the brake pedal has traveled 20 mm (3/4 in.).

3. To make the light come on earlier, hold the switch body (**Figure 50**) and turn the adjusting nut *clockwise* as viewed from the top. Turn *counterclockwise* to delay the light from coming on.

NOTE
Some riders prefer the light to come on a little early. This way, they can tap the pedal without braking to warn drivers who are following too closely.

ELECTRICAL COMPONENTS

This section contains information on electrical components other than switches.

Brake and Taillight Sensor Testing

1. Remove both side covers and the seat as described in Chapter Eleven.

2. Turn the ignition switch ON (**Figure 51**) and disconnect the brown wire at the sensor. Refer to **Figure 52**. The brake and taillight warning light on the indicator panel should come ON.

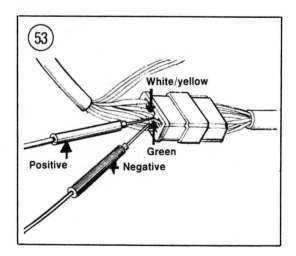

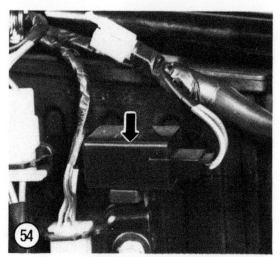

3. If the warning light does not come on, perform the following at the 6-pin connector and 3 loose wires:

   a. Use a 0-20 V *DC* voltmeter and measure the voltage between the black/brown (+) terminal and the green terminal (–) (**Figure 52**). There should be voltage (Honda does not provide voltage specifications). If no voltage is present, check out and repair the source circuit.

   b. If there is voltage at the black/brown terminal and the green terminal, measure the voltage between the white/yellow (+) and green (–) terminals (**Figure 53**). The specified voltage is 9-14 volts. If there is no voltage between the white/yellow and green terminals the sensor unit is faulty and must be replaced.

4. Reconnect the loose brown wire to the sensor.

5. Install the seat and side covers.

Turn Signal Relay Replacement

Remove the left-hand side cover. Pull the turn signal relay (**Figure 54**) out of the rubber mount.

Transfer the wires to the new relay and install the relay in the rubber mount. Install all parts removed.

Instrument Panel
Removal/Installation

1. Remove the right-hand side panel.

2. Disconnect the battery negative lead.

3. Remove the headlight and headlight housing as described in this chapter.

4. Remove the fuse cover and fuse holder.

5. From the fuse holder disconnect the 5-pin connector (containing 3 wires).

6A. On CB550 models, within the headlight case disconnect two 6-pin black connectors (containing 5 wires).

6B. On CB650 models, within the headlight case disconnect two 6-pin black connectors (containing 5 wires) and the 6-pin mini connector (gear position indicator).

7. Also in the headlight case, disconnect the following individual wires:

   a. Blue (high beam indicator).

   b. Orange (left-hand turn signal indicator).

   c. Light blue (right-hand turn signal indicator).

8. Carefully pull the connectors (within the headlight housing) out through the rear of the headlight housing.

9. Disconnect the speedometer cable from the meter housing.

10. Remove the nuts securing the instrument panel to the upper fork bridge.

11. Install by reversing these removal steps. Make sure all connectors are free of corrosion and are tight.

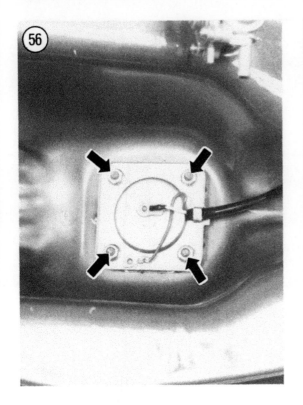

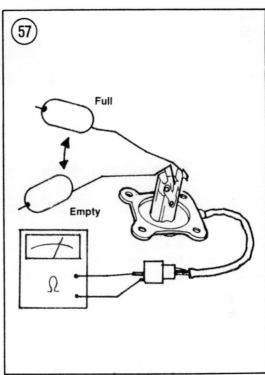

Horn Removal/Installation

1. Disconnect the connectors from the horns (**Figure 55**).
2. Remove the bolt securing each horn to the hydraulic brake line 3-way joint on the lower fork bridge and remove them.
3. Install by reversing these removal steps. Make sure the connections are tight and free of corrosion.

Horn Testing

Remove the horn as described in this chapter. Connect a 12-volt battery to the horn. If the horn is good, it will sound. If not, replace it.

Fuel Level Sensor
Removal/Testing/Installation

1. Remove the fuel tank as described in Chapter Six.
2. Drain all fuel from the tank into a clean sealable metal container. This fuel can be reused if kept clean.
3. Turn the fuel tank upside down on a blanket or soft cloths to protect the tank's finish.
4. Remove the nuts (**Figure 56**) securing the fuel level sensor to the bottom of the fuel tank.
5. Carefully remove the sensor and O-ring from the fuel tank. Be careful not to damage or bend the float arm during removal.

6. Use an ohmmeter and check the resistance between the green and the yellow/white wires (**Figure 57**). Move the arm from the full to the empty position. The specified resistance is as follows:
  a. Full: 4-10 ohms.
  b. Empty: 90-100 ohms.
If the fuel sensor does not meet these specifications the unit must be replaced.
7. If the fuel sensor checks out all right, connect the fuel sensor connector to the wire harness. Turn the ignition switch ON and perform Step 8.

NOTE
In the following test, the battery must be fully charged or the test results will be incorrect.

8. Move the float from the full (float at top) to empty (float at bottom) position and observe the fuel gauge indications. If the fuel gauge does not indicate the proper level the fuel gauge must be replaced.

Fuse Panel Removal/Installation

Refer to **Figure 58** for CB550 models or **Figure 59** for CB650 models.

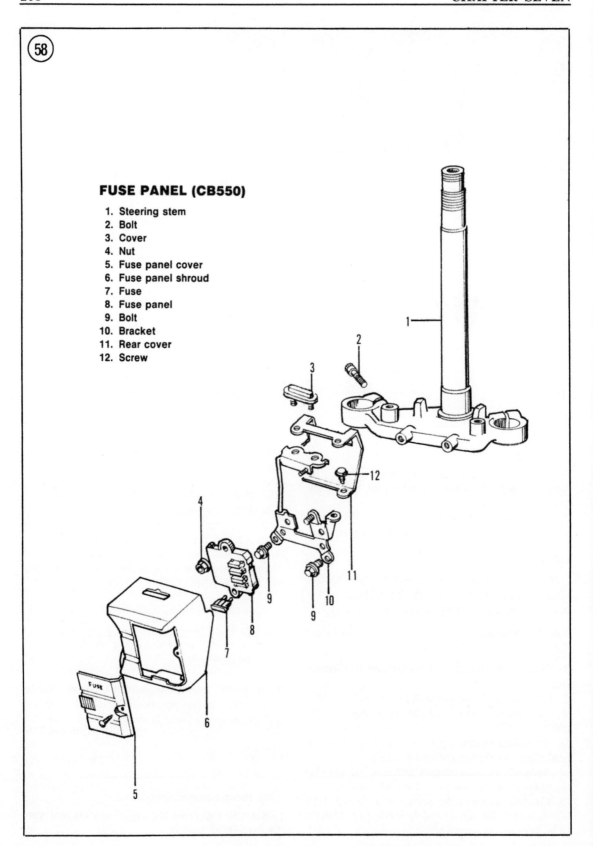

58

FUSE PANEL (CB550)

1. Steering stem
2. Bolt
3. Cover
4. Nut
5. Fuse panel cover
6. Fuse panel shroud
7. Fuse
8. Fuse panel
9. Bolt
10. Bracket
11. Rear cover
12. Screw

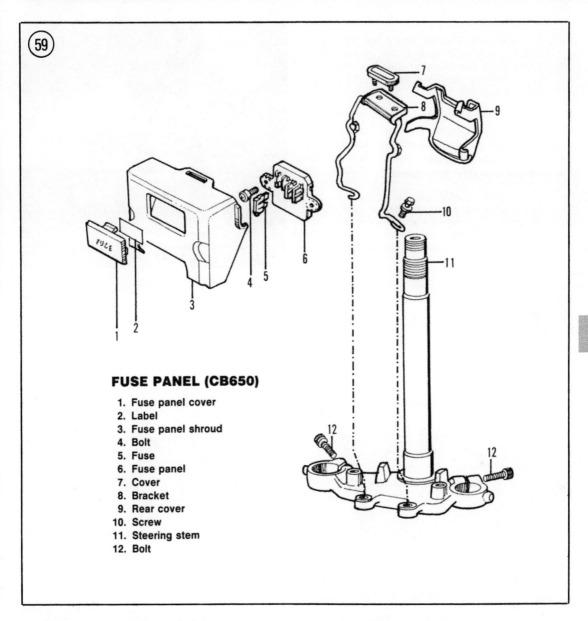

FUSE PANEL (CB650)

1. Fuse panel cover
2. Label
3. Fuse panel shroud
4. Bolt
5. Fuse
6. Fuse panel
7. Cover
8. Bracket
9. Rear cover
10. Screw
11. Steering stem
12. Bolt

1. Remove the right-hand side cover and disconnect the battery negative lead.

2. Remove the headlight and headlight housing (A, **Figure 60**) as described in this chapter.

3. Remove the fuse cover (B, **Figure 60**).

4. Remove the bolts securing the fuse holder to the bracket.

5. Pull the fuse holder forward enough to reach the connectors on the backside.

6. Disconnect each connector and note its location on the fuse panel.

7. Remove the fuse holder.

8. Install by reversing these removal steps. Make sure all connectors are free of corrosion and tight.

Fuses

There are 5 fuses. The main 30 amp fuse (fusible link) is located next to the starter solenoid and the remaining 4 are located in the fuse panel.

If the main fusible link blows, disconnect the connector (**Figure 61**) and open the fuse door. Remove the Phillips screws securing the fusible link and replace it (**Figure 62**). There is a spare link inside the panel.

The remaining fuses (all 15 amp) are located under the lid (**Figure 63**) on the fuse panel cover next to the horns on the front fork (**Figure 64**). Always carry spare fuses.

NOTE
The fuses have a unique shape (not the typical glass tube with metal ends). Carry extra fuses in your tool box as this type fuse may not be available everywhere.

Whenever a fuse blows, find out the reason for the failure before replacing the fuse. Usually the trouble is a short circuit in the wiring. This may be caused by worn-through insulation or a disconnected wire shorted to ground.

CAUTION
Never substitute aluminum foil or wire for a fuse. Never use a higher amperage fuse than specified. An overload could cause a fire and complete loss of the motorcycle.

Table 1 CHARGING SYSTEM OUTPUT TEST

rpm	Amperage output
1983	
2,500	2 amps
2,000-2,100	0 ± 1 amp
1,500	-5 ± 1 amp
1,000	-10 ± 1 amp
1984-ON	
2,500	2 amps
1,700-1,800	0 ± 1 amp
1,500	-3 ± 1 amp
1,000	-9 ± 1 amp

Table 2 STARTER TROUBLESHOOTING

Symptom	Probable Cause	Remedy
Starter does not work	Low battery	Recharge battery
	Worn brushes	Replace brushes
	Defective relay	Repair or replace
	Defective switch	Repair or replace
	Defective wiring connection	Repair wire or clean connection
	Internal short circuit	Repair or replace defective component
Starter action is weak	Low battery	Recharge battery
	Pitted relay contacts	Clean or replace
	Worn brushes	Replace brushes
	Defective connection	Clean and tighten
	Short circuit in commutator	Replace armature
Starter runs continuously	Stuck relay	Replace relay
Starter turns; does not turn engine	Defective starter clutch	Replace starter clutch

Table 3 REPLACEMENT BULBS

Item	Wattage	Number
Headlight (quartz bulb)	12V 60/55	H4 (Phillips 12342/99 or equivalent)
Tail/brakelight	12V 8/27W	SAE No. 1157
Turn signals		
Front	12V 23/8W	SAE No. 1034
Rear	12V 23 W	SAE No. 1073
Instrument lights	12V 3W	SAE No. 57
Indicator lights	12V 3W	SAE No. 57
High beam indicator	12V 3W	SAE No. 57
Neutral indicator	12V 3W	SAE No. 57
Oil pressure warning	12V 3W	SAE No. 57
Gear position light	12V 8W	SAE No. 1034

7

Table 4 GEAR POSITION SWITCH TEST

Gear position	Continuity between ground and wire color
CB550	
N	Green
6th	Blue
CB650	
1st	Yellow
N	Green
2nd	Blue
3rd	White
4th	Red
5th	Brown
6th	Black

CHAPTER EIGHT

FRONT SUSPENSION AND STEERING

This chapter describes repair and maintenance procedures for the front wheel and tire, forks and steering components.

Front suspension torque specifications are covered in **Table 1**. **Tables 1-4** are at the end of this chapter.

FRONT WHEEL

Removal

1. Place the bike on the centerstand or place wood block(s) under the engine or frame to support it securely with the front wheel off the ground.
2. Remove the speedometer cable setscrew. Pull the speedometer cable (**Figure 1**) free from the speedometer gear box.

NOTE
On dual-disc models, it is necessary to remove only one of the caliper assemblies, not both.

3. To remove the left-hand caliper assembly, perform the following:
  a. Remove the bolt (A, **Figure 2**) securing the left-hand brake caliper assembly to the front fork.
  b. Pivot the caliper assembly up on the pivot bolt (B, **Figure 2**) and off the brake disc.
  c. Remove the caliper assembly and tie it up to the front fork.

NOTE
Insert a piece of vinyl tubing or wood in both calipers in place of the brake discs. That way if the brake lever is inadvertently squeezed, the piston will not be forced out of the cylinder. If this does happen, the caliper may have to be disassembled to reseat the piston and the system will have to be bled. By using the wood, bleeding the brake is not necessary when installing the wheel.

4. Remove the chrome cap (**Figure 3**) from the top of the axle pinch bolt.
5. Remove the axle pinch bolt. Unscrew and withdraw the front axle (**Figure 4**).
6. Pull the wheel down and forward and remove it. Don't lose the axle spacer on the right-hand side.

CAUTION
*Do not set the wheel down on the disc surface as the disc may get scratched or warped. Set the sidewalls on 2 wood blocks (**Figure 5**).*

Installation

1. Make sure the axle bearing surfaces of the fork slider and axle are free from burrs and nicks.
2. Remove the vinyl tubing or pieces of wood from the brake calipers.

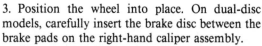

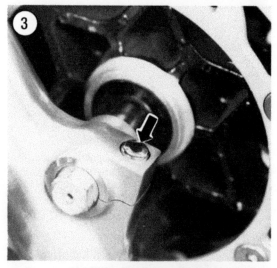

3. Position the wheel into place. On dual-disc models, carefully insert the brake disc between the brake pads on the right-hand caliper assembly.

4. Align the speedometer housing with the tang on the left-hand fork slider.

5. Make sure the axle spacer is in place (**Figure 6**).

6. Insert the front axle from the right-hand side and screw it into the left-hand fork leg.

7. Tighten the front axle to the torque specification listed in **Table 1**.

8. Install the pinch bolt and tighten it finger-tight only.

9. To install the left-hand caliper assembly, perform the following:

    a. Position the caliper assembly onto the pivot bolt and push the assembly all the way on.

    b. Pivot the caliper assembly down, being careful not to damage the brake pads.

    c. Install the bolt (A, **Figure 2**) securing the left-hand brake caliper assembly to the front fork and tighten to the torque specifications listed in **Table 1**.

10. Slowly rotate the wheel and install the speedometer cable into the speedometer housing. Install the cable setscrew.

11A. On single-disc models, tighten the pinch bolt to the specification in **Table 1**.

11B. On dual-disc models, perform the following:

    a. With a flat feeler gauge, measure the distance between the outside surface of the disc and the inside surface of the right-hand caliper holder (**Figure 7**). The clearance must be 0.7 mm (0.028 in.) or more.

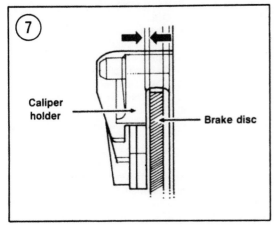

Caliper holder

Brake disc

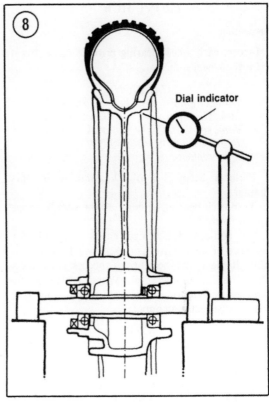

Dial indicator

8

b. If clearance is insufficient, pull the left-hand fork leg out until this dimension is achieved.

c. Tighten the pinch bolt and nut to the specification listed in **Table 1**.

12. After the wheel is completely installed, rotate it and apply the brakes a couple of times to make sure it rotates freely and the brake pads are against the disc(s) correctly.

Inspection

Measure the axial and radial runout of the wheel with a dial indicator as shown in **Figure 8**. The maximum axial and radial runout is 2.0 mm (0.08 in.). If the runout exceeds this dimension, check the wheel bearing condition.

If the wheel bearings are okay, the alloy wheel will have to be replaced as it cannot be serviced. Inspect the wheel for signs of cracks, fractures, dents or bends. If it is damaged in any way, it must be replaced.

WARNING
Do not try to repair any damage to an alloy wheel as it will result in an unsafe riding condition.

Check axle runout as described under *Front Hub Inspection* in this chapter.

FRONT HUB

Inspection

Inspect each wheel bearing prior to removing it from the wheel hub.

> *CAUTION*
> *Do not remove the wheel bearings for inspection purposes as they will be damaged during the removal process. Remove wheel bearings only if they are to be replaced.*

1. Perform Steps 1-3 of *Disassembly* in this chapter.
2. Turn each bearing by hand. Make sure bearings turn smoothly.
3. On non-sealed bearings, check the balls for evidence of wear, pitting or excessive heat (bluish tint). Replace the bearings if necessary; always replace as a complete set. When replacing the bearings, be sure to take your old bearings along to ensure a perfect matchup.

> *NOTE*
> *Fully sealed bearings are available from many bearing specialty shops. Fully sealed bearings provide better protection from dirt and moisture that may get into the hub.*

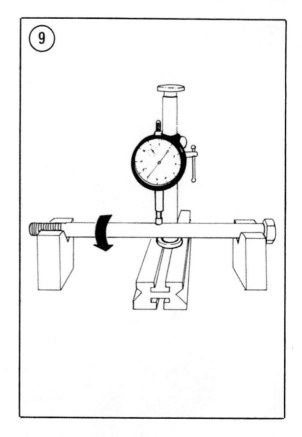

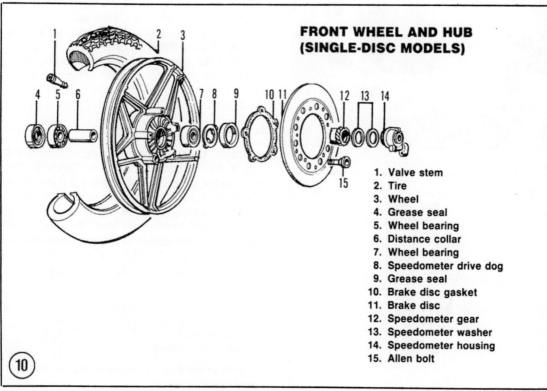

FRONT WHEEL AND HUB (SINGLE-DISC MODELS)

1. Valve stem
2. Tire
3. Wheel
4. Grease seal
5. Wheel bearing
6. Distance collar
7. Wheel bearing
8. Speedometer drive dog
9. Grease seal
10. Brake disc gasket
11. Brake disc
12. Speedometer gear
13. Speedometer washer
14. Speedometer housing
15. Allen bolt

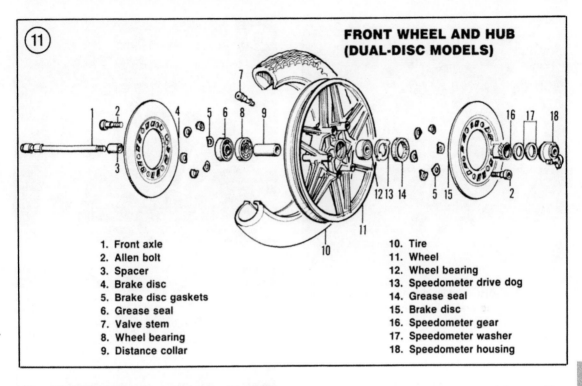

FRONT WHEEL AND HUB (DUAL-DISC MODELS)

1. Front axle
2. Allen bolt
3. Spacer
4. Brake disc
5. Brake disc gaskets
6. Grease seal
7. Valve stem
8. Wheel bearing
9. Distance collar
10. Tire
11. Wheel
12. Wheel bearing
13. Speedometer drive dog
14. Grease seal
15. Brake disc
16. Speedometer gear
17. Speedometer washer
18. Speedometer housing

8

4. Check the axle for wear and straightness. Use V-blocks and a dial indicator as shown in **Figure 9**. If the runout is 0.2 mm (0.01 in.) or greater, the axle should be replaced.

Disassembly

Refer to **Figure 10** for single-disc models or **Figure 11** for dual-disc models for this procedure.
1. Remove the front wheel as described in this chapter.
2. Remove the spacer (**Figure 12**) and grease seal (**Figure 13**) from the right-hand side.
3. Remove the speedometer housing, the grease seal and speedometer drive dog (**Figure 14**) from the left-hand side.
4. Before proceeding further, inspect the wheel bearings as described in this chapter. If they must be replaced, proceed as follows.
5A. On single-disc models, remove the bolts securing the brake disc. Remove the disc and the single damping shim located between the disc and the hub.

NOTE
On dual-disc models, each disc is designed to work on one side of the wheel. They are marked with an "R" (right-hand side) or "L" (left-hand side). Refer to **Figure 15**. *The discs must be reinstalled on the correct side of the wheel.*

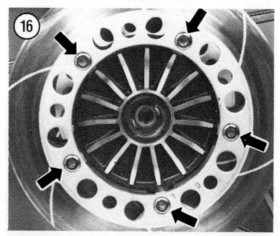

5B. On dual-disc models, remove the bolts (**Figure 16**) securing the brake disc. Remove the disc and the individual damping shims (at each bolt hole) located between the disc and the hub. Remove both discs.

6A. A special Honda tool set-up can be used to remove the wheel bearings as follows:

   a. Install the 15 mm bearing remover (Honda part No. 07746-0050400) into the right-hand bearing.

   b. Turn the wheel over (left-hand side up) on the workbench so the bearing remover is touching the workbench surface.

   c. From the left-hand side of the hub, install the bearing remover expander (Honda part No. 07746-0050100) into the bearing remover. Using a hammer, tap the expander into the bearing remover.

   d. Stand the wheel in a vertical position.

   e. Tap on the end of the expander and drive the right-hand bearing out of the hub. Remove the bearing and the distance collar.

   f. Repeat for the left-hand bearing.

6B. If special tools are not available, perform the following:

   a. To remove the right- and left-hand bearings and distance collar, insert a soft aluminum or brass drift into one side of the hub.

   b. Push the distance collar over to one side and place the drift on the inner race of the lower bearing.

   c. Tap the bearing out of the hub with a hammer, working around the perimeter of the inner race.

   d. Repeat for the other bearing.

7. Clean the inside and the outside of the hub with solvent. Dry with compressed air.

Assembly

1. On non-sealed bearings, pack the bearings with a good quality bearing grease. Work the grease in between the balls thoroughly; turn the bearing by hand a couple of times to make sure the grease is distributed evenly inside the bearing.

2. Blow any dirt or foreign matter out of the hub prior to installing the bearings.

> *CAUTION*
> *Install non-sealed bearings with the single sealed side facing outward. Tap the bearings squarely into place and tap on the outer race only. Use a socket (**Figure 17**) that matches the outer race diameter. Do not tap on the inner race or the bearing might be damaged. Be sure the bearings are completely seated.*

3. Install the right-hand bearing and press the distance collar into place.

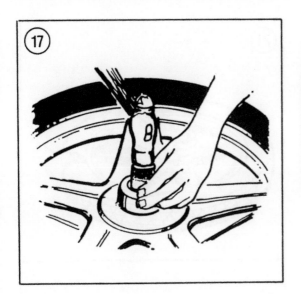

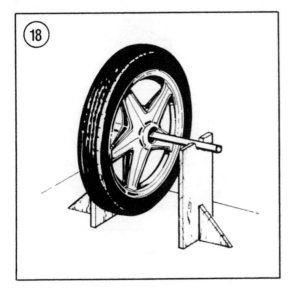

7. Align the tangs of the speedometer drive gear with the drive dog in the hub and install the speedometer gear box.

8. Install the spacer on the right-hand side.

9. Install the front wheel as described in this chapter.

WHEEL BALANCE

An unbalanced wheel is unsafe. Depending on the degree of unbalance and the speed of the motorcycle, the rider may experience anything from mild vibration to a violent shimmy which may even result in loss of control.

On alloy wheels, weights are attached to the rim. A kit of Tape-A-Weight or equivalent may be purchased from most motorcycle supply stores. This kit contains test weights and strips of adhesive-backed weights that can be cut to the desired weight and attached directly to the rim.

Before you attempt to balance the wheel, check to be sure the wheel bearings are in good condition and properly lubricated and that the brakes do not drag. The wheel must rotate freely.

1. Remove the wheel as described in this chapter or Chapter Nine.

2. Mount the wheel on a fixture such as the one shown in **Figure 18** so it can rotate freely.

3. Give the wheel a spin and let it coast to a stop. Mark the tire at the lowest point.

4. Spin the wheel several more times. If the wheel keeps coming to rest at the same point, it is out of balance.

5. Tape a test weight to the upper (or light) side of the wheel.

6. Experiment with different weights until the wheel, when spun, comes to a rest at a different position each time.

7. Remove the test weight and install the correct size adhesive-backed or clamp-on weight (**Figure 19**).

4. Install the left-hand bearing.

5A. On single-disc models, install the single damping shim on the hub and then install the brake disc. Install the bolts and tighten to the specification listed in **Table 1**.

5B. On dual-disc models, perform the following:

a. Position the brake disc on the correct side of the wheel (**Figure 15**). Discs are marked "R" (right-hand side) or "L" (left-hand side).

b. Install the individual damping shims onto the hub at each bolt hole and then install the brake disc.

c. Install the bolts and tighten to the specification listed in **Table 1**.

d. Repeat for the other disc.

6. Install the grease seal on the right-hand side.

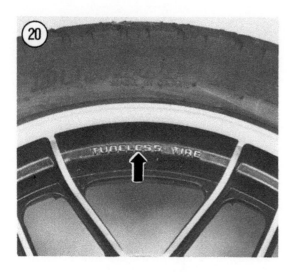

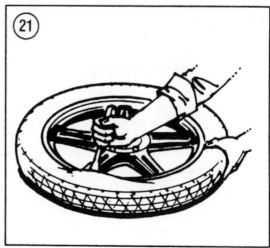

TIRE CHANGING

The rim of the alloy wheel is aluminum and the exterior appearance can easily be damaged. Special care must be taken with tire irons when changing a tire to avoid scratches and gouges to the outer rim surface. Insert scraps of leather between the tire iron and the rim to protect the rim from gouges. Honda offers rim protectors (part No. 07772-0020200) for this purpose that are very handy to use. All models are factory-equipped with tubeless tires and wheels designed specifically for use with tubeless tires.

> *WARNING*
> *Do not install tubeless tires on wheels designed for use only with tube-type tires. Personal injury and tire failure may result from rapid tire deflation while riding. Wheels for use with tubeless tires are so marked (**Figure 20**).*

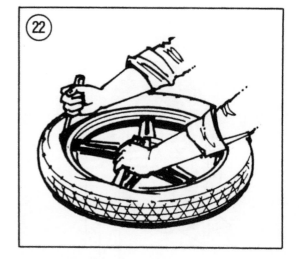

Removal

1. Remove the valve core to deflate the tire.
2. Press the entire bead on both sides of the tire into the center of the rim. Lubricate the beads with soapy water.
3. Insert the tire iron under the bead next to the valve (**Figure 21**). Force the bead on the opposite side of the tire into the center of the rim and pry the bead over the rim with the tire iron.
4. Insert a second tire iron next to the first to hold the bead over the rim. Then work around the tire with the first tire iron, prying the bead over the rim (**Figure 22**).
5. Stand the tire upright. Insert the tire iron between the second bead and the side of the rim that the first bead was pried over (**Figure 23**). Force the bead on the opposite side from the tire iron

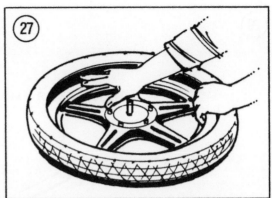

8

into the center of the rim. Pry the second bead off the rim, working around as with the first.

6. Honda recommends the tire valve stem be replaced whenever the tire is removed from the wheel.

Installation

1. Carefully inspect the tire for any damage, especially inside.

2. A new tire may have balancing rubbers inside. These are not patches and should not be disturbed. A colored spot near the bead indicates a lighter point on the tire. This spot (**Figure 24**) should be placed next to the valve stem.

3. Lubricate both beads of the tire with soapy water.

4. Place the backside of the tire into the center of the rim. The lower bead should go into the center of the rim and the upper bead outside. Work around the tire in both directions (**Figure 25**). Use a tire iron for the last few inches of bead (**Figure 26**).

5. Press the upper bead into the rim opposite the valve (**Figure 27**). Pry the bead into the rim on both sides of the initial point with a tire iron, working around the rim to the valve (**Figure 28**).

HANDLEBAR AND STEERING STEM

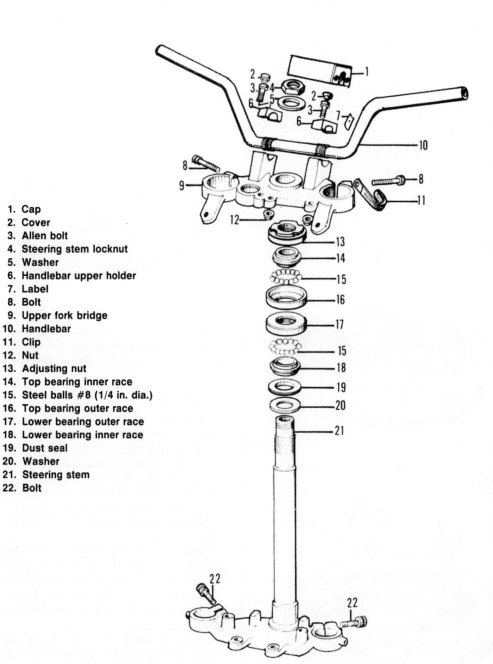

1. Cap
2. Cover
3. Allen bolt
4. Steering stem locknut
5. Washer
6. Handlebar upper holder
7. Label
8. Bolt
9. Upper fork bridge
10. Handlebar
11. Clip
12. Nut
13. Adjusting nut
14. Top bearing inner race
15. Steel balls #8 (1/4 in. dia.)
16. Top bearing outer race
17. Lower bearing outer race
18. Lower bearing inner race
19. Dust seal
20. Washer
21. Steering stem
22. Bolt

6. Check the bead on both sides of the tire for even fit around the rim.

7. Bounce the wheel several times, rotating it each time. This will force the tire beads against the rim flanges. After the tire beads are in contact with the rim evenly, inflate the tire to seat the beads.

NOTE
If you are unable to get an airtight seal this way, install an inflatable band around the circumference of the tire. Slowly inflate the band until the beads are seated against the rim flanges, then inflate the tire. If you still encounter trouble, deflate the inflation band and the tire. Apply additional lubricant to the beads and repeat the inflation procedure. Also try rolling the tire back and forth while inflating it.

8. Inflate the tire to more than the recommended inflation pressure for initial seating of the rim flanges. Once the beads are seated correctly, deflate the tire to the correct pressure. Refer to **Table 2**.

WARNING
Never exceed 4.0 kg/cm² (56 psi) inflation pressure as the tire could burst causing severe injury. Never stand directly over the tire while inflating it.

TIRE REPAIRS

Patching a tubeless tire on the road is very difficult. If both beads are still in place against the rim, a can of pressurized tire sealant may inflate the tire and seal the hole. The beads must be against the wheel for this method to work.

Another solution is to carry a spare inner tube that could be temporarily installed and inflated. This will enable you to get to a service station where the tire can be correctly repaired. Be sure that the tube is designed for use with a tubeless tire.

Honda and the tire industry recommend that the tubeless tire be patched from the inside. Therefore, do not patch the tire with an external type plug. If you find an external patch on a tire, it is recommended that it be patch-reinforced from the inside.

Due to the variations of material supplied with different tubeless tire repair kits, follow the instructions and recommendations supplied with the repair kit.

Honda recommends that the valve stem be replaced each time the tire is removed from the wheel.

HANDLEBAR

Removal

Refer to **Figure 29** this procedure.

1. Remove the right-hand side cover.
2. Disconnect the battery negative lead.
3. Remove the right-hand rear view mirror (A, **Figure 30**).
4. Disconnect the brake light switch electrical connector (B, **Figure 30**).
5. Remove the screws securing the right-hand handlebar switch assembly (C, **Figure 30**) and remove the electrical wires from the clips (D, **Figure 30**) on the handlebar.

CAUTION
Cover the frame with a heavy cloth or plastic tarp to protect it from accidental spilling of brake fluid. Wash any spilled brake fluid off any painted or plated surface immediately, as it will destroy the finish. Use soapy water and rinse thoroughly.

6. Remove the 2 bolts (E, **Figure 30**) securing the brake master cylinder and lay it over the frame. Keep the reservoir upright to minimize loss of brake fluid and to keep air from entering into the brake system. It is not necessary to remove the hydraulic brake line.

7. Remove the throttle assembly (F, **Figure 30**) and carefully lay the throttle assembly and cables over the fender or back over the frame. Be careful that the cables do not get crimped or damaged.

8. Remove the left-hand rear view mirror (A, **Figure 31**).

9. Disconnect the clutch switch wires (B, **Figure 31**).

10. Remove the 2 bolts securing the clutch master cylinder (C, **Figure 31**) and lay it over the frame. Keep the reservoir upright to minimize loss of hydraulic fluid and to keep air from entering into the clutch system. It is not necessary to remove the hydraulic line.

11. Disconnect the choke cable from the choke lever (D, **Figure 31**).

12. Remove the screws securing the left-hand handlebar switch assembly (E, **Figure 31**) and remove the electrical wires from the clips on the handlebar.

13. Remove the plastic plugs (**Figure 32**) and remove the Allen bolts (**Figure 33**) securing the handlebar upper holders in place. Remove the handlebar upper holders. Remove the handlebar.

14. To maintain a good grip on the handlebar and to prevent it from slipping down, clean the knurled section of the handlebar with a wire brush. It

8

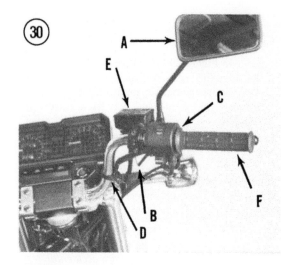

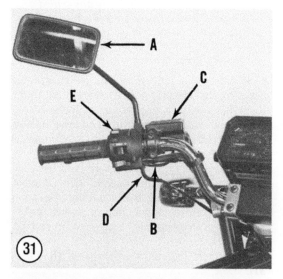

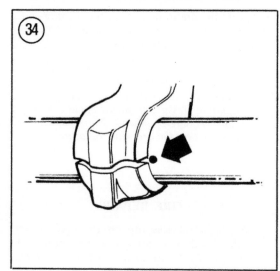

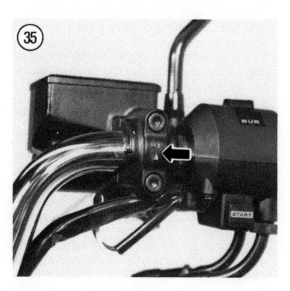

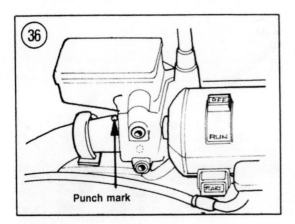

Punch mark

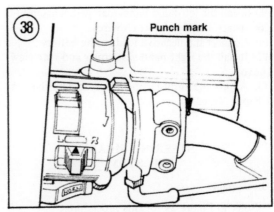

Punch mark

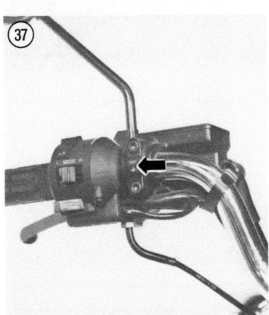

4. Apply a light coat of multipurpose grease to the throttle grip area on the handlebar prior to installing the throttle grip assembly.

> *NOTE*
> *When installing all assemblies, align the punch mark on the handlebar with the slit on the mounting bracket (**Figure 34**).*

5. Install the throttle grip assembly and right-hand switch assembly.
6. Install the brake master cylinder on the handlebar. Install the clamp with the punch mark facing down or with the "UP" arrow (**Figure 35**) facing up and align the clamp mating surface with the punch mark on the handlebar (**Figure 36**). Tighten the upper bolt first and then the lower bolt.

> *WARNING*
> *After installation is completed, make sure the brake lever does not come in contact with the throttle grip assembly when it is pulled on fully. If it does the brake fluid may be low in the reservoir; refill as necessary. Refer to **Front Disc Brakes** in Chapter Ten.*

7. Attach the choke cable to the choke lever.
8. Install the clutch master cylinder onto the handlebar. Install the clamp with the punch mark facing down or with the "UP" arrow (**Figure 37**) facing up and align the clamp mating surface with the punch mark on the handlebar (**Figure 38**). Tighten the upper bolt first and then the lower bolt.

> *WARNING*
> *After installation is completed, make sure the clutch lever does not come in contact with the hand grip assembly when it is pulled on fully. If it does the hydraulic fluid may be low in the reservoir; refill as necessary. Refer to **Clutch Master Cylinder** in Chapter Five.*

should be kept rough so it will be held securely by the holders. The holders should also be kept clean and free of any metal gouged loose by handlebar slippage.

Installation

1. Position the handlebar on the upper fork bridge so the punch mark on the handlebar is aligned with the top surface of the raised portion of the upper fork bridge.
2. Install the handlebar holders and install the Allen bolts. Tighten the forward bolts first and then the rear bolts. Tighten all bolts to the specification listed in **Table 1**. Install the plastic plugs.
3. After installation is complete, recheck the alignment of the handlebar punch mark.

9. Install the left-hand handlebar switch assembly.

10. Attach the clutch switch wires.

11. Connect the negative lead to the battery.

12. Install the right-hand side cover and rear view mirrors.

13. Adjust the throttle operation as described in Chapter Three.

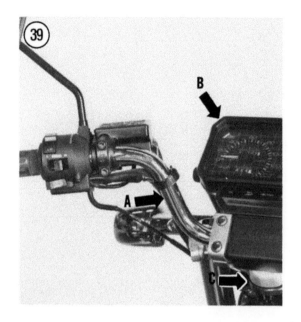

STEERING HEAD AND STEM

Disassembly

Refer to **Figure 29** for this procedure.

1. Remove the front wheel as described in this chapter.

2. Remove the handlebar (A, **Figure 39**) as described in this chapter.

3. Remove the headlight assembly as described in Chapter Seven.

4. Remove the instrument cluster (B, **Figure 39**) as described in Chapter Seven.

5. Remove the fuse panel as described in Chapter Seven.

6. Disconnect the electrical connector from the horns and remove the horns.

7. Remove the ignition switch as described in Chapter Seven.

8. Loosen the upper fork bridge bolts.

9. Remove the front fender and front forks as described in this chapter.

10. Remove the hydraulic brake 3-way hose connector assembly from the lower portion of the steering stem assembly. It is not necessary to disconnect the hydraulic lines. If the lines are disconnected or loosened, the brake system will have to be bled as described in Chapter Ten.

11. Remove the steering stem nut and washer (C, **Figure 39**) and remove the upper fork bridge.

12. Remove the steering stem adjust nut. To loosen the adjust nut, use a large drift and hammer or use the easily improvised tool shown in **Figure 40**.

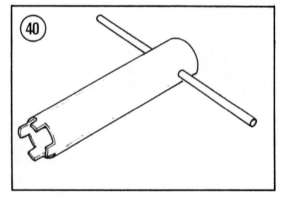

13. Have an assistant hold a large pan under the steering stem to catch any loose balls that may fall out while you carefully lower the steering stem.

14. Lower the steering stem assembly down and out of the steering head.

15. Remove the ball bearings from the upper and lower race. There are 37 ball bearings total (18 in the upper race and 19 in the lower race).

Inspection

1. Clean the bearing races in the steering head and the bearings with solvent.

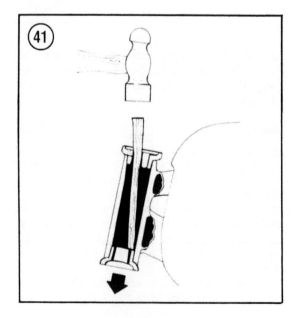

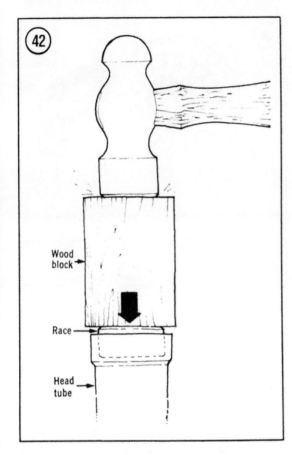

2. Check the welds around the steering head for cracks and fractures. If any are found, have them repaired by a competent frame shop or welding service.

3. Check the balls for pitting, scratches or discoloration indicating wear or corrosion. Replace them in sets if any are bad.

4. Check the races for pitting, galling and corrosion. If any of these conditions exist, replace the races as described in this chapter.

5. Check the steering stem for cracks and check its race for damage or wear. If this race or any race is damaged, the bearings should be replaced as a complete bearing set. Take the old races and bearings to your dealer to ensure accurate replacement.

Steering Head Bearing Races

The headset and steering stem bearing races are pressed into place. Because they are easily bent, do not remove them unless they are worn and require replacement.

***Headset bearing race
removal/installation***

> *NOTE*
> *The top and bottom bearing races are
> the same size.*

To remove the headset race, insert a hardwood stick or soft punch into the head tube (**Figure 41**) and carefully tap the race out from the inside. After it is started, tap around the race so neither the race nor the head tube is damaged.

To install the headset race, tap it in slowly with a block of wood, a suitable size socket or piece of pipe (**Figure 42**). Make sure the race is squarely seated in the headset race bore before tapping it into place. Tap the race in until it is flush with the steering head surface.

***Steering stem bearing
race and grease seal
removal/installation***

Refer to **Figure 43** for this procedure.

1. To remove the steering stem race (bottom bearing lower race) try twisting and pulling it up by hand. If it will not come off, carefully pry it up with a screwdriver; work around in a circle, prying a little at a time.

2. Remove the bottom bearing lower race, dust seal and dust seal washer.

3. Install the dust seal washer and dust seal. Slide the bottom bearing lower race over the steering stem with the bearing surface pointing up.

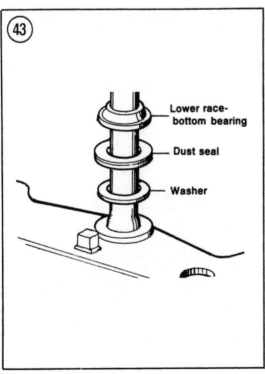

4. Tap the lower race down with a piece of hardwood; work around in a circle so the race will not be bent. Make sure it is seated squarely and is all the way down.

Assembly

Refer to **Figure 29** for this procedure.

1. Make sure the steering head and stem races are properly seated.

2. Apply a coat of cold grease to the upper bearing race cone and fit 18 ball bearings around it (**Figure 44**).

3. Apply a coat of cold grease to the lower bearing race cone and fit 19 ball bearings around it (**Figure 45**).

4. Install the steering stem into the head tube and hold it firmly in place.

5. Install the upper race of the top bearing.

6. Install the steering stem adjust nut and tighten it until it is snug against the upper race, then back it off 1/8 turn.

> *NOTE*
> *The adjusting nut should be just tight enough to remove both horizontal and vertical play (**Figure 46**), yet loose enough so the assembly will turn to both lock positions under its own weight after an assist.*

7. Install the upper fork bridge, washer and steering stem nut.

> *NOTE*
> *Steps 8-10 must be performed in this order to assure proper upper and lower fork bridge to fork alignment.*

8. Slide the fork tubes into position and tighten the lower fork bridge bolts to the specification listed in **Table 1**.

> *NOTE*
> *Install the fork tubes so the top of the fork tube aligns with the top surface of the upper fork bridge (**Figure 47**).*

9. Tighten the steering stem nut to the specification listed in **Table 1**.

10. Tighten the upper fork bridge bolts to the specification listed in **Table 1**.

11. Install the ignition switch as described in Chapter Seven.

12. Install the fuse panel and then the horns as described in Chapter Seven.

13. Install the brake 3-way hose connector assembly to the lower steering stem assembly. If any of the lines were disconnected or loosened, the brake system will have to be bled as described in Chapter Ten.

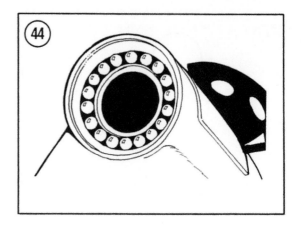

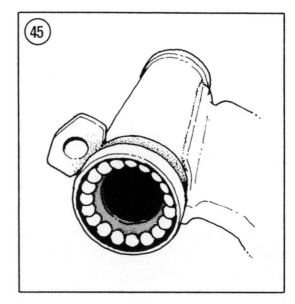

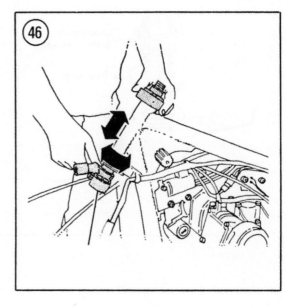

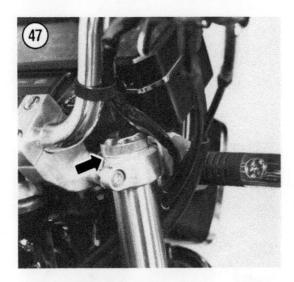

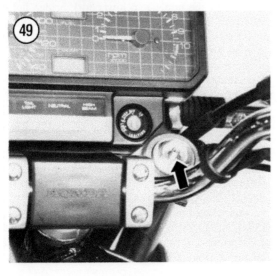

14. Install the instrument cluster and headlight as described in Chapter Seven.

15. Install the handlebar and front wheel as described in this chapter.

16. After a few hours of riding, the bearings have had a chance to seat; readjust the free play in the steering stem with the steering stem adjusting nut. Refer to Step 6.

Steering Stem Adjustment

If play develops in the steering system, it may only require adjustment. However, don't take a chance on it. Disassemble the stem and look for possible damage. Then reassemble and adjust as described in Step 6 of the assembly procedure.

FRONT FORK

The front suspension is a spring controlled, hydraulically damped, telescopic fork with air assist. On some models an anti-dive feature is built into the left-hand fork leg; this is covered separately in this chapter.

Before suspecting major trouble, drain the front fork oil and refill with the proper type and quantity; refer to Chapter Three. If you still have trouble, such as poor damping, a tendency to bottom or top out or leakage around the rubber seals, follow the service procedures in this section.

To simplify fork service and to prevent the mixing of parts, the legs should be removed, serviced and installed individually.

Removal

1. Remove the air valve cap (**Figure 48**) and *bleed off all air pressure* by depressing the valve stem (**Figure 49**).

> *WARNING*
> *Always bleed off all air pressure; failure to do so may cause personal injury when disassembling the fork assembly.*

> *WARNING*
> *Release the air pressure gradually. If released too fast, fork oil will spurt out with the air. Protect your eyes and clothing accordingly.*

> *NOTE*
> *The Allen bolt at the base of the slider has been secured with Loctite and is often very difficult to remove because the damper rod will turn inside the slider. It sometimes can be removed with an air impact driver. If you are unable to remove it, take the fork tubes to a dealer and have the screws removed.*

2. If the fork assembly is going to be disassembled, perform the following:

   a. Have an assistant hold the front brake on, and compress the front forks.

   b. Using a 6 mm Allen wrench, slightly loosen the Allen bolt at the base of the slider. If the bolt is loosened too much, fork oil may start to drain out of the slider.

   c. Release the forks and front brake.

3. Remove the caliper assembly(ies) as described in Chapter Ten. Tie the caliper assembly(ies) up to the frame.

4. Remove the front wheel as described in this chapter.

5. Remove the chrome cover caps. Remove the bolts securing the fork brace (A, **Figure 50**) and remove the fork brace.

6. Remove the bolts securing the front fender (B, **Figure 50**) and remove the fender.

7. Loosen, but do not remove, the fork top cap bolts.

8. Loosen the upper and lower fork bridge bolts (**Figure 51**).

9. Remove the fork tube. It may be necessary to slightly rotate the fork tube while pulling it down and out.

Installation

> *NOTE*
> *On models so equipped, be sure to install the fork leg with the anti-dive (TRAC) mechanism on the left-hand side of the bike.*

1. Insert the fork tube up through the lower and upper fork bridges.

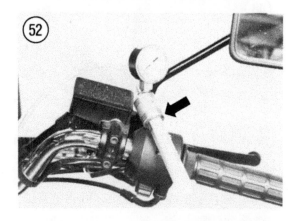

2. Align the top of the fork tube with the top surface of the upper fork bridge (**Figure 47**).

3. Tighten the upper and lower fork bridge bolts loosely at this time—just tight enough to hold them in place.

4. Tighten the upper and lower fork bridge bolts to the torque specifications listed in **Table 1**.

5. Install the fork brace and tighten the bolts to the torque specification listed in **Table 1**. Install the trim caps into the bolts.

6. Install the front fender and tighten the bolts securely.

7. Install the front wheel as described in this chapter.

8. Install the brake caliper assembly(ies) as described in Chapter Ten.

9. Make sure the front wheel is off the ground and inflate the forks to 0-0.4 kg/cm² (0-6 psi). Do not use compressed air, only use a small hand-operated air pump (**Figure 52**).

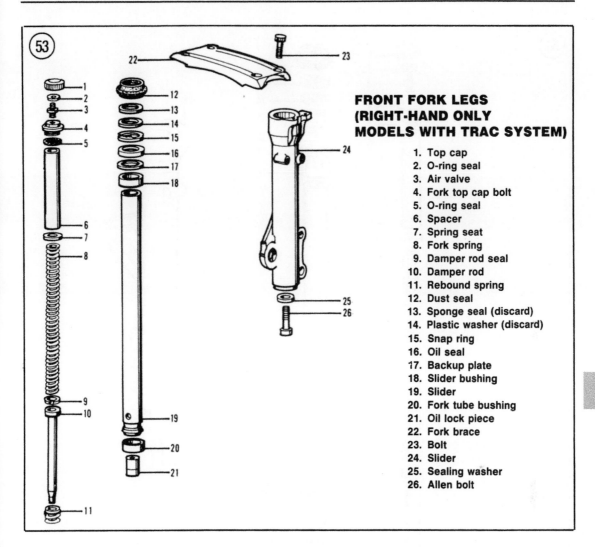

**FRONT FORK LEGS
(RIGHT-HAND ONLY
MODELS WITH TRAC SYSTEM)**

1. Top cap
2. O-ring seal
3. Air valve
4. Fork top cap bolt
5. O-ring seal
6. Spacer
7. Spring seat
8. Fork spring
9. Damper rod seal
10. Damper rod
11. Rebound spring
12. Dust seal
13. Sponge seal (discard)
14. Plastic washer (discard)
15. Snap ring
16. Oil seal
17. Backup plate
18. Slider bushing
19. Slider
20. Fork tube bushing
21. Oil lock piece
22. Fork brace
23. Bolt
24. Slider
25. Sealing washer
26. Allen bolt

WARNING
Never use any type of compressed gas as an explosion may be lethal. Never heat the fork assembly with a torch or place it near an open flame or extreme heat, as this will also result in an explosion.

CAUTION
Never exceed an air pressure of 3.0 kg/cm² (43 psi) as damage may occur to internal components of the fork assembly.

10. Take the bike off of the centerstand, apply the front brake and pump the forks several times. Recheck the air pressure and readjust if necessary.

Disassembly

On models *without* the TRAC system, refer to **Figure 53** for both the right- and left-hand fork legs. On models with the TRAC system refer to **Figure 53** for the right-hand fork leg and to **Figure 54** for the left-hand fork leg during the disassembly and assembly procedures.

1. Clamp the slider in a vise with soft jaws.

2. If not loosened during the fork removal sequence, loosen the Allen bolt on the bottom of the slider.

NOTE
This screw has been secured with Loctite and is often very difficult to remove because the damper rod will turn inside the slider. It sometimes can be removed with an air impact driver. If you are unable to remove it, take the fork tubes to a dealer and have the screws removed.

3. Remove the Allen bolt and gasket from the slider.

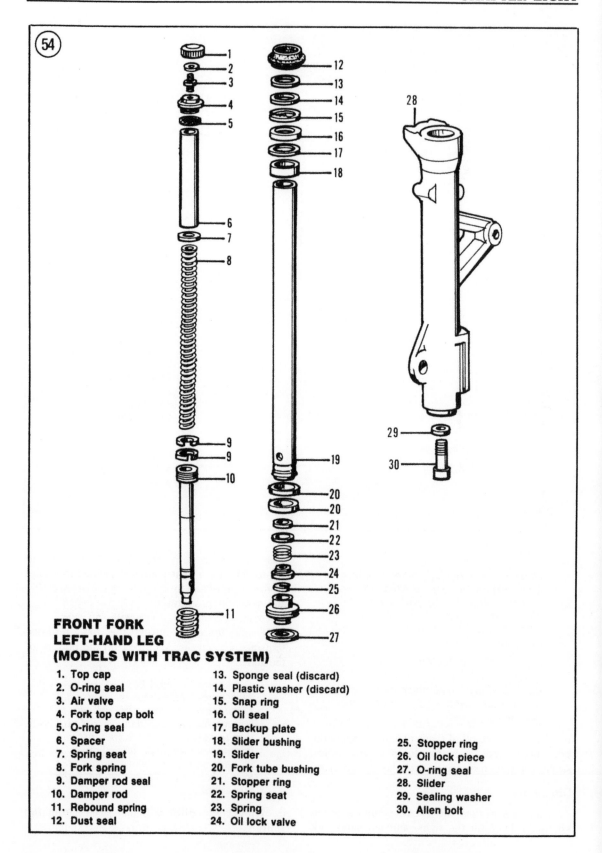

**FRONT FORK
LEFT-HAND LEG
(MODELS WITH TRAC SYSTEM)**

1. Top cap
2. O-ring seal
3. Air valve
4. Fork top cap bolt
5. O-ring seal
6. Spacer
7. Spring seat
8. Fork spring
9. Damper rod seal
10. Damper rod
11. Rebound spring
12. Dust seal
13. Sponge seal (discard)
14. Plastic washer (discard)
15. Snap ring
16. Oil seal
17. Backup plate
18. Slider bushing
19. Slider
20. Fork tube bushing
21. Stopper ring
22. Spring seat
23. Spring
24. Oil lock valve
25. Stopper ring
26. Oil lock piece
27. O-ring seal
28. Slider
29. Sealing washer
30. Allen bolt

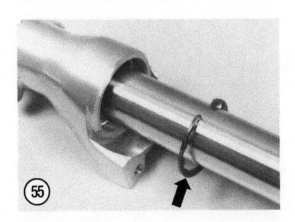

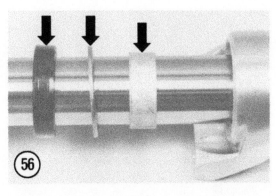

4. Hold the upper fork tube in a vise with soft jaws and loosen the fork top cap bolt/air valve assembly (if it was not loosened during the fork removal sequence).

WARNING
Be careful when removing the fork top cap bolt as the spring is under pressure. Protect your eyes accordingly.

5. Remove the fork top cap bolt from the fork.
6. Remove the spacer, the spring seat and the fork spring.
7. Remove the fork from the vise, pour the fork oil out and discard it. Pump the fork several times by hand to expel most of the remaining oil.
8. Remove the dust seal from the slider.

NOTE
*The Honda factory has determined that the sponge seal may work its way down into the oil seal and give the appearance of a worn or leaking oil seal. Therefore do **not** reinstall the sponge seal and plastic washer under the dust seal during the assembly procedure. If you purchase a new seal kit that still has these 2 parts in it, discard them. They are not to be used.*

9. Remove the sponge seal, the plastic washer and the circlip (**Figure 55**). Discard the sponge seal and plastic washer as they are not to be reinstalled.

NOTE
On this type of fork, force is needed to remove the fork tube from the slider.

10. Install the fork slider in a vise with soft jaws.
11. There is an interference fit between the bushing in the fork slider and the bushing on the fork tube. In order to remove the fork tube from the slider, pull hard on the fork tube using quick in and out strokes. Doing this will withdraw the bushing, backup ring and oil seal from the slider.

NOTE
It may be necessary to slightly heat the area on the slider around the oil seal prior to removal. Use a rag soaked in hot water; do not apply a flame directly to the fork slider.

12. Withdraw the fork tube from the slider.

NOTE
Do not remove the fork tube bushing unless it is going to be replaced. Inspect it as described in this chapter.

13. Turn the fork tube upside down and slide off the oil seal, backup ring and slider bushing (**Figure 56**) from the fork tube.

NOTE
Do not discard the slider bushing at this time. It will be used during the installation procedure.

14A. On models with the TRAC system, perform the following:
  a. On the right-hand fork slider, remove the oil lock piece, the damper rod and rebound spring.

NOTE
On the left-hand fork leg the oil lock piece and its O-ring will stay in the fork slider and cannot be removed.

  b. On the left-hand fork slider, remove the circlip, oil lock valve, spring and the spring seat from the damper rod. Remove the damper rod from the slider.
14B. On all other models, remove the oil lock piece, the damper rod and rebound spring on both fork legs.
15. Inspect the components as described in this chapter.

Assembly

1. Coat all parts with fresh DEXRON automatic transmission fluid or fork oil prior to installation.

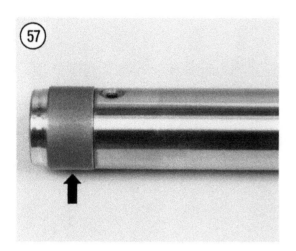

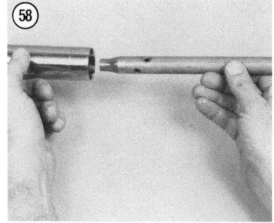

2. If removed, install a new fork tube bushing (**Figure 57**).

3A. On models with the TRAC system, perform the following:

  a. Into the right-hand fork slider, install the rebound spring onto the damper rod and insert this assembly into the fork tube (**Figure 58**).

  b. Into the left-hand fork slider, install the rebound spring onto the damper rod and insert this assembly in the fork tube (**Figure 59**). On the damper rod, install the spring seat, the spring, the oil lock valve and the circlip. Refer to **Figure 60** and **Figure 61**.

  c. Temporarily install the fork spring, spring seat, the spacer and fork top cap bolt to hold the damper rod in place.

  d. On the right-hand fork leg, install the oil lock piece onto the damper rod (**Figure 62**).

> *NOTE*
> *On the left-hand fork leg the oil lock*
> *piece is still inside the fork slider.*

  e. Install the upper fork assembly into the slider. Refer to **Figure 63** for the right-hand fork leg or to **Figure 64** for the left-hand fork leg.

3B. On all other models, perform the following:

  a. Into both the right- and left-hand fork slider, install the rebound spring on the damper rod and insert this assembly in the fork tube (**Figure 58**).

  b. Temporarily install the fork spring, spring seat (**Figure 65**), spacer and fork top cap bolt to hold the damper rod in place.

  c. On both fork legs, install the oil lock piece on the damper rod (**Figure 62**).

  d. Install the upper fork assembly into the slider (**Figure 63**).

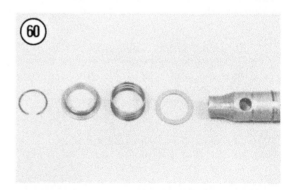

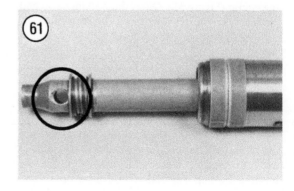

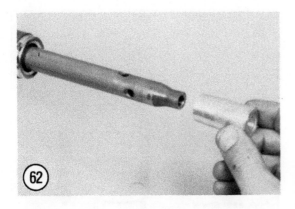

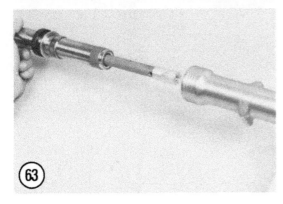

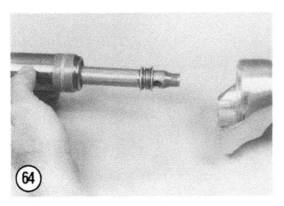

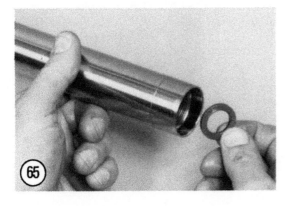

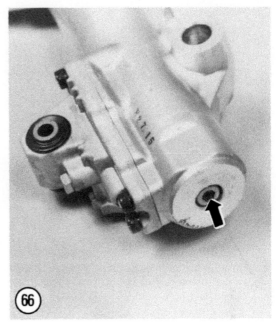

NOTE
Perform Steps 4-19 for one of the fork assemblies, then repeat Steps 4-19 for the other fork assembly.

4. Make sure the gasket is on the Allen head screw.
5. Apply Loctite Lock N' Seal to the threads of the Allen bolt prior to installation. Install it in the fork slider (**Figure 66**) and tighten to the specification in **Table 1**.
6. Slide the new fork slider bushing down the fork tube and rest it on the slider.
7. Slide the fork slider backup ring (flange side up) down the fork tube and rest it on top of the fork slider bushing.
8. Place the old fork slider bushing on top of the backup ring. Drive the bushing in the fork slider with Honda special tool Fork Seal Driver (part No. 07947-4630100). Drive the bushing in place until it seats completely in the recess in the slider. Remove the installation tool and the old fork slider bushing.

NOTE
*A piece of 2 in. galvanized pipe can also work as a tool. If both ends are threaded (a close nipple pipe fitting), wrap one end with duct tape (**Figure 67**) to prevent the threads from damaging the interior of the slider.*

9. To prevent damage to the inside of the new fork seal during installation, wrap the groove in the top of the fork tube with clear tape (something smooth and non-abrasive—do not use duct or masking tape).

10. Coat the new seal with ATF (automatic transmission fluid). Position the seal with the marking facing upward and slide it down on the fork tube. Drive the seal in the slider with Honda special tool Fork Seal Driver (part No. 07947-4630100); refer to **Figure 68**. Drive the oil seal in until the groove in the slider can be seen above the top surface of the oil seal. Remove the tape from the top of the fork tube.

NOTE
The slider seal can be driven in with a homemade tool as described in the NOTE following Step 8.

11. Install the circlip (**Figure 55**) sharp side up. Make sure the circlip is completely seated in the groove in the fork slider.

12. Install the dust seal. Remember, do *not* install the plastic washer and the sponge seal. Discard them if they are included in a new seal kit that you may have purchased. Refer to the Note regarding these items in the *Disassembly* procedure.

NOTE
Figure 69 *shows the correct placement of all components installed during Steps 6-12.*

13. Remove the fork top cap bolt, the spacer, the spring seat and the fork spring.

14. Fill the fork tube with the correct quantity of DEXRON automatic transmission fluid or fork oil. Refer to in Chapter Three.

15. Install the fork spring with the closer wound coils toward the top of the fork tube.

16. Install the fork seat and the spacer.

17. Inspect the O-ring seal (**Figure 70**) on the fork top cap bolt/air valve assembly; replace if necessary.

18. Install the fork top cap bolt/air valve assembly while pushing down on the spring. Start the bolt slowly, don't cross-thread it.

19. Place the slider in a vise with soft jaws and tighten the top fork cap bolt to the specification listed in **Table 1**.

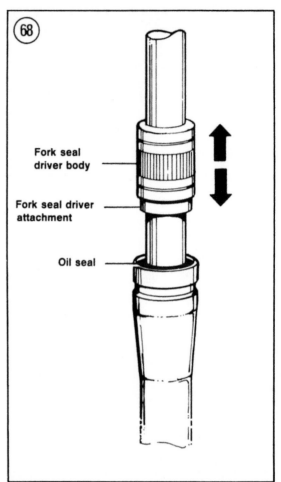

Fork seal driver body

Fork seal driver attachment

Oil seal

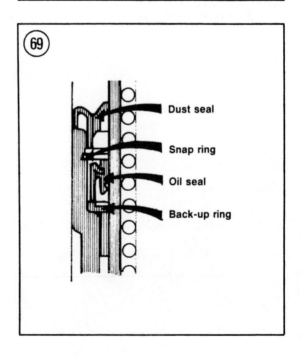

Dust seal

Snap ring

Oil seal

Back-up ring

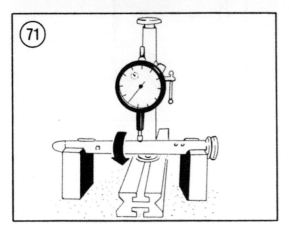

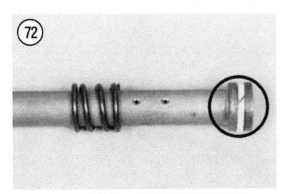

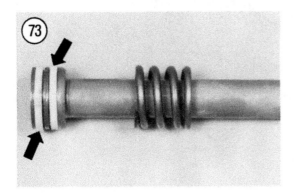

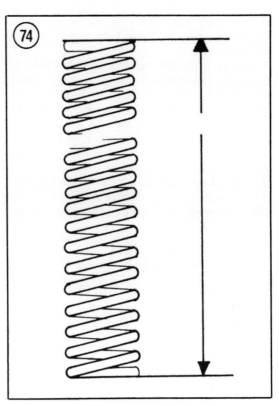

8

20. Perform Steps 4-19 for the other fork assembly.

21. Install the fork assemblies as described in this chapter.

Inspection

1. Thoroughly clean all parts in solvent and dry them. Check the fork tube for signs of wear or scratches.

2. Check the damper rod for straightness. **Figure 71** shows one method. The rod should be replaced if the runout is 0.2 mm (0.008 in.) or greater.

3. Carefully check the damper rod and piston ring(s) for wear or damage (**Figure 72**).

> *NOTE*
> *On models with the TRAC system, the damper rod on the left-hand side is equipped with 2 piston rings (**Figure 73**). The right-hand damper rod has only one.*

4. Check the upper fork tube for straightness. If bent or severely scratched, it should be replaced.

5. Check the lower slider for dents or exterior damage that may cause the upper fork tube to hang up during riding. Replace if necessary.

6. Measure the uncompressed length of the fork spring (not rebound spring) as shown in **Figure 74**.

If the spring has sagged to the service limit dimensions listed in **Table 3** the spring must be replaced.

7. Inspect the slider and fork tube bushings. If either is scratched or scored they must be replaced. If the Teflon coating is worn off so the copper base material is showing on approximately 3/4 of the total surface, the bushing must be replaced. Also check for distortion on the check points of the backup ring; replace as necessary. Refer to **Figure 75**.

8. Any worn or damaged parts should be replaced. Simply cleaning and reinstalling unserviceable components will not improve performance of the front suspension.

ANTI-DIVE
FRONT SUSPENSION

On models so equipped, the TRAC (Torque Reactive Anti-dive Control) system is integrated in the left-hand fork leg (**Figure 76**). The system

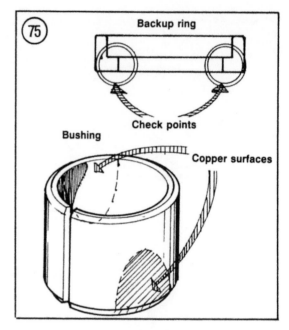

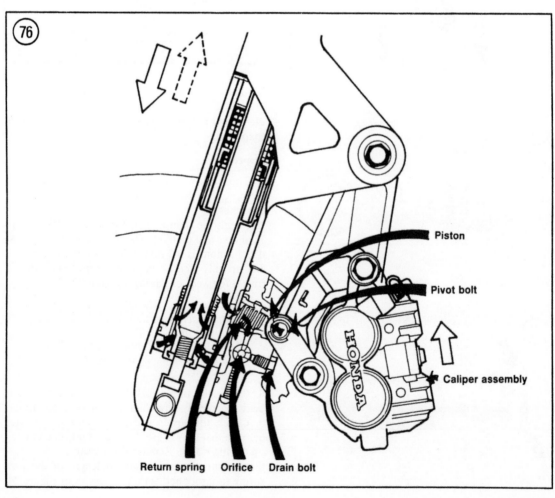

reacts to the forward weight transfer of the bike and rider(s) during braking. This system is strictly mechanical as opposed to some other systems that rely on brake fluid pressure.

The left-hand caliper assembly is pivot-mounted on the left-hand fork slider. As the brake is applied the caliper tries to move with the disc, thus pivoting the caliper assembly toward the TRAC unit. This action forces a tab on the caliper assembly against the piston and main spring in the TRAC unit.

As the TRAC piston moves, it uncovers the oil control orifice to restrict the fork leg's

compression-damping passageway, thus diverting the fork oil through a small secondary valve (oil control orifice). The internal damping action increases, the fork resists compression and the anti-dive action is created. The harder the brake is applied, the further the valve moves and the greater the anti-dive action. The secondary valve is adjustable and controls the damping rate. There are 4 different settings from soft to extra firm; the adjustment procedure is covered in this chapter.

If the forks encounter a bump when the brake is applied, the hydraulic pressure inside the fork leg progressively forces the main valve to open. By doing this the fork can move to absorb the shock.

Damping Adjustment

The fork damping rate can be adjusted to 4 different settings from soft to extra firm. The oil control orifice has 4 different diameter holes that control the flow rate of the fork oil, to either increase or decrease the damping rate.

Turn the oil control orifice (**Figure 77**) with a screwdriver to the desired damping position. Refer to **Table 4** for the different settings and their damping effect.

Disassembly/Assembly

Refer to **Figure 78** for this procedure.
1. Remove the left-hand fork leg and drain the fork oil as described in this chapter.

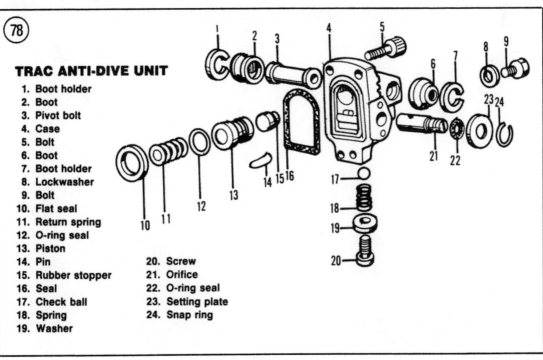

TRAC ANTI-DIVE UNIT

1. Boot holder
2. Boot
3. Pivot bolt
4. Case
5. Bolt
6. Boot
7. Boot holder
8. Lockwasher
9. Bolt
10. Flat seal
11. Return spring
12. O-ring seal
13. Piston
14. Pin
15. Rubber stopper
16. Seal
17. Check ball
18. Spring
19. Washer
20. Screw
21. Orifice
22. O-ring seal
23. Setting plate
24. Snap ring

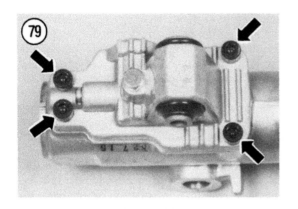

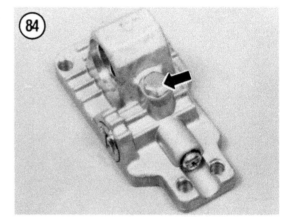

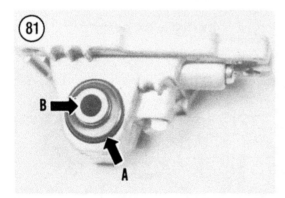

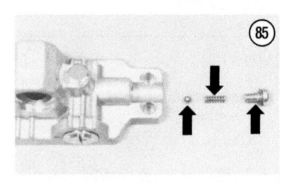

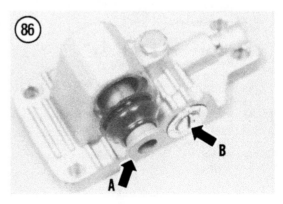

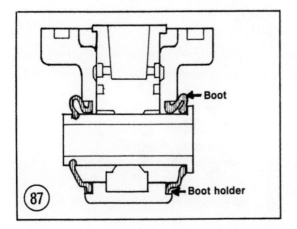

Boot

Boot holder

87

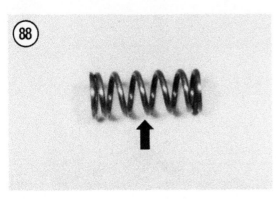

88

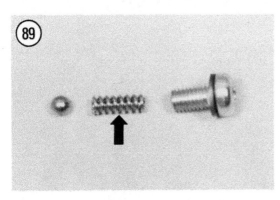

89

90

2. Remove the Allen bolts (**Figure 79**) securing the anti-dive case to the fork slider.

3. Remove the flat seal (**Figure 80**) from the fork slider.

4. Remove the case, the piston and the return spring from the slider.

5. Remove the boot and boot holders (A, **Figure 81**) from each side of the pivot bolt. Remove the pivot bolt (B, **Figure 81**).

6. Remove the pin (**Figure 82**) securing the oil control orifice.

7. Withdraw the oil control orifice (**Figure 83**) from the case.

8. Remove the drain screw (**Figure 84**).

9. Remove the screw, washer and check ball (**Figure 85**).

10. Assemble by reversing these removal steps, noting the following.

11. Apply Loctite Lock N' Seal to all screw and Allen bolt threads prior to installation.

12. Apply automatic transmission fluid to all O-ring seals prior to installation.

13. Apply a light coat of silicone grease to the pivot bolt collar prior to installation.

14. Install the pivot bolt collar with the large end (A, **Figure 86**) on the same side as the oil control orifice setting plate (B, **Figure 86**).

15. Install the pivot bolt collar boot holder as shown in **Figure 87**.

16. Tighten all screws and Allen bolts securely.

8

Inspection

1. Clean all parts in solvent and thoroughly dry with compressed air.

2. Inspect the piston return spring (**Figure 88**) and the check ball spring (**Figure 89**) for wear or damage.

3. Inspect the O-ring seal on the piston (**Figure 90**) and the oil control orifice (**Figure 91**) for wear or deterioration. Replace if necessary.

4. Inspect the flat seal on the fork leg (**Figure 92**) for wear or deterioration. Replace if necessary.

5. Inspect the pivot bolt collar boots and holders (**Figure 93**) for wear or deterioration. Replace if necessary.

6. Make sure the oil flow holes (**Figure 94**) in the oil control orifice and case (**Figure 95**) are clean and unobstructed. Blow out with compressed air; do not use a piece of wire as it may gouge the interior surface and disrupt the flow path.

7. Inspect the O-ring seal on the case (**Figure 96**) for wear or deterioration. Replace if necessary.

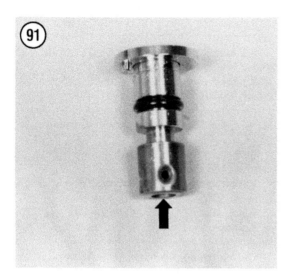

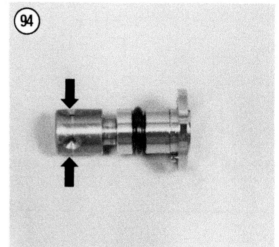

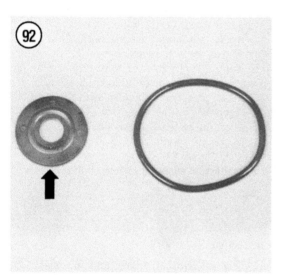

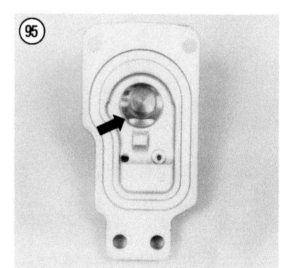

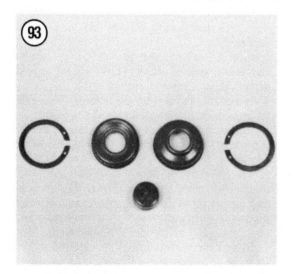

Table 1 FRONT SUSPENSION TORQUE SPECIFICATIONS

Item	N·m	ft.-lb.
Front axle	55-65	40-47
Front axle pinch bolt	15-25	11-18
Caliper mounting bolts (single-disc models)		
Upper mounting bolt	35-45	25-33
Lower mounting bolt	20-25	14-18
Caliper bolts (dual-disc models)		
Right-hand	30-40	22-29
Left-hand side		
Pivot bolt	25-35	18-22
Mounting bolt	20-25	14-18
Piston pin bolt	20-25	14-18
Caliper bracket bolt	35-45	25-33
Brake system union bolts	25-35	18-25
Brake disc bolts	35-40	25-29
Handlebar holder bolts	20-30	14-22
Fork bridge bolts		
Upper	9-13	7-9
Lower	45-55	33-40
Fork cap bolt	15-30	11-22
Fork brace Allen bolts	18-28	13-20
Fork slider Allen bolt	15-25	11-18
Steering stem nut	90-120	65-87

8

Table 2 TIRE INFLATION PRESSURE (COLD)

Tire size	Normal	Maximum load limit*
Front 100/90-19		
CB550	28 psi (2.00 kg/cm²)	28 psi (2.00 kg/cm²)
CB650	32 psi (2.25 kg/cm²)	32 psi (2.25 kg/cm²)
Rear 130/90-16		
CB550	28 psi (2.00 kg/cm²)	36 psi (2.50 kg/cm²)
CB650	32 psi (2.25 kg/cm²)	40 psi (2.80 kg/cm²)

* Up to maximum load limit of 200 lbs (90 kg) including total weight of motorcycle with accessories, rider(s) and luggage.

Table 3 FRONT FORK SPRING LENGTH

Standard	Service limit
CB550 551.5 mm (21.71 in.)	540.5 mm (21.28 in.)
CB650 522.9 mm (21.71 in.)	512.4 mm (20.2 in.)

Table 4 ANTI-DIVE ADJUSTMENT CHART*

Position	Damping effect
1	Soft
2	Standard
3	Firm
4	Extra firm

* The adjuster must be exactly on one of the numbered detents for the adjustment to be accurate.

CHAPTER NINE

REAR SUSPENSION AND FINAL DRIVE

This chapter includes repair and replacement procedures for the rear wheel, rear suspension components and the final drive unit. Tire service and wheel balancing are described in Chapter Eight.

Power from the engine is transmitted to the rear wheel by a drive shaft and the final drive unit.

Refer to **Table 1** for rear suspension torque specifications. **Tables 1-2** are located at the end of this chapter.

REAR WHEEL

Removal/Installation

1. Place the bike on the centerstand or block up the engine so the rear wheel clears the ground.
2. Completely unscrew the rear brake adjusting nut (**Figure 1**).
3. Depress the brake pedal and remove the brake rod from the pivot joint in the brake arm. Install the pivot joint and adjusting nut onto the brake rod to avoid misplacing them.
4. Remove the cotter pin, nut, washer and rubber washer from the rear brake torque link (**Figure 2**). Don't lose the bolt in the torque link.
5. Loosen the axle pinch bolt (A, **Figure 3**).
6. Remove the rear axle self-locking nut (**Figure 4**).

7. Remove the lower bolt on the right-hand shock absorber. Move the end of the shock up and out of the way.
8. Insert a drift or screwdriver into the hole in the end of the rear axle and withdraw the axle (B, **Figure 3**) from the right-hand side.
9. Slide the wheel to the right to disengage it from the hub drive splines and remove the wheel.
10. Don't lose the axle spacer in the rear brake panel.

Inspection

Measure the axial and radial runout of the wheel with a dial indicator as shown in **Figure 5**. The maximum axial and radial runout is 2.0 mm (0.08 in.). If the runout exceeds this dimension, check the wheel bearing condition.

If the wheel bearings are okay, the wheel will have to be replaced, as it cannot be serviced. Inspect the wheel for signs of cracks, fractures, dents or bends. If it is damaged in any way, it must be replaced.

> *WARNING*
> *Do not try to repair any damage to an alloy wheel as it will result in an unsafe riding condition.*

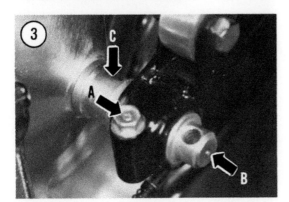

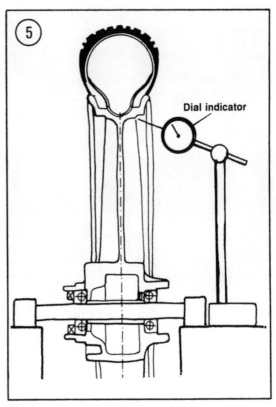

Dial indicator

Check axial runout as described under *Rear Hub Inspection* in this chapter.

Installation

1. Apply a light coat of grease (lithium based NLGI No. 2 grease with molybdenum disulfide) to the final driven flange spline (**Figure 6**) and to the rear wheel ring gear (**Figure 7**).

2. Position the rear wheel so the splines of the final driven flange and the final drive align. If necessary, turn the wheel a little to align the splines. Push the wheel to the left until it completely seats.

3. Loosen the final drive case nuts (**Figure 8**).

4. Make sure the axle spacer is installed between the rear brake panel and the swing arm (C, **Figure 3**).

5. Install the rear axle from the right-hand side and install the axle nut only finger-tight.

6. Move the brake torque link up into position and install the bolt (if removed), rubber washer, washer and nut. Tighten the nut to the torque specifications listed in **Table 1**.

7. Install a new cotter pin and bend the ends over completely.

8. Install the rear axle nut.

9. Insert a drift into the hole in the axle to keep the axle from turning.

9

10. Tighten the rear axle nut to the torque specifications listed in **Table 1**.

11. Tighten the final drive gear case nuts, then the axle pinch bolt and the brake panel stopper bolt to the torque specifications listed in **Table 1**.

12. Make sure the return spring is installed on the brake rod and reinstall the brake rod in the pivot joint. Install the adjusting nut.

13. After the wheel is installed, completely rotate it and apply the brake several times to make sure it rotates freely and the brakes work properly.

14. Adjust the rear brake free play as described in Chapter Three.

REAR HUB

Inspection

Inspect each wheel bearing prior to removing it from the wheel hub.

CAUTION
Do not remove the wheel bearings for inspection as they will be damaged during removal. Remove wheel bearings only if they are to be replaced.

1. Perform Step 1 and Step 2 of *Disassembly* in this chapter.

2. Turn each bearing by hand. Make sure the bearings turn smoothly.

3. On non-sealed bearings, check the balls for evidence of wear, pitting or excessive heat (bluish

tint). Replace the bearings if necessary; always replace as a complete set. When replacing the bearings, be sure to take your old bearings along to ensure a perfect matchup.

NOTE
Fully sealed bearings are available from many bearing specialty shops. Fully sealed bearings provide better protection from dirt and moisture that may get into the hub.

4. Check the axle for wear and straightness. Use V-blocks and a dial indicator as shown in **Figure 9**. If the runout is 0.2 mm (0.01 in.) or greater, the axle should be replaced.

5. Inspect the splines of the final driven flange. If any are damaged the flange must be replaced.

Disassembly

Refer to **Figure 10** for this procedure.

1. Remove the rear wheel as described in this chapter.

2. Remove the bolts securing the final driven flange and remove the flange (**Figure 7**).

3. Before proceeding further, inspect the wheel bearings as described in this chapter. If they must be replaced, proceed as follows.

4A. A special Honda tool set-up can be used to remove the wheel bearings as follows:

   a. Install the 17 mm bearing remover (Honda part No. 07746-0050500) into the right-hand bearing.

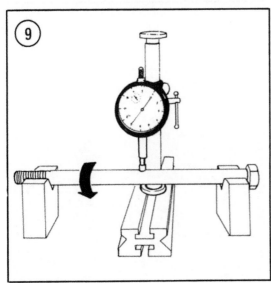

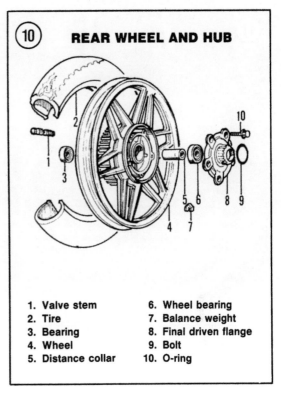

REAR WHEEL AND HUB

1. Valve stem	6. Wheel bearing
2. Tire	7. Balance weight
3. Bearing	8. Final driven flange
4. Wheel	9. Bolt
5. Distance collar	10. O-ring

b. Turn the wheel over (left-hand side up) on the workbench so the end of the bearing remover is touching the workbench surface.

c. From the left-hand side of the hub, install the bearing remover expander (Honda part No. 07746-050100) into the bearing remover. Using a hammer, tap the expander into the bearing remover with a hammer.

d. Stand the wheel in a vertical position.

e. Tap on the end of the expander and drive the right-hand bearing out of the hub. Remove the bearing and the distance collar.

f. Repeat for the left-hand bearing.

4B. If special tools are not available, perform the following:

a. To remove the right- and left-hand bearings and distance collar, insert a soft aluminum or brass drift into one side of the hub.

b. Push the distance collar over to one side and place the drift on the inner race of the lower bearing.

c. Tap the bearing out of the hub with a hammer, working around the perimeter of the inner race.

d. Repeat for the other bearing.

5. Clean the inside and outside of the hub with solvent. Dry with compressed air.

6. Clean the inside and the outside of the final driven flange with solvent. Remove and discard the O-ring seal at the base of the splines. Dry with compressed air.

7. Inspect the splines. If any are damaged the final driven flange must be replaced.

Assembly

1. On non-sealed bearings, pack the bearings with a good quality bearing grease. Work the grease in between the balls thoroughly; turn the bearing by hand a couple of times to make sure the grease is distributed evenly inside the bearing.

2. Blow any dirt or foreign matter out of the hub prior to installing the bearings.

3. Pack the hub with multipurpose grease.

9

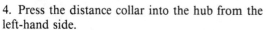

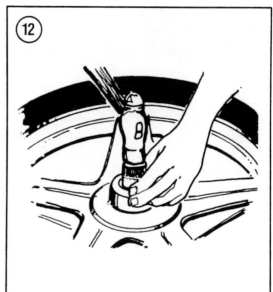

4. Press the distance collar into the hub from the left-hand side.

CAUTION
Install the standard bearings (they are sealed on one side only) with the sealed side facing out (Figure 11). Tap the bearings squarely into place and tap only on the outer race. Use a socket (Figure 12) that matches the outer race diameter. Do not tap on the inner race or the bearing will be damaged. Be sure to tap the bearings in until they seat completely.

5. Install the left-hand bearing into the hub.
6. Install the right-hand bearing into the hub.
7. Install the final driven flange and bolts. Tighten the bolts to the torque specifications listed in **Table 1**.
8. Install a new O-ring seal onto the base of the splines on the final driven flange.
9. Install the rear wheel as described in this chapter.

FINAL DRIVE UNIT

Removal

1. Remove the rear wheel as described in this chapter.
2. Drain the final drive unit oil as described in Chapter Three.
3. Remove the lower nut and washer (**Figure 13**) securing the left-hand shock absorber to the final

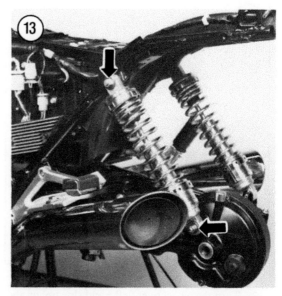

drive unit. Pivot the shock absorber up and out of the way.
4. Remove the nuts and washers (**Figure 8**) securing the final drive unit to the swing arm.
5. Pull the final drive unit and drive shaft straight back until it is disengaged from the splines on the output shaft.

Inspection

The final drive unit and drive shaft require a considerable number of special Honda tools for

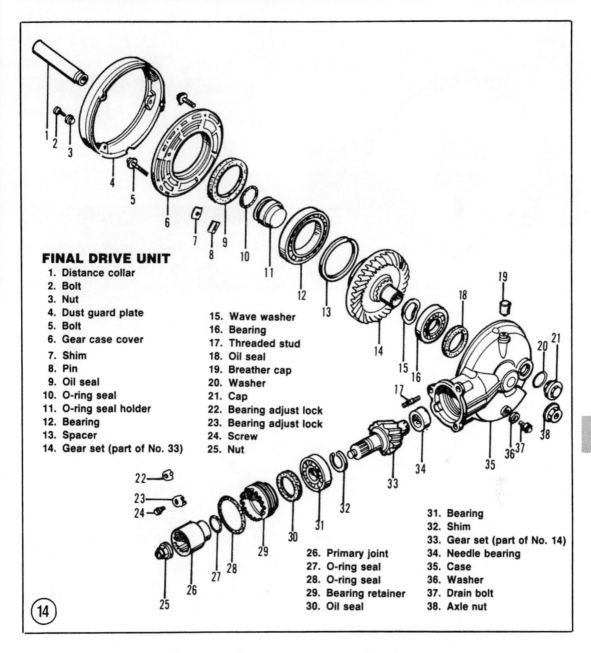

FINAL DRIVE UNIT
1. Distance collar
2. Bolt
3. Nut
4. Dust guard plate
5. Bolt
6. Gear case cover
7. Shim
8. Pin
9. Oil seal
10. O-ring seal
11. O-ring seal holder
12. Bearing
13. Spacer
14. Gear set (part of No. 33)
15. Wave washer
16. Bearing
17. Threaded stud
18. Oil seal
19. Breather cap
20. Washer
21. Cap
22. Bearing adjust lock
23. Bearing adjust lock
24. Screw
25. Nut
26. Primary joint
27. O-ring seal
28. O-ring seal
29. Bearing retainer
30. Oil seal
31. Bearing
32. Shim
33. Gear set (part of No. 14)
34. Needle bearing
35. Case
36. Washer
37. Drain bolt
38. Axle nut

(14)

disassembly and assembly. The price of all of these tools could be more than the cost of most repairs or seal replacement by a dealer.

Figure 14 shows the internal components of the final drive unit.

1. Check that the dust cover flange bolt (A, **Figure 15**) is in place and is tight.

2. Inspect the splines on the final driven ring gear (B, **Figure 15**). If they are damaged or worn the ring gear must be replaced. If these splines are damaged, also inspect the splines on the rear wheel final driven flange; it may also need to be replaced.

3. Inspect the splines for the universal joint on the drive shaft (**Figure 16**). If they are damaged or worn, the drive shaft must be replaced. If these splines are damaged, also inspect the splines in the output shaft; it may also need to be replaced.

4. Inspect the threads on the mounting studs (**Figure 17**) for wear or damage. Replace any damaged studs.

5. Check that gear oil is not leaking from either side of the unit (ring gear side or pinion joint side). If there are traces of oil leakage, take the unit to a dealer for oil seal replacement.

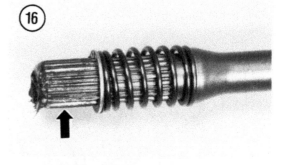

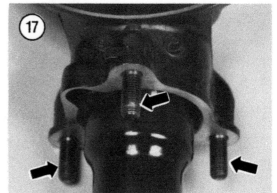

Installation

1. Apply a light coat of molybdenum disulfide grease (NGLI No. 2) to the splines of the drive shaft joint and the final driven spline.

2. Shift the transmission into NEUTRAL.

3. Pull back the rubber boot at the front end of the swing arm to gain access to the universal joint.

4. Install the final drive unit and drive shaft into the swing arm. Slightly rotate the universal joint to align the splines of the drive shaft with the universal joint and push the final drive unit and drive shaft all the way in until they stop.

5. Install the final drive unit nuts only finger-tight at this time. Do not tighten the nuts until the rear wheel and rear axle are in place.

6. Install the rear wheel as described in this chapter. Tighten the final drive unit nuts to the specifications listed in **Table 1**.

7. Install the left-hand shock absorber lower washer and nut and tighten to the torque specifications listed in **Table 1**.

8. Refill the final drive unit with the correct amount and type of gear oil. Refer to Chapter Three.

UNIVERSAL JOINT

Removal/Inspection/Installation

1. Remove the swing arm as described in this chapter.

2. Remove the universal joint from the engine output shaft.

3. Clean the universal joint in solvent and thoroughly dry with compressed air.

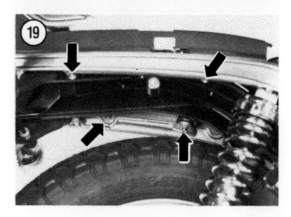

REAR SHOCK ABSORBER (CB550)

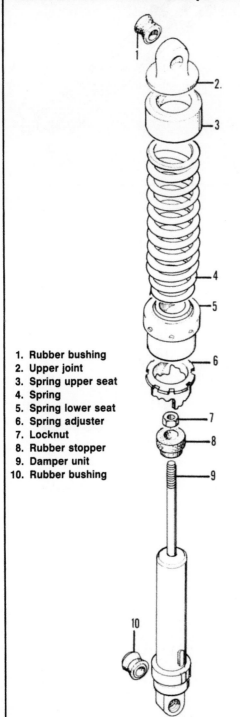

1. Rubber bushing
2. Upper joint
3. Spring upper seat
4. Spring
5. Spring lower seat
6. Spring adjuster
7. Locknut
8. Rubber stopper
9. Damper unit
10. Rubber bushing

4. Inspect the universal joint pivot points for play. Rotate the joint in both directions. If there is noticeable side play the universal joint must be replaced.

5. Inspect the splines at each end of the universal joint. If they are damaged or worn, the universal joint must be replaced.

NOTE
If these splines are damaged, also inspect the splines in the final drive unit and the engine output shaft; they may also need to be replaced.

6. Apply a light coat of molybdenum disulfide grease (NGLI No. 2) to both spline ends.

7. Install the universal joint onto the engine output shaft.

8. Install the swing arm as described in this chapter.

SHOCK ABSORBERS

Removal/Installation

Removal and installation of the rear shocks is easier if done separately. The remaining unit will support the rear of the bike and maintain the correct relationship between the top and bottom shock mounts.

1. Place the bike on the centerstand.

2. Remove both side covers and the seat as described in Chapter Eleven.

3. On CB650 models, perform the following:
   a. Remove the bolts (**Figure 18**) securing the rear hand grip and remove the grip.
   b. Remove the bolts (**Figure 19**) securing the rear handrail assembly and remove the handrail assembly.
   c. Partially remove the handrail assembly and disconnect all electrical connectors to the rear turn signals and brake/taillight units.

4. Adjust both shocks to their softest setting, completely counterclockwise.

5. Remove the nuts or bolts (**Figure 13**) securing the upper and lower end of the shock absorber.

6. Pull the shock straight off the upper mounting studs on the frame and remove the shock.

7. Install by reversing these removal steps. Tighten the upper mounting nut and lower mounting bolt or nut to the torque specifications listed in **Table 1**.

8. Repeat for the other side.

**Disassembly/Inspection/
Assembly (CB550)**

Refer to **Figure 20** for this procedure.

9

The shock is spring-controlled and hydraulically damped. The shock damper unit is sealed and cannot be serviced. Service is limited to removal and replacement of the damper unit and the spring.

> *WARNING*
> *Without the proper tool, this procedure can be dangerous. The spring can fly loose, causing injury. For a small bench fee, a dealer can do the job for you.*

> *NOTE*
> *Two additional components have to be added to the basic compressor tool. They are included in a kit (Honda part No. 07959-MB10000).*

1. Replace the base, the spring guide and the clevis of the shock compressor with the new parts included in the kit.
2. Install the shock absorber in a compression tool as shown in **Figure 21**. This is a special tool available from Honda dealers. It is the Rear Shock Absorber Compressor Tool (Honda part No. 07959-3290001).

> *CAUTION*
> *Be sure the compressor tool base is properly adjusted to fit the shock spring seat and that the clevis pin is screwed all the way into the clevis.*

3. Compress the shock spring just enough (approximately 30 mm) to gain access to the locknut.
4. Place the upper joint in a vise with soft jaws and loosen the locknut (**Figure 22**).
5. Completely unscrew the upper joint. This part may be difficult to break loose as Loctite Lock N' Seal was applied during assembly.
6. Release the spring tension and remove the shock from the compression tool.
7. Remove the spring upper seat, spring, spring lower seat and the spring adjuster from the damper unit.
8. Measure the spring free length (**Figure 23**). The spring must be replaced if it has sagged to the service limit listed in **Table 2** or less.
9. Check the damper unit for leakage and make sure the damper rod is straight.

> *NOTE*
> *The damper unit cannot be rebuilt; it must be replaced as a unit.*

10. Inspect the rubber bushings in the upper and lower joints. Replace if necessary.
11. Inspect the rubber stopper. If it is worn or deteriorated, remove the locknut and slide off the rubber stopper. Replace with a new one.

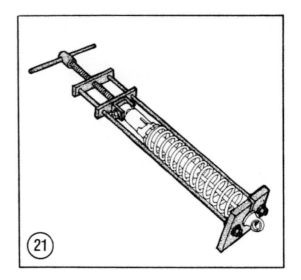

Upper joint   Locknut
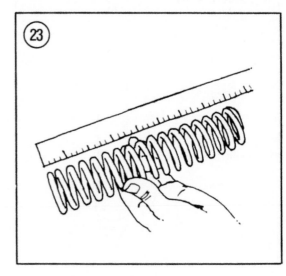

REAR SHOCK ABSORBER (CB650)

1. Adjuster stop ring
2. Washer
3. Adjuster cover
4. Spring
5. Damper adjuster
6. Rubber bushing
7. Upper joint
8. Washer
9. Nut
10. Steel ball
11. Spring
12. Steel ball
13. O-ring
14. Upper retainer
15. Adjust rod
16. Spring
17. Spring lower seat
18. Label
19. Spring adjuster
20. Locknut
21. Rubber stopper
22. Damper unit
23. Bolt
24. Nut
25. Washer
26. Cap nut
27. Washer
28. Shock absorber (complete)
29. Rubber bushing
30. Collar

(24)

12. Assembly is the reverse of these disassembly steps, noting the following.

13. Install the spring with the closer wound coils toward the top.

14. Apply Loctite Lock N' Seal to the threads of the damper rod prior to installing the locknut. Temporarily screw the locknut all the way down and tight against the end of the threads.

15. Apply Loctite Lock N' Seal to the threads of the damper rod prior to installing the upper joint. Screw the upper joint on all the way. Secure the upper joint in a vise with soft jaws and tighten the locknut along with the damper rod against the upper joint.

> *NOTE*
> *After the locknut is tightened completely the locknut must be against the bottom surface of the upper joint and against the end of the threads on the damper rod.*

16. Align the spring upper seat to the upper joint when releasing the spring compressor tool.

Disassembly/Inspection/Assembly (CB650)

Refer to **Figure 24** for this procedure.

The shock is spring-controlled and hydraulically damped. The shock damper unit is sealed and cannot be serviced. Service is limited to removal and replacement of the damper unit and the spring.

> *WARNING*
> *Without the proper tool, this procedure can be dangerous. The spring can fly loose, causing injury. For a small bench fee, a dealer can do the job for you.*

1. Compress the spring just enough (approximately 30 mm) to gain access to the adjuster stop ring. Remove the stop ring.

2. Hold the shock in the upright position and remove the washer and the adjuster cover.

3. Remove the damper adjuster.

4. Note the location of the steel balls in the upper retainer. Mark their location with a permanent marker pen so they will be installed in the exact same location.

5. Remove the steel balls and adjuster springs.

> *NOTE*
> *One additional component has to be added to the basic compressor tool. It is the attachment (Honda part No. 07967-KC10000).*

6. Insert the attachment (Honda part No. 07967-KC10000) in the shock's spring at the upper

9

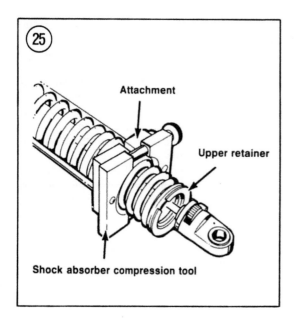

Attachment

Upper retainer

Shock absorber compression tool

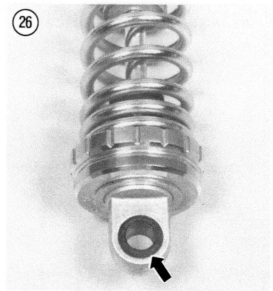

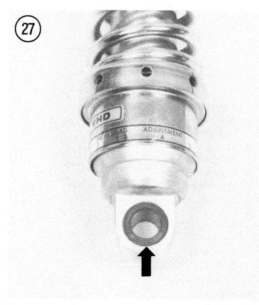

end of the shock (**Figure 25**). Install the shock absorber in a compression tool as shown in **Figure 21**. This is a special tool available from Honda dealer. It is the Rear Shock Absorber Compressor Tool (Honda part No. 07959-3290001).

7. Compress the shock spring just enough (approximately 30 mm) to gain access to the upper retainer. Remove the upper retainer.

8. Release the spring tension and remove the shock from the compression tool.

9. Remove the spring upper seat, spring, spring lower seat and spring adjuster.

10. Measure the spring free length (**Figure 23**). The spring must be replaced if it has sagged to the service limit listed in **Table 2** or less.

11. Check the damper unit for leakage and make sure the damper rod is straight.

NOTE
The damper unit cannot be rebuilt; it must be replaced as a unit.

12. Inspect the rubber bushings in the upper (**Figure 26**) and lower joints (**Figure 27**). Replace if necessary.

13. Inspect the rubber stopper (**Figure 28**). If it is worn or deteriorated, remove the locknut and slide off the rubber stopper. Replace with a new one.

14. Assembly is the reverse of these disassembly steps, noting the following.

15. Install the spring with the closer wound coils toward the top.

16. Install the steel balls into their correct location as noted in Step 4. Install the adjuster springs.

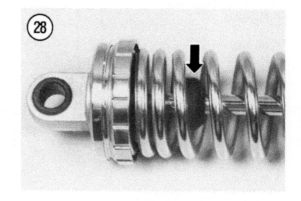

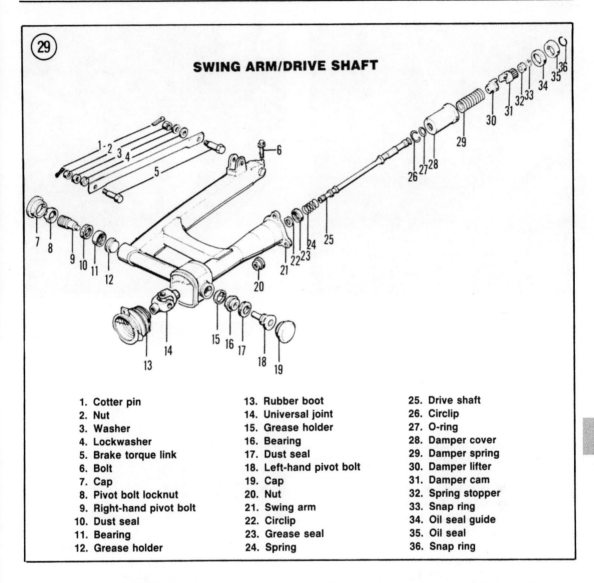

SWING ARM/DRIVE SHAFT

1. Cotter pin	13. Rubber boot	25. Drive shaft
2. Nut	14. Universal joint	26. Circlip
3. Washer	15. Grease holder	27. O-ring
4. Lockwasher	16. Bearing	28. Damper cover
5. Brake torque link	17. Dust seal	29. Damper spring
6. Bolt	18. Left-hand pivot bolt	30. Damper lifter
7. Cap	19. Cap	31. Damper cam
8. Pivot bolt locknut	20. Nut	32. Spring stopper
9. Right-hand pivot bolt	21. Swing arm	33. Snap ring
10. Dust seal	22. Circlip	34. Oil seal guide
11. Bearing	23. Grease seal	35. Oil seal
12. Grease holder	24. Spring	36. Snap ring

SWING ARM

In time, the roller bearings will wear and will have to be replaced. The condition of the bearings can greatly affect handling performance and if worn parts are not replaced they can produce erratic and dangerous handling. Common symptoms are wheel hop, pulling to one side during acceleration and pulling to the other side during braking.

A Honda special tool is required for loosening and tightening of the pivot adjusting bolt locknut. The tool is the Swing Arm Pivot Locknut Wrench (Honda part No. 07908-ME90000). This tool is required for proper and safe installation of the swing arm. If this locknut is not tightened correctly it may allow the adjusting bolt to work loose. This

could result in the swing arm working free from the right-hand side of the frame causing a serious accident.

Refer to **Figure 29** for this procedure.

Removal

1. Place the bike on the centerstand.
2. Remove both side covers and remove the seat as described in Chapter Eleven.
3. Remove the exhaust system as described in Chapter Six.
4. Remove the rear wheel as described in this chapter.
5. Remove the final drive unit and drive shaft as described in this chapter.
6. Remove the lower mounting bolt or nut and washer securing each shock absorber.

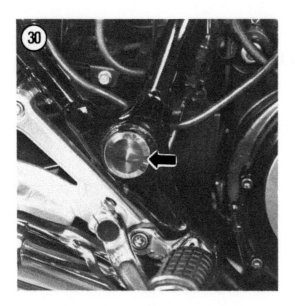

NOTE
It is not necessary to remove the shock absorber units, just pivot the units up and out of the way.

7. Grasp the rear end of the swing arm and try to move it from side to side in a horizontal arc. There should be no noticeable side play. If play is evident and the pivot adjusting bolt is tightened correctly, the bearings should be replaced.

8. Pull the rubber boot free from the output gear case on the engine.

9. Remove the right-hand pivot cap (**Figure 30**).

10. Use the special tool, Swing Arm Pivot Locknut Wrench (Honda part No. 07908-ME90000), to loosen the locknut (A, **Figure 31**) on the right-hand side.

11. Use a 17 mm Allen wrench and remove the right-hand adjusting bolt (B, **Figure 31**).

12. Remove the left-hand pivot cap.

13. Remove the left-hand pivot bolt (**Figure 32**).

14. Pull back on the swing arm, free it from the frame and remove it from the frame.

Installation

1. Position the swing arm into the mounting area of the frame. Align the holes in the swing arm with the holes in the frame.

2. Apply a light coat of grease to the inner end of both the right- and left-hand pivot bolts. Install the right- and left-hand pivot bolts.

3. If removed, install the rubber boot onto the swing arm with the "UP" mark facing up.

4. Make sure the swing arm is properly located in the frame and then tighten the left-hand pivot bolt to the torque specifications listed in **Table 1**.

5. Loosen the left-hand pivot bolt and retighten to the correct torque specification.

6. Tighten the right-hand pivot bolt to the torque specifications listed in **Table 1**. Loosen it and retighten to the correct torque specification.

7. Move the swing arm up and down several times to make sure all components are properly seated.

8. Retighten the right-hand pivot bolt to the correct torque specification.

9. On the right-hand side, use the special tool, Swing Arm Pivot Locknut Wrench (Honda part No. 07908-ME90000), to tighten the locknut (A, **Figure 31**) to the torque specification listed in **Table 1**. Hold the right-hand pivot bolt with a 17 mm Allen wrench to make sure the pivot bolt does not move while tightening the locknut.

10. Install the final drive unit and drive shaft assembly as described in this chapter.

11. Install the rear shock absorbers as described in this chapter.

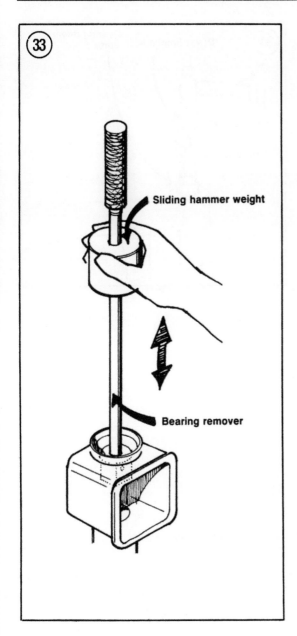

Sliding hammer weight

Bearing remover

The bearing outer race must be removed with special tools available from a Honda dealer. The special tools are as follows:

  a. Bearing remover: Honda part No. 07936-4150000.
  b. Handle: Honda part No. 07936-3710100.
  c. Slide hammer weight: Honda part No. 07936-3710200.
  d. Driver handle A: Honda part No. 07749-00100000.
  e. Bearing driver outer: Honda part No. 07746-0010200.

1. Remove the swing arm as described in this chapter.
2. Remove the dust seal and bearing assembly from each side of the swing arm.
3. Secure the swing arm in a vise with soft jaws.

> *NOTE*
> *These special tools grab the outer race and then withdraw it from the swing arm with the use of a tool similar to a body shop slide hammer.*

4. Remove the left-hand bearing race first (**Figure 33**). To remove the left-hand bearing race, perform the following:

  a. Remove the attachment from the bearing remover.
  b. Install the bearing remover through the hole in the bearing and install a 29 mm (OD) washer and the attachment on the shaft.
  c. Install the slide hammer and handle onto the bearing remover.
  d. Slide the weight on the hammer several times to move the race out slightly. Slide the weight up and down until the bearing race is removed.
  e. Remove the grease holder.

5. Turn the swing arm over in the vise and repeat for the other end.
6. Thoroughly clean out the inside of the swing arm with solvent and dry with compressed air.
7. Apply a light coat of waterproof grease to all parts prior to installation.
8. Install a new grease holder into the bearing receptacle.

> *NOTE*
> *Either the right- or left-hand bearing race can be installed first.*

9. To install the new roller bearing outer race, place the bearing driver outer over the bearing race

12. Install the rear wheel as described in this chapter.
13. Install the exhaust system as described in Chapter Six.

Bearing Replacement

The swing arm is equipped with a roller bearing at each end. The inner race and roller bearing will come right out (no force needed) after the grease seal is removed. The bearing outer race is pressed in place and has to be removed with force. The race will get distorted when removed, so don't remove it unless absolutely necessary.

9

and drive the race into place with the driver handle A and a hammer (**Figure 34**). Drive the race into place slowly and squarely. Make sure it is properly seated.

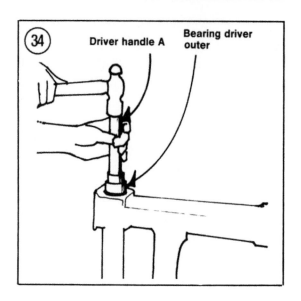

> *CAUTION*
> *Never reinstall a bearing outer race that has been removed. During removal it becomes slightly damaged and is no longer true to alignment. If installed, it will damage the roller bearing assembly and create an unsafe riding condition.*

10. Repeat Step 9 for the other bearing race.

11. Install a new roller bearing and dust seal on each end of the swing arm.

12. Install the swing arm as described in this chapter.

Table 1 REAR SUSPENSION TORQUE SPECIFICATIONS

Item	N·m	ft.-lb.
Rear axle nut	60-80	43-58
Rear axle pinch bolt	20-30	14-22
Shock absorber mounting nut and bolt	30-40	22-29
Brake torque link bolt	18-25	13-18
Final drive unit nuts	60-70	43-51
Swing arm		
Left-hand pivot bolt	80-120	58-87
Right-hand pivot bolt	8-12	6-9
Right-hand pivot locknut	80-120	58-87

Table 2 REAR SHOCK ABSORBER SPRING FREE LENGTH

Standard	Service limit
CB550SC 228.2 mm (8.98 mm)	223.6 mm (8.80 in.)
CB650SC 217.6 mm (8.57 mm)	213.2 mm (8.40 in.)

CHAPTER TEN

BRAKES

The brake system consists of a either a single or dual disc on the front wheel and a drum brake on the rear.

Refer to **Table 1** for brake specifications and **Table 2** for torque specifications. **Table 1** and **Table 2** are located at the end of this chapter.

FRONT DISC BRAKE

The front disc brake(s) is actuated by hydraulic fluid and is controlled by a hand lever on the master cylinder. As the brake pads wear, the brake fluid level drops in the reservoir and automatically adjusts for wear.

When working on hydraulic brake systems, it is necessary that the work area and all tools be absolutely clean. Any tiny particles of foreign matter and grit in the caliper assembly or the master cylinder can damage the components. Also, sharp tools must not be used inside the caliper or on the piston. If you have any doubt about your ability to correctly and safely carry out major service on the brake components, take the job to a dealer or brake specialist.

MASTER CYLINDER

Removal/Installation

1. Remove the rear view mirror (A, **Figure 1**) from the master cylinder.

> *CAUTION*
> *Cover the fuel tank and instrument cluster with a heavy cloth or plastic tarp to protect them from accidental brake fluid spills. Wash brake fluid off any painted or plated surfaces or plastic parts immediately, as it will destroy the finish. Use soapy water and rinse completely.*

2. Pull back the rubber boot (A, **Figure 2**) and remove the union bolt (B, **Figure 2**) securing the brake hose to the master cylinder. Remove the brake hose. Tie the brake hose up and cover the end to prevent the entry of foreign matter.
3. Disconnect the front brake light switch wires (C, **Figure 2**).
4. Remove the clamping bolts (B, **Figure 1**) and clamp securing the master cylinder to the handlebar and remove the master cylinder.
5. Install by reversing these removal steps, noting the following.
6. Install the clamp with the "UP" arrow (**Figure 3**) facing up. Align the face of the clamp with the punch mark on the handlebar (**Figure 4**). Tighten the upper bolt first, then the lower to the torque specification listed in **Table 2**.
7. Install the brake hose onto the master cylinder. Be sure to place a sealing washer on each side of

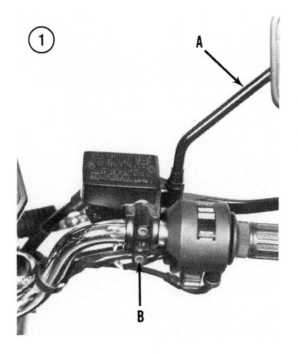

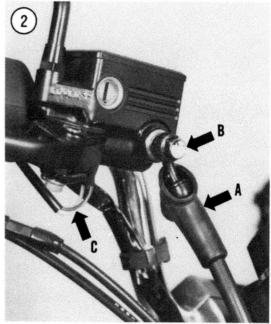

the fitting and install the union bolt. Tighten the union bolt to the torque specifications listed in **Table 2**.

8. Bleed the brake as described in this chapter.

Disassembly

Refer to **Figure 5** for this procedure.

1. Remove the master cylinder as described in this chapter.

2. Remove the bolt and nut securing the brake lever and remove the lever.

3. Remove the screws securing the cover and remove the cover and diaphragm; pour out the brake fluid and discard it. *Never* reuse brake fluid.

4. Remove the rubber boot from the area where the hand lever actuates the internal piston.

5. Using circlip pliers, remove the internal circlip from the body.

6. Remove the secondary cup and the piston assembly.

7. Remove the primary cup and spring.

8. Remove the brake light switch if necessary.

Inspection

1. Clean all parts in denatured alcohol or fresh brake fluid. Inspect the cylinder bore and piston contact surfaces for signs of wear and damage. If either part is less than perfect, replace it.

2. Check the end of the piston for wear caused by the hand lever. Replace if worn.

3. Replace the piston if the secondary cup requires replacement.

4. Inspect the pivot hole in the hand lever. If worn or elongated it must be replaced.

5. Make sure the passages in the bottom of the brake fluid reservoir are clear. Check the reservoir cap and diaphragm for damage and deterioration and replace as necessary.

6. Inspect the threads at the brake line connection.

7. Check the hand lever pivot lugs on the master cylinder body for cracks.

8. Measure the cylinder bore (**Figure 6**). Replace the master cylinder if the bore exceeds the specifications given in **Table 1**.

9. Measure the outside diameter of the piston as shown in **Figure 7** with a micrometer. Replace the piston assembly if it is less than the specifications given in **Table 1**.

Assembly

1. Soak the new cups in fresh brake fluid for at least 15 minutes to make them pliable. Coat the inside of the cylinder with fresh brake fluid prior to the assembly of parts.

> *CAUTION*
> *When installing the piston assembly, do not allow the cups to turn inside out as they will be damaged and allow brake fluid leakage within the cylinder bore.*

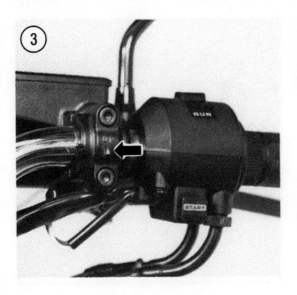

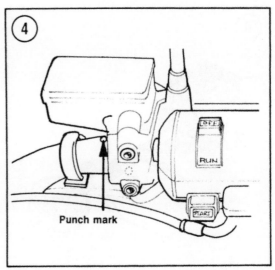

Punch mark

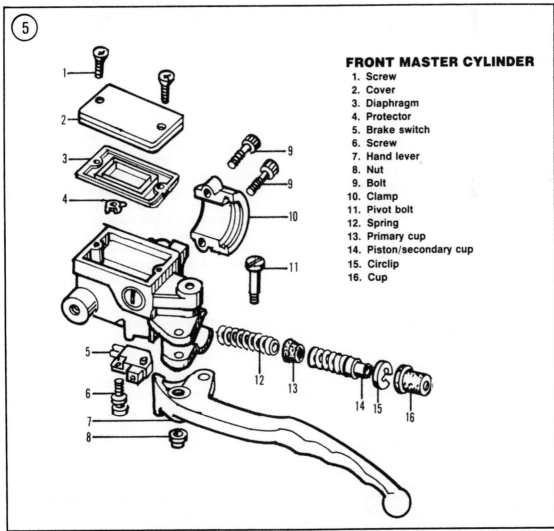

FRONT MASTER CYLINDER
1. Screw
2. Cover
3. Diaphragm
4. Protector
5. Brake switch
6. Screw
7. Hand lever
8. Nut
9. Bolt
10. Clamp
11. Pivot bolt
12. Spring
13. Primary cup
14. Piston/secondary cup
15. Circlip
16. Cup

10

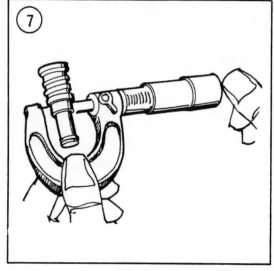

2. Install the spring, primary cup and piston assembly into the cylinder together. Install the spring with the tapered end facing toward the primary cup.

NOTE
Be sure to install the primary cup with the open end in first, toward the spring.

3. Install the circlip and slide in the rubber boot.
4. Install the diaphragm and cover. Do not tighten the cover screws at this time as fluid will have to be added later when the system is bled.
5. Install the brake lever on the master cylinder body.
6. If removed, install the brake light switch.
7. Install the master cylinder as described in this chapter.

BRAKE PAD REPLACEMENT

There is no recommended mileage interval for changing the friction pads in the disc brake. Pad wear depends greatly on riding habits and conditions. The pads should be checked for wear every 6,400 km (4,000 miles) and replaced when the wear indicator reaches the edge of the brake disc. To maintain an even brake pressure on the disc always replace both pads in each caliper at the same time.

CAUTION
Check the pads more frequently when the wear line approaches the disc. On some pads the wear line is very close to the metal backing plate. If pad wear happens to be uneven for some reason the backing plate may come in contact with the disc and cause damage.

Refer to **Figure 8** for single-disc models or **Figure 9** for dual-disc models for this procedure.
1A. On single-disc models and the right-hand caliper on dual-disc models, perform the following:
   a. Remove the bolts securing the caliper assembly to the front fork.
   b. Remove the caliper assembly from the brake disc.
1B. On the left-hand caliper on dual disc models, perform the following:
   a. Remove the bolt (A, **Figure 10**) securing the brake caliper assembly to the front fork.
   b. Pivot the caliper assembly up on the pivot bolt (B, **Figure 10**) and off the brake-disc.
   c. Remove the caliper assembly.
2. Remove the bolt (A, **Figure 11**) securing the pad pin retainer to the caliper assembly and remove the pad pin retainer (B, **Figure 11**).
3. Remove both pad pins and both brake pads.
4. Clean the pad recess and the end of the pistons with a soft brush. Do not use solvent, a wire brush or any hard tool which would damage the cylinders or pistons.
5. Carefully remove any rust or corrosion from the disc.
6. Lightly coat the end of the pistons and the backs of the new pads (*not* the friction material) with disc brake lubricant.

NOTE
When purchasing new pads, check with your dealer to make sure the friction compound of the new pad is compatible with the disc material. Remove any roughness from the backs of the new pads with a fine-cut file; blow them clean with compressed air.

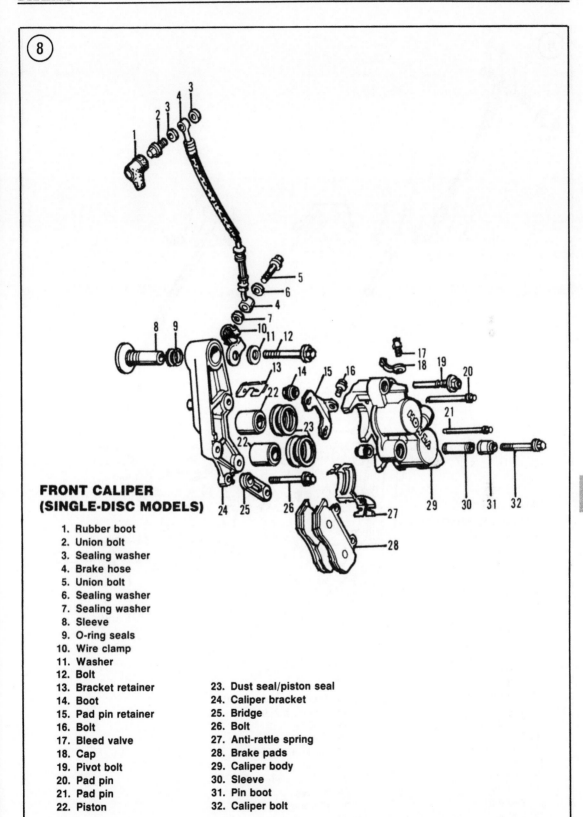

⑧

FRONT CALIPER
(SINGLE-DISC MODELS)

1. Rubber boot
2. Union bolt
3. Sealing washer
4. Brake hose
5. Union bolt
6. Sealing washer
7. Sealing washer
8. Sleeve
9. O-ring seals
10. Wire clamp
11. Washer
12. Bolt
13. Bracket retainer
14. Boot
15. Pad pin retainer
16. Bolt
17. Bleed valve
18. Cap
19. Pivot bolt
20. Pad pin
21. Pad pin
22. Piston

23. Dust seal/piston seal
24. Caliper bracket
25. Bridge
26. Bolt
27. Anti-rattle spring
28. Brake pads
29. Caliper body
30. Sleeve
31. Pin boot
32. Caliper bolt

10

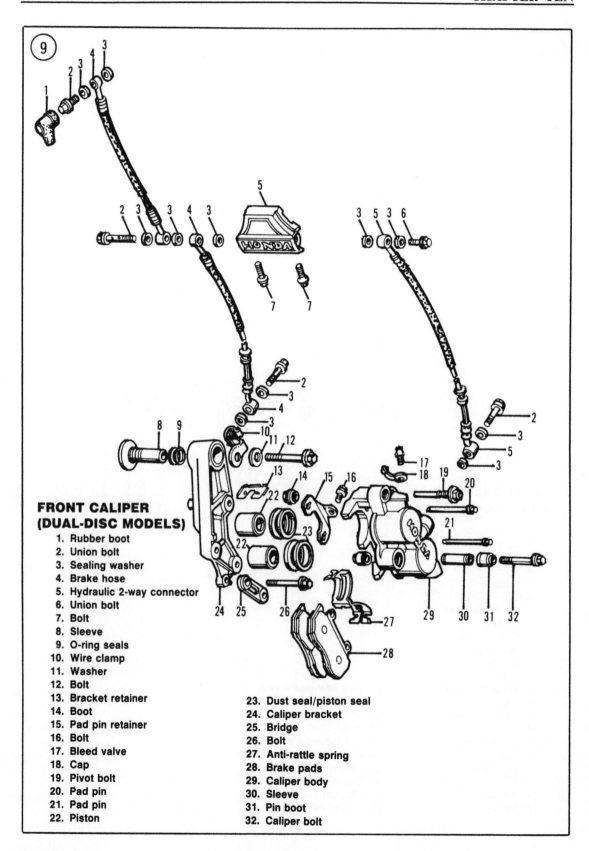

**FRONT CALIPER
(DUAL-DISC MODELS)**

1. Rubber boot
2. Union bolt
3. Sealing washer
4. Brake hose
5. Hydraulic 2-way connector
6. Union bolt
7. Bolt
8. Sleeve
9. O-ring seals
10. Wire clamp
11. Washer
12. Bolt
13. Bracket retainer
14. Boot
15. Pad pin retainer
16. Bolt
17. Bleed valve
18. Cap
19. Pivot bolt
20. Pad pin
21. Pad pin
22. Piston
23. Dust seal/piston seal
24. Caliper bracket
25. Bridge
26. Bolt
27. Anti-rattle spring
28. Brake pads
29. Caliper body
30. Sleeve
31. Pin boot
32. Caliper bolt

7. When new pads are installed in the caliper the master cylinder brake fluid level will rise as the caliper pistons are repositioned. Perform the following:

    a. Clean the top of the master cylinder of all dirt and foreign matter.

    b. Remove the cap (**Figure 12**) and diaphragm from the master cylinder and slowly push the caliper pistons into the caliper. Constantly check the reservoir to make sure brake fluid does not overflow. Remove fluid, if necessary, prior to it overflowing.

    c. The pistons should move freely. If they don't and there is evidence of them sticking in the cylinder, the caliper should be removed and serviced as described in this chapter.

8. Push the caliper pistons in all the way to allow room for the new pads.

9. Install the anti-rattle spring as shown in **Figure 13**.

10. Partially install the pad pins (**Figure 14**).

11. Install the outboard pad (**Figure 15**) and partially install the pins through that pad.

12. Install the inboard pad (**Figure 16**).

13. Push the pins all the way through both pads and into the other side of the caliper.

14. Install the pad pin retainer (B, **Figure 11**) onto the ends of the pins. Push the pin retainer down and make sure it seats completely in the groove in each pin.

15. Install the pad pin retaining bolt (A, **Figure 11**).

16A. On single-disc models and the right-hand caliper on dual-disc models, perform the following:

    a. Install the caliper assembly onto the disc, being careful not to damage the brake pads.

    b. Install the bolts securing the brake caliper assembly to the front fork and tighten to the torque specifications listed in **Table 2**.

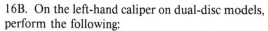

16B. On the left-hand caliper on dual-disc models, perform the following:
    a. Lubricate the caliper upper pivot bolt and pivot boot on the caliper bracket with silicone grease.
    b. Position the caliper assembly pivot bolt into the receptacle in the caliper bracket and push the assembly all the way on.
    c. Pivot the caliper assembly down, being careful not to damage the brake pads.
    d. Install the bolt (A, **Figure 10**) securing the brake caliper assembly to the front fork and tighten to the torque specifications listed in **Table 2**.
17. On dual-disc models, repeat Steps 1-16 for the other caliper assembly.
18. Place wood blocks under the engine or frame so the front wheel is off the ground. Spin the front wheel and activate the brake lever as many times as it takes to refill the cylinder in the caliper and correctly locate the pads.
19. Refill the master cylinder reservoir, if necessary, to maintain the correct fluid level. Install the diaphragm and top cap.

> *WARNING*
> *Use brake fluid from a sealed container clearly marked DOT 3. Other types may vaporize and cause brake failure. Always use the same brand name; do not intermix as many brands are not compatible. Do not intermix silicone based (DOT 5) brake fluid as it can cause brake component damage leading to brake system failure.*

> *WARNING*
> *Do not ride the motorcycle until you are sure the brakes are operating correctly with full hydraulic advantage. If necessary, bleed the brake as described in this chapter.*

20. Bed the pads in gradually for the first 80 km (50 miles) by using only light pressure. Immediate hard application will glaze the new friction pads and greatly reduce the effectiveness of the brake.

CALIPER

Removal/Installation

Refer to **Figure 8** for single-disc models or **Figure 9** for dual-disc models for this procedure.
It is not necessary to remove the front wheel in order to remove either or both caliper assemblies.

> *CAUTION*
> *Do not spill any brake fluid on the painted portion of the front wheel. Wash off any spilled brake fluid immediately, as it will destroy the finish. Use soapy water and rinse completely.*

1. Place a container under the brake line at the caliper. Remove the union bolt and sealing washers (A, **Figure 17**) securing the brake line to the caliper assembly. Remove the brake line and let the brake fluid drain into the container. Dispose of this brake fluid—never reuse brake fluid. To prevent the entry of moisture and dirt, cap the end of the brake line and tie the loose end up to the forks.
2A. On single-disc models and the right-hand caliper on dual-disc models, perform the following.
    a. Loosen the bolts securing the brake caliper assembly to the front fork gradually in several steps. Push on the caliper while loosening the bolt to push the pistons back into the caliper.
    b. Remove the bolts securing the brake caliper assembly to the front fork.
    c. Remove the caliper assembly from the brake disc.
2B. On the left-hand caliper on dual-disc models, perform the following:

(17)

a. Loosen the bolt (B, **Figure 17**) securing the brake caliper assembly to the front fork gradually in several steps. Push on the caliper while loosening the bolt to push the pistons back into the caliper.

b. Remove the bolt (B, **Figure 17**).

c. Pivot the caliper assembly up on the pivot bolt (C, **Figure 17**) and off the brake disc.

d. Remove the caliper assembly.

3. Remove the caliper assembly.

4. On dual-disc models, repeat Steps 1-3 for the other caliper assembly.

5. Install by reversing these removal steps, noting the following.

6A. On single-disc models and right-hand caliper on dual-disc models, perform the following:

a. Carefully install the caliper assembly on the disc being careful not to damage the brake pads.

b. Install the bolts securing the brake caliper assembly to the fork and tighten to the torque specifications listed in **Table 2**.

6B. On the left-hand caliper on dual-disc models, perform the following:

a. Lubricate the caliper upper pivot bolt and pivot boot on the caliper bracket with silicone grease.

b. Position the caliper assembly pivot bolt into the receptacle in the caliper bracket and push the assembly all the way on.

c. Pivot the caliper assembly down, being careful not to damage the brake pads.

d. Install the bolt (A, **Figure 10**) securing the brake caliper assembly to the front fork and tighten to the torque specifications listed in **Table 2**.

7. Install the brake hose, with a sealing washer on each side of the fitting, onto the caliper. Install the union bolt and tighten to the torque specifications listed in **Table 2**.

8. Bleed the brake as described in this chapter.

WARNING
Do not ride the motorcycle until you are sure the brakes are operating properly.

Rebuilding

If the caliper leaks, the caliper should be rebuilt. If the pistons stick in the cylinders, indicating severe wear or galling, the entire unit should be replaced. Rebuilding a leaky caliper requires special tools and experience.

Caliper service should be entrusted to a dealer, motorcycle repair shop or brake specialist. Considerable money can be saved by removing the caliper yourself and taking it in for repair.

BRAKE HOSE REPLACEMENT

There is no factory-recommended replacement interval but it is a good idea to replace all brake hoses every four years or when they show signs of cracking or damage.

Refer to **Figure 8** for single-disc models or **Figure 9** for dual-disc models for this procedure.

CAUTION
Cover the front wheel, fender and fuel tank with a heavy cloth or plastic tarp to protect them from spilled brake fluid. Wash off any brake fluid from any painted or plated surface or plastic parts immediately, as it will destroy the finish. Use soapy water and rinse completely.

1. Place a container under the brake hose at the caliper. Remove the union bolt and sealing washers (A, **Figure 17**) securing the brake hose fitting to the caliper assembly.

2. Remove brake hose from the clip on the fender stay.

3. Remove the brake hose and let the brake fluid drain out into the container. To prevent the entry of moisture and dirt, plug the brake hose inlet in the caliper.

WARNING
Dispose of this brake fluid—never reuse brake fluid. Contaminated brake fluid can cause brake failure.

4. On dual-disc models, repeat Steps 1-3 for the other caliper.

10

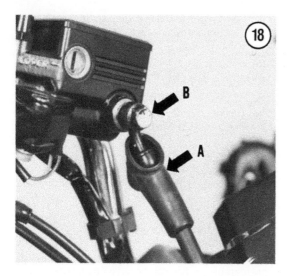

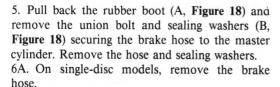

5. Pull back the rubber boot (A, **Figure 18**) and remove the union bolt and sealing washers (B, **Figure 18**) securing the brake hose to the master cylinder. Remove the hose and sealing washers.

6A. On single-disc models, remove the brake hose.

6B. On dual-disc models, perform the following:

    a. Remove the union bolt and sealing washers (**Figure 19**) securing the left-hand brake hose to the 2-way joint.

    b. Remove the union bolt and sealing washers (**Figure 20**) securing the upper hose and the right-hand lower hose to the 2-way joint and remove them and the sealing washer.

7. Install new hoses, sealing washers and union bolts in the reverse order of removal. Be sure to install new sealing washers in the correct positions; refer to **Figure 8** for single-disc models or **Figure 9** for dual-disc models.

8. Tighten all union bolts to torque specifications listed in **Table 2**.

9. Refill the master cylinder with fresh brake fluid clearly marked DOT 3 only. Bleed the brake as described in this chapter.

> *WARNING*
> *Use brake fluid from a sealed container clearly marked DOT 3. Other types may vaporize and cause brake failure. Always use the same brand name; do not mix as many brands are not compatible. Do not mix silicone-based (DOT 5) brake fluid as it can cause brake component damage leading to brake system failure.*

> *WARNING*
> *Do not ride the motorcycle until you are sure the brakes are operating properly.*

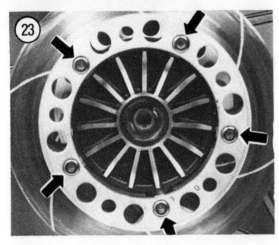

BRAKE DISC

Removal/Installation

1. Remove the front wheel as described in Chapter Eight.

> *NOTE*
> *Place a piece of wood or vinyl tube in the calipers in place of the disc. This way, if the brake lever is squeezed the pistons will not be forced out of the cylinders. If this happens, the caliper might have to be disassembled to reseat the pistons and the system will have to be bled. By using the wood or vinyl tube, bleeding the system is not necessary when installing the wheel.*

> *CAUTION*
> *Do not set the wheel down on the disc surface, as the disc may get scratched or warped. Set the wheel on 2 blocks of wood (**Figure 21**).*

2. Remove the speedometer housing from the left-hand side and the spacer from the right-hand side.

3. On dual-disc models, the discs are marked with either an "R" (right-hand side) or "L" (left-hand side); refer to **Figure 22**. Be sure to install the disc on the correct side during installation.

4. Remove the Allen bolts (**Figure 23**) securing the brake disc to the hub and remove the disc.

5A. On single-disc models, remove the single gasket between the disc and the hub.

5B. On dual-disc models, remove the individual gaskets between the disc and each bolt hole on the hub.

6. On dual-disc models, if necessary, repeat Step 4 and Step 5 for the disc on the other side of the wheel.

7. Install by reversing these removal steps, noting the following.

8. Install the gasket(s) between the disc and the hub.

9. Tighten the disc mounting Allen bolts to the torque specifications listed in **Table 2**.

Inspection

It is not necessary to remove the disc from the wheel to inspect it. Small marks on the disc are not important, but radial scratches deep enough to snag a fingernail reduce braking effectiveness and increase brake pad wear. If these grooves are found, the disc should be replaced.

1. Measure the thickness of the disc at several locations around the disc with a micrometer or vernier caliper (**Figure 24**). The disc must be

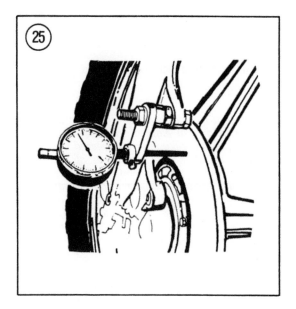

replaced if the thickness in any area is less than that specified in **Table 1**.

2. Make sure the disc bolts are tight prior to this check. Check the disc runout with a dial indicator as shown in **Figure 25**. Slowly rotate the wheel and watch the dial indicator. If the runout exceeds that listed in **Table 1** the disc(s) must be replaced.

3. Clean the disc of any rust or corrosion and wipe clean with lacquer thinner. Never use an oil-based solvent that may leave an oil residue on the disc.

BLEEDING THE SYSTEM

This procedure is not necessary unless the brakes feel spongy, there has been a leak in the system, a component has been replaced or the brake fluid has been replaced. When bleeding the front system, do one caliper at a time.

> *NOTE*
> *On dual-disc models, bleed the caliper farthest from the master cylinder (left-hand caliper) first, then the other caliper. This will minimize air bubbles in the system.*

1. Remove the dust cap from the brake bleed valve.

2. Connect a length of clear tubing to the bleed valve on the caliper (**Figure 26**).

3. Place the other end of the tube in a clean container.

4. Fill the container with enough fresh brake fluid to keep the end submerged. The tube should be long enough so a loop can be made higher than the bleed valve to prevent air from being drawn into the caliper during bleeding.

> *CAUTION*
> *Cover the fuel tank and instrument cluster with a heavy cloth or plastic tarp to protect it from spilled brake fluid. Wash off brake fluid from any painted or plated surface or plastic parts immediately, as it will destroy the finish. Use soapy water and rinse completely.*

5. Clean the cover of the master cylinder of all dirt and foreign matter. Remove the screws securing the top cover and remove the cover and diaphragm. Fill the reservoir almost to the top lip; insert the diaphragm and the cover loosely. Leave the cover in place during this procedure to prevent the entry of dirt.

> *WARNING*
> *Use brake fluid from a sealed container clearly marked DOT 3. Other types may vaporize and cause brake failure. Always use the same brand name; do not mix as many brands are not compatible. Do not mix silicone-based (DOT 5) brake fluid as it can cause damage leading to brake failure.*

6. Insert a 20 mm (3/4 in.) spacer between the handlebar grip and the brake lever. This will prevent over-travel of the piston within the master cylinder.

7. Slowly apply the brake lever several times. Hold the lever in the applied position.

8. Open the bleed valve about one-half turn. Allow the lever to travel to its limit against the

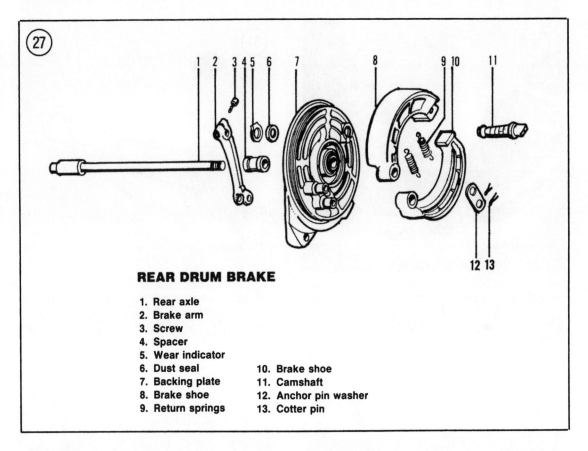

REAR DRUM BRAKE

1. Rear axle
2. Brake arm
3. Screw
4. Spacer
5. Wear indicator
6. Dust seal
7. Backing plate
8. Brake shoe
9. Return springs
10. Brake shoe
11. Camshaft
12. Anchor pin washer
13. Cotter pin

installed spacer. When this limit is reached, tighten the bleed screw.

9. As the fluid enters the system, the level will drop in the reservoir. Maintain the level at about 3/8 inch from the top of the reservoir to prevent air from being drawn into the system.

10. Continue to pump the lever and fill the reservoir until the fluid emerging from the hose is completely free of bubbles.

NOTE
Do not allow the reservoir to empty during the bleeding operation or more air will enter the system. If this occurs, the entire procedure must be repeated.

11. Hold the lever in, tighten the bleed valve, remove the bleed tube and install the bleed valve dust cap.

12. If necessary, add fluid to correct the level in the reservoir. It should be to the upper level line.

13. Install the reservoir cover and tighten the screws.

14. Remove the spacer that was installed in Step 6 from the brake lever. Test the feel of the brake lever. It should be firm and should offer the same resistance each time it's operated. If it feels spongy,

it is likely there still is air in the system and it must be bled again. When all air has been bled from the system and the fluid level is correct in the reservoir, double-check for leaks and tighten all the fittings and connections.

WARNING
Before riding the motorcycle, make certain the brakes are operating correctly by operating the lever several times.

REAR DRUM BRAKE

Pushing down on the brake foot pedal pulls the rod which in turn rotates the camshaft. This forces the brake shoes out into contact with the brake drum.

Pedal free play must be maintained to minimize brake drag and premature brake wear and maximize braking effectiveness. Refer to Chapter Three for complete adjustment procedure.

Disassembly

Refer to **Figure 27** for this procedure.

1. Remove the rear wheel as described in Chapter Nine.

10

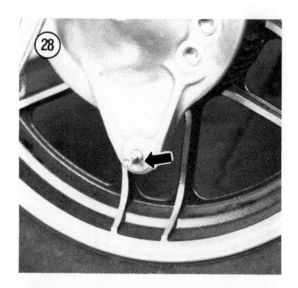

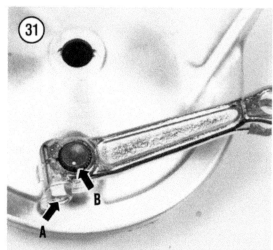

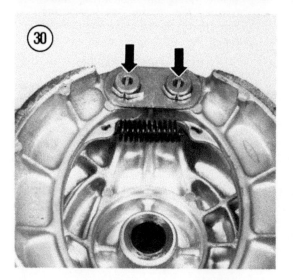

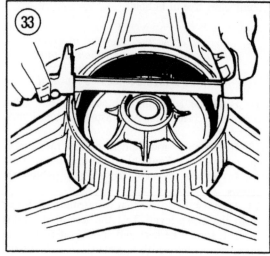

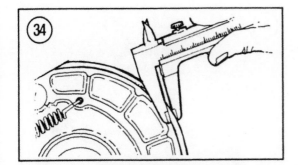

2. Remove the torque link bolt (**Figure 28**) from the brake assembly.

3. Pull the brake assembly straight up and out of the brake drum (**Figure 29**).

4. Remove the cotter pins and washer from the brake backing plate (**Figure 30**).

5. Remove the bolt and nut (A, **Figure 31**) securing the brake arm and remove the brake arm, wear indicator and dust seal. Withdraw the camshaft from the backing plate.

6. Using needlenose pliers, remove the return spring (next to the camshaft) from the brake linings. Remove the other return spring in the same manner.

Inspection

1. Thoroughly clean and dry all parts except the brake linings.

2. Check the contact surface of the drum (**Figure 32**) for scoring. If there are grooves deep enough to snag your fingernail the drum should be reground.

3. Measure the inside diameter of the brake drum with vernier calipers (**Figure 33**). If the measurement is greater than the service limit listed in **Table 1** the rear wheel must be replaced; the brake drum is an integral part of the wheel.

4. If the drum can be turned and still stay within the maximum service limit diameter, the linings will have to be replaced and the new ones arced to conform to the new drum contour.

5. Measure the brake linings with a vernier caliper (**Figure 34**). They should be replaced if the lining portion is worn to the service limit dimension or less (**Table 1**).

6. Inspect the linings for imbedded foreign material. Dirt can be removed with a stiff wire brush. Check for any traces of oil or grease; if the linings are contaminated they must be replaced.

7. Inspect the cam lobe and pivot pin area of the backing plate (**Figure 35**) for wear or corrosion. Minor roughness can be removed with fine emery cloth.

8. Inspect the brake shoe return springs for wear. If they are stretched, they will not fully retract the brake shoes. Replace as necessary.

Assembly

1. Grease the camshaft (**Figure 36**) with a light coat of molybdenum disulfide grease. Install the cam into the backing plate from the backside.

2. From the outside of the backing plate install the dust seal (**Figure 37**).

3. Align the wear indicator to the camshaft as shown in **Figure 38** and push it down all the way to the backing plate (**Figure 39**).

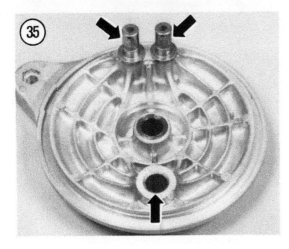

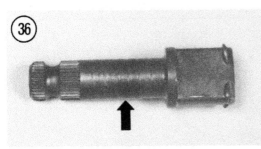

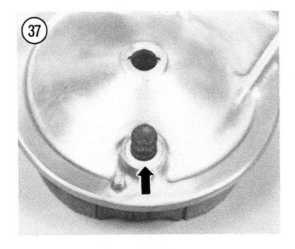

10

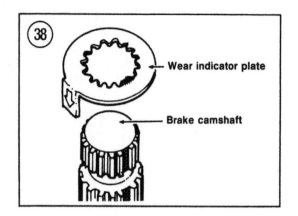

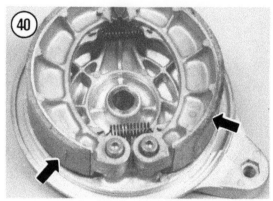

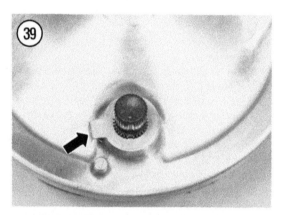

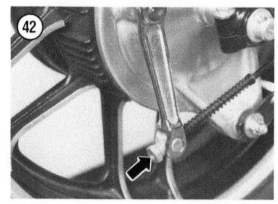

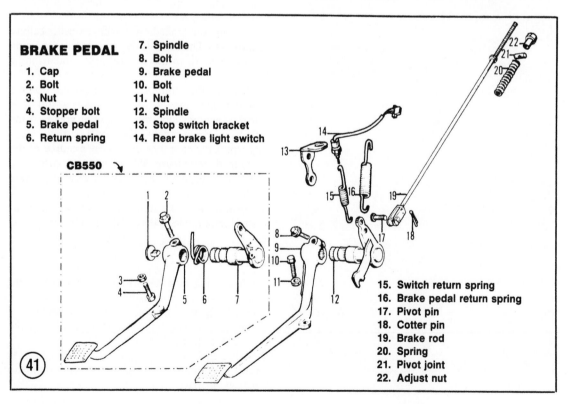

BRAKE PEDAL

1. Cap
2. Bolt
3. Nut
4. Stopper bolt
5. Brake pedal
6. Return spring
7. Spindle
8. Bolt
9. Brake pedal
10. Bolt
11. Nut
12. Spindle
13. Stop switch bracket
14. Rear brake light switch

15. Switch return spring
16. Brake pedal return spring
17. Pivot pin
18. Cotter pin
19. Brake rod
20. Spring
21. Pivot joint
22. Adjust nut

CB550

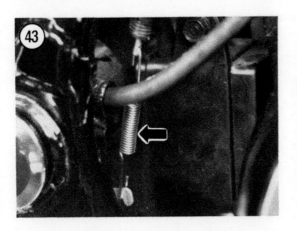

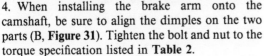

4. When installing the brake arm onto the camshaft, be sure to align the dimples on the two parts (B, **Figure 31**). Tighten the bolt and nut to the torque specification listed in **Table 2**.

5. Grease the camshaft and pivot post with a light coat of molybdenum disulfide grease; avoid getting any grease on the brake backing plate where the brake linings may come in contact with it.

6. Hold the brake shoes in a "V" formation with the return springs attached and snap them into place on the brake backing plate. Make sure they are firmly seated on it (**Figure 40**). Install the double lockwasher and new cotter pins. Bend the ends over completely.

7. Install the brake panel assembly into the brake drum.

8. Install the rear wheel as described in Chapter Nine.

9. Adjust the rear brake as described in Chapter Three.

REAR BRAKE PEDAL

Removal/Installation

Refer to **Figure 41** for this procedure.

1. Completely unscrew the adjustment nut (**Figure 42**) on the brake rod.

2. Push down on the brake pedal and remove the brake rod from the pivot joint in the brake arm. Install the pivot joint on the brake rod and reinstall the adjustment nut to avoid losing any small parts.

3. Disconnect the brake light switch return spring (**Figure 43**) and the brake pedal return spring from the brake lever.

4. Remove the cotter pin and pivot pin securing the brake cable/rod assembly to the pivot shaft arm.

5. Remove the plastic plug (A, **Figure 44**) from the brake pedal.

6. Remove the bolt (B, **Figure 44**) clamping the brake pedal to the pivot shaft arm and remove the brake pedal.

7. On CB650 models, disconnect the pedal return spring from the pivot shaft arm.

8A. On CB550 models, remove the pivot shaft arm and return spring from the frame.

8B. On CB650 models, remove the pivot shaft arm from the frame.

9. Install by reversing these removal steps, noting the following.

10. Apply a light coat of multipurpose grease to all pivot areas prior to installing any components.

11. Install the brake pedal. Align the punch marks on the brake pedal and the brake pivot shaft.

12. Adjust the brake pedal height and free play as described in Chapter Three.

10

Table 1 BRAKE SPECIFICATIONS

Item	Specification	Wear limit
Master cylinder		
Cylinder bore ID	15.870-15.913 mm (0.6248-0.6265 in.)	15.93 mm (0.627 in.)
Piston OD	15.827-15.854 mm (0.6231-0.6242 in.)	15.82 mm (0.623 in.)
Front caliper		
Cylinder bore ID	30.148-30.280 mm (1.1901-1.1921 in.)	30.290 mm (1.1925 in.)
Piston OD	30.230-30.280 mm (1.1902-1.1913 in.)	30.140 mm (1.187 in.)
Front brake disc thickness	4.8-5.2 mm (0.19-0.20 in.)	4.0 mm (0.16 in.)
Disc runout	—	0.3 mm (0.12 in.)
Rear brake drum ID	160.0-160.3 mm (6.30-6.31 in.)	161 mm (6.34 in.)
Rear brake shoe thickness	4.9-5.0 mm (0.19-0.20 in.)	2.0 mm (0.08 in.)

Table 2 BRAKE TORQUE SPECIFICATIONS

Item	N•m	ft.-lb.
Brake hose union bolts	25-35	18-25
Front master cylinder cover screws	1-2	0.7-0.9
Caliper mounting bolts (single-disc models)		
Upper mounting bolt	35-45	25-33
Lower mounting bolt	20-25	14-18
Caliper bolts (dual-disc models)		
Right-hand	30-40	22-29
Left-hand side		
Pivot bolt	25-35	18-22
Mounting bolt	20-25	14-18
Piston pin bolt	20-25	14-18
Caliper bracket bolt	35-45	25-33
Brake disc mounting bolts	35-40	25-29
Rear brake torque link bolt	18-25	13-18

CHAPTER ELEVEN

FRAME AND REPAINTING

This chapter includes replacement procedures for miscellaneous components attached to the frame.

This chapter also describes procedures for completely stripping the frame. Recommendations are provided for repainting the stripped frame.

KICKSTAND (SIDESTAND)

Removal/Installation

1. Place a wood block(s) under the frame to support the bike securely.
2. Raise the kickstand and disconnect the return spring (A, **Figure 1**) from the pin on the frame with Vise Grips.
3. From under the frame, remove the bolt and nut (B, **Figure 1**) and remove the kickstand from the frame.
4. Install by reversing these steps. Apply a light coat of multipurpose grease to the pivot surfaces of the frame tab and the kickstand yoke prior to installation.

CENTERSTAND

Removal/Installation

1. Place a wood block(s) under the frame to hold the bike securely in place.
2. Raise the centerstand and use Vise Grip pliers to unhook the return spring for the centerstand.

3. Unscrew the bolt on each side securing the centerstand to the frame. Don't lose the pivot collar between the frame and centerstand where the bolts attach.
4. Remove the centerstand from the frame.
5. Remove the pivot collar from each pivot area on the centerstand.
6. Install by reversing these removal steps, noting the following.
7. Apply multipurpose grease to the pivot collar and the pivot area of the centerstand where the pivot collar rides.

FOOTPEGS

Replacement

Remove the cotter pin and washer securing the footpeg to the bracket on the frame. Remove the pivot pin and footpeg. Refer to **Figure 2** for the front footpeg and **Figure 3** for the rear footpeg.

Make sure the spring is in good condition and not broken. Replace as necessary.

Lubricate the pivot point and pivot pin prior to installation. Install a new cotter pin and bend the ends over completely.

To remove the entire footpeg assembly, remove the bolts securing the assembly to the crankcase and remove the assembly.

11

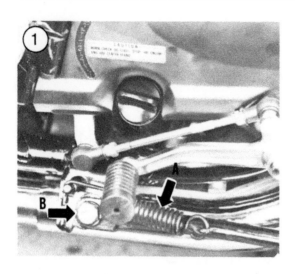

SIDE COVERS
AND SEAT

Removal/Installation (CB550)

1. Pull out on the bottom of the side cover and remove the side covers from the rubber mounts in the frame tabs.
2. At the back of the seat pull on the seat release mechanism to unhook the rear of the seat.
3. Pull the rear seat toward the rear and unhook the front of the seat.
4. Remove the seat.
5. Install by reversing these steps.

Removal/Installation (CB650)

1. Pull out on the bottom of the side cover (**Figure 4**) and remove the side covers from the rubber mounts in the frame tabs.
2. Remove the bolt (**Figure 5**) on each side securing the rear seat.
3. Pull the seat straight up and off the frame.

REAR FENDER

Removal/Installation (CB550)

Refer to **Figure 6** for this procedure.
1. Remove both side covers and seat as described in this chapter.
2. Remove the fuel tank as described in Chapter Six.
3. Disconnect the electrical connectors to both rear turn signals, the taillight/brake light, license plate light and the taillight sensor.
4. Loosen the shock absorber upper mounting nut on each side.
5. Remove the nut securing each turn signal assembly to the side grab rail. Remove both turn signal assemblies.

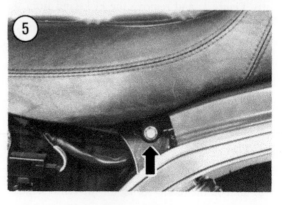

⑥

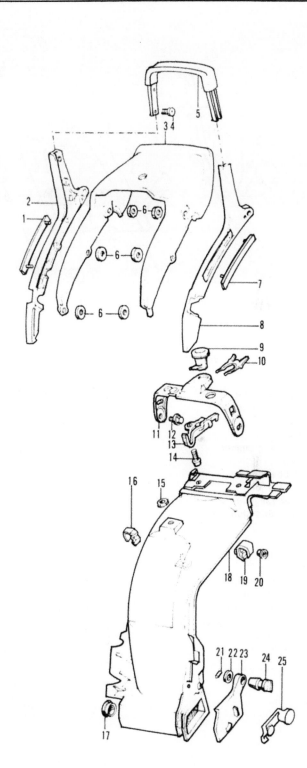

REAR FENDER (CB550)

1. Reflector
2. Right-hand grab rail
3. Fender cowl
4. Bolt
5. Rear grab rail
6. Rubber bushing
7. Reflector
8. Left-hand grab rail
9. Seat lock assembly
10. Clip
11. Bracket
12. Bolt
13. Seat catch hook
14. Bolt
15. Nut
16. Cable clamp
17. Rubber plug
18. Rear fender
19. Cable clip
20. Rubber plug
21. Pin
22. Washer
23. Tool box lid
24. Catch
25. Cover

11

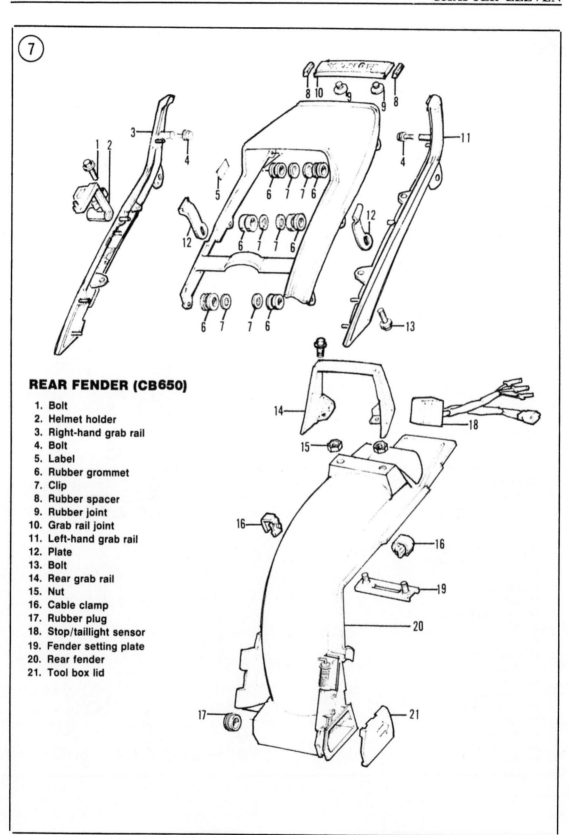

REAR FENDER (CB650)

1. Bolt
2. Helmet holder
3. Right-hand grab rail
4. Bolt
5. Label
6. Rubber grommet
7. Clip
8. Rubber spacer
9. Rubber joint
10. Grab rail joint
11. Left-hand grab rail
12. Plate
13. Bolt
14. Rear grab rail
15. Nut
16. Cable clamp
17. Rubber plug
18. Stop/taillight sensor
19. Fender setting plate
20. Rear fender
21. Tool box lid

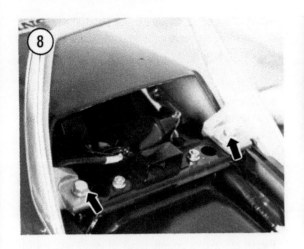

6. Remove the bolts securing the rear grab rail and remove the rear grab rail.

7. Remove the screws securing the tail section and side grab rail assembly. Remove the tail section and side grab rail assembly.

8. Remove the bolts securing the rear fender to the frame stay.

9. Carefully pull the rear fender assembly slightly up and to the rear and out of the frame.

10. Install by reversing these removal steps.

Removal/Installation (CB650)

Refer to **Figure 7** for this procedure.

1. Remove both side covers and the seat as described in this chapter.

2. Remove the fuel tank as described in Chapter Six.

3. Remove the bolts (**Figure 8**) securing the rear grab rail and the tail cover above the taillight. Remove the rear grab rail.

4. Remove the bolts (**Figure 9**) securing the tail section and side grab rail assembly.

5. Partially remove the tail section and disconnect the electrical connectors to both rear turn signals, the taillight/brake light and the taillight sensor.

6. Remove the tail section and side grab rail assembly.

7. Remove the bolts securing the rear fender to the frame stay.

8. Carefully pull the rear fender assembly slightly up and to the rear and out of the frame.

9. Install by reversing these removal steps.

FRAME

The frame does not require routine maintenance. However, it should be inspected immediately after any accident or spill.

Component Removal/Installation

1. Remove the seat, side covers and fuel tank.

2. Remove the engine as described in Chapter Four.

3. Remove the front wheel, steering head and front forks as described in Chapter Eight.

4. Remove the rear wheel, shock absorber and swing arm as described in Chapter Nine.

5. Remove the battery as described in Chapter Three.

6. Remove the wiring harness.

7. Remove the kickstand and footpegs as described in this chapter.

8. Remove the centerstand as described in this chapter.

9. Remove the steering head races from the steering head tube as described in Chapter Eight.

10. Inspect the frame for bends, cracks or other damage, especially around welded joints and areas that are rusted.

11. Assemble by reversing these removal steps.

Stripping and Painting

Remove all components from the frame. Thoroughly strip off all old paint. The best way is to have it sandblasted down to bare metal. If this is not possible, you can use a liquid paint remover and steel wool and a fine, hard wire brush.

> *CAUTION*
> *Some of the fenders, side covers, frame covers and air box are molded plastic. If you wish to change the color of these parts, consult an automotive paint supplier for the proper procedure. Do not use any liquid paint remover on these components as it will damage the surface. The color is an integral part of some of these components and cannot be removed.*

11

When the frame is down to bare metal, have it inspected for hairline and internal cracks. Magnaflux is the most common and complete process.

Make sure that the primer is compatible with the type of paint you are going to use for the finish color. Spray on one or two coats of primer as smoothly as possible. Let it dry thoroughly and use a fine grade of wet sandpaper (400-600 grit) to remove any flaws. Carefully wipe the surface clean and then spray a couple of coats of the final color. Use either lacquer or enamel base paint and follow the manufacturer's instructions.

A shop specializing in painting will probably do the best job. However, you can do a surprisingly good job with a good grade of spray paint. Spend a few extra dollars and get a good grade of paint as it will make a difference in how good it looks and how long it will stand up. It is a good idea to shake the can and make sure the ball inside is loose when you purchase the paint. Shake the can as long as is stated on the can. Then immerse the can upright in a pot or bucket of warm water (not hot-not over 120° F).

WARNING
Higher temperatures could cause the can to burst. Do not place the can in direct contact with any flame or heat source.

Leave the can in the water for several minutes. When thoroughly warmed, shake the can again and spray the frame. Be sure to get into all the crevices where there may be rust problems. Several light mist coats are better than one heavy coat. Spray-painting is best done in temperatures of 70-80° F (21-26° C); any temperature above or below this will give you problems.

After the final coat has dried completely, at least 48 hours, any overspray or orange peel may be removed with a light application of Dupont rubbing compound (red color) and finished with Dupont polishing compound (white color). Be careful not to rub too hard or you will go through the finish.

Finish off with a couple coats of good wax prior to reassembling all the components. It is a good idea to keep the frame touched up with fresh paint if any minor rust spots or scratches appear.

An alternative to painting is powder coating. The process involves spraying electrically charged particles of pigment and resin on the object to be coated, which is negatively charged. The charged powder particles adhere to the electrically grounded object until heated and fused into a smooth coating in a curing oven. Powder coated surfaces are more resistant to chipping, scratching, fading and wearing than other finishes. A variety of colors and textures are available. Powder coating also has advantages over paint as no environmentally hazardous solvents are used.

INDEX

12

1983 CB5500SC

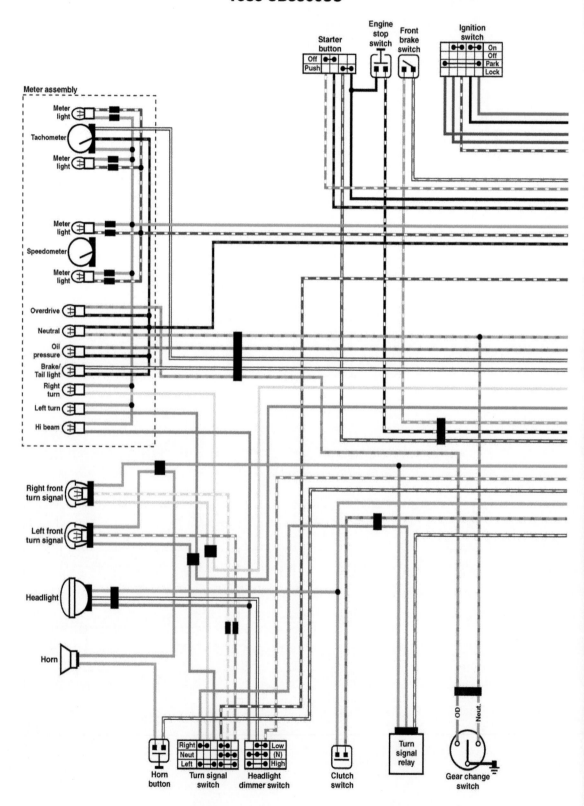

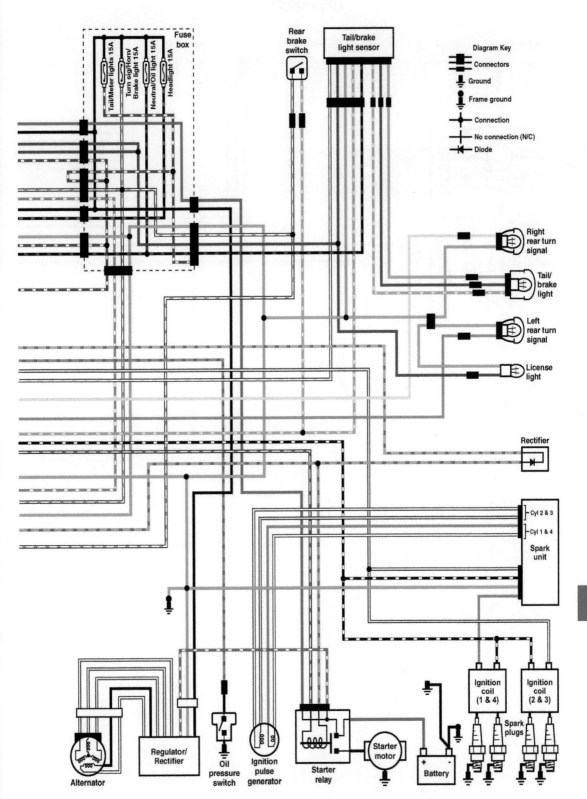

13

1983 CB650SC

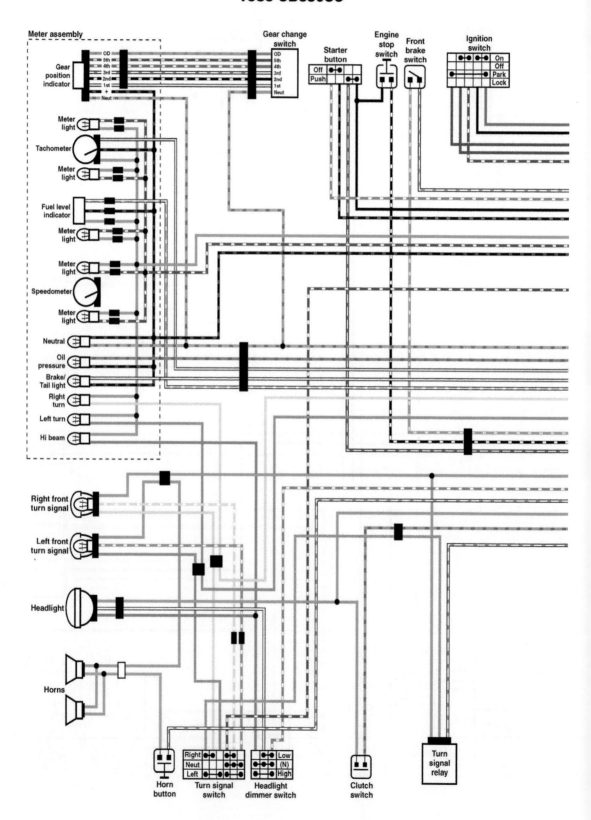

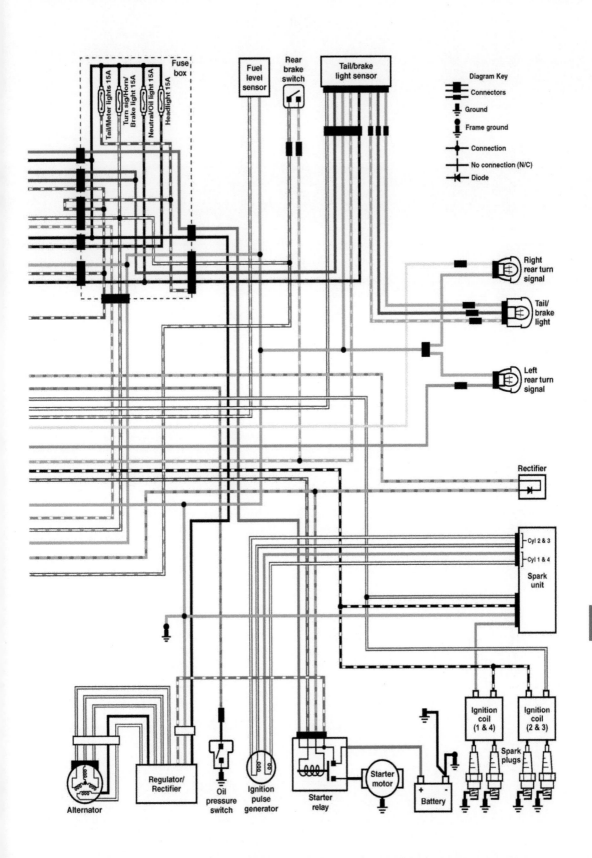

NOTES

NOTES

NOTES

NOTES

NOTES

MAINTENANCE LOG

Date	Miles	Type of Service

MAINTENANCE LOG

Date	Miles	Type of Service